The Gates of Africa

The Pharaoh's Shadow
Shooting the Breeze
Lifting the Veil
Florence Nightingale's Letters from Egypt

The Gates of
Africa

DEATH, DISCOVERY,
AND THE SEARCH FOR TIMBUKTU

Anthony Sattin

St. Martin's Press ⚏ New York

Chapter heading illustrations by Rex Nicholls
based on images from antique maps
Maps by John Gilkes

www.stmartins.com

ISBN 0-312-33643-8
EAN 978-0312-33643-1

First published in Great Britain by HarperCollins*Publishers*

First U.S. Edition: January 2005

10 9 8 7 6 5 4 3 2

For Sylvie,
ever my inspiration,
and for Johnny and Felix,
our young adventurers

CONTENTS

vii

ILLUSTRATIONS

Sir Joseph Banks, 'the godfather of exploration', painted by John Russell, R.A., in 1788. *(Private Collection. Photograph by Alex Saunderson)*

Soho Square in 1812 by George Shepherd. *(Dixson Galleries, State Library of New South Wales)*

Frances Rawdon, the Earl of Moira, in 1789 by Sir Joshua Reynolds. *(The Royal Collection © 2003, Her Majesty Queen Elizabeth II)*

Bryan Edwards Esq. *(By courtesy of the National Portrait Gallery, London)*

Major James Rennell by John Opie. *(Private Collection. Photograph courtesy of Southampton Oceanography Centre)*

John Ledyard, the first great American traveller. *(Dartmouth College Library)*

Sidi Hassan, the dashing late Bey of Tripoli. *(Title page of* Letters Written during a Ten Years' Residence at the Court of Tripoli *by Miss Tully, 3rd edition, 2 vols. Colburn, London, 1819)*

Murzuq in the Fezzan, now southern Libya. *(Drawn by J.M. Bernatz from a sketch by Dr Barth. From* Travels and Discoveries in North and Central Africa *by Henry Barth. Longman Green, 1857)*

Mungo Park by Thomas Rowlandson. *(By courtesy of the National Portrait Gallery, London)*

Medina, the Wuli capital. *(From* Travels in Western Africa *by William Gray. John Murray, London, 1825)*

The capital of Bondo. *(From* Travels in Western Africa *by William Gray. John Murray, London, 1825)*

A View of Ali's Tent at the Camp of Benowm. (J.C. Barrow, from a sketch by Mungo Park. From Travels in the Interior of Africa *by Mungo Park, 2nd edition, 1799)*

Mungo Park having just reached the River Niger: the way it looked in

London. *(By Lady Elizabeth Foster. From* Travels in the Interior of Africa *by Mungo Park, 2nd edition, 1799)*

A view of Kamalia. *(J.C. Barrow, from a sketch by Mungo Park. From* Travels in the Interior of Africa *by Mungo Park, 2nd edition, 1799)*

The Battle of Heliopolis by Leon Cogniet, c.1850. *(Courtesy Mathaf Gallery, 24 Motcomb St, London SW1)*

The Pyramids and Giza Plateau, by Henry Salt. *(Private Collection)*

Portrait of Henry Salt by Joseph Bonomi. *(Reproduced by kind permission of Hisham Khatib)*

Jean Louis Burckhardt, Swiss gentleman, before leaving for Africa. *(Etched by Angelica Clarke, from the original drawing by Slater. From* Travels in Nubia *by J.L. Burckhardt. John Murray, 1822)*

Burckhardt as he appeared in 1817. Portrait by Henry Salt. *(Reproduced by kind permission of Hisham Khatib)*

Abu Simbel, Ramses II's great temple complex. Sketch by Linant de Bellefonds. *(Reproduced by kind permission of The National Trust/ The Bankes of Kingston Lacy & Corfe Castle Archives, Dorset Record Office. NT/BKL (unnumbered). Photograph © The British Museum)*

William Martin Leake. *(Portrait by Christian Albrecht Jensen. By courtesy of the National Portrait Gallery, London)*

John Barrow. *(Portrait attributed to John Jackson. By courtesy of the National Portrait Gallery, London)*

Major Alexander Gordon Laing.

Réné Caillié. *(Engraved on stone by C. Hamburger. From* Travels through Central Africa to Timbuctoo *by Réné Caillié. Colburn & Bentley, London, 1830)*

Timbuktu as it was during the age of the African Association. *(Engraved by J. Clark. From* Travels through Central Africa to Timbuctoo *by Réné Caillié. Colburn & Bentley, London, 1830)*

Kano, one of the Hausa cities, a city of such sophistication and colour that Lieutenant Hugh Clapperton's naval dress uniform failed to turn heads. *(Drawn by J.M. Bernatz from a sketch by Dr Barth. From* Travels and Discoveries in North and Central Africa *by Henry Barth. Longman Green, 1857)*

MAPS

CHRONOLOGY

1787   Settlement of freed British slaves creates a colony at Sierra
        Leone

1788   The African Association is formed and sends John Ledyard
        to Cairo with instructions to cross the Sahara from east to
        west. Simon Lucas heads for Tripoli to cross the Sahara from
        north to south

1790   Daniel Houghton sails up the Gambia River to cut inland to
        the Niger and Timbuktu

1792   W.G. Browne independently sets out for the Nile and
        Abyssinia

1795   Mungo Park sails to the Gambia River to cut inland to the
        Niger and Timbuktu

1797   Frederick Hornemann arrives in Cairo en route to Fezzan
        and Timbuktu

1804   Creation of the Peul Empire of Sokoto, to the detriment of
        the Hausa States

1805   Henry Nicholls is sent to Calabar to travel north towards the
        Niger. Mungo Park sets out for the Niger again, backed by
        the British government, advised by the African Association

1807   The slave trade is outlawed by British Parliament. British
        government takes over Sierra Leone as colony

1809   Henry Salt travels to Abyssinia. Jean Louis Burckhardt leaves
        for the Middle East and then Timbuktu

1816   Tuckey's expedition to the mouth of the Congo

1818   Lyon and Ritchie sail to Tripoli to cross the Sahara to the
        Niger

1821   Creation of Société de Géographie de France. Captain
        Gordon travels up the White Nile

1822   Clapperton, Denham and Oudney leave Tripoli to cross the
            Sahara

1825–27   Laing leaves Tripoli for Timbuktu. Clapperton and Lander
            in Sokoto

1826–28   Linant de Bellefonds (French) travels up the White Nile

1830   Henry Welford travels up the White Nile. Geographical
            Society of London (soon the Royal Geographical Society) is
            founded

1831   The African Association is merged with the Royal Geographi-
            cal Society

A NOTE ON SPELLING

In spite of the fact that Samuel Johnson's *Dictionary of the English Language* was already into its sixth edition by the time the African Association was founded, correspondents used a variety of English spellings and were liberal, and at times random, in their use of capital letters. Throughout I have tried to find a balance between veracity, ease and modern understanding. I have left original spellings intact – for your pleasure – whenever I have quoted from contemporary sources. Spelling of foreign and particularly Arabic words seems to have no logic to it. A shaykh can be spelled shek, sheikh, sheik and so on. As there is no universally agreed convention on the transliteration of Arabic words (surely something Sir Joseph Banks or one of his friends would have seen to by now), I have adopted my own – al not el, *sharif* not *shereef*. There is a similar range of place names, with Timbuktu spelled Tambuta, Tombooctoo, Timkitoo and a range of other variants. For these I have used modern spellings wherever possible, so Hausa not Houssa, Bondo not Boundou. I hope the result retains some of the original character, but is not so opaque as to be confusing.

'To lovers of adventure and novelty,
Africa displays a most ample field.'

James Rennell

Talking Timbuktu

'To EXPLORE. v.a. [exploro, Latin]
To try; to search into; to examine by trial.'
Samuel Johnson, *A Dictionary of the English Language* (1785)

Beyond the crenellated towers of Cairo's thousand-year-old Bab an-Nasr, Gate of Victory, stands a cemetery. Known as the City of the Dead, this swathe of tombs has become part of the city of the living, as its large tomb chambers look increasingly desirable in a city filled to bursting. There are always people milling around the main road into the cemetery, flower-sellers with wreaths and bouquets wrapped in palm fronds, chanters ready to recite *suras* from the Koran for a few notes, muscled grave-diggers, black-robed women ready to mourn on demand and a few guardians, keys hanging from their robes like jailers. Behind them, the cemetery is a maze of small tombs, shacks, graves, huts, cafés, storerooms and the occasional grand mausoleum. Once off the main street and into this confusion, it is easy to lose yourself, as I did, wanting to pay my respects to a man known both as Jean Louis Burckhardt and as Shaykh Ibrahim ibn Abdallah.

There are no written records of who is buried where in Bab an-Nasr. Instead the guardians store the knowledge and then pass it like an heirloom from father to son. Burckhardt, Shaykh Ibrahim, died almost two hundred years ago. According to the guidebook I had consulted, his tomb was lost. It seemed unlikely that a foreigner would ever find it, but Cairo is a city of wonders and one Eid, the feast at the end of the fasting month of Ramadan, I went to look. There is a tradition of visiting the cemetery during the Eid, so the place was crowded and people had better things to do than to guide a foreigner around the tombs. But passed from one guardian to the next, I did eventually find a small nineteenth-century mausoleum containing a low white marble grave inscribed with Burckhardt's titles as a *hajj* (one who has performed the pilgrimage to Mecca), as a *shaykh* and as *al Lausani*, the man from Lausanne. To this the guardian added the title of *al Muslimayn*, the two Muslims, which he meant as an indication of Burckhardt's sanctity.

Let's now jump back to the mid-nineteenth century, to 1853, when a thirty-two-year-old Anglo-Irishman disguised as an Afghani Muslim passed through that same massive gate. Then as now, the cemetery was 'a favourite resort' during the Eid. The man was Richard Burton. Fluent in Arabic, easy in his disguise, Burton found himself in a crowd of 'jugglers, buffoons, snake-charmers, dervishes, ape-leaders, and dancing boys habited in women's attire'.[1] Expelled from Oxford University, and then disgraced as an officer in the East India Company's army, Burton was passing through Cairo on his way to perform the pilgrimage to Mecca. Burton knew that Burckhardt had made the pilgrimage some forty years earlier, and it seems there was an element of homage in his mention of the Swiss traveller's 'humble grave'. Burton reported that some £20 had been raised among the city's foreign community to cover the grave with what he called a fitting monument. 'Some objection, however, was started, because Moslems are supposed to claim Burckhardt as one of their own saints.'[2]*

Who was this Lausani *shaykh*, this Swiss traveller still revered in Cairo more than two hundred years after his death? Jean Louis Burckhardt came from a wealthy Swiss family whose business and domestic harmony was destroyed in the 1790s when they fell foul of an occupying French revolutionary army. The young Burckhardt grew up longing for a place where life and liberty were respected;

---

* The marble cladding was added in the 1880s, apparently paid for by Europeans in Cairo. The small house that now covers the tomb was added in the 1920s or 1930s by the Burckhardt family in Switzerland, who continue to look after its upkeep. All very touching, though there is some doubt as to whether the great traveller's bones lie beneath the cenotaph, or somewhere else in the cemetery.

as more of Europe fell to Napoleon Bonaparte, only England seemed to offer what he wanted. Burckhardt arrived in London in the summer of 1806 and, strange as it may sound, was introduced to a man who suggested he might like to become an explorer and who offered to send him into Africa to search for answers to questions about the rise of rivers, the extent of deserts, the state of empires and the whereabouts of goldfields. Burckhardt accepted. On his way there, he became the first European since the Crusaders to set eyes on the ancient Nabataean city of Petra and the first since antiquity to see the magnificent pharaonic temples at Abu Simbel. He also travelled further up the Nile than any recorded European before him. These were all remarkable achievements, but the object of his journey, the reason he had been sent, lay across the burning Sahara in Timbuktu.

Burton, who acknowledged Burckhardt as his favourite travel writer, certainly knew all about these achievements, as he did about Burckhardt's groundbreaking pilgrimage to Mecca. That year of 1853, Burton travelled east from Cairo and made his own pilgrimage to Mecca. The following year he was in Abyssinia's holy city of Harar, officially closed to non-Muslims, and five years later, with the backing of the Royal Geographical Society, he and his partner John Hanning Speke cut inland from the malarial Swahili coast in search of the source of the Nile and ensured their names would live on by becoming the first recorded Europeans to reach lakes Tanganyika and Victoria.

Books on the history of African geography are dominated by the stories of Burton and Speke and their contemporaries, particularly Livingstone and Stanley, Grant, and Samuel and Florence Baker. The names that stand out are almost exclusively Victorian. If an earlier African traveller is mentioned, it is likely to be James Bruce, a resourceful Scottish laird who travelled through the Ethiopian highlands in the 1760s in search of the source of the Nile. But Bruce is a man with an unfortunate reputation. In his own time he was accused of having made up the entire story of his travels: his critics suggested that instead of risking his life in Africa he had spent years in happy, peaceful seclusion somewhere around the Mediterranean before returning to Britain. An extended vacation in the south might have seemed tempting to his tormentors, but not, one suspects, to the irascible Bruce. Later critics dismissed Bruce for believing that the source he had reached was that of the White Nile, when in reality it was the Blue. Nevertheless his journey was one of the turning points in European involvement in Africa, for it demonstrated that one man could go a long way inland and live to tell the tale. In Bruce's case, home proved to be more dangerous than the wilds of Africa, for in 1794 he slipped on the stairs of his country house, struck his head and died, four years after the publication of his *Travels*. But what happened between Bruce and Burton, between the 1770s and 1850s? Burckhardt's adventures provided a clue.

For years I collected information and anecdotes about him, talked about him in libraries in London and cafés in the Middle East, followed him on some of his journeys and kept an eye out for new sources of information. But the closer I came to Burckhardt, the more curious I became about the men who set him on his way. Who were they? Why were they prepared to spend time and money to solve the mysteries of the African interior? And how far did they succeed? My initial curiosity about Burckhardt eventually led me to the fantastic, improbable, tragic story that follows.

ACKNOWLEDGEMENTS

Jean Louis Burckhardt reckoned that 'It is a less fatiguing duty to perform travels than to write them down,' but I have loved both the travelling and the writing. Both were made easier and more fun thanks to the help, hospitality and friendship of many people, from Moloko and Cherif of the Casa di Mansa drum group in Abene, Senegal, who taught me a few beats and a few other things about West Africa at the start of the journey, to staff at the Rare Books Department of the British Library, who let me work with Sir Joseph Banks' original books, to friends who read an earlier draft in wintry London and to others who turned away from blue sea and blowing volcanoes to read the proofs on Salina.

In the UK, these include Neil Chambers, Director of the Sir Joseph Banks Archive Project at the Natural History Museum, London; Roger Charity; Douglas of the Linnaean Society; Angela Fisher; Dr Rita Gardner, Director of the RGS; Ben Gibson; Mark Hudson; Deborah Manley; Philip Mansel; Dr John Parker of SOAS; Tom Porteous, then of the BBC World Service; Peta Rée; Susan Strong, archivist of the RGS; Richard Trillo; Bruce Wannell and Albee Yend. Staff at the British Library, Cambridge University Library, the London Library, the Royal Geographical Society and the Sutro Library, San Francisco, have all given generous – and essential – support, as have Christopher Phipps, Arthur Murfitt and the regulars in the London Library's reading room.

In West Africa, I was particularly helped by Ali Farke Touré in Niafunké; the retiring Egyptian librarian of the Ahmed Baba Library in Timbuktu; Professor Boubacar Barry of Shaykh Anta Diop University, Dakar; Malika Beraud in Banjul (and elsewhere!); Stephane Brabant and Bruno Brunetti in Dakar; Jenny Cathcart; Issa Balobo Maiga of the Action Sociale, Timbuktu; staff at the Municipal Library, St Louis; Ibrahima Tapo – Mr Fixit of Mopti; Raymond and Lisa at the Casamar; Hamdool of Radio Timbuktu (Alfarouk); Will Wenham, my travelling companion to Timbuktu; and Silla and Amadou who looked after us for a week on the Niger.

Elsewhere, thanks to Mme Pascale Linant de Bellefonds and Marcel Kurz in Paris, to Professors John Rodenbeck and Jason Thompson at AUC, and Nicholas Warner in Cairo; in the US to Marian Todd and other relatives of John Ledyard, Cassandra Vivian and to Martha Whittaker at the Sutro Library in San Francisco; in Australia to John Gascoigne of the University of New South Wales.

Tracking down maps and illustrations was at times another journey off the map, and I owe a great debt to the inimitable Francis Herbert, Keeper of Maps at the RGS, whose job was not helped by the locking of the Society's map collection during most of the period of my research. Generous advice and help was also provided by Lord Brabourne, Mike Conquer of Southampton University's Oceanography Centre, Dartmouth College's Sarah Hartwell, Kathleen O'Malley and Joshua Shaw, Dr Hisham Khatib in Jordan, Robert Jones of the Government Art Collection, Deborah Manley, Dr Tim Moreton of the National Portrait Gallery, Lord Rennell of Rodd and Jane Taylor, Patricia Usick of the British Museum's Egyptology Department.

I am much indebted (again!) to Christine Walker of the *Sunday Times*, Sarah Spankie of *Condé Nast Traveller* and Sara Jane Hall at the BBC for commissioning stories that helped with my travels in Africa. Gareth Abbott, Kate Fenhalls and Jos Teughels provided me with places to write when I needed some peace and quiet, while Brigid Keenan provided a house in France where key chapters were written. The team at HarperCollins have been wonderful and attentive to my needs and whims: many thanks to Cathie Arrington, Vera Brice, Helen Ellis, Caroline Hotblack, Rachel Nicholson and to photographer Alex Saunderson. Nicholas Crane, Stanley Stewart and Rose Baring generously made time to read the manuscript at an early stage – their comments were crucial – while eagle-eyed Robert Lacey has transformed my pages into this book. Above all I must thank my agent, Gillon Aitken, who encouraged me to put aside my obsession with Burckhardt and to look at the bigger picture; Michael Fishwick, editor extraordinaire at HarperCollins, who saw what it might grow into; and Sylvie Franquet, who has walked, talked, breathed, eaten, smelled and, I know, also suffered years of eighteenth-century Africa with me these past few years.

Anthony Sattin
London, August 2003

The Gates of Africa

1

Exploration's Godfather

'Wide as the world is, traces of you are to be found
in every corner of it.'
Lord Hobart to Joseph Banks, 18 October 1793[1]

London, 9 June 1788

WHAT ADVENTURES these hands have had. They bear witness
to the day he shimmied down a rope to escape a Portuguese block-
ade in the bay at Rio and another when he stroked the shapely
curves of a girl on Tahiti – she had fire in her eyes, he later wrote,
and he incurred the anger of a queen to enjoy her favours. They are
plump, white, well-attended gentleman's hands, protruding from a
frilled cuff, and yet they have wielded knives to cut plant specimens
around the world, held pencils to sketch, brushes to colour, pos-
itioned instruments to observe the transit of Venus and worked a
pump to save Captain Cook's ship from sinking. More recently –
the previous year – they began to swell and ache with the onset of
gout. Now, as he sits for the artist and Royal Academician John
Russell, these hands are holding a sheet of paper on which is drawn
an image of the moon.

The man is Sir Joseph Banks, the year 1788, and the irony of the
situation is not lost on him. There is no chance that he will ever
set foot on the moon and yet, thanks to the telescope created by
his friend William Herschel (who has recently discovered the planet

1

Uranus), he is able to observe its surface in some detail. On the other hand, he has set foot in Africa. He has walked through the lushness of old fruit trees, enjoyed the generosity of palms and discovered the necessity of shade trees. He has also seen some of its murderous stretches of treeless desert. Geographers and earlier travellers have pointed to a great desert, stretching across the northern half of the continent, from the Atlantic Ocean to the Red Sea, pierced from south to north by the Nile. And below that, it was rumoured that there was a great river, the Niger, running across the latitudes. He can imagine the extremes, the withering sands, the vertiginous rocks, the torrential rivers, the vast scrublands scattered with shade trees, the lush tropical pastures and forests, the dusty villages, petty kingdoms, seasonal trading posts and, it is rumoured, the great empires . . . and yet neither Herschel with his telescope nor any other Fellow of the Royal Society can devise a way for him to know for sure what lies in the interior of Africa.

The lexicographer Dr Samuel Johnson, another of Sir Joseph Banks' good friends, has recently defined a map as 'a geographical picture on which lands and seas are delineated according to the longitude and latitude'.[2] Yet this does not describe the pages being sold in London, Paris or anywhere else on earth in 1788. In this, the twenty-seventh year of the glorious reign of the soon-to-be-mad King George III, a map of Africa still owes more to the hopeful imaginings of ancient and medieval geographers than to the lie of the land as it exists in this, the Age of Enlightenment.

In the middle of the map, the interior of the continent, some lines trace the course of rivers; several curves represent mountains. Near the edge of the outline, the names of many towns and a few great cities are written, among them Cairo and Morocco (Marrakesh). At the heart of the continent lies Timbuktu, legendary city of gold, capital of a mighty empire. But history, legend, rumour and deduction all suggest that there is much else beside. The seventeenth-century anthologist Samuel Purchas spelled it out when he wrote that 'the richest Mynes of Gold in the World are in Africa . . . and I cannot but wonder, that so many have sent so many, and

spent so much in remoter voyages to the East and West and neglected Africa in the midst'.[3]

There are several reasons for this sorry state of affairs. To Banks
and his contemporaries Africa appears to be geographically hostile.
In South America, they can sail up the Amazon, as the Spaniards
have done. They can cut deep into North America along the Missis-
sippi with the same ease, and cross much of Europe on the Rhône
and the Rhine. But although ancient geographers have written of the
Niger and the Nile, no European in the Age of Enlightenment has
managed to get very far into Africa without running into trouble with
the continent's geography. Green, precipitous mountains, withering
desert sands, blasting hot in summer, freezing in winter, torn apart
by winds and sandstorms at other times of the year, mangrove
swamps, tropical forests, rivers blocked by rapids, seasonal floods . . .
And to add to this geographical hostility, in many places they have
also had to deal with the hostility of Africans, often caused by a mis-
trust of Christians by Muslims or by a well-founded suspicion that
white-skinned foreigners bring trouble and steal trade.

There is more: even if the landscape or natives don't hold them
up, the rains do, and with the rains come deadly diseases.* It is
possible that some outsiders have made it deep into the continent
– the sixteenth-century Portuguese certainly had a go, and two
Italian priests were rumoured to have crossed from Tripoli to
Katsina in modern-day Nigeria in 1711. But it is safe to say that
most foreigners who have attempted to travel to the interior have
died along the way, while the few survivors have left no detailed
descriptions of where they have been or of what they found there.
Or if they have, their descriptions are lost, misfiled, hidden, untrans-
lated or otherwise not yet come into the hands of Sir Joseph Banks
and his Enlightened friends.

This dearth of information might have halted the movement of
Europeans into the interior of Africa, but it has not stopped geographers from pontificating on its secrets. Almost unanimously, they

---

* Eighteenth-century man, for all his advances, has yet to discover that the good Lord has
given mosquitoes the ability to carry a virus by the name of malaria.

3

have drawn two great river systems that bisect the continent like clock hands pointing to nine o'clock. Wisdom – very ancient wisdom, at that – has it that the Niger River, the hour hand, runs parallel to the equator, and that somewhere to the east of centre of the continent it joins up with the Nile, the minute hand, which climbs due north. On some maps, a third great river, the Congo, is shown as a dash or an arc through the centre. To these dominant features, noble geographers have added other details. They are on safe ground along the coast, where they can plot towns and cities whose character and extent are known for a fact. But what to do with the interior? There are mountains, though no one in Europe knows where they begin or end; to these they have given fanciful names such as the Mountains of the Moon and the Mountains of Kong. Around them have been placed a clutch of kingdoms that some geographers have imagined as savage and barbarous. Others have conceived of noble capitals and mighty empires, worthy partners to Europe's own kingdoms. Beyond this, mapmakers must choose between flights of fancy, or empty white spaces.

In recent years, Europeans, among them our Joseph Banks – the knighthood came in 1781, long after his travelling days – have sailed the seven seas, set foot on Australia, skirted both the north and south ice caps, observed the transit of Venus, escorted Tahitian royalty to London and even looked with some detail at the surface of the moon. Yet they and he remain surprisingly, frustratedly ignorant of Africa. Now they want to know more. Ever since James Bruce's return to Europe, their curiosity has been growing. 'Africa is indeed coming into fashion,' the chronicler Horace Walpole noted at the time. 'There is just returned a Mr Bruce, who has lived three years in the Court of Abyssinia, and breakfasted every morning with the maids of honour on live oxen. Otaheite [the Tahitian prince whom Cook brought to London] and Mr Banks are quite forgotten.'[4]*

* Walpole went on: 'Mr Blake I suppose will order a live sheep for supper at Almack's, and ask whom he shall help to a piece of the shoulder. Oh yes, we shall have negro butchers, and French cooks shall be laid aside. My Lady Townsend, after the rebellion, said, everybody was so bloodthirsty, that she did not dare to dine abroad, for fear of meeting with a rebel pie – now one shall be asked to come and eat a bit of raw mutton. In truth, I do think we are ripe for any extravagance.'

In London's salons, trading houses and government offices, the same questions are being asked: What does Africa consist of? Where are its legendary riches, the fields with their harvests of gold and precious stones? What of the achievements of its people? What do they grow there? What could Europeans grow there? What of their past, their future? A few, Sir Joseph among them, are also asking another question: How can they find out? He has to know.

We come to these questions at the other end of history, after the exploration of the continent and the subsequent scramble by European governments first to control Africa and then to colonise it. The oppression of the majority of Africans by a tiny minority of Europeans, the struggle for independence, the post-colonial catastrophes and the chaos and confusion that exists in many African countries today is a long, long way in the future.

We look at this puzzle of what lies in the interior of Africa from another point of view, coloured by the fact that Africa is now seen, in the words of a British prime minister, as 'a scar on the conscience of the world'. How hard it is to forget all that, but how essential if we are to understand this story. It takes a great leap of imagination to appreciate how tantalising the African questions appear to Sir Joseph Banks in 1788 as he puts down the detailed map of the moon and picks up the sketchy map of the African interior.

A year and a half earlier, in January 1787, fifty-four years after the satirist Jonathan Swift's attack on geographers who 'in Afric maps,/With savage pictures filled their gaps,/And o'er unhabitable downs,/Placed elephants for want of towns', the cartographer Samuel Boulton published a four-sheet map of Africa. Mapmaking is a matter of painstaking evolution. Scraps of information, gathered often in bizarre or dangerous circumstances, allow geographers to effect detailed corrections and minute expansions. Two paces forwards, one backwards. Boulton took as his starting point a map of Africa published in 1749 by the brilliant French geographer

Rennell's map
showing Herodotus'
knowledge of Africa

The
WORLD,
as known to
HERODOTUS,
on
A Spherical Projection;
and with its
Parts *in their just relative* Positions,
and Proportions.

Published according to Act of Parliament, by James Rennell, 20th Feb.r 1800.

Müller sculp.t

Jean-Baptiste Bourguignon d'Anville. In this, he behaved no differ-
ently to the mapmakers who had gone before him. Even the great
d'Anville had used an earlier map as his starting point and was, in
effect, drawing heavily on medieval and classical geographers. The
Frenchman had gone a long way towards removing those elephants
and beasts from the map; Boulton now attempted to go one step
further. In keeping with an age that prided itself on the rigour of
its scientific enquiries, he decided to remove every town, port and
geographical feature, whether mountain, river or desert, of whose
existence he was not certain.

Another Frenchman, de Mornes, had tried this on his own map
of Africa just sixteen years earlier, in 1761, but was led astray by his
love of rationality. Instead of putting down what was known for
certain from first-hand sources, he attempted to accommodate the
stuff of legends: 'It is true,' de Mornes wrote on his map by way
of explanation, 'that the centre of the continent is filled with burning
sands, savage beasts, and almost uninhabitable deserts. The scarcity
of water forces the different animals to come together to the same
place to drink. Finding themselves together at a time when they
are in heat, they have intercourse with one another, without paying
regard to the differences between species. Thus are produced those
monsters which are to be found there in greater numbers than in
any other part of the world.'[5] Geography, it will be clear from this,
is a long and dangerous road, full of traps, ready to ensnare the
well-intentioned but unwary traveller.

Like d'Anville and de Mornes, Boulton explained that he was
including 'all [Africa's] states, kingdoms, republics, regions, islands,
&c.' Crucially, however, there were to be no more elephants, no
dragons or two-headed beasts to cover up his lack of knowledge.
Out went the Garamantes, whose speech the Greek historian Herodotus had described as resembling 'the shrieking of a bat rather
than the language of men'. (Herodotus, it should be pointed out,
did visit North Africa but did not get as far south as the land of the
Garamantes.) Out too went the Blemmyes, whom the first-century
Roman scholar Pliny the Elder described as having 'no head but
mouth and eyes both in their breast'. The only decorations Boulton

8

allowed on his map of Africa were some ships under sail in the oceans and a few African figures draped around the title, which pretty much summed up the *status quo* as far as Europeans were concerned. If he did not know something, he would rather leave a blank than hazard a guess. It proved to be more of a challenge than a cartographer in the Age of Enlightenment might have expected.

Since the Portuguese adventurer Lopes de Sequeira sailed around the continent 270 years earlier, there has been a regular and growing traffic between Europe and ports along Africa's west coast and around the Cape of Good Hope. European sea captains have returned with charts, maps and soundings, gold, ivory and slaves and, perhaps most potent, a rich fabric woven from legends and hearsay. In West Africa, British traders have made headway up the Gambia River and their French rivals have done the same along the more northerly Senegal River. Plenty of Europeans have cut inland from the coast, some certainly making it a few hundred miles up the rivers, perhaps some of them even reaching the Niger and Timbuktu. A few have even sat down and written about their experiences, among them Richard Jobson, who sailed three hundred miles up the Gambia River in 1620 and returned to write *The Golden Trade, or a Discovery of the River Gambia and the Golden Trade of the Aethiopians.* Jobson clearly enjoyed his journey, describing how he shared 'familiar con-versation, fair acceptance, and mutual amity' with people along the river, particularly with a local trader by the name of Bucknor Sano. From Sano, Jobson heard of a city, two months' journey inland, 'the houses whereof are covered only with gold'. Other travellers returned with tales of snow-capped mountains, vast rivers, terrible deserts, miraculous lakes . . .

But even if their experiences reached the ears of geographers, almost nothing they had to report advanced the cause of science, because they saw little of it first-hand. Even when they did see it, they took no bearings and recorded no distances between places, making it difficult and sometimes impossible for geographers to profit from their experiences. All this left Boulton having to explain in a box on his map that: 'The Inland Parts of Africa being but very little known and the Names of the Regions and Countries which fill that vast Tract of Land being for the Greatest part placed by Conjecture It may be judged how Absurd are the Divisions Traced in some Maps and why they were not followed in this.' As a result, the interior of Boulton's map has more white than black, more virgin page than printer's ink.

So matters stand on this June day in 1788 when Sir Joseph Banks, middle-aged, solidly-built, hair curled around his temples, powdered and puffed on top, steps out of his home, a corner house – number 32 – and into Soho Square.* The seventeen years that have passed since he was in Africa have transformed him, and nothing about his appearance suggests that he is anything other than a man of wealth and privilege. Outwardly, at least, the English gentleman and *amateur* have eclipsed the globetrotting man of action. In 1771, when he returned from his round-the-world voyage as the scientist on Cook's voyage, Banks was hailed as a hero and revelled in his new-found status of celebrity traveller. In 1774, by which time he had made a voyage to Iceland, the chronicler James Boswell described him as 'an elephant, quite placid and gentle, allowing you to get upon his back or play with his proboscis'.[6] By 1788, however, age and now gout have begun to sap some of his vigour. No longer a world traveller, Banks is now a grandee, a friend of the King and President of his Royal Society. He is a famous man. Extraordinarily well connected, he counts key politicians, big bankers, bankrupt old money, grand titles, leading businessmen and some of the most brilliant brains of the day among his circle

* Banks bequeathed the house to his librarian, Robert Brown, who rented part of it to the Linnaean Society. It was demolished in 1936 and the site is now covered by the London offices of 20th Century-Fox.

of close friends. But for all that, it is the world beyond his island that continues to shape him and that has provided posterity with the material with which it has fashioned his image as the patron of travellers, the godfather of exploration and the caretaker of much of Britain's colonial policy.

In the seventeen years since his return, the world has also changed: perhaps most significant, the American colonies have won their independence from the British crown. While mandarins in London's ministries continue to respond to the loss like wounded parents, Sir Joseph has moved on. He spawns his own plans for new British interests abroad, fosters those of others and lends time, money and credibility to anything he thinks will further the interests of the country he loves so dearly. Increasingly his attention is drawn to Africa, and he remembers its remarkable richness and seductive promise. As he prepares to make the half-mile journey across the centre of London to St Alban's Street, he does so knowing that he has a workable idea of how to improve the map of Africa. It is an idea that he will foster for the remainder of his long life and that will allow him to continue to exercise his love of both intellectual and – vicariously at least – of physical adventure.

Perhaps as he leaves home this day he remembers, as many of us do, the things he has not completed. Much has already been achieved, but so much more remains to be done. The First Fleet of convicts and settlers sailed from England the previous year and should by now be settled in the colony he has dreamed up, lobbied for and helped to equip at Australia's Botany Bay (the name Captain Cook gave to the bay where Banks went botanising). Seeds and cuttings are sent with increasing regularity from a range of contacts he has fostered around the world. As they arrive, they are stored in his Soho Square herbarium or planted out, propagated and studied at the botanical gardens he has helped to create at Kew. But the founding of the Royal Horticultural Society is in the future, as is the safekeeping of Linnaeus' collection, the development of his own botanical garden, the advising of the King, his seat on the Privy Council and the boards of Trade and Longitude. The future will indeed be fertile.

To maintain all his contacts, he has had to become a prodigious letter writer. Each morning a pile of correspondence is gone through in the study at Soho Square, Banks sitting at one of the desks in front of a sofa, the fireplace and a dozen good portraits in oil. A great deal of his correspondence concerns the Royal Society and its ever-widening range of interests, for he is guided by the visionary principle of universal knowledge and by his belief that resources should be pooled, advances shared and science in all its many branches should be fostered across national borders.

In this year of 1788 he is forty-five years old and has already been President of the Royal Society, the home of England's finest scientists, for ten years. During this time, dissenters have complained that a heavy-drinking, adventure-loving botaniser is a far from worthy successor to a chair once occupied by the likes of Isaac Newton. But he has weathered their protests as he will weather others, with stoicism, confident that he can shrug them off.

The Royal Society met in its new quarters at Somerset House in the Strand, as usual, the previous evening and, as usual before the meeting, Sir Joseph opened his home both to members of the Society and to members of society. Three rooms in Soho Square were filled with scientists and philosophers, adventurers, business-men and foreigners, all of them bearing seeds, whether physical or metaphorical, botanical or philosophical.* There are letters to write on this Monday morning as a result of the Society's meeting: among others, to the botanist Johann Hedwig, Professor of Medicine at Leipzig, whom he wants to congratulate for having been elected 'a foreign member of our Royal Society'. There is always too much correspondence to deal with, too many other tasks to be done, but now he puts them aside, or instructs others to continue with them, for he has a meeting to attend that will help to shape the future of Africa.

---

* As T.J. Mathias put it in *The Pursuits of Literature* (1812), 'Sir Joseph Banks has instituted a meeting at his house in Soho Square, every Sunday evening, at which the literati and men of rank and consequence, and men of no consequence at all, find equally a polite and pleasing reception from that justly distinguished man'.

2

The Charge of Ignorance

'No other part of the world abounds with gold and silver in greater degree . . . and it is surprising that neither the ancient or modern Europeans notwithstanding their extraordinary and insatiable thirst after gold and silver, should have endeavoured to establish themselves effectively in a country much nearer to them than either America or the East Indies and where the object of their desires are to be found in equal, if not greater plenty.'

Encyclopaedia Britannica, second edition (1788)

London, 9 June 1788

THE CAPITAL is a mad, crowded jumble, its inhabitants gripped by a fever of activity. While Sir Joseph is on his way to his rendezvous in St Alban's Street, Their Most Britannic (and still quite Germanic) Majesties King George III and Queen Charlotte Sophia are reviewing a troop of Dragoons. Mr Pitt the Younger, the twenty-eight-year-old Prime Minister, is immersed in the cares and affairs of State, turning over the debates in Parliament and deliberating on tensions in Europe. The Lord Chancellor is in his office appointing a new Lord Chief Justice – it isn't something he has done before: the previous incumbent, the Earl of Mansfield, held the post for thirty-two years. Like His Lordship, the new Chief Justice will have no trouble filling the prisons. Sir Joseph Banks knows all about this problem of overcrowding. The three female cells in London's Newgate Jail are crammed with many more than the seventy prisoners they were intended to hold, as convicts sentenced to 'Transportation to Parts Beyond the Seas' wait for the arrival of ships to take them to Botany Bay, Sir Joseph's Australian project.

The Times has just called London 'an emporium of all the world and the wonder of foreigners'. Plenty of these 'wondering' foreigners appear to be installed in the capital. 'London abounds with an incredible number of these black men,' one commentator notes this year of 1788,[1] while to the poet William Wordsworth's eyes:

> *Among the crowd all specimens of man,*
> *Through all the colours which the sun bestows,*
> *And every character of form and face:*
> *The Swede, the Russian; from the genial south,*
> *The Frenchman and the Spaniard; from remote*
> *America, the Hunter-Indian; Moors,*
> *Malays, Lascars, the Tartar, the Chinese,*
> *And Negro Ladies in white muslin Gowns.*[2]

The world's largest city reaches out beyond the shores of Albion with more than just prison ships. There is plenty of movement through the port during these early days of June as ships arrive from Norway, Cadiz, Nantes, Venice and several tropical ports. 'Just landed,' trills an advert for Young's Italian Warehouse on the front page of the paper this day, 9 June, 'a large quantity of very curious Salad Oil, from Provence, Lucca, and Florence; Olives, Anchovies, Capers; Parmesan, Gruyer, and other foreign Cheese; Macaroni . . .' Some Londoners clearly have a taste for the finer things in life. There is foreign intelligence, too: news just in that the states of Massachusetts, Connecticut, Pennsylvania, Delaware, New Jersey and Georgia – British colonies until eleven years ago – have agreed to join something called the United States of America. It is more salt in the festering wound of the mother nation. There is no appetite now for colonies if this is how the successful ones behave.

One other snippet of foreign intelligence reported this day has a bearing on our story: there is early news of an insurrection in France as demands grow for the King to make sweeping concessions and share power. A revolution is in the making.

Parliament, keen to break for summer recess as soon as its work is done, has its sights on matters abroad as well as near at hand. On this day, as Sir Joseph heads for his meeting, Honourable Members hear about the plight of American Loyalists, the problems in Scottish boroughs and the dilemma of the English Episcopal Church in Amsterdam. But the main debate concerns evidence given to support a 'Bill for regulating the transportation of Slaves from Africa to America'. Here is a topic guaranteed to split the House as it is splitting the country, or at least that part of the country with moral, economic or political interest in such matters. *The Times* in its editorial has taken the side of Sir William Dolben, the politician who has sponsored the Bill, thundering that, 'For Englishmen to chain their innocent fellow-creatures together, and keep them in bondage for life, is much more repugnant to Christianity, than cutting off the ears of the enemy is barbarity, in the followers of Mahomet.'[3] That afternoon, however, had the Honourable Members looked out of their windows they would have seen a very different sort of fleet sailing upstream past the Houses of Parliament as pleasure boats massed to contest the Annual Silver Cup and Cover.

Across the river in Croydon, a well-known boxer from Birmingham by the name of Futerel is failing to live up to his reputation as a destroyer of men. The contest, held in an impromptu ring, lasts an hour and ten minutes, which sounds reasonable enough, but according to reports Futerel spends much of this time 'lying for a few minutes' or pretending to be 'a lump of doe in a sack'. The Prince of Wales and his attendant Major Hanger happen to be among the disgusted audience. Suspicions of a fix are rife.

Nor is London lacking in artistic endeavour these bright days of June. At the Poet's Gallery in Fleet Street, Mr Macklin is showing new work by a range of artists, among them Sir Joshua Reynolds and his rival, Thomas Gainsborough, now fighting a losing battle against cancer. The Theatre Royal in Covent Garden is spreading out the dust sheets as its audience flees to their country estates to escape the coming hot weather, but Sadler's Wells, which attracts a different sort of public and has only just opened for the summer season, is staging performances by a ten-year-old boy known as the Infant Hercules, while another character known as the Little Devil dances across a tightrope. Meanwhile, down at the Theatre Royal on Drury Lane, the actor Mr Smith is pulling down the final curtain on a glorious thirty-five-year stage career by performing in Sheridan's *School for Scandal*. After the performance, the socialite Lady Lucan is heard to say to Mrs Sheridan, the playwright's wife: 'You must certainly be a happy woman, Madam, who have the felicity of pleasing the man that pleases all the world.' The comment is worthy of one of Sheridan's characters, because it is common knowledge that for some time the playwright has been looking elsewhere for his sexual pleasures.

Later, after the lights have gone out on anyone who has laid their head in a palace, a mansion, a house, an apartment, a lodging or a share of a bed in a doss-house, after the homeless have collapsed into a gin-induced haze in the city's parks or beneath its bridges, just as the clocks are striking midnight, an athletic man by the name of Foster Powell is seen leaving the capital for the northern city of York, hoping to get there and back by Saturday midnight, five full days. He is accompanied by two men on horseback and one on foot, presumably to ensure that he is not held up along the way – robbery on the King's highway remains a common complaint. Powell intends to travel from midnight until eleven the next morning, rest until 5 p.m. and then walk through the night. To succeed, he needs to walk just over sixty-six miles a day. Long before the clock chimes and Powell sets out on his adventure, Sir Joseph Banks has embarked upon one of his own.

Mr Hunt, the obsequious proprietor of the St Alban's Tavern, is an old hand at greeting the rich and famous at his establishment, for his rooms are a popular venue for political meetings and fashionable dinners, among them the regular though far from frequent meetings of the Saturday's Club. Little is known of the Club before this memorable day, not even whether it usually meets on a Saturday: after all, this is a Monday. But there is nothing unusual about its existence, for we are in the great age of clubs and societies. An active man about town can expect to belong to several of them, although perhaps not so many as Sir Joseph Banks, who is an esteemed member of the Royal Society Club, the Society of Dilettanti, the Society of Arts, the Society of Antiquaries, the Engineers' Society, the Society for the Improvement of Naval Architecture and others. Most of these provide a good excuse for a social gathering of sometimes learned, usually entertaining, often heavy-drinking and invariably like-minded men. In this, the Saturday's Club is unexceptional; until this day, when something of immense and long-lasting consequence happens.

Banks turns off Pall Mall, enters the St Alban's Tavern, is shown up the stairs and into a room rented for the occasion for a guinea. Only nine of the Club's dozen members are able to attend. After the greetings and an exchange of news, glasses are filled and a good dinner served.

Banks' companions are all wealthy men with significant political and intellectual influence. Henry Beaufoy is a Quaker and Member of Parliament. The son of a vinegar manufacturer, he has shown more interest in politics than commerce and published his first paper, *The Effects of Civilisation on the Real Improvement and Happiness of Mankind*, before his twentieth birthday. When Gainsborough painted him, he chose to portray him as a romantic, a dandified English gentleman, his hair a little wild and swept back, left hand hidden in the breast of a blue, big-buttoned frock-coat, breeches tucked into riding boots, right hand resting on a cane. He possesses formidable debating skills, as one would expect of a founder of the Dissenting Academy, and is preparing to make a thundering speech in Parliament damning the captains of slaving vessels for mistreating their human cargoes and damning their defenders in Parliament with what he will call 'the stigma of everlasting

17

dishonour'.[4] It will be one more step, he hopes, on the road to the abolition of slavery.

Alongside him is General Conway. At seventy, the General is the oldest of the group, a former Secretary of State, a retired army top brass, an amateur botanist and, like Banks and Beaufoy, an improver – he commissioned the bridge over the Thames at Henley. Surprisingly, he is also a linguist: a performance is announced for this very evening of a French play he has translated.

One of the youngest members of the Saturday's Club is the Irish aristocrat Francis Rawdon. Soon he will inherit the title Earl of Moira, and then earn that of Marquis of Hastings, will become an intimate of the Prince of Wales and be appointed Governor-General of India. But at this stage, at thirty-three years of age, he is merely a rising star, a tall man with a commanding manner who has come home from the American War of Independence with a reputation for being a reliable officer and with the rank of lieutenant colonel.

The other members are no less remarkable. William Pulteney is one of the richest men in the country, and Sir William Fordyce a doctor who has published works on subjects as varied as venereal diseases and the medical properties of rhubarb. Friends describe Fordyce as an unassuming, convivial man who seldom dines alone. The Earl of Galloway, on the other hand, is joyfully outspoken, particularly about his twin passions of agriculture and the abolition of slavery. Here too is the Commissioner for Trade and Plantations, Sir Adam Ferguson, and Andrew Stuart, a lawyer and sometime Member of Parliament, both government advisers. Of the three members who are unable to attend, Sir John Sinclair has been called 'the most indefatigable man in England' – he will go on to create the Board of Agriculture and sit on the Privy Council – the Earl of Carysfort is a scholarly evangelist, while the most unusual man among them, Richard Watson, the Bishop of Llandaff, has had the honour of occupying the chairs of both Divinity and Chemistry at Cambridge University. Between them, these dozen men wield great influence in many spheres of life, from government to commerce and science. Seven are members of the elevated Royal Society, eight have seats in Parliament and most own significant estates or control extensive business interests.

The records of this meeting are of a general nature, and although they tell us what is decided upon, they do not reveal who says what or in which order. It seems certain that mention is made of the Slavery Bill currently being discussed in Parliament, and from slavery conversation will naturally enough have turned to Africa.

Banks is the only member of the Saturday's Club who has been to Africa. Since his return he has funded several botanical expeditions to examine the continent's rich flora. He has also received several proposals from people interested in making journeys into the interior and a suggestion that an Arabic-speaking slave from the West Indies be shipped back to Africa to travel inland. But he is not the only one to be interested in Africa, as is suggested by the fact that 1200 people subscribed to the first edition of *The Letters of Ignatius Sancho*,* a freed slave. Another account of slavery, written by Olaudah Equiano,† the son of a West African chief, is just now being prepared for the printers, backed among others by General Conway and Lord Rawdon, both now present in this upstairs room at the tavern.

If Banks has provided the original idea, Henry Beaufoy now pushes it forward. The geographer James Rennell, who is not present but who knows most of the members, will write later that Beaufoy smoothed the way for the Association, 'a path which, more than any other person, he had contributed to open, and render smooth'.[5] Sir John Sinclair seems to have been the other key player – his son will later claim that he took 'a leading part' – although he is not present now as matters come to a head and the following resolution is made:

---

* Sancho was born on a slave ship, soon orphaned and handed to three 'maidens' in Greenwich who were happy to keep him in a state of ignorance. He came to the attention of the Duke and Duchess of Montagu, who employed him as their butler, educated him and, when he was too old to serve, set him up as a grocer. Sancho's son William worked for a time as Sir Joseph Banks' librarian before setting himself up as a bookseller.

† Equiano was enslaved and shipped to the West Indies, but ended up as an educated, Christ-loving author pleading in London for the abolition of slavery.

At an adjourned Meeting of the Saturday's Club, at the St. Alban's Tavern, on the 9th of June, 1788.

PRESENT

Earl of Galloway	Sir Adam Ferguson	Mr. Pulteney
Lord Rawdon	Sir Joseph Banks	Mr. Beaufoy
General Conway	Sir William Fordyce	Mr. Stuart

ABSENT MEMBERS

Bishop of Llandaff	Sir John Sinclair
Lord Carysfort	

Resolved,
That as no species of information is more ardently desired, or more generally useful, than that which improves the science of Geography; and as the vast continent of Africa, notwithstanding the efforts of the ancients, and the wishes of the moderns, is still in a great measure unexplored, the members of this Club do form themselves into an Association for promoting the discovery of the inland parts of that quarter of the world.[6]

The resolution oozes optimism, as does a four-page brochure the members publish soon after. This serves as a statement of intent, a sales document in which the full Plan of the Association is laid out. Both the minutes and the Plan are written by Henry Beaufoy, Secretary of the new Association; Banks, who has been appointed Treasurer, approves the text before it goes to the printers. In the Plan, Beaufoy explains the geographical attractions of Africa: 'Of the objects of inquiry which engage our attention the most, there are none, perhaps, that so much excite continued curiosity, from childhood to age; none that the learned and unlearned so equally wish to investigate, as the nature and history of those parts of the world, which have not, to our knowledge, been hitherto explored.'

So far, so good. There follows something of an over-simplification: 'To this desire the Voyages of the late Captain Cook have so far afforded gratification, that nothing worthy of research by Sea, the Poles themselves excepted, remains to be examined.' Then Beaufoy gets to the point of the Association: much of Asia and America has recently been explored, as has the area north of Cape Town, while traders have made inroads up the rivers of West Africa. 'But notwithstanding the progress of discovery on the coasts and borders of that vast continent, the map of its interior is still but a wide extended blank.' He ends his introduction thus: 'Desirous of rescuing the age from a charge of ignorance, which, in other respects, belongs so little to its character, a few individuals, strongly impressed with the practicability and utility of thus enlarging the fund of human knowledge, have formed the plan of an Association for promoting the discovery of the interior parts of Africa.'[7]

Being British, they have also drawn up rules to regulate function and behaviour. They have committed themselves to paying a subscription of five guineas a year each for three years. During the Association's first year, they are invited to put forward the names of people they think will make suitable members – they clearly want the Association to grow, but they are not going to let in just anybody. And before they leave the tavern, they hold a ballot to choose a Committee: Banks and Beaufoy are elected along with Rawdon, Stuart and the Bishop of Llandaff. The Committee is then given responsibility for 'the choice of the persons who are to be sent on the discovery of the interior parts of Africa, together with the Society's correspondence, and the management of its funds'.[8] With that, the meeting is adjourned, the room empties, the friends part, perhaps unaware of the significance of their resolution.

London is awash with Associations – there is one 'for preserving Liberty and Property against Republicans and Levellers' and another 'for reducing the exorbitant Price of Butcher's Meat'.[9] But this one is different. Until now, exploration has relied on the patronage of kings or governments, on trading companies and on the occasional enlightened, wealthy or speculative individual. This organisation is to be funded by a group of friends whose purpose is neither political nor commercial, although they will not deny that they have interests in both. The African Association has been created to mount expeditions and collect information that will lead to geographical advances and open up the continent. It is the start of a new era.

At this point it is worth pausing to consider to what purpose any new findings might be put. Sir John Sinclair's son provided a blunt but also a neat answer. 'Hitherto,' he observed, 'Europeans had visited Africa to plunder, to oppress, and to enslave;– the object of this society was to promote the cause of science and humanity; to explore the mysterious geography, to ascertain the resources, and to improve the condition of that ill-fated continent.'[10]

Promoting the cause of science and humanity encapsulates a large number of possibilities. Take the slave trade, for instance. Several members of the Association are active in the campaign to end slavery; those who are not are at least aware of predictions for the future of Britain's trans-Atlantic trade. This trade depends on three points of contact. Britain exports cloth, metal (including guns) and other products of its growing industries to the West African coast. Trade between Britain and West Africa is clearly profitable: between 1720 and 1772 it grew from sixty-five ships carrying £130,000 worth of cargo (now roughly equivalent to £6.5 million) to 175 ships – a departure every two days – carrying £866,000 worth of goods (£43.3 million).[11]

By 1788 these figures are considerably higher, and West Africa has become one of Europe's major trading partners. But there is a limit to how much trade can grow between the two continents, as Africa has only a limited ability to pay for European goods. Gold dust, ivory, animal skins and senna* are all accepted as objects of barter, but the vast and growing majority of European goods are paid for in Africa with slaves. These are then shipped across the Atlantic, where they are traded for sugar, rum and the other good things of the Caribbean, which are then brought back and sold in England. The development of Britain's growing industries as well as the wealth of the West Indies depend on this triangular trade.

---

* Senna, a leaf grown south of the Sahara and Timbuktu, among other places, was in great demand in pre-fibre Europe for its laxative properties.

If the sale of slaves is to be outlawed, how will West Africans pay for cloth and guns? The answer is obvious to anyone, such as Banks or Rennell, who knows their history, and it has a direct bearing on the Association's activities.

In 1324, Mansa Kankan Musa, the Emperor of Mali, decided to fulfil his articles of faith by making a pilgrimage to Mecca. He and his considerable entourage crossed the dessert and were treated royally by the Sultan when they arrived in Cairo. Horses and camels, food and water were then provided to smooth their way to Mecca and back to Egypt. The Emperor was so pleased with this treatment that, in the words of one observer, when he returned to the Nile he spread 'upon Cairo the flood of his generosity: there was no person, officer of the court or holder of any office of the sultanate who did not receive a sum of gold from him. The people of Cairo earned incalculable sums from him, whether by buying and selling or by gifts. So much gold was current in Cairo that it ruined the value of money . . .'[12] While it took a generation for the price of gold to recover in Cairo, the legend of Mali's immense gold reserves lasted at least until the summer of 1788.

Mansa Musa's extravagance (in the end, he spent so much that he was obliged to borrow money to get home) is not the only African story to have reached the Saturday's Club's eyes and ears. To them as to many in Europe at this time, West Africa, and particularly Mali, is a land of golden promise, another El Dorado. Al-Idrissi, the twelfth-century geographer, has described many civilised cities of central Africa, among them Kaugha, 'a populous City, without Walls, famous for Business and useful for Arts for the Advantage of its People'; Kuku, where 'the Governors and Nobility are covered with Sattin'; and Ghana, where the King, for decoration, had 'an Lump of Gold, not cast, nor wrought by any other Instruments, but perfectly formed by the Divine Providence only, of thirty Pounds Weight'. Leo Africanus, four hundred years later, had this to say of Timbuktu: 'The Inhabitants, and especially the Strangers that reside there, are very rich, insomuch that the present King gave both his Daughters in Marriage to two rich Merchants . . . The rich King of Tombuto has in his Possession many golden Plates and Scepters, some whereof are 1300 Ounces in Weight, and he keeps a splendid and well-furnished Court ... The King at his own Expense liberally maintaineth here great Numbers of Doctors, Judges, Priests, and other learned Men. There are Manuscripts, or written Books, brought hither out of Barbary, which are sold for more Money than any other Merchandize. Instead of Money, they use Barrs of Gold ...'[13] Instead of slaves, so the thinking goes, they could pay for imported European goods with these 'Barrs of Gold'.

All this has made an impression on the imaginations of members of the Saturday's Club, as is clear from Beaufoy's prediction that 'Their mines of gold (the improvable possession of many of the inland states) will furnish, to an unknown, and probably boundless extent, an article that commands, in all the markets of the civilized world, a constant and unlimited scale.'[14] This might have been true several centuries ago, but by the end of the eighteenth century the gold reserves which Mansa Musa and the kings of Timbuktu had exploited are exhausted. What's more, the great empires they supported have recently been torn apart by a reforming Islamic *jihad*. The great cities of Sudan have been reduced and their kings left in fear of their lives, while the internal trade has shrunk to a shadow of its former glory. All this, Beaufoy and the other members of the Association have yet to discover.

The lure of gold, the campaign to abolish slavery, the need to find new trading partners all add to the keenly felt desire to know what lies at the heart of Africa. By the end of the eighteenth century, breathtaking scientific advances have forced Europeans to reconsider their relationship with the world. The past is being uncovered – classical sites such as Pompeii are even now being excavated – the natural world is being classified by the likes of Linnaeus, while Cook's voyages have shown that the physical world can also be known. In such a rampant intellectual climate, can the secrets of the African interior remain hidden for much longer?

Africa is a large continent, too large even for the ambitions of the Association: they must choose an area of interest within it. It is now beyond the bounds of possibility to resurrect their discussions or determine the way in which they reached this decision, but it is possible to look at the ideas that have informed their choices.

Beaufoy gives some pointers when he explains in the Plan of the Association how much of the rest of the world has been explored and recorded. Even parts of Africa are well known – he notes that the Swedish traveller Dr André Sparrman, a member of Cook's second trans-global expedition, has travelled some way inland from Cape Colony in the south of the continent; the English translation of his *Voyage to the Cape of Good Hope, towards the Antarctic Polar Circle and round the World; but chiefly into the Country of the Hottentots and Caffres, from the Year 1772, to 1776* appeared two years earlier, in 1786. Colonel Gordon, in charge of the Dutch garrison at the Cape, has since travelled inland as far as the Orange River, and perhaps his account will appear before long. In East Africa, James Bruce's long-awaited, five-volume *Travels to Discover the Source of the Nile* is expected at any moment, although in the event it is not published until 1790. But little progress has been made in the inland parts of West Africa since early in the eighteenth century, when an Englishman by the name of Francis Moore and a Frenchman, André Brue, sailed up the Senegal and Gambia rivers. Of the interior of sub-Saharan Africa, the area loosely called Sudan (not to be confused with the present country further to the east), almost nothing new has been learned since the sixteenth-century descriptions of Leo Africanus.

Leo's work on the interior stands out from earlier accounts, from the twelfth-century Nubian al-Idrissi for instance, from the Roman and Greek maps, even from the second-century Alexandrian geographer Ptolemy, because he actually visited many of the places he described. Born into a wealthy Moorish family in Granada in the 1490s and brought up in Fez after the fall of the Moorish kingdoms in Spain, he was taken travelling at an early age. By the time he was twenty he had already visited Tabriz in Persia and had crossed to Timbuktu on the southern side of the Sahara. Later, though it is not clear in which year, he returned south, revisited Timbuktu and then made a tour of the countries or territories of central North Africa. From Djenne and Gao in Mali, he travelled through Agadez, Kano and Burnu before making his way to Egypt. Then in 1518, on his way back to Morocco from Egypt, Italian pirates took him prisoner and his life changed. There was a chance that he might have been killed or sold as a slave, but his captors seem to have recognised that he was a man of learning and presented him to the Medici Pope Leo X. Leo, a shrewd judge of character and a notable patron of the arts, recognised the value of the tale the Moor had to tell. He went to great lengths to keep him in Rome, cosseting him with luxury and privilege, and going so far as to adopt him as his own godson. Renamed after his benefactor, baptised in the Christian faith and given the distinguishing name of Africanus, Leo the Moor sat down to write an account of the things he had seen and heard on his travels. His *Descrittione dell'Africa*, published in 1550 and translated into English as *A Geographical Historie of Africa* in 1600, became the authority on African geography.

'I saw 15 kingdoms of the Negroes myself,' Leo writes of the interior of the continent, 'but there are several others which I never saw, but the Negroes know them well.'[15] Of the geography of the region to the south of the Sahara, he has this to say:

> In the Country of the Negroes, there is a noble river called Niger, which beginneth Eastward from a Desart, named by the Natives Seu. Others affirm that the Niger springs out of a Lake, and so goeth on Westward till it empties itself into the Sea. Our Cosmographers say that it comes out of Nilus, and that for some Space it is hid in the Earth, and afterwards pours forth in such a Lake as is before mentioned. Some other people think that the Beginning of this River is to the West-ward, and so running East formeth that great Lake: But that is not probable, because they go with the Stream in Boats Westward from Tombuto [Timbuktu] to Ghinea [Ghana], and Melli [Mali], for those Kingdoms are situated to the West of Tombuto.[16]

Banks and his circle recognise that Leo offers no certainties. Even though he visited the region and sailed along the Niger, he still cannot place the river's source with any certainty. Nor has he correctly remembered the direction of its flow. But he has provided them with their challenge: they need to clarify, verify or find an alternative to Leo's account of the interior. And so the Committee agrees to direct its first geographical mission south of the Sahara to Bambuk, where they will look for the Niger River and sail along it to Timbuktu, Borno and the other places associated with the legendary and now exhausted goldfields. Their plan is typical of the imagination of an age of genius, breathtaking in both scope and ambition. It calls for two travellers to be commissioned. One is to sail to Tripoli on the North African coast and travel south across the Sahara. The other is to approach from the east, through what is now the state of Sudan, and cross to the west coast.

By slicing through the northern part of the continent, top to bottom and side to side, Banks and Beaufoy hope to find answers to the questions that have puzzled geographers for millennia. Where do the two great rivers rise? Where does the Niger end? Where are the mighty empires of central Africa? And where are their goldfields? As Banks watches his fellow Committee members leave Soho Square on Tuesday, 16 June 1788, he is confident that it is now only a matter of time before they fill in those blanks on Samuel Boulton's map.

3

A Friend to Mankind

'In furtherance of their designs, they employed able and ingeni-
ous travellers to penetrate into the interior, and collect information upon all subjects interesting to the philosopher or the
philanthropist.'

Rev. John Sinclair, *Memoir of the Life and Works of Sir John Sinclair*[1]

London, May 1788

THERE WAS A PRICE to pay for success, particularly for achieving
it so young. Joseph Banks was twenty-seven when he came home
from the round-the-world voyage with Captain Cook to find he
was famous, and just thirty-five when he followed Isaac Newton
and a line of other remarkable men into the President's chair at
the Royal Society. The darling of salon and club, he was also a
favourite of cartoonists and satirists, who coined a number of ripe
nicknames for him, among them the Fly Catching Macaroni, the
Great South Sea Caterpillar, the Intellectual Flea and the President
of Frogs and Flies.[2] There were many others. The lampooner John
Wolcot, writing under the name of Peter Pindar, filled page after
page with insulting verse along the lines of: 'A nutshell might
with perfect ease enclose/Three-quarters of his sense, and all his
learning.'[3]

Banks took this in his stride. He never replied to, nor even
commented on any of these attacks, at least not in public. Perhaps

28

he found them amusing. Perhaps he recognised that criticism confirmed his significance in the run of things: the Grub Street hacks didn't waste their poison on just anybody. And even Pindar, a man whose pen was more poisoned than most, had to salute Banks' legendary hospitality:

> To give a breakfast in Soho,
> Sir Joseph's very bitterest foe
> Must certainly allow him peerless merit;
> Where, on a wag-tail, and tom-tit,
> He shines, and sometimes on a nit,
> Displaying pow'rs few Gentlemen inherit.[4]

With the notable exception of a brothel known as Hooper's Hotel that counted the Prince of Wales among its patrons, Sir Joseph's townhouse was the busiest in Soho Square. It was one of the largest, too, and certainly ought to have been more than adequate to contain his household; but it is a golden rule that collectors never have enough space.

The forty-five-year-old knight had been married for nine years to Dorothea Hugessen,* a woman described as 'comely and modest' – in a portrait painted by the Royal Academician John Russell in 1788 she appears as a dark-haired, round-faced, gentle-looking woman in frills and flounces. She was also an heiress. Not that Banks needed the money – he was in his own right among the three or four hundred richest men in the country. Perhaps more important for him was her readiness to accommodate his many interests. She liked to collect porcelain, so will have understood his obsessive hoarding instincts. She was also prepared to accommodate his sister, Sarah Sophia, a tall, 'handsome' and above all forceful woman who indulged plenty of her own eccentricities, passions and obsessive urges, among them a desire to collect coins. It was clearly a happy

---

* There were rumours that Banks had become engaged to a young woman named Harriet Blosset before sailing with Cook. She certainly believed they were betrothed, and spent the years of his absence embroidering waistcoats for him. He had other ideas, as is indicated by a comment he made at the time about the women of South Africa: 'had I been inclined for a wife I think this is the place of all others I have seen where I could have best suited myself' (Lyte, p.141).

arrangement: as late as 1818, Dorothea wrote of her husband and sister-in-law that 'no two people ever contributed more to the happiness of others than they both have to mine. They are everything to me.'[5] In considerable harmony and happiness, then, they filled the house with cupboards and chests and boxes, with porcelain and coins, plants and seeds, dried creatures and pinned insects, rocks, antiquities, exotica of all sorts and souvenirs from Sir Joseph's travels, not just around the world with Cook, but an earlier journey to Labrador and Newfoundland and a later one to Iceland. But the thing that took up most room in the house was his library, which he built into one of the finest in the country. The catalogue alone ran to 2464 pages.[*]

These collections, particularly the library, were unique resources and not ones that Banks thought of keeping to himself.[†] As a result of this and because of his range of connections and interests, his house became one of the social and intellectual hubs of the city. A steady stream of people passed through his door, among them regular visitors who had access whenever they wanted and scholars and intellectuals from around the country and across Europe. Many of these people were also welcome at the breakfasts that Banks held each Thursday morning during the Royal Society's season. As *Feltham's Picture of London* noted in 1805:

> *Sir Joseph Banks, President of the Royal Society, Receives his friends, members of the society and gentlemen introduced by them, at a public breakfast, at his house in Soho-square. The literary, and much more, the scientific news of the day, are the topics of the conversations which then take place. New and curious specimens of subjects in antiquities, in natural history, &c., are often produced for the inspection of the persons who then assemble. On every Sunday evening, too, during the meetings of the Royal Society, the same gentleman*

[*] Until his death at the house in 1782, Daniel Solander also lived at Soho Square. One of Banks' assistants on the Cook voyage, he later became his librarian and keeper of the natural history collection at the British Museum.
[†] Banks would bequeath the majority of his library, herbarium, manuscripts, drawings, engravings and all his other significant collections to the British Museum.

*opens his house for the reception of a conversation-assembly
of his literary and philosophical friends, and of all gentlemen,
whether natives of the country or foreigners, whom his friends
introduce.*

Historians tend to portray Banks as gout-ridden and cantankerous,
a massive, brooding presence with great influence but increasingly
outdated views. All that was to come later, when he was in his
seventies and had become jowly, swept his grey hair off his face
and packed a considerable belly in his dark frock-coat. But in 1788,
when we first meet him, he is in middle age. Convivial and connected, he is also up-to-date in his thinking, good-humoured,
quick-witted and still physically active, equally enthusiastic about
riding his horses and fishing on the Thames. At this stage, he looks
like a man who has a great deal more to accomplish.

In manners, Banks can be somewhat brusque – he is more a
country squire than a courtier, and small talk is not his forte, as
Fanny Burney, the novelist and Second Keeper of the Queen's
Robes, discovered. Meeting him at a Windsor tea party she complained that he was 'so exceedingly shy that we made no acquaintance at all. If, instead of going round the world, he had fallen from
the moon, he could not appear less versed in the usual modes of
a tea-drinking party. But what, you will say, has a tea-party to do
with a botanist, a man of science, and the President of the Royal
Society?'[6] Not that his lack of tea-party manners deterred Fanny,
for she was still happy to join friends and relations, the great and
the good, petitioners, porters carrying packages fresh off the mail
coach, retainers bringing food, papers and news from his country
estate in Yorkshire and all the other visitors who knocked at the
door of his house in Soho Square.

Standing out from this crowd one day in May 1788 was a tall,
fit, fair-haired man who, according to one account, was dressed in
rags. In spite of his appearance he was not begging and, contrary
to what might have been expected, he had no trouble in getting
past the doorman. The visitor was John Ledyard, a young American
explorer whom Banks had met several years earlier and for whom

31

he had provided both money and influence. Ledyard had just returned from a gruelling overland journey to Siberia, and with no one else to turn to, he had come to Banks for help. The godfather of exploration explained that he hoped to have a proposition for him soon enough.

A month after Ledyard's arrival, on 17 June, Lord Rawdon, Henry Beaufoy and the lawyer Andrew Stuart met at Banks' house to select the African Association's first geographical missionary. Several offers had been received during the previous weeks, even before the Association had been created, but they were no match for Ledyard once Banks talked up his proposal and past achievements. The Committee took their Treasurer's advice and concluded that 'the employment of Mr. Ledyard may be eminently useful to the purposes of the Association'.[7] Nine days later, his selection was confirmed and Beaufoy and Banks drafted a more precise resolution.

Ledyard was to travel overland to Marseilles and from there sail to Egypt, make his way over the desert to Suez, cross the Red Sea to Mecca in present-day Saudi Arabia and then cross back again to Nubia. Such an itinerary would have been enough to convince most people that they were dealing with madmen. But whatever Ledyard might suffer getting to Nubia, it was only then that the mission – and the dangers – would really start. From the Red Sea coast, he was to cut inland across the withering Nubian Desert, ford the Nile, negotiate the southern Libyan Desert and prepare to face the Sahara. He was then instructed to continue westward 'as nearly as possible in the direction of the Niger, with which River, and with the Towns and Countries on its borders, he shall endeavour to make himself acquainted'. After that? Well, it was up to him: he was free to find his own way to the Atlantic coast and then sail back to England.

It was a tall order, more than two thousand miles over some of the world's most challenging terrain, and it was fraught with difficulties. Perhaps the biggest challenge would be to locate the River Niger, since no one could be quite certain where it lay. Happily Ledyard's employers were aware of the difficulty. 'If the abovementioned Plan should be found altogether impracticable, he shall proceed to the discovery of the Inland parts of Africa, by the rout [sic] which may appear to him the best suited to the purpose.'[8]

Sailing from England to Egypt could hardly be called exploration in the eighteenth century – there was regular traffic across the Mediterranean, though the going was often far from easy. European interests in India and further east meant that frequent caravans crossed the desert between Cairo and Suez (the Suez Canal was still eighty years away). Although there was a risk of attack by Bedouin tribes, whom the Pasha in Cairo was powerless to control, Ledyard could be confident of passing that barrier. Assuming that he got this far, his problems would just be beginning. For one thing, Christians had long been banned from sailing on the Red Sea. The official explanation for this was the desire to protect the purity of the Muslim holy places at Mecca and Medina, although there was certainly an equally strong desire to keep European traders away from the lucrative Red Sea trade. James Bruce claimed to have persuaded the Egyptian Pasha, Muhammad Bey Abu Dahab, to allow British ships to sail to Suez. And as Bruce had been in touch with Banks since his return to Britain, it is likely that Ledyard also knew about this agreement. What he perhaps did not know was that since Bruce's visit to Egypt, the Ottoman authorities had issued a *Hatti Sharif*, an instruction to the Pasha, judges, imams and indeed just about anyone else with any authority over the Egyptian Red Sea coast: 'The Sea of Suez is destined for the noble pilgrimage to Mecca,' it began unequivocally. 'To suffer Frank [European] ships to navigate therein, or to neglect opposing it, is betraying your Sovereign (the Ottoman Emperor), your religion, and every Mahometan.'[9]

It was going to be an achievement just to reach the Nubian shore. A quick look at the map of Africa will help to point up some of the hazards of the proposed journey: Ledyard's route lay through the Nubian Desert, over the Nile and then thousands of miles across

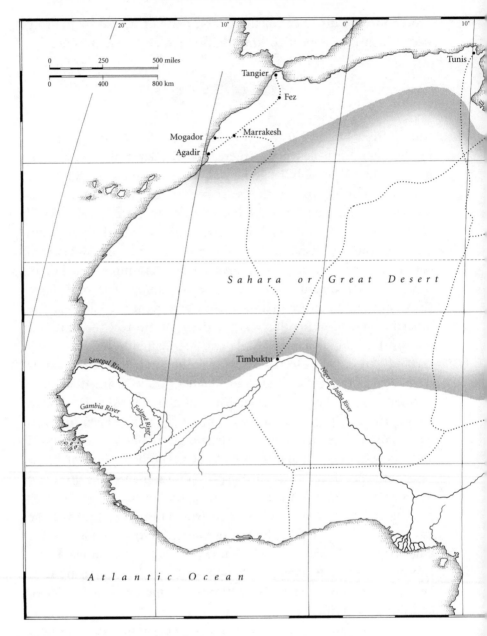

*Ledyard in Cairo on his way to Suakin, Lucas in Tripoli: a grand plan
to bisect the northern half of Africa in 1788*

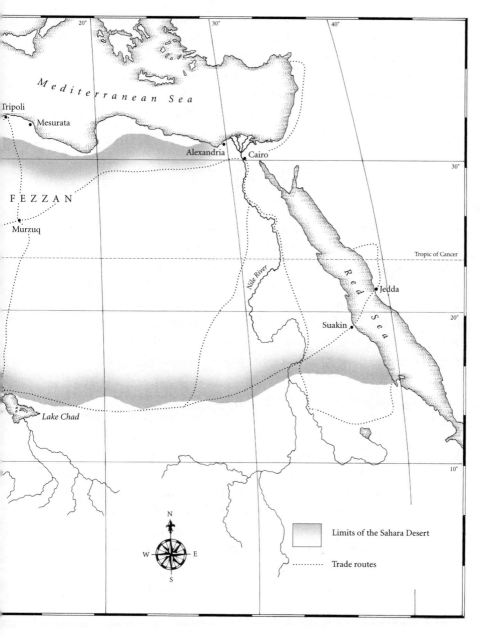

Mediterranean Sea

Tripoli

Mesurata

Alexandria   Cairo

FEZZAN

Murzuq

Tropic of Cancer

Nile River

Red Sea

Jedda

Suakin

Lake Chad

N

W — E

S

Limits of the Sahara Desert

Trade routes

the entire breadth of the Sahara, through countries whose political situation was completely unknown to the Association and, indeed, to just about anyone else outside Africa. To guide himself through all this, Ledyard had a map drawn using speculation, hearsay and wishful thinking. What sort of man would agree to a mission of this sort, which others might have regarded as an elaborate form of suicide?

Connecticut-born John Ledyard was already famous as independent America's first explorer, but then travel was in his blood: his father was a sea captain who traded between Boston and the West Indies. After his father's early death in 1762, Ledyard's upbringing was as unsettled as the times, and there was something inevitable about his signing up with one of his father's friends and sailing out of New England.* In 1775, now twenty-four years old, he crossed to England in the hope of making his way in the world, which he did, though not as he had expected.

In England Ledyard heard of Captain Cook's preparations for his third voyage to the Pacific. Cook, already a legend as a navigator and explorer, was going in search of a northern passage between the Atlantic and Pacific oceans, and Ledyard decided to join him. Marine Corporal Ledyard sailed out of Plymouth on Cook's ship the *Resolution* in July 1776, and sailed back in the autumn of 1780. He had been on the beach on Hawaii when Cook was murdered, opened negotiations with Russian fur traders in the north-west Pacific, been promoted to sergeant and made a name for himself as a solid and reliable member of the expedition. He had also discovered his path in life. He was, he explained, not a philosopher but 'a traveller and a friend to mankind'.[10]

'My ambition,' Ledyard wrote to his mother in his usual convol-

---

* In 1999, the John Ledyard Scholarship Foundation was created in the US to honour students who follow the traveller's example by dropping out of college and travelling more than two thousand miles from home at least three times.

uted style after the *Resolution* voyage, 'is to do every thing, which my disposition as a man, and my relative character as a citizen, and, more tenderly, as the leading descendant of a broken and distressed family, should prompt me to do . . . My prospects at present are a voyage to the East Indies, and eventually round the world. It will be of two or three years' duration. If I am successful, I shall not have occasion to absent myself any more from my friends; but, above all, I hope to have it in my power to minister to the wants of a beloved parent . . . Tell [my sisters] I long to strew roses in their laps, and branches of palms beneath their feet.' He would be a sybarite, a poet, a man of means. First he wanted a share of the 'astonishing profit' to be had buying furs in the American north-west. But how was he to get there?

At that time, neither Europeans nor members of the newly united states of America had found an overland route across the American continent to the Pacific. Ledyard first looked for an American backer to help him sail south around the Americas to the west coast. When that plan was unsuccessful he moved to Europe, looking for backers first in Spain and then in France. By the time he reached Paris, it was becoming clear, even to a man of his irrepressible optimism, that no one was going to provide him with a ship to go and trade in furs.

Before leaving the States Ledyard had written a book, *A Journal of Captain Cook's Last Voyage*. Its publication had established him as a celebrity, even in Europe, where he was fêted as the first American explorer. Marooned in Paris, he at least had the consolation of becoming part of the city's American community and enjoying the patronage of the American Consul, Thomas Jefferson. The Consul clearly liked the young man, whom he described as having 'genius, an education better than the common, and a talent for useful & interesting observation'.[11] Perhaps it was Jefferson's patriotic influence that began to rub off on Ledyard during this period. Still determined to reach the American north-west, he wrote to his family with more enthusiasm than clarity that 'the American Revolution invites to a thourough [sic] discovery of the Continent. But a Native only could feel the pleasure of the Atchievement [sic].

It was necessary that an European should discover the Existance [sic] of that Continent, but in the name of Amor Patria. Let a Native of it Explore its Boundary. It is my wish to be the Man.'

Ledyard now changed his plans, and in the autumn of 1786, with a little money provided by Banks, to whom he had been recommended, he left Paris. His plan was to travel overland through Europe to Russia, although the Russian Empress Catherine the Great had already refused him permission to travel through her lands, assuming he was a threat to the Russian monopoly on the fur trade. In this she was right, because from Russia he intended to sail to the American north-west and make contact with the fur traders he had met when travelling with Captain Cook. At this point Ledyard confessed to an even greater ambition: Siberia was not the goal but a step on the way. He wanted to be the first person to circumnavigate the world by land.

If desire alone were enough he would have succeeded, but weather and politics conspired against him. During the winter of 1786 he crossed from Stockholm to St Petersburg and in June 1787 left for Siberia. Three months and six thousand miles later, having travelled much of the way on foot, he reached the Okhotsk Sea, but was unable to cross to Kamchatka, where he intended to join the fur traders, because the sea had frozen. He travelled back to Yakutsk to sit out the winter as best he could on meagre resources. He probably would have survived until the thaw. But in March 1788 his luck ran out: the Empress's agents caught up with him and he was arrested, accused of being a French spy, marched back across Russia to the Polish frontier and warned that he would be executed if he dared to enter Russian territory again without Imperial permission. He used the last of his money to reach Königsberg (present-day Kaliningrad), where he found someone prepared to lend him £5 on Sir Joseph Banks' credit. From there, he headed for Soho Square.

The day he reached Yakutsk – it was 18 September 1787 – Ledyard had felt the profits from fur dealing, and the possibilities they would create, to be within his reach. In pensive mood, thinking of the journeys ahead, he confided to his journal, 'I have but two long frozen Stages more [from Yakutsk to the coast and then across the Pacific] and I shall be beyond the want or aid of money, until emerging from her deep deserts I gain the American Atlantic States and then thy glow[i]ng Climates, Africa explored, I lay me down and claim a little portion of the Globe I've viewed.'[12] The American journey was not to be, but there was something prophetic about the mention of Africa.

When Ledyard appeared in Soho Square, Banks scribbled a note of introduction in his spidery hand and sent him around to Henry Beaufoy's house in Great George Street. Beaufoy was impressed. 'Before I had learned from the note the name and business of my visitor,' he wrote later, describing that meeting for the Association's subscribers, 'I was struck with the manliness of his person, the breadth of his chest, the openness of his countenance, and the inquietude of his eye.'[13] Elsewhere he described Ledyard as being of 'middling size', though 'remarkably expressive of activity and strength. His manners, though unpolished, were neither uncivil nor unpleasing.' You can hear the affectionate patronage with which the Englishman viewed the brash American.

'I spread the map of Africa before him,' Beaufoy went on, 'and tracing a line from Cairo to Sennar [he had clearly forgotten about the deviation to Mecca], and from thence westward in the latitude and supposed direction of the Niger, I told him that was the route, by which I was anxious that Africa might, if possible, be explored.'

Thinking that at last things were going his way, Ledyard admitted that he felt 'singularly fortunate to be entrusted with the adventure'.[14]

'When will you set out?' Beaufoy asked.

Led on by breezy optimism, the American told Beaufoy he would be ready to leave in the morning.

The Association, however, required more time to prepare for the adventure. Letters of recommendation and credit needed to be arranged and, most important, money had to be raised to pay for the journey. At the inaugural meeting on 9 June the dozen founding Saturday's Club members had each committed themselves to paying an annual subscription of five guineas. Within a fortnight, membership had more than doubled: among the new members were Lord Rawdon's uncle the Earl of Huntingdon, Baron Loughborough, Richard Neave, the Governor of the Bank of England and Chairman of the West India Merchants, the Prince of Wales' friend the Duke of Northumberland and two more anti-slavery campaigners. But even if they all paid their subscriptions when asked, which was unlikely, the Association could still only call on £136.10s., and although that may have paid the annual salaries of the servants who ran Banks' house, it clearly was not going to be enough to fund two separate expeditions into Africa.

Banks had anticipated the problem. On 17 June he had suggested that each of the five Committee members should advance the Association £50 on top of their annual subscriptions. Even then there were not sufficient funds, so the Committee – principally Banks – now agreed to advance the Association a total of £453. Once the money was in place, a number of instructions had to be issued to people such as Mr Baldwin, the British Consul in Alexandria, asking him to act as banker and to honour Ledyard's letter of credit.

While the practicalities were being sorted out, the traveller was busy preparing for his departure and attending a round of meetings, briefings and dinners. Among them is likely to have been a dinner at the Royal Society Club – the Society's social arm – similar to this one described by a passing Frenchman called Barthélemy Faujas de Saint-Fond:

> *The dishes were of the solid kind, such as roast beef, boiled beef and mutton prepared in various ways, with abundance of potatoes and other vegetables, which each person seasoned as he pleased with the different sauces which were placed on the table in bottles of different shapes. The beefsteaks and the roast beef were at first drenched with copious bumpers of strong beer, casked porter, drunk out of cylindrical pewter*

pots, which are much preferred to glasses, because one can swallow a whole pint at a draught.

This prelude being finished, the cloth was removed and a handsome and well-polished table was covered, as if it were by magic, with a number of fine crystal decanters filled with the best port, madeira and claret; this last is the wine of Bordeaux. Several glasses, as brilliant in lustre as fine in shape, were distributed to each person and the libations began on a grand scale, in the midst of different kinds of cheese, which rolling in mahogany boxes from one end of the table to the other, provoked the thirst of the drinkers.[15]

After the cheese, Saint-Fond relates with a sneaking sense of admiration, the serious drinking began.

Ledyard enjoyed all these preparations and revelled in the attention he received in London, some of which clearly touched his vanity. In a letter to his family, he mentions that his portrait had been painted by the Swedish artist Breda and was now hanging at Somerset House, home to both the Royal Society and the Royal Academy of Art: the catalogue for the Academy's annual exhibition that summer lists the portrait and notes that Ledyard 'has undertaken to travel round the world on foot'. In a letter to his cousin, Ledyard described the Association as 'a Society of Noblemen & Gentlemen who had for some time been fruitlessly enquiring for somebody that would undertake to travel through the continent of Africa. My arrival,' he added pompously, 'has made it a reality.'[16] He seemed to have had an equally inflated opinion of the Association's immediate importance, claiming that it already had a membership of two hundred. 'It is a growing thing,' he wrote, '& the King privately promoting & encouraging it will make its objects more extensive than at first thought of. The king has told them that no expense should be spared.'[17] There is no evidence that the King ever even mentioned it, but Ledyard clearly believed that money should be forthcoming.

In Paris hoping for a ship to take him to the American north-west, Ledyard had equipped himself with two big dogs and a hatchet, but he had very different plans for Africa. Beaufoy had advanced him thirty guineas as soon as he accepted the mission. Two guineas were spent on his lodgings, the rest going to pay for his wardrobe, which included '6 fine Shirts, 1 Suit of Cloaths [sic], 1 Hat [which cost him a guinea], 1 Pocket Book, 1 Shaving case, 2 pair silk stockings, 2 pair ditto, 1 pair shoes, 1 pair Buckles, 1 pair bag, 1 pair Boots, 1 Watch, Waistcoat & breeches, Ditto ditto black silk, 1 pair black silk stockings, 2 white cravats, 1 Silk Handkerchief'. By 17 June he had run up another bill, this time of some £16, and was the proud owner of '2 pair leather pantaloons, new black stock & razor strap, a dozen shirts, 4 hatchets, pair of boots, umbrella, 2 silk handkerchiefs'.[18]

Perhaps sensing that Ledyard's spending was getting out of hand, Banks and Beaufoy met on 26 June to settle his financial arrangements. In all, they were prepared to allow him one hundred guineas to buy clothes and equipment and to get himself to Cairo. In Cairo, Consul Baldwin was authorised to advance £50. This was supposed to be enough to get Ledyard across Africa, although, if Baldwin thought it necessary, he could draw a further £30. The Committee had two reasons for wanting Ledyard to keep his spending to a minimum. For one thing they were short of funds. But more important, they were convinced 'that in such an Undertaking Poverty is a better protection than Wealth, and that Mr. Ledyard's address [appearance and manner] will be more effectual than money, to open to him a passage to the Interior of Africa'.[19]

Around this time, Ledyard wrote to his mother in Connecticut explaining his new commission. 'I have trampled the world under my feet, laughed at fear, and derided danger. Through millions of fierce savages, over parching deserts, the freezing north, the everlasting ice, and stormy seas, have I passed without harm. How good is my God . . . I am going away into Africa to examine that continent. I expect to be absent three years. I shall be in Egypt as soon as I can get there, and after that go into unknown parts.'[20] Ledyard was due to leave London on the Dover coach on 30 June. Not being one to let a dramatic moment pass unexploited, that morning he left Beaufoy with a speech guaranteed to stir his sponsors:

I am accustomed to hardships. I have known both hunger and nakedness to the utmost extremity of human suffering. I have known what it is to have food given me as a charity to a madman; and I have at times been obliged to shelter myself under the miseries of that character to avoid a heavier calamity. My distresses have been greater than I have ever owned, or ever will *own to any man. Such evils are terrible to bear; but they never yet had power to turn me from my purpose. If I live, I will faithfully perform, in its utmost extent, my engagement to the Society; and if I perish in the attempt, my* honour *will still be safe, for death cancels all bonds.*[21]

It was a momentous occasion. For Ledyard, this was the fulfilment of his hopes and ambitions, a dangerous journey backed by some of the most important people in Britain and providing an opportunity for him to return to fame and, he hoped, some fortune. For members of the Association, just three weeks to the day after that first meeting in the St Alban's Tavern they watched their first explorer set off on a geographical mission that they hoped would reveal to them the mysteries of the interior of Africa. Men of science, men of experience what's more, they should have known better than to have let their enthusiasm run away with them. The approach they had chosen, bisecting the continent, was hugely ambitious and carried no guarantee of success. Yet they viewed this departure with excitement and imagination, and with a rare humanity: 'Much, undoubtedly, we shall have to communicate [to people in Africa],' Beaufoy was to write, 'and something we may have to learn.'[22]

Ledyard was in Paris by 4 July, for he sent his compliments to his former patron, the American Consul Thomas Jefferson. Writing from the Hôtel d'Aligre on the rue d'Orléans, he explained in a formal note that 'he is now on his way to Africa to see what he can do with that continent'.[23] Jefferson, it seems, was unimpressed that Ledyard had signed up with a British organisation; Ledyard in turn was stung by his mentor's criticism. This, rather than the cold that Ledyard claimed, may explain why the two men did not meet to celebrate the anniversary of American independence during the week the traveller spent in the French capital. Sailing from Marseilles some days later, Ledyard arrived in Alexandria early in August.

Alexandria looms large in the imagination. Its ancient glory, the reputation that clings to the extravagance of Cleopatra, the plight of its library and the brilliance of its scholars – the geographer Claudius Ptolemy among them – have inspired historians, poets and adventurers. But the port Ledyard sailed into displayed few obvious traces of this glorious past beyond a standing pillar wrongly ascribed to Caesar's friend Pompey and a fallen obelisk credited to Cleopatra (since removed to London). Alexandria had been the Egyptian capital in the seventh century when conquering Arab armies crossed the Nile, but it had been left to rot in favour of a new settlement at Cairo and its ancient buildings were now buried beneath rubble, used as foundations for meaner houses. What European travellers called 'the Turkish town', huddled over the formerly glorious seafront quarter of Alexander's city, now contained a mere four thousand people.

The Sultan's palace stood a little way off from the Turkish town, as did the houses of the few European residents. The only lively part of town was the port, where goods were landed en route to the Red Sea. The size of this transit trade had increased throughout the eighteenth century as British and French interests developed in India and the East. Trade was one of the main reasons why the British Consul, George Baldwin, and his beautiful wife were installed in Alexandria when Ledyard arrived. Another reason was a matter of health. Spring was the season of plague in Egypt, but Alexandria seemed to suffer less severely than Cairo and to rid itself of the disease sooner. In the summer, the season of Ledyard's arrival, Cairo bubbled under a relentless sun, but in Alexandria one could find relief from the cooling sea breezes.

Baldwin offered the traveller hospitality and accommodation, but Alexandria was not to the American's taste. He described it as a place of 'poverty, rapine, murder, tumult, blind bigotry, cruel persecution, pestilence! A small town built in the ruins of antiquity, as remarkable for its miserable architecture, as I suppose the place once was for its good and great works of that kind.'[24] He visited the sights, recovered from his journey and moved on. Seven weeks after leaving England, he was in Cairo.

Carlo Rossetti, the fifty-two-year-old Venetian Consul, was a long-time resident of Egypt. He had made a fortune from assisting cargo being shipped along the overland route between Alexandria and Suez and now wielded great influence, both with Egyptians and foreign governments: among the many posts he held at the time of Ledyard's arrival was that of British Chargé d'Affaires. Rossetti greeted the new arrival warmly enough, but gave 'no very pressing invitation' for Ledyard to stay with him, so the American settled in one of the city's convents, which were usually open to passing Europeans. Rossetti proved to be more generous with his introductions than he had been with his house, and took Ledyard to meet Aga Muhammad, one of Egypt's power-brokers. This meeting was crucial, for although the entire region as far south as Nubia was officially under the control of Istanbul, it was the Egyptian Pasha who wielded real authority in the south.

Fifteen years earlier, the previous ruler of Egypt, Muhammad Bey Abu Dahab, had expressed surprise, wonder even, at James Bruce wanting to travel up the Nile. When the Pasha asked why he wanted to make the journey, Bruce had answered that he was travelling merely for the pleasure of seeing where the river began. For the Pasha this simply did not make sense. To make the pilgrimage to Mecca or to undertake a journey to trade were things he could understand. But to travel just to look . . .

'You are not an India merchant?' Bruce reported the Bey as having asked him.

> I said, 'No.'
> 'Have you no other trade nor occupation but that of travelling?'
> I said, 'That was my occupation.'

> '*Ali Bey, my father-in-law,*' *replied he,* '*often observed there never was such a people as the English; no other nation on earth could be compared to them, and none had so many great men in all professions, by sea and land: I never understood this till now; that I see it must be so when your king cannot find other employment for such a man as you, but sending him to perish by hunger and thirst in the sands, or to have his throat cut by the lawless barbarians of the desert.*'

And all that just to see where the river began.

The King of Sennar had asked Bruce the same question. Bruce had refined his answer to suit local sensibilities and replied that he was travelling to atone for past sins. And how long had he been travelling? Some twenty years, he explained. 'You must have been very young,' the King observed, some of his harem behind him, 'to have committed so many sins, and so early; they must all have been with women?' Bruce, with unusual modesty, explained that only some of them were.

Seventy years later the traveller Alexander Kinglake met with a similar response: 'The theory is that the English traveller has committed some sin against God and his conscience, and that for this the Evil Spirit has hold of him, and drives him from his home like a victim of the old Greek Furies, and forces him to travel over countries far and strange, and most chiefly over deserts and desolate places, and to stand upon the sites of cities that once were, and are no more, and to grope among the tombs of dead men.'[25]

The Association's first geographical missionary appears to have had no such grilling, and reported to his masters in London that Aga Muhammad 'gave me his hand to kiss, and with it the promise of letters, protection, and support, through Turkish Nubia, and also to some chiefs far inland'.

The Aga had never travelled as far south as Ledyard was intending to go. Nevertheless, he had very definite ideas about who and what he would meet on his way. Among them would be people who had the power to turn into strange animals. Ledyard tried to hide his amusement at the Aga's credulity and replied that the prospect of meeting these bizarre people 'rendered me more anxious to be on my voyage'.[26] The Aga was also curious to know how Ledyard was going to communicate with the people he would meet on his journey. 'I told him, with vocabularies.'[27] Which means that he was travelling with books as well as the leather pantaloons, hatchets and the rest of the paraphernalia he had bought in England. The Aga looked stunned. This was not the sort of foreigner he was used to seeing in Cairo.

Not that there was a shortage of foreigners in the city. Estimates vary like the population itself, which was frequently ravaged by plague, but Cairo at the end of the eighteenth century had a native population in the region of 250,000. The city was divided into three distinct areas, the Nile port of Boulak, 'Old Cairo' upstream from the port around the Roman and Arab settlements, and 'Grand Cairo', the medieval city at its heart, overlooked by the citadel, the home of the country's rulers. Some European visitors described it as being as large in area as Paris. But unlike European cities, Cairo was reaching the low point of a long decline. It could boast fewer palaces, and fewer schools, than three or four hundred years earlier, and what had survived was mostly in a state of decrepitude. Only one aspect of the city's life was thriving: the international transit trade. Thanks to Europe's growing need to move people and cargo quickly to the East – thanks, too, to men such as Baldwin and Rossetti – there was considerable traffic between Alexandria and Suez. And Cairo was still also one of the hubs of the North African trade, with caravans arriving from Nubia and Abyssinia in the south, Fezzan and Tripoli in the west and, less common, from the heart of the continent. It was from these people that Ledyard hoped to glean some news of his intended final destination.

Ledyard was far from idle in his first week in the Egyptian capital, as he was quick to point out in his letters to Banks and Beaufoy. He had made various social calls to important Cairenes and had wandered the souks in search of traders from the south. 'I have made the best inquiries I have been able . . . of the nature of the country before me; of Sennar, Darfoor, Wangara, of Nubia, Abyssinia, of those named, or unknown by name. I should have been happy to have sent you better information of those places than I am yet able to do. It will appear very singular to you in England, that we in Egypt are so ignorant of countries which we annually visit: the Egyptians know as little of geography as the generality of the French; and, like them, sing, dance, and traffic, without it.' But there was one source of geographical information he was able to tap. These were people whom Ledyard calls 'Jelabs', and they were traders who had come from the interior to sell slaves in Cairo. He was clearly pleased with what they had to tell him and boasted, 'I have a better idea of the people of Africa, of its trade, of the position of places, the nature of the country, manner of travelling, &c. than ever I had by any other means; and, I believe, better than any other means would afford me.'[28]

By 25 October, more than two months after his arrival in Cairo, Ledyard appeared to be set; with Rossetti's help he had made arrangements to travel with a caravan heading south to Sennar. There is an irony in a man sent by a group clearly opposed to the slave trade preparing to travel with a slave caravan, but it is one that escaped the traveller himself. 'The King of Sennar,' he wrote, 'is himself a merchant, and concerned in the Sennar caravans. The merchant here who contracts to convey me to Sennar, is Procurer at Cairo to the King of Sennar; this is a good circumstance, and one that I knew not of till to-day. Mr. Rossetti informed me of it. He informed me also, that this year the importation of Negro slaves into Egypt will amount to 20,000.'[29] As well as slaves, the traders brought camels, ostrich feathers, elephant teeth and gum Sennar, which, like gum Arabic, was tapped from acacia trees. The south-bound caravan that Ledyard was going to join would be carrying a shipment of soap, antimony, red linen, razors, scissors, mirrors and beads.

Jared Sparks, Ledyard's early-nineteenth-century biographer, states that by this time the American had adopted 'a dress suited to the character he was to assume'. In other words, he was dressed as a Levantine traveller. But his disguise was clearly far from perfect, because on a visit to the slave market he was 'rudely treated' by some Turks, who recognised him as a 'Frank'. Around this time he also 'began in earnest to study the manners of the people around him, and particularly of the traders in the caravans, which were then at Cairo'.[30] From them he collected plenty of information that he thought worth sending back to London. 'A caravan goes from here to Fezzan, which they call a journey of fifty days; and from Fezzan to Tombuctou [Timbuktu], which they call a journey of ninety days. The caravans travel about twenty miles a day, which makes the distance on the road from here to Fezzan, one thousand miles; and from Fezzan to Tombuctou, one thousand eight hundred miles. From here to Sennar is reckoned six hundred miles.' Some of this information was almost accurate: it is around 1200 miles in a straight line from Cairo to Fezzan, and twice that to Timbuktu. But Ledyard's calculation for Sennar is woefully short – it is more like 1200 miles south of Cairo.

The prospect of the journey from Cairo must have seemed easy to the man who had crossed Russia with little money and without Imperial permission; Ledyard should be forgiven for thinking that the interior of Africa was within his reach, that fame was at hand and with it the means to settle back home in Connecticut and throw roses in his sisters' laps. But although he had learned many things on his travels, he had not acquired the essential Oriental quality of patience. The Sennar caravan delayed its departure, and then again. And then again. As time passed, Ledyard became increasingly desperate to begin his African journey. Some of this is understandable: the man who had wanted to leave London the day after meeting Beaufoy had now been held up for some three months in the Egyptian capital. The false starts, delayed departures and repeated disappointments began to eat away at him; his letters and reports, entrusted to European sea captains, are full of warnings to himself that he must resist any urge towards 'rashness'. Around this time he wrote to Beaufoy that 'A Turkish sopha has no charms for me: if it had, I could soon obtain one here. I could to-morrow take the command of the best armament of Ishmael Bey* – I should

---

* Ishmael, or more correctly Ismail, Bey was at that time the *Shaykh al-Balad*, the most powerful of the *beys* or nobles who wielded power in Egypt.

be sure of success, and its consequential honours. Believe me, a single well-done from your Association has more worth in it to me, than all the trappings of the East.'

At the end of October, Ledyard was sufficiently confident of his departure to assure Beaufoy that his next letter would be from Sennar or somewhere further into the continent. If his calculation of the distance between Cairo and Sennar was right, and if the caravan really did manage to cover twenty miles a day, then the journey might take around thirty days. To this would need to be added at least another month for his letter to reach London from Cairo – his first letter from Alexandria, sent in early August, didn't reach Beaufoy until 18 October. The members of the Association might therefore have to wait until late January before receiving his news from Sennar. But some time early in January, before the Committee had received word from either Ledyard, Rossetti or Baldwin, rumours began to circulate in London that Ledyard was dead. Certainly he had not left Cairo when he intended, for he had written another farewell letter on 15 November, this time to Thomas Jefferson in Paris. He was, he said, 'doing up my baggage for the journey'. But again he did not leave. Instead he became sick.

Late in November 1788, Ledyard began to suffer from what Beaufoy described as a bilious complaint – most likely some sort of gastric infection, so common among visitors to Egypt now as then. To speed up his recovery, he treated himself with what was, at the time, a common remedy, vitriolic or sulphuric acid. In his eagerness to be cured, he seems to have taken an overdose. Realising from the chronic burning pains in his gut that he had made a mistake, he tried to counteract the acid with tartar emetic, a toxic and irritating salt which, he must have hoped, would force him to vomit out the acid. But the damage was already done, as was clear from his continued internal bleeding.

Rossetti was there and offered what Beaufoy called 'generous friendship',[31] as were Cairo's finest doctors. But nothing they could suggest was effective against the damage done by the chemicals and exacerbated, in Beaufoy's view, by the anxiety Ledyard felt at his failure to leave Cairo. By the end of November, according to Sparks – on 17 January, according to an announcement in the *Gentleman's Magazine* – the great American survivor, the man who had returned home unharmed when Captain Cook had fallen, who had crossed Russia in defiance of a ban from the Empress Catherine, the African Association's first geographical missionary was dead. 'He was decently interred,' Beaufoy assured the Association's members, 'in the neighbourhood of such of the English as had ended their days in the capital of Egypt.'[32]

Beaufoy, in writing of Ledyard's end, stressed the American's suitability for his mission – 'he appeared to be formed by Nature for achievements of hardihood and peril'.[33] Yet privately he could be forgiven for wondering whether Ledyard had been properly prepared for his mission. He might also have wondered what else the Association's travellers would have to learn before they would be able to reveal the mysteries of the African interior. Neither Beaufoy nor Banks seemed to have reached the point, yet, when they would question their choice of route into the interior or the practicability of their ambitious plan to bisect the northern half of the continent. But then, at this stage they did not need to, because their second traveller was already in the court of the Bashaw (Pasha) of Tripoli, arranging permission and protection for his journey into the interior.

4

The Oriental Interpreter

'MR LUCAS, ORIENTAL INTERPRETER, whose salary
is £80 *per ann*, offers to proceed, by the way of Gibralter [sic]
& Tripoli to Fezan, provided his Salary is continued to him
during his Absense.'

Undated and unsigned note in the African Association's papers,
possibly written by Henry Beaufoy[1]

SIMON LUCAS, King George III's Arabic interpreter, volunteered
his services as soon as the Association was created, convinced that
he was uniquely qualified to be a geographical missionary. The
Committee seemed to agree. They discussed his proposal at their
first meeting and noted his obvious qualities. It was proposed that
Banks would ask Viscount Sydney, the Secretary of State for the
Home Department, to obtain the King's permission for Lucas to
travel. His Majesty, it appears, had no objections to his interpreter
going absent, nor to paying his salary while he was away, and so
Lucas' proposition was accepted. Banks and Beaufoy, fired with
enthusiasm for their new project, felt they had made a great catch
in securing his services, for his knowledge of north-west Africa was
unrivalled in England. How he came by this knowledge was an
oft-repeated story.

Like Beaufoy, Lucas' father had been a London wine merchant.
While Lucas was still in his teens – the dates are vague and some
accounts refer to his still being a boy – his father sent him to Cadiz

to learn the wine trade first-hand. Everything passed off well until he was on his way home at the end of this apprenticeship, when calamity struck: the ship in which he was sailing was attacked by the infamous 'Sallee Rovers'. Of the many corsairs who operated along the Barbary Coast, the pirates from Morocco's Atlantic port of Sali had a reputation for being the most ruthless and the most savage. But they were also businessmen and, when they could, would rather sell their captives as slaves than torment or torture them. This is exactly what they did with the young Englishman they hauled off the London-bound ship: Lucas was sold to the Emperor of Morocco, Sultan Sidi Muhammad.*

Lucas spent three years in the Sultan's service. The great Imperial court at Meknes was more of a royal city than a palace, a labyrinth of enclosures, courtyards and chambers, the large harem at its centre protected by the Sultan's feared Negro bodyguard. In this environment, surrounded by officials and functionaries, the young Englishman found that the only way to survive was to learn the language and adapt to the ways of the Moors. When he was finally able to leave, he didn't get very far. On his release, he quickly made the short hop from the so-called Pillars of Hercules to Gibraltar, already held by the British. There he came to the attention of General Cornwallis, who recognised the value of his Moroccan experience and asked him to go back – not as a slave, this time, but in the service of his own King. The offer of so dramatic a reversal of fortune was too sweet for Lucas to resist and so, instead of sailing home to London, he returned to the Moroccan Emperor Sidi Muhammad's court as British Vice-Consul and Chargé d'Affaires. Clearly the place and his position in it agreed with him, as he stayed for some sixteen years. When he finally returned to London, his knowledge of Arabic, of the manners and customs of the Moroccans, of the layout of their country and the functioning of their court was unrivalled in England and helped him to secure the post of Oriental Interpreter to King George III. Given his expertise, it would

---

* Sultan Sidi Muhammad was later to abandon the corsair *jihad* against Christian shipping and negotiate protection treaties under which people such as Lucas were able to sail the seas without fear of threat from Moroccan pirates. All that was in the future.

have made more sense for the African Association to have sent Lucas to Tangier or to the Atlantic port of Mogador (now known as Essaouira) and asked him to travel inland from there. But Lucas knew that Morocco was not safe to travel through, as did Banks, thanks to his correspondence with the current British Consul to the Emperor's court, James Matra.

Matra had sailed with Banks and Captain Cook. While Banks returned to fame in London and the presidency of the Royal Society, Matra, who could count on neither contacts nor fortune, secured a posting as a secretary at the British Embassy in Constantinople. Eight years later, he asked Banks to help him find other employment, although without result. Back in London and living, as he wrote to Banks, 'the life of a solitary fugitive',[2] various avenues were explored, several proposals suggested, but again without success. Then, in 1787, the post of British Consul in Morocco became free and Banks pulled strings to secure the appointment for Matra.

Matra's opinion on the viability of travellers heading south from Morocco was unequivocal. 'All investigation of the interiour [sic] part of Africa,' he wrote to Banks in 1788, 'as far as this Empire is concerned, is an *absolute impossibility*.'[3] The situation was unfortunate, but north-west Africa was out. In the meantime another option presented itself.

In 1786, Hajj Abd ar-Rahman, Foreign Minister to Ali Karamanli, Bashaw of Tripoli, arrived in London on an official mission that was to last fifteen months. During this time, he relied on Lucas both to help him on court matters and to assist him around the city. Lucas was hoping that Abd ar-Rahman would remember their friendship and cooperation and return the favour by ensuring his welcome in Tripoli. He was also counting on the Minister to persuade the Bashaw to offer his protection for the journey to the Fezzan, a place over which the Bashaw claimed nominal sovereignty. In *The Proceedings of the Association*, Beaufoy explained the plan. 'To Mr. Lucas, in consideration of the knowledge which he possessed of the Language and Manners of the Arabs, they [the Committee] allotted the passage of the Desert of Zahara, from Tripoli to Fezzan; for they had learned from various information, that with this kingdom, which in some measures is dependent on Tripoli, the traders of Agadez and Tombuctou, and of other towns in the Interior of Africa, had established a frequent and regular intercourse.'[4] Accordingly, Lucas was instructed to sail to Tripoli, cross the Sahara to the Fezzan and from there continue to the Gambia or the coast of Guinea. To get him there, in addition to his salary of £80, which the King had agreed to continue paying, the Association voted £100 to cover equipment, transport to Tripoli and to buy presents as sweeteners for the Bashaw and others at his court, the most popular of which turned out to be pairs of double-barrelled pistols. In addition, he was provided with letters of credit, to be drawn against Sir Joseph Banks. This credit – a total of £250 if he needed it – was to provide funds for his journey into the interior.

Unlike Ledyard, Lucas took time to prepare for his departure. He kitted himself out easily enough, packing a pocket compass, a thermometer, a pair of brass-mounted pistols and a silver watch. He also charged the Association for a scarlet kerseymere shawl, a crimson waistcoat with blue lining and gold lace trim and a matching skullcap, a crimson and blue sash, yellow slippers and white robes. But court obligations and illness delayed him, and it was not until 25 October that Lucas sailed from Marseilles.

Like Cairo and Damascus, Tripoli owed nominal allegiance to the Turkish sultans. But in 1711 the Tripolitan Viceroy Ahmed Karamanli had declared his independence and established a dynasty that was in its third generation by the time Simon Lucas' ship tied up in the city's fortified harbour. For this reason, Tripoli offered a warmer welcome to foreigners than many other ports along the turbulent North African coast. Its harbour was busy with sailing ships from around the Mediterranean, while its souks and caravanserais were crowded with Moorish traders who had brought their cargoes of spices, slaves, ivory and other exotica so much in demand in Europe.

Although it claimed control over vast territory stretching deep into the continent, whatever power and splendour Tripoli had once enjoyed had long since faded, and Ali Karamanli, the present Bashaw, had trouble maintaining the loyalty of his subjects. Beaufoy, always quick to point up a moral, wrote that 'if he [the traveller] reflects on the nature of a despotic government, ever incompatible with permanent prosperity, he will not be surprised when he finds, on a nearer view, that the city ... exhibits through all its extent, the marks of a rapid decay'.[5] Moral decay, he insisted, was mirrored in physical decay.

Tripoli was unlike the Cairo Ledyard had visited or the ports of Morocco with which Lucas was familiar. Where Cairo could rely on its position on the increasingly busy trade route between Europe and the East, and Morocco dominated the west Saharan trade, as it had once controlled the golden city of Timbuktu, Tripoli depended for its survival on the spoils of the Barbary corsairs and on profits from caravan trading between the Mediterranean and central Africa.

Two thousand years earlier, the North African coast around Tripoli had flourished under Roman supervision, the coastal plains made fertile, the ports of Tripolitania kept busy. Under the loosening grip of the Bashaw Ali, however, the country was both unproductive and unstable, while the city was increasingly decrepit. It looked its best from the sea – 'the whole of the town appears in a semicircle, some time before reaching the harbour's mouth', according to a visitor of Lucas' time. 'The extreme whiteness of square flat buildings covered with lime, which in this climate encounters the sun's fiercest rays, is very striking.'[6] The European consulates all looked out to sea, which helped consuls monitor the arrival of ships and also gave them the luxury of relieving sea breezes in the summer.

Beyond the port, consulates, palace and state mosque, the city was a jumble. The treasures of Africa were displayed in the covered bazaar: stacks of ostrich feathers, sacks of gums, lines of elephant tusks and hoards of gold. Once a week, in a long vaulted enclosure, there was also the pitiful sight of the slave market: European captives were stood on small platforms, while Africans, who had already been marched across the Sahara, now walked up and down to catch the eye of buyers who sat drinking coffee. Further inland, the city turned in on itself, a series of long unbroken walls hiding houses, the occasional square offering relief in the shape of a mosque or public bath. Beyond this, seasonal pastures provided grazing for goats and camels, and then gave way to the dust, shrub, rock and sand of the desert.

Lucas arrived in Tripoli knowing he could count on Richard Tully, the British Consul, and Hajj Abd ar-Rahman, the Minister of Foreign Affairs. Abd ar-Rahman had returned to his city the previous year, and was still Foreign Minister. According to Miss Tully, the Consul's sister, he 'bears here so excellent a character that he is universally beloved by Christians, as well as Moors, and is adored by his family'.[7] He also seems to have been a notable exception to the rule that everyone involved in North African court business was obliged to spin a web of intrigue and deceit.

The following morning the Minister took Lucas to meet the Bashaw, Ali Karamanli. Beaufoy had exaggerated when he called the palace 'a mouldering ruin', although it paled in comparison with the palaces of Sicily or Naples. Its forty-foot walls were pierced only by a few windows and a heavily guarded gate; its Chinese-tiled rooms were linked by dark, rank passages which exuded the stink of decay and an aura of gloom. Lucas was anxious as he passed through the outer public chambers and along these passages into the Bashaw's audience hall. The coming interview was crucial to the success of his mission, for there was no chance of leaving for the south without the Bashaw's permission; yet Ali was bound to be suspicious of the foreigner's motives for wanting to make the journey.

The audience began with the usual formalities and exchange of greetings, and Lucas then presented the pair of double-barrelled pistols he had brought out from London. The Bashaw was a short, tubby, white-haired man, not yet fifty years old. He was pleased by the pistols, for no blacksmith in North Africa could produce such elaborate and dependable work. He was less thrilled by the request that accompanied them. Lucas wanted to be allowed to travel to the Fezzan, but no Christian the Bashaw knew of had ever been so far south of Tripoli. What, he asked, was a man like Lucas, a gentleman and courtier, going to do in such a Godforsaken place?

Lucas knew better than to tell the truth – that he wanted to follow the trade routes across the Sahara to Timbuktu – because he doubted whether the Bashaw would believe that the African Association was interested only in Africa's geography. The Bashaw's government still depended to some extent on the revenue earned from taxing trade caravans that passed through his lands. Whatever the Association's motives, it was clearly not in the Bashaw's interest to have the current situation disturbed by any outsiders.

Understanding this, Lucas lied. He made no mention of trade routes, maps or fabled cities of gold. Instead, he talked about the curiosity of scholars in London and of rumours of significant Roman antiquities in the Bashaw's southernmost lands. It was these, he explained, that he had been sent to visit. On the way, he added, hoping to throw the Bashaw off the scent entirely, he had also been asked to look out for certain medicinal plants that could not be found in Europe.

The Bashaw was well aware that these Europeans had ulterior motives. He appears also to have realised that delay would be easier than refusal. Accordingly, he declared himself fascinated by Lucas' proposed journey and eager to help in any way he could; Lucas would be free to leave as soon as safe transport could be arranged. What he had omitted to mention was that his guest might have to wait a long time before the route south would be considered safe, because at that moment the Arab tribes who lived between Tripoli and Fezzan had risen up against the Bashaw and had attacked several caravans, one of them only a few miles from the city. No sooner had he left the Bashaw's presence than Lucas was apprised of the political situation: there were rumours that the Bashaw was raising an army of some five or six thousand men to go and settle scores. It immediately became clear that no permission would be granted for southbound travel. He was trapped in Tripoli.

In the end, his friend Abd ar-Rahman found a way out of this predicament by introducing him to two men newly arrived from the Fezzan. These men, who had brought a cargo of slaves and senna, were no ordinary traders, but members of the Fezzani royal family and *sharifs*, men who claimed to be of the bloodline of the Prophet Muhammad. As such, they commanded the respect of all Muslims, of whatever tribe or nationality. The elder of these two *sharifs*, Imhammad, was a prince of Fezzan, a short, dark-skinned man of some fifty years of age. The other *sharif*, a younger, taller, copper-skinned man named Fuad, was the King of Fezzan's son-in-law.

Lucas immediately recognised the possibilities these two presented for him to make some progress into the interior. The *sharifs* announced that if the Englishman were willing to travel with them, they would guarantee his safe arrival in Fezzan. Once there, Fuad assured him, his father-in-law would be delighted to meet a Christian, as none had ever managed to travel so far south into the desert. As a way of sealing their agreement, Lucas offered the men a pair of pistols each, along with enough powder, ball and flints to keep them in use for some time. All that was needed now was for the Bashaw to approve of the *sharifs'* offer. Any anxiety Lucas might have had on this front was dispelled when a good riding mule arrived from the royal stables and a Jewish tent-maker, also sent by the Bashaw, arrived to make a suitable tent for the Englishman's rigorous journey. Encouraged by this, Lucas laid in supplies, dressed himself in Turkish clothes – he would obviously not be able to travel as an Englishman – and ordered a magnificent robe that he intended to give as a present to the King of Fezzan.

At 8.30 on the morning of Sunday, 1 February 1789, with Ledyard already dead and buried in Cairo, Lucas passed through the gates of Tripoli bound for the interior, armed with a recommendation from the Bashaw. With twenty-one camels to carry their cargo and baggage, the caravan consisted of the younger Sharif Fuad and three other merchants on horseback, the older Sharif Imhammad on an ass, Lucas' black servant on a camel and a dozen men of Fezzan on foot. Walking along with them were three freed slaves and their wives, on their way to their homes across the desert. For his part, the African Association's missionary now wore his hair so long that he looked, in his own words, 'like a London Jew in deep mourning'.[8] Dressed in his Turkish robes and riding the Bashaw's fine mule, travelling in the company of descendants of the Prophet and a relative of the King of Fezzan, assured of the protection of the

Bashaw of Tripoli and the friendship of his Foreign Minister, Lucas was as secure in his saddle as any eighteenth-century European traveller could be. Another traveller in his place would have been more optimistic about his chances of success. But Lucas was well aware that he was better suited to the rituals and intrigues of the court than the challenge of the desert.

There was a direct route south of Tripoli to Fezzan, but the *sharifs*, hoping to save themselves both trouble and money, had had their merchandise shipped to the port of Mesurata, about a hundred miles east of Tripoli. So the small caravan followed the coast and a week later found their merchandise arrived safely at Mesurata. So far, so good, but the travellers now discovered that there were no camels to carry their cargo to Fezzan. The camels that were usually available for hire belonged to Bedouin who were now off in the desert fighting the Bashaw's forces. Even if the Bedouin could be found, they were going to be loath to rent out their pack animals at such an unstable time to someone travelling under the Bashaw's protection. Various compromises were attempted, but by early March, a month after leaving Tripoli, it was clear that the *sharifs* were not going to find transport for their bales of goods. By then the hot weather had started and the season for crossing the desert was over.

'Wearied by fruitless expectations of a peace,' Beaufoy explained to the members of the Association, 'disappointed in their expedients, and warned by the increasing heat, that the season for a journey to Fezzan was already past, the Shereefs [sic] now resolved to proceed to the intended places of their summer residence. The Shereef Fouwad [sic] retired to Wadan, his native town; and the Shereef Imhammed, with tears in his eyes, and an earnest prayer that he might see his friend Mr. Lucas again in November, retired to the mountains, where he had many acquaintance, and could live at small expense.'[9]

What was Lucas to do? There is no doubt that he could have gone on. He had money, connections and willing companions in the returning slaves, who were still keen to make the journey, in spite of the heat. He could speak the language, knew the customs,

60

and no doubt looked even more like 'a London Jew in deep mourning' after a month out and a week on the move than he had when
he left Tripoli. He also had plenty of transport, for although the
twenty-one camels they had brought from Tripoli were not enough
to carry the *sharifs*' cargo – they reckoned they needed another 130
– they were more than enough to carry all that Lucas would need
for the desert crossing. Ledyard would have gone on, as would most
of the Association's later travellers. But Lucas was not a man of
action.

Abandoned by the two men who had guaranteed his safety on
the journey into the desert, faced with the prospect of being caught
in the Sahara during the summer – and remember, as far as he
knew, no white man had ever been so far into the great desert in
any season – fearful of passing through country in which the Bashaw
was conducting a campaign of attrition against rebellious desert
tribes, Lucas decided to turn back. On 20 March, as Beaufoy
recorded in the Association's *Proceedings*, 'Mr. Lucas took leave of
the Governor, to whose civilities he had been much indebted, and
having accompanied a small caravan as far as Lebida, embarked on
a coasting vessel at the neighbouring village of Legatah, and went
by sea to Tripoli.'[10] The Bashaw was clearly delighted to have this
troublesome foreigner out of the desert, accepted the return of his
mule and wished Lucas better luck for another year. Even then
Lucas could have spent the summer on the coast. Had he done so,
he might have become a celebrated traveller, in spite of himself,
for in July the inhabitants of Tripoli were thrilled by the rare
appearance of a prince of Borno, an entertaining, well-informed
man with a taste for large pearls and jewel-encrusted earrings. This
prince might have invited Lucas to visit his country. But Lucas did
not stay. On 6 April he sailed out of Tripoli, spent an extended
quarantine on Malta (there was a suspicion that there was plague
in Mesurata), continued to Marseilles and was back in England by
26 July, some ten months after he had left. Unexpectedly, although
he had failed to travel more than a few miles away from the African
coast, he was not going home empty-handed.

Lucas had found it easier to strike up a conversation with the chatty fifty-year-old Imhammad than with his younger companion. The Englishman knew that Imhammad had travelled widely across the Sahara on slaving missions for the King of Fezzan, and when he realised he was not going to be able to cross the desert himself, he looked for a way of persuading Imhammad to share some of his knowledge of the south.

One evening in Mesurata, when the younger *sharif* Fuad was sitting elsewhere, Lucas unfolded the map of Africa he had brought from London. Imhammad's curiosity got the better of him, and he asked if he could have a look at this drawing. The *sharif* had evidently never seen a map before, and Lucas was only too happy to explain what it represented and how useful it could be. Then came his masterstroke. He explained that he had brought it as a gift for the King of Fezzan, but was embarrassed to present it in its current state because he suspected that it contained many errors. Perhaps, the Oriental Interpreter now suggested, the *sharif* could help him correct those errors. Lucas would then be able to draw another map and would make two copies, one for the King and another for the *sharif*.

Under the circumstances Imhammad could hardly refuse to share his knowledge. Lucas led him over to a small dune a little way from the tents, so they would not be disturbed, and there, in the sand, began to question him about the geography of the land to the south, of Fezzan and the other kingdoms of the Sahara and of what lay beyond the desert. As the old Fezzani gave his answers, turning over in his mind memories of journeys he had made through the fiery heart of the continent, Lucas scribbled notes, drew sketches and wrote down the figures that represented the catch, the treasure, the achievement that he snatched from Africa and took with him back to his employers in London.

5

The Moors' Tales

'The inland geography of that vast continent [is] an obscure scene which has been less invisible to the Arabian Moors than to any other nation of the ancient or modern world.'

Edward Gibbon, *Of the Position of the Meridional Line* (1790–91)[1]

London, May 1789

CAREFUL READERS of the *Gentleman's Magazine* of May 1789 will have spotted the following announcement, tucked away between a list of His Royal Highness, the Duke of Clarence's household and notice of a meeting to decide whether a Coldstream Guards officer had behaved like a gentleman:

A general meeting of the subscribers to the association for promoting the discovery of the interior parts of Africa, was held at the St. Alban's Tavern, when an account of the proceedings of the committee during the past year, and of the interesting intelligence which had been received in the course of it, particularly from the late Mr. Ledyard, was submitted to their consideration. By this intelligence, every doubt is removed of the practicability of the object for which the society was instituted; and as several persons have offered themselves as candidates to succeed the late Mr. Ledyard in the service of the Association, there is reason to suppose, that the knowledge already obtained will soon be followed by more extensive discoveries.[2]

The claim that 'every doubt is removed of the practicability' of getting to the interior was an exaggeration of epic proportions. The grand plan of bisecting northern Africa west of Sudan and south of Tripoli had come to nothing. And if Ledyard's meagre report was the most important of the Association's discoveries to date, then little had been achieved. But if the Committee took liberties in their announcement in the *Gentleman's Magazine*, it was because it was intended as a rallying cry, a membership drive.

When they created the Association in June of the previous year, Banks, Beaufoy and the other Saturday's Club members gave no indication of how large an organisation they envisaged. Within the first fortnight of its existence, fifteen names were added to those of the dozen founding members. Following the announcement in the *Gentleman's Magazine*, word spread through salons, drawing rooms and clubs; membership was soon up to sixty. With members committed to paying the five-guinea subscription, the Association could now count on an annual income of at least £315, more than enough to keep a traveller in the field.

The new members were a more eclectic group than the founders, but they still reflected the areas of influence and interest of the five-man Committee, in particular of its key players, Banks, Beaufoy and Lord Rawdon. There was a large group of nobility, among them the Duke of Grafton and the Earl of Bute, both former prime ministers. Rawdon had signed up some of his relations, including his father, the Earl of Moira, and his uncle the Earl of Huntingdon. More surprising was the arrival of the Countess of Aylesbury. A woman in the club? In 1789? Indeed so, and neither by chance, mistake or manipulation. While some twenty-first-century London clubs continue to refuse female membership, in May 1789 the Committee of the African Association reached the enlightened conclusion that 'The Improvement of Geographical knowledge is not unworthy the attention, or undeserving the Encouragement of the Ladies of Great Britain.'

Among this first intake of women, alongside the Countess of Aylesbury and Lady Belmore, was a Mrs Child, a useful addition: she might not have had a title, but she was married to one of London's wealthiest bankers. Thomas Coutts, founder of the financial house that still bears his name, was also attracted to the project and became the Association's banker of choice. Four members of the Hoare banking dynasty signed up too, three of them Evangelists and strongly opposed to the slave trade: Samuel Hoare Jr, the Quaker, was one of the original members of the 1785 Abolitionist Committee. Other notable new names included the potter Josiah Wedgwood, the historian Edward Gibbon – he had just published the final volume of *The Decline and Fall of the Roman Empire* – the Orientalist William Marsden and John Hunter, reputed to be the finest surgeon at work in England. A considerable number of members were also Fellows of the Royal Society, unsurprising given that Banks was the President. Equally unsurprising, considering the anti-slavery sentiments of the Committee, many of these new members were actively working towards the abolition of slavery. Of this group, one man stands out, a visionary by the name of Dr John Lettson,* a Quaker who had already taken the decisive step of freeing slaves on a West Indian plantation he inherited. But Richard Neave, a leader of the West India Merchants and a man inevitably involved in the slave trade, was also admitted, which points to a tension between the conflicting interests of abolitionists and planters.

Had these new recruits discovered the bungling nature of the Association's first missions, of Ledyard's unfortunate death in Cairo and Lucas' lame approach to the Sahara, they might have disagreed with Beaufoy's claim that 'every doubt has been removed'. Some might have gone so far as to suggest that the Association's cause was hopeless. But they had not been given all of the details and neither would they be, at least not for some time, because the Committee had included in their founding charter a resolution to

---

* Lettson studied medicine under Sir William Fordyce, one of the Association's original members. He went on to found the Royal Humane Society and the Philosophical Society of London.

share with the members only that information which 'in the opinion of the committee, may, without endangering the object of their Association, be made public'.[3] But even though they had covered their backs, there was a new urgency about the cause. Results were needed. All eyes turned to the south.

The Oriental Interpreter knew nothing of this as he watched the domes and minarets of Tripoli's skyline disappear beyond the horizon. Even so, he must have had some anxiety about returning home without having seen the longed-for interior of the continent, and will have taken comfort from the knowledge that he would arrive in London in midsummer, when many members of the African Association would have fled the dust and stink and general rot of the overheated capital. The dust sheets would be on the furniture in Soho Square, Sir Joseph Banks would be in Yorkshire, revelling in the soothing greenery of his country seat of Revesby Abbey, while Henry Beaufoy would have returned to his country house near Beaconsfield in Buckinghamshire. But Lucas' predictions were confounded: at the end of July, the shutters were still open at 32 Soho Square and Beaufoy was still in residence at Great George Street. What had kept them up in town out of season?

While Lucas was settling into Consul Tully's house in Tripoli the previous October, his employer, King George III, discovered that his eyes had become yellow, his urine brown, his mind disordered. Over a period of a couple of weeks His Britannic Majesty was reduced from a proud monarch to a man who cried to his children that he was going mad. The King's ill health sparked a constitutional crisis as his son, George, Prince of Wales, was made Regent. The monarchy crisis touched each of the Association's inner members, either as Members of Parliament or, as with Banks, because they were regulars at court. But by the time Lucas reached London, the King had recovered, a thanksgiving service had been held at St Paul's Cathedral and a series of grand dinners and balls thrown at Windsor and across London to celebrate George's return to form. No sooner was the English King out of trouble than his French counterpart, Louis XVI, was in it.

On 14 July, twelve days before Lucas set foot on English soil, citizens of Paris stormed the Bastille prison, murdered the governor and emptied its crowded cells. The French King's inability to restore order fanned the hopes and the audacity of the revolutionaries. The game was up for the *ancien régime*, something Georgiana, the Duchess of Devonshire recognised even before the Bastille fell: in Paris on 8 July, she had dressed in mourning to visit the King and Queen at Versailles. The sentiment was accurate, though in the event, it was not until January 1793 that the republicans forced Louis to bow before M. Guillotine's monstrous contraption.

To a man of Banks' character, the fall of the French King was a reflection of the sickness of the world. Whatever the failings of Louis XVI, or of George III for that matter, Banks and many around him believed that progress, whether intellectual, social or economic, was most likely to be achieved under the guidance of a king, with the solid support of the nobility and land-owners and with the efforts of a contented workforce. Reports flooding in from France, where the revolution quickly spread out of the capital and chaos gripped the country, merely served to confirm Banks' view.

In this year of revolution, 1789, over two hundred ships left England's ports bound for Africa. Many of them returned bringing people as well as goods. Not slaves, for the law in England now discouraged that: any Africans shipped as slaves were instantly transformed into free men when they touched the shores of Albion. The Africans arriving in England in 1789 were a mixed bunch of traders, petitioners and adventurers, all drawn by the economic might as much as the social right of England and its capital, the world's greatest city. Among them was a Moroccan named Ben Ali.

It is a measure of the Association's fast-growing reputation that soon after his arrival in England, news of its mission came to the ears of Ben Ali. It is perhaps also a sign of their openness that the Committee were prepared to listen to what the Moor had to say: early in June, while Lucas was quarantined in the *lazaretto* of Malta, Ben Ali was invited to meet Banks, Lord Rawdon and other members of the Committee. An English Barbary trader by the name of Dodsworth, who was fluent in Magrebi Arabic, acted as interpreter.

The Moor began by laying out his credentials. He was a respected trader from the Atlantic coastal town of Safi, for many centuries one of the principal markets for Morocco's trans-Saharan trade, and he believed he could help the Association's missionaries reach the heart of Africa. On several occasions in the course of business, Ben Ali had crossed the Sahara. Timbuktu, the Niger and Bambara, places that had become a grail for the Association, were familiar to him. He was known there and had good contacts. What's more, he would be happy to share his knowledge. He even had a proposition to make: for a fee, something the Association had not offered until now, and with certain guarantees, he would be happy to take two Europeans to Timbuktu.

Sitting in the luxurious surroundings of Sir Joseph Banks' house, some of the world's riches scattered around the room, the Moor must have calculated that if these men were at all serious about wanting to reach the African interior, they would pay him well. But the situation was not in fact so clear-cut. Banks wanted results, but experience as a traveller had taught him to treat such offers with caution. Money was not the issue: he had ample means to fund Ben Ali's trip and had already paid considerably more to support other voyages of discovery. But this was Association business, and as Treasurer he knew they were already financially over-extended. So instead of producing a purse of gold from his breast pocket, as the Moor seems to have expected, Sir Joseph offered golden words and insisted that, for the moment at least, the Committee could offer nothing more. 'We place Confidence in you,' Ben Ali was told. 'You should place some Confidence in us.'

The Moroccan, who had also seen something of the world, knew that reassurances and confidences would fill neither his belly nor his pocketbook. But rather than walk away from the Association, he tried a different approach. For reasons that are not clear, he singled out Lord Rawdon. Perhaps because the Irish peer was the youngest member of the Committee, perhaps because he appeared more sympathetic during the Committee hearing, or perhaps because Ben Ali believed he was the most trustworthy, or the most gullible – whatever the reason, on Wednesday, 10 June, Rawdon received a letter from a Dr W. Thomson. 'At the desire of Said Aben Ali I write this . . . He talks of making with your Lp [Lordship] *personally*, a Covenant before God with *Bread and Salt.*' Thomson was clearly reluctant to be writing the letter. 'I endeavoured to explain to him,' he continued, 'that it was not for me to determine, either how far your L'p might be inclined to pledge your Honour as an Individual, considered apart from the Society, or to submit to any other Rites in giving your Word than what was usual with a British Nobleman.'[4]

The Moor had miscalculated: Rawdon had no intention of entering into any sort of rite. Instead, two days later, the peer met Banks and Beaufoy in Soho Square and between them they agreed to offer Ben Ali 'an allowance'[5] of three guineas a week for as long as it took Dodsworth, his interpreter, to write down his account of the interior of Africa. Ben Ali agreed, the work soon started and continued for the next seven weeks.

The notes of Ben Ali's interviews have not survived, but the Committee were clearly convinced by him, for they now tentatively agreed to his offer to take two of their missionaries into the interior. The proposed route was another departure for them: Ben Ali did not want to approach Africa by way of Cairo, Tripoli or even his native Morocco. Instead, he suggested that they abandoned their planned bisection of northern Africa and approached from the west, sailing up the River Gambia and then continuing overland to

Timbuktu. For the Committee, this was a radical change in their approach to the continent, but it was less of a problem than the terms Ben Ali demanded. For his part in the adventure, he wanted the Association to provide him with £300 in cash or gold. With this, he would buy goods to trade in the interior, which would serve two crucial purposes: proceeds from the sale of these goods would pay for their travel deeper into the interior and, just as important, would also give credibility to their disguise as merchants. There was one other demand: if the mission was successful, if he and the two travellers reached Timbuktu and made it back to London, he wanted the Association to provide him with a pension of £200 a year.

The terms were steep. Ledyard's mission had cost just over £237 and Lucas' account, although the Committee didn't know it at this point, had topped £400, so Ben Ali's mission costs were not unexpected. But neither of the Association's previous missionaries had received a salary or the promise of a pension. Apart from the money, there were concerns about the Moor's reliability, and therefore also about the safety of whoever they sent out with him. The Committee argued the matter. Discussions went on for some weeks, and while they continued three more characters entered the story.

François Xavier Swediaur was a forty-year-old doctor, born in Austria of Swedish parents, who for some years had been practising medicine in London. He counted among his friends Sir William Fordyce, one of the Association's founders; through Fordyce, Swediaur heard of Ben Ali. The Moor's offer struck a chord: he had long wanted to do something different with his life, and this was the sort of opportunity he could not let pass. A few days later he volunteered to be the Association's next geographical missionary, and recommended that a friend of his, Mr Hollen Vergen, be allowed to accompany him.

To Banks, Swediaur and Hollen Vergen offered a way out of the impasse the Committee had reached with Ben Ali. He could not bring himself to trust the Moor with the Association's money, convinced there was a real possibility – a probability, even – that they would never hear from him again. If that were to happen, the Association's credibility would be seriously compromised. But Banks and Fordyce had known Swediaur for years. They trusted him, and through him they could see a way to make the Moor's proposition work.

Beaufoy still had his doubts. On 23 July he wrote to Banks that he had seen Swediaur and had told him, much to the doctor's satisfaction, 'that you seem inclined to place him at the head of the Gambia adventure and to give him the aid of the Moor, as a useful but subordinate partner in the business of the Journey'.[6] Beaufoy was happy for Swediaur and Hollen Vergen to represent the Association, though like Banks he mistrusted Dodsworth and Ben Ali. As the success of the mission depended on Ben Ali, whatever Swediaur's role, Beaufoy continued to raise objections, arguing that risking some £300 of the Association's money in this way was 'equally inconsistent with the state of our funds and with the common maxims of Mercantile prudence'.[7] Banks now found a way around this impasse by introducing to the Committee someone who knew a great deal more than any of them about mercantile prudence.

Philip Sansom had made a fortune from trading abroad, and in the process had acquired a reputation in the City as a man of sound commercial sense. He was, as Banks also knew, very much in favour of abolishing slavery.* At this stage, in the summer of 1789, Sansom was not a member of the Association – he didn't sign up until 1791 – but Banks knew him well enough to make an approach, and Sansom appeared to be happy to help: together with several business colleagues he offered to send out a cargo of £500 worth of goods in the care of one of his own men. When they reached Timbuktu, Swediaur would be allowed to trade with these goods. Presumably Sansom and his partners thought it was worth risking £500 on a venture that might give them a toehold in the Timbuktu trade.

Banks was delighted. The plan, as laid out in the Committee's minutes, ran as follows: Swediaur and Hollen Vergen, 'being animated by an earnest desire of promoting the great object of the

---

* Sansom later served as Deputy Chairman of the Sierra Leone Company, the philanthropic organisation that helped to establish a settlement for freed slaves in West Africa in 1787.

Association for the discovery of the Interior parts of Africa', were to sail to the Gambia with Ben Ali as their guide and interpreter. While they made the much-longed-for journey to Timbuktu, Sansom's cargo would remain on the Atlantic coast. Once the missionaries reached Timbuktu, the cargo would be sent on and Swediaur and Hollen Vergen would sell the goods. The financial arrangements had also fallen neatly into place: the Association would pay £300 travelling expenses for the three men, £125 to equip Swediaur and Hollen Vergen, £50 a year (for a maximum of three years) to Hollen Vergen and £100 to Swediaur if he reached Timbuktu and lived to tell the tale. Swediaur would also earn a commission on the sale of Sansom's cargo. The only person who might possibly have been unhappy with the deal was Ben Ali, who had both a greater role and a greater reward in mind when he first approached the Association. But that kind of concern quickly became irrelevant on 6 August, when Sir Joseph scribbled a hasty note to Beaufoy: 'The Moor is missing.'[8]

Dodsworth, who was still translating and, to some extent, chaperoning Ben Ali, had brought the bad news to Soho Square, announcing that the Moor had simply vanished, leaving his rooms and taking nothing with him. Not knowing of any other motive, Dodsworth assumed that he had killed himself 'from his uneasiness of mind'.[9] But Beaufoy quickly made enquiries and heard otherwise. Ben Ali, it seems, was lying low in Hampstead, forced into hiding by the appearance of an angry pregnant woman pressing paternity claims on him. She was not the first, and perhaps, like the others, she would not have managed to disrupt the Moor's – and therefore the Association's – plans had she not brought the police along with her. Dodsworth had already posted bail to keep Ben Ali out of jail on one occasion, but could see no way to help him now.

When Banks heard the news, he suffered one of his periodic eruptions of moral outrage. 'How,' he demanded to know, 'is this Consonant with an intention of travelling in our service?'[10] The answer was obvious: it was not.

Ben Ali simply disappeared from Hampstead, leaving a couple of angry women and fatherless children, and was never heard of again. A month or two later, Dr Swediaur collapsed: repeated bouts of colic forced him to give up any hopes of travelling to Timbuktu. As a result, Philip Sansom withdrew his offer of cargo and the plan on which Banks, Beaufoy and Rawdon had spent considerable time and energy was dead. But as soon became apparent, their efforts were not wasted.

They had not found the River Niger, nor had they seen Timbuktu. They knew nothing more about the course of the River Nile, nor of the extent of the great lakes they believed would be found in the centre of the continent. But Simon Lucas had returned safe and sound, thank God, and had brought a thorough description of the route south of Tripoli as given to him by Imhammad and confirmed by the Governor of Mesurata. Meanwhile, members in London had done their part in trying to redraw Boulton's 1787 map by trawling for useful information.

Among the many people Banks contacted was James Matra in Morocco. Matra, who had already warned of the 'absolute impossi-bility' of exploring Africa through Morocco, now repeated his reser-vations in a letter from Gibraltar, explaining that, 'After all my hopes [of providing new information] I am obliged to tell you my expectations of procuring you intelligence of the route thro [sic] the interior of this Country are wonderfully disappointed – I have Paper in abundance, but not to the purpose...'[11] If he wasn't able to deliver new intelligence, Matra could at least offer general encouragement: 'By what I hear of Tombucktoo [sic], called by the Moors Timkitoo, it seems a Country well worth examining.'[12] But at the same time as he was insisting that he had nothing new to tell Banks, Matra was writing a detailed account of the trade through Morocco for Lord Sydney, the Secretary of State for the Home Department and for the Barbary States of North Africa.

The previous October, most likely at Banks' suggestion, Sydney had written to the British consuls in the Barbary States asking them to report on trade and trading routes into the Sahara and central Africa. Neither Tully in Tripoli nor Consul Logie in Algiers replied to His Lordship's request, but Matra sent in a lengthy report from Tangier, which included this overview: 'The Caravan Trade from Morocco to Guinea proceeds no further South than to Tambuctoo, the Capital of Negroland. This Town, I believe, is a general Rendez-vous not only for the people of this Country [Morocco] but likewise for the Traders of Algiers, Tunis and Tripoli . . .' He then offered the sort of details he had told Banks were unavailable. The meat of it was this: caravans of up to three hundred people carried European products – cloths, beads, spices, brassware and needles – to the interior and brought tobacco and salt, gold dust, ivory, slaves and gum back to the north. As far as he could tell, as many as four thousand slaves were being marched across the desert to Morocco each year, among them eunuchs 'of a Country called Bambara',[13] whose king was said to be happy to exchange some twenty of them for a good horse. Perhaps most tantalising for the African Association was news that the region of Timbuktu was inhabited 'by a civilized and quiet People and abounds with large unfortified Towns . . . The Country is fruitful and produces much Corn and Rice near the Rivers or Lakes, I suppose, for I am informed it never rains there: It abounds likewise with Cattle and Sheep . . .'[14]

Much of this new information was published in *The Proceedings of the Association for Promoting the Discovery of the Interior Parts of Africa*, a report written by Beaufoy and published in 1790. Running to 115 quarto pages, it contains a remarkable amount of detail on the country previously marked on maps as Nigritia or Bilad as-Sudan (both terms refer to 'the Land of the Blacks'). In the margin, beside each statement, Beaufoy identified the principal source of information, either Imhammad or Ben Ali. Here, at last, were men of the south describing their lands, the season for Saharan travel, the measures to be taken when travelling by camel, the distances that could reasonably be covered in a day – 'three miles in the hour' for 'seldom more than seven or eight [hours] in a day'.[15] Here too was confirmation of the existence of the great kingdoms of Katsina and Borno, of cities and towns – Murzuq, Domboo, Kanem, Ganatt, Assouda and Weddan – that had previously been known only by hearsay, and lists of hitherto unknown tribes, the Kardee, the Serrowah, the Showva, Battah, Mulgui and others. And here too was the first mention in any account of North Africa of a place called Tibesti, several hundred miles across the desert and described as mountainous, home to a wild tribe and to 'vales fertile in corn and pasturage for cattle, of which they have numerous herds'.[16] Their camels were said to be the finest in Africa.

There was much here to reassure the Committee, such as, for instance, Lucas' claim that 'travelling through all this part of Africa is considered as so secure, that the Shereef Imhammed, with the utmost chearfulness [sic] and confidence of safety, proposed to accompany and conduct Mr. Lucas, by the way of Fezzan and Cashna [Katsina], across the Niger, to Assenté [Ashanti], which borders on the Coast of the Christians'.[17] Wishful thinking, but perhaps not impossible. Everything the Association had learned from its sources suggested that once a way into the interior was found, their problems would be over because, according to these accounts at least, food and water were abundant so long as you knew where to look for them. At the heart of these reports, unsurprisingly considering the informants were merchants, were descriptions of a lucrative trade in gold, salt, cotton, senna, ivory, ostrich feathers and a host of other commodities. Mention was also made of firearms: according to Imhammad, they were unknown in the inland states south of the Niger for the simple reason that 'the Kings in the neighbourhood of the coast, [are] persuaded that if these powerful instruments of war should reach the possession of the populous inland States, their own independence would be lost'.[18]

Perhaps the most significant information concerns the Niger, and on this, as on much else, Imhammad and Ben Ali concur. 'Of this river,' Beaufoy wrote, 'which in Arabic is sometimes called Neel il

Kibeer, or the Great Nile, and at others, Neel il Abeed, or the Nile of the Negroes, the rise and termination are unknown, but the course is from East to West.' Here we have it: Leo Africanus, the sixteenth-century traveller and writer, was refuted and the Age of Enlightenment had resolved, in theory at least, one of the enduring mysteries of African geography. There were other revelations as well: the elephants and savage beasts were to be replaced on the map by mountains of stupendous height, wide rivers and vast salt-water lakes. Much of this was simply wrong. But in London in that summer of revolution, neither Banks, Beaufoy nor anyone else suspected the magnitude of their errors.

The Committee were clearly disappointed at Lucas' lack of endeavour, but equally they were delighted that he had returned and brought with him such corroboration. Whatever the cooling off between the missionary and his masters – and there is no further mention of Lucas' mission in the Committee's minute books – the *Proceedings* put a positive spin on the journey and generously explained that it had ended because he was 'deprived of all prospect of arriving this year at Fezzan'.[19] That may have been the end of Lucas, at least in our story, had not fortune brought to Beaufoy's attention another North African with a story to sell.

Asseed El Hage Abd Salam Shabeeny (As Sayyid al Hajj Abd Salam Shabeni) – Shabeni for short – was born in Tetouan, a Moroccan town that looks down to the Mediterranean from the Rif Mountains. Like Leo Africanus and Ben Ali, Shabeni was the son of a merchant. At fourteen years of age his father took him travelling, and for much of the next thirteen years he lived in Timbuktu. On his return to Tetouan, the young man decided it was time to make his mark and to branch out on his own. He travelled to Egypt and from there made the pilgrimage to Mecca, hence his title of el Hage, or al Hajj, the Pilgrim. Several years later, back in Tetouan, he set himself up as a merchant.

In this guise, as a trader, he travelled to Hamburg in 1789 to buy linen and anything else on which he could turn a profit back home. When his purchases had been baled up and a passage agreed, he boarded ship for the south. On their second day out of port, sailing through the North Sea, they were attacked (by whom he omits to say) and Shabeni was captured. Taken off the ship, he was landed at Ostend where, after almost seven weeks of captivity, he managed to secure his release. Instead of being home in Morocco in December 1789, Shabeni found himself in London, where he soon came to the attention of the African Association, an answer to Banks' and Beaufoy's prayers. He had spent thirteen years living in and travelling around the northern half of Africa, and he held out to the Association the prospect of an even more accurate and detailed description of the place.

Early in the spring of 1790, Beaufoy put aside his parliamentary duties to interview Shabeni and one of his companions. As with Ben Ali, Beaufoy offered Shabeni a deal: the Association would pay him twenty-five guineas in return for all he could tell them about the interior. As Shabeni spoke little or no English and Beaufoy knew even less Arabic, an interpreter was needed; Lucas was the obvious choice. Whatever Beaufoy had heard from Imhammad and Ben Ali now paled into insignificance as Shabeni described to his eager audience the great city of Timbuktu. It is easy to imagine the scene at Beaufoy's house on Great George Street, the royal residences on one side and the Palace of Westminster, home of Parliament, on the other. When Shabeni started to talk, he transported them out of the room crowded with carved furniture, large oil paintings and knotted rugs and into the legendary African city. He began by describing its defences, a wide trench some twelve feet deep and a mud wall 'sufficiently strong to defend the town against the wild Arabs'.[20] There were three gates, lined with camel skin and 'so full of nails that no hatchet can penetrate them; the front appears like one piece of iron'.[21] Inside the walls, the Sultan lived in his considerable palace with an equally considerable harem. He was secure and wealthy, protected by a standing army of five thousand men and with such a store of wealth that he handed out gold dust to all and sundry, even his slaves. If this was good to hear, what came next was even better.

South-east of Timbuktu, eight or ten days downstream as he remembered it and around twelve hours' journey inland from the river, Shabeni had entered a city that no one in Europe had ever even heard of. Hausa, he explained to the startled Beaufoy, was nearly as large as London. In fact it was so big that although he had lived there for two years, he never managed to see all of it. The King's palace was equally imposing, hidden behind an eight-mile wall and protected by an army of 180,000 soldiers. Gold was found nearby, not by mining, for there were no mountains to excavate, but simply by digging up and refining the sand. There was a just government, conditions were stable, trade was profitable (caravans came from as far afield as India) and, perhaps most encouraging of all, unlike in many other places foreign merchants were required to pay neither tax nor duty to the Sultan, 'as the Housaeens think they ought to be encouraged'.[22] Even without any direct income from the foreigners, the royal revenue 'is supposed to be immense'. Beaufoy suspended his disbelief and listened to this story with all the wonder of a child hearing a fairy tale. It was everything he and the Association had hoped for – civilisation, wealth and an enlightened ruler deep in the heart of Africa.

By the time the Committee published its *Proceedings* in 1790, membership had risen to ninety-five. But apart perhaps from Sir Joseph Banks, none of these eminent people had the slightest claim to be considered a geographer. Happily, one was at hand. James Rennell enters the story with a considerable reputation: he was the outstanding geographer of his generation, referred to as 'the English d'Anville'. This did not do him justice, for in many ways he was a far greater geographer than the French master. He was now, in 1790, forty-eight years old, and travel and maps were his life. By

1792 he had become the Association's official geographer and been offered its first honorary membership.

Rennell had lost his parents while still a child and been enlisted into the Royal Navy before his fifteenth birthday. This gave him the opportunity to travel and also provided the circumstances where his talent for surveying and drawing maps was brought out and recognised. He started as a conscript, but within six years had risen to the grand title of Surveyor-General of the East India Company's dominions in Bengal. By the time he was twenty-one, he was responsible for mapping large swathes of India. There was excitement as well as responsibility – in 1770, he wrote to a friend, 'I must not forget to tell you that about a Month ago, a large Leopard jumped at me, and I was fortunate enough to kill him by thrusting my Bayonet down his Throat. Five of my young Men were wounded by him; four of them very dangerously. You see I am a lucky Fellow.' Six years later, with huge areas of 'Hindostan' mapped, his luck ran out near Bhutan when he was severely wounded in a skirmish with fakirs. He survived the attack, but the wounds never properly healed and the following year he was forced to resign his commission through ill health.

Rennell was back in London by 1778. A portrait by John Opie shows him to have a high forehead, long nose and sharp eyes. He looks like the sort of person who loves nothing better than to get involved in a tough but good-natured intellectual wrangle, although the words 'diffident', 'unassuming', 'candid' and 'grave yet sweet' crop up in descriptions of his character. He had returned from India with the rank of major and a pension – when the East India Company finally deigned to pay it – of £2000 a year (some £100,000 now), which meant he would not have to worry about money. Not that he was going to be idle. In 1778 he published a series of charts and maps of South Africa. Three years later the *Bengal Atlas* was published and in 1783 he celebrated the appearance of his masterwork, *A Memoir of a Map of Hindostan*, the first reliable map of India. By then he had been elected a Fellow of the Royal Society and was on friendly terms with Banks and several other members of the African Association: it was only a matter of time before they approached him to cast a geographer's eye over the new information they had received and to see what light it threw on the map of Africa.

Rennell published his interpretations of the new information, his *Construction of the Map of Africa*, in 1790 as a companion piece to Beaufoy's *Proceedings*. He began by noting that d'Anville used second- and twelfth-century geographers to fill in the centre of Africa and questioned why it had proved so difficult to obtain fresh information about the continent. The reason, he concluded, owed 'more to natural causes, than to any absolute want of attention on the part of Geographers':[23]

> *Africa stands alone in a geographical view! Penetrated by no inland seas, like the Mediterranean, Baltic, or Hudson's Bay; nor overspread with extensive lakes, like those of North America; nor having in common with the other Continents, rivers running from the center to the extremities: but, on the contrary, its regions separated from each other by the least practicable of all boundaries, arid Desarts [sic] of such formidable extent, as to threaten those who traverse them, with the most horrible of all deaths, that arising from thirst! Placed in such circumstances, can we be surprised at our ignorance of its Interior Parts?*[24]

Rennell's new map of Africa used the latest intelligence collected by the Association. He still took d'Anville, Leo and al-Idrissi as his starting point, but he went on to test their findings against those of his travellers. Inevitably, given his enduring fascination with ancient geography, the *Elucidations* are sprinkled with references to the ancient writers he so revered, to Herodotus and Pliny, Arrian and Strabo. Often he agreed with them, as with the location of Murzuq, the main town of Fezzan, which Lucas had failed to reach. But there are several places where information gathered by the Association allowed Rennell the sweet sensation of breaking new ground by providing fresh plottings, among them the location of the Niger, Timbuktu and the oasis of Siwa, site of the ancient oracle of Jupiter Ammon. Nor could he resist trying to chart the course of the Niger:

The river known to Europeans by the name of Niger, runs on the South of the kingdom of Cashna, in its course towards Tombuctou; and if the report which Ben Alli heard in that town, may be credited, it is afterwards lost in the sands on the South of the country of Tombuctou.

On his map, Rennell marked the known part of the Niger with a continuous line, the speculative part – the run-off into the desert – with a dotted one. But he then went on to assert that 'the Africans have two names for this river; that is, Neel il Abeed, or River of the Negroes; and the Neel il Kibeer, or the Great River. They also term the Nile (that is, the Egyptian River) Neel Shem: so that the term Neel, from whence our Nile, is nothing more than the appellative of River; like Ganges, or Sinde.'[25] In this he was completely wrong. The Egyptian Nile is known as the Nil al Kabir; above Khartoum, the western branch of the river is known as the Nil al Abiat (hence his Abeed), or White Nile, the eastern branch along which James Bruce had already explored, being known as the Blue Nile. The word Nil or Neel referred solely to the Nile.

The Sharif Imhammad, Ben Ali and Shabeni had all used a day's march as a measure of distance and, in the absence of any readings of longitude or latitude, Rennell had no choice but to use these to create geographical facts. It was a difficult task, perhaps ultimately an impossible one, as he realised when he tried to plot the whereabouts of Timbuktu. But 'in using materials of so coarse a kind', he apologised, 'trifles must not be regarded'.[26]

In what way had this new information changed their understanding of Africa? While Ledyard was rotting in his Cairene grave, Lucas becoming reacquainted with the rituals of court life and Banks busy keeping the minds of government ministers on the fate of the Botany Bay colonists (and while they all watched with horror the unfolding terror in France), Beaufoy sat at his desk in Westminster

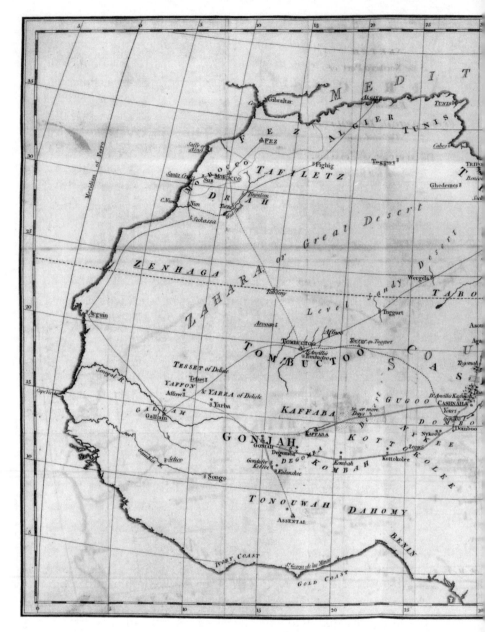

Rennell's map of Africa, 1790

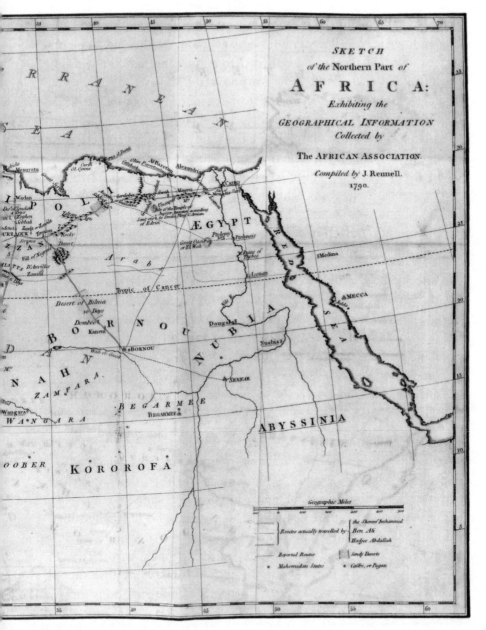

and drew 'conclusions of an important and interesting nature'.[27] Having summed up the Association's advances and dwelled on some of the minutiae of the facts, he turned to something he knew would touch his audience directly: the British Grand Tourist, he suggested, might consider 'exchanging the usual excursion from Calais to Naples, for a Tour more extended and important'.[28] The location of this place? None other than Fezzan. Here, he assured his readers, the *amateur* of archaeology would find fulfilment and the lover of Nature could discover much that was so far unknown in Europe. All of which was probably true, only first the traveller had to find a way of reaching Fezzan, something Lucas had failed to do.

For the more adventurous tourist, the possibilities seemed endless, even if the destinations were unknown:

> *The powerful Empires of Bornu and Cashna will be open to his investigation; the luxurious City of Tombuctou, whose opulence and severe police attract the Merchants of the most distant States of Africa, will unfold to him the causes of her vast prosperity; the mysterious Niger will disclose her unknown origin and doubtful termination; and countries unveiled to ancient and modern research will become familiar to his view.*[29]

It was wishful thinking, of course. How was a Grand Tourist to swap Naples for central Sahara when Rennell was still struggling to locate with certainty Borno, Katsina or any of the other powerful empires? And how was an English lord or gentleman to succeed when a traveller of John Ledyard's experience, who had sailed the world with Cook and crossed Siberia alone, had managed to go no further than Cairo and Simon Lucas hardly left sight of the coast?

The Association's first resolution, drafted by Beaufoy that summer day back in 1788, stated that 'no species of information is more ardently desired, or more generally useful, than that which improves the science of Geography'.[30] Their area of enquiry was clearly fixed on the interior of the northern half of Africa, in particular the River Niger, the east–west trans-continental caravan routes and the whereabouts of Timbuktu. But Beaufoy now extended the bounds of the Association's interests from geography and history to trade. And given that the flag followed trade just as much as trade followed the flag, he was also moving the Association into the realm of politics.

Beaufoy concluded by laying out the commercial possibilities the Association's researches had exposed. 'Of all the advantages to which a better acquaintance with the Inland Regions of Africa may lead, the first in importance is, the extension of the Commerce, and the encouragement of the Manufactures of Britain ... One of the most profitable manufactures of Great Britain',[31] he went on, was firearms. These were currently traded along the coast. The rulers of the coastal states had effectively stopped the movement of weapons into the interior for the obvious reason that guns gave them an edge over their more powerful inland neighbours. If their rivals were able to buy European-made weapons, the coastal states would be overrun. British traders, Beaufoy seemed to be suggesting, need have no scruples about arming both sides in this conflict, nor about disturbing the balance of power. Perhaps he believed that this might in some way stop the flow of slaves from the interior to the coast.

As well as musing on the sale of firearms, Beaufoy drew some larger conclusions about the African trade. Merchants from Morocco, Tripoli, Egypt and elsewhere, he noted, went to the considerable expense of mounting caravans and making extraordinary journeys across the Sahara, with all the costs and dangers that this entailed, and were still able to turn a good profit. Millions of pounds were mentioned. And here the idea first suggested by Ben Ali reappears. Imagine, Beaufoy went on, how much profit British traders might make if they cut inland from the coast south of the Sahara, much less than half the journey of the northern African traders. This, of course, ignored the fact that no European he knew of had made that journey and lived to tell the tale. 'Associations of Englishmen should form caravans, and take their departure from the highest navigable reaches of the Gambia [River], or from the settlement which is lately established at Sierra Leone.' There would, he knew, be setbacks, as there always are with new ventures. But consider the market: appearing to pluck a figure from the air, for he had nothing more substantial to base it on, he estimated the population in the interior, of Katsina, Borno, Timbuktu and all those other places Rennell had recently plotted on his map, at 'probably more than one hundred millions of people'.[32] 'The gain would be such as few commercial adventures have ever been found to yield.'[33]

After all these exhortations, it comes as no surprise that the Association's next missionary was sent to find a route between the Gambia River, the Niger and 'luxurious', gold-plated Timbuktu.

6

The Gambia Route

'On Saturday the African Club [the Committee] dined at the
St Alban's Tavern. There were a number of articles produced
from the interior parts of Africa, which may turn out very
important in a commercial view; as gums, pepper, &c. We
have heard of a city ... called *Tombuctoo*: gold is there so
plentiful as to adorn even the slaves; amber is there the most
valuable article. If we could get our manufactures into that
country we should soon have gold enough.'

Sir John Sinclair, 1790[1]

IN 1782, six years before the Association was formed, Sir Joseph
Banks found himself faced with a situation of the utmost delicacy.
A Fellow of the Royal Society, a wealthy chemist by the name of
John Price, announced that he had found a way of converting
mercury into gold. Price's claim caused a sensation, not least
because it appeared to be verified by witnesses of great character:
he had conducted the experiment at his Surrey laboratory, where,
in the presence of their lordships Palmerston, Onslow and King,
he produced a yellow metal that was proved, upon testing, to be
gold. When word got out, Price quickly became a national hero,
fêted throughout the land; Oxford University, perhaps a little
opportunistically, even offered him an honorary degree. Barely aud-
ible over the clamour and adulation, Sir Joseph and some of his
colleagues at the Royal Society announced that they simply didn't

believe him. Rather than draw more attention to the man, the Fellows decided to do nothing, in the hope that he would soon be exposed or forgotten. The opposite happened. Price published an account of his experiment, although not the actual formula for making the precious metal, and the book quickly sold out. Banks decided this story had gone far enough, and asked its author to be so kind as to repeat the experiment for the scrutiny of the Royal Society. Price agreed and, on the appointed day, welcomed three eminent Fellows into his lab. Instead of alchemy, they witnessed a different sort of experiment: Price swallowed a phial of poison and died before their eyes.

The Price episode was unusual but by no means unique. In an age of trial and error, when some scientists were making such huge advances, it seemed as though anything was possible, even the creation of gold from base metal. In such a climate, the idea of sending explorers off to an area that others had already visited and asking them to locate towns, rivers and goldfields that were known to exist must have seemed a low-risk adventure. And yet, for their third mission, the Association reigned in some of its ambition. The grand plan of bisecting the northern half of Africa, of sending one explorer to cross it from east to west and another from north to south, was abandoned. The next geographical missionary was to follow up the Hajj Shabeni's suggestion and cut a passage through from the Atlantic coast to the Niger River. This plan was more specific than the previous one and, the Committee must have reckoned, more likely to succeed. Their traveller would head up the Gambia River and cut inland to the kingdoms of Bondo and Bambuk, both bywords for gold and lying in an area in which the French had been trying to open trade with the Atlantic. Beyond Bambuk lay the route to Timbuktu, a place where 'gold is . . . so plentiful as to adorn even the slaves', Committee member Sir John Sinclair noted, echoing the reports of earlier centuries. But if deciding on new routes of exploration was easy, choosing the right man for the job was not.

There was no shortage of volunteers – Banks' archive is littered with applications – but the Committee had been criticised for their first choice of missionaries and also for the routes they had chosen, so this time they were going to take more care. In March 1789, James Bruce had warned Banks about Ledyard: 'I am afraid,' he wrote from his family seat in Kinnaird, Scotland, 'your African or rather Nubian traveller will not answer your expectations . . . He is either too high or too low; for he should join the Jellaba at Suakim . . . or else he should have gone to Siout or Monfalout in Upper Egypt from Cairo, and, having procured acquaintance and accommodations there, set out with the great Caravan of Sudan, traversing first the desert of Selima to Dar Four, Dar Selé, and Bagirma, so on to Bournu, and down to Tombucto to the Ocean at Senega or the Gambia.'[2] Harsh, perhaps, but history proved him right.

Not everyone was so critical of Ledyard, however. Thomas Jefferson, his patron in Paris, continued to refer to his 'genius', while the opinion-making *Gentleman's Magazine*, considering his mission in its issue of July 1790, thought that 'Such a person as Mr. Ledyard was formed by Nature for the object in contemplation; and, were we unacquainted with the sequel [his death in Cairo], we should congratulate the Society in being so fortunate as to find such a man for one of their missionaries.' But then in January 1792, W.G. Browne, a traveller we shall meet in the field in the next chapter, wrote that 'Ledyard, the Man employed by the society on the Sennar expedition, was a very unfit person; and, tho' he had lived, would not have advanced many leagues on the way, if the judgement of people in Egypt concerning him be credited.'[3]

Lucas attracted just as much criticism. When news of his failure to get beyond the Libyan coast reached Tangier, James Matra, the Consul, wrote to Banks, 'I am sorry for Lucas' miscarriage, but his expedition has ended as ever I feared it would. He is nothing but a good natured fellow. It is very certain that a Moorish education [which Lucas had had as a slave to the Emperor of Morocco] plays the devil with us. Were you to take one from the first stock of Heroes and bring [him] up here, timidity would be the most certain though by far not the worst consequence of it.'[4] Another of the Association's missionaries, meeting Lucas several years later, wrote, 'I don't know if the Committee believes his excuses for his returning to England, or if they give them so little a credit as I do myself . . .'[5]

The obvious conclusion to be drawn in 1790 was that in their haste to get their first two missions off to Africa, the Committee had chosen men who were either inappropriate for the task they had been given, as in the case of Lucas, or insufficiently prepared, as could be said of Ledyard. It was clear that more than languages, which had been Lucas' strength, or travel experience, which had recommended Ledyard, were needed to crack open the African shell. But then, consider the problems the Association's missionaries faced. Apart from the fact that they were uncertain of where they were going and of what they would find when they got there, they needed to have a great facility with languages – take a trip along the River Niger in Mali now and you will find your boatman speaking at least half a dozen quite distinct languages or dialects in the course of a normal day, including Mandekan, Soninke, Wolof, Fulani and Songhay. They also needed extraordinary physical strength and what Banks would have called rude health. After all, they were being sent to an area that later came to be known as the white man's grave. A long list of preventatives are recommended today to protect travellers in the region against cholera, yellow fever, typhoid, meningitis, polio, tetanus, diphtheria, hepatitis A and B, rabies and malaria, none of which had even been identified in the late eighteenth century. Diplomacy was another essential skill for the Association's travellers. Throughout Africa there was great suspicion of Europeans and Americans. Why were they there? Were they preparing for an invasion? Were they going to take over local trade? Was it gold that drew them so far from home? Certainly no one in West Africa was going to be convinced by the sort of explanation Bruce and Ledyard offered in Cairo, that they were travelling out of curiosity, just to see where rivers rose, to know what lay across deserts. European involvement in the slave trade had revealed the brutish side of the Christian spirit and had shown how easily visitors could become raiders. If there had ever been any romantic speculation about white men in West Africa, it was long gone.

Miraculously, in the summer of 1790 the Committee received an offer of 'services' from someone who seemed to possess just about all of the experience and qualities they now knew they wanted. In July 1788, Banks' friend and colleague at the Royal Society, the lawyer Sir William Musgrave, had written to suggest that a man by the name of Daniel Houghton might be of use to the Association. Nothing came of it at the time because Ledyard and Lucas had already been commissioned. But Houghton kept his eye on the Association's progress, and when two years later he heard that the Committee were planning a new expedition, he was quick to repeat his offer.

Houghton certainly seemed to have the credentials for the job. Born into an Irish military family in 1740, at the age of eighteen he had enlisted as an ensign in his father's regiment, the 69th Regiment of Foot. The following year he was promoted to lieutenant, and later saw action in the West Indies. In 1772, stationed in Gibraltar, he had been sent to the Emperor of Morocco by General Cornwallis,* his commanding officer, in an attempt to normalise relations between the two countries. According to Houghton's later testimonial – there seem to be no other records of this adventure – he succeeded in calming the Emperor's stormy character. Whatever the truth, Cornwallis died soon after and, much to his annoyance, Houghton never received the recognition or reward he felt he was owed. 'There is no Beast in the Creation half so remorseless,' he later wrote in regard to Cornwallis, 'as the hardened Heart of an ungenerous Person.'[6]

The following year, 1773, he took the traditional route to promotion and bought himself a company in his father's old regiment, but debt soon forced him to sell. Five years later, desperate to change his circumstances, he prepared to sail for India to take up the post of Engineer to the Nawab of Arcot, a small principality seventy-five

---

* This was the same Cornwallis who had sent Lucas back to Morocco in a diplomatic role soon after he had been freed from slavery there.

miles inland from Madras. 'I have some overtures made me here,' he wrote to his wife Mary* while waiting at Cowes for a boat in June 1778, 'but my mind is engaged for greater schemes in India.'[7] This Indian adventure was supposed to be a turning point, but his run of bad fortune was not over yet: he sailed just as Britain and France went to war and the ship he was travelling in was forced to abandon its journey and put in at Gorée, a tiny dot of an island just off the African coast and now within sight of the Senegalese capital of Dakar.

Apart from a brief British occupation in 1693, the French had held Gorée for more than a century. With the reopening of hostilities between the two countries in 1778 and as a reflection of Britain's greater naval strength, the French evacuated the island and the British moved in. In these changed circumstances Houghton was offered the post of Fort-Major at Gorée. Without other means or options, he accepted the job and remained on the island for four years, until Britain handed it back to the French as part of the peace treaty of 1783.

Houghton already had the idea of making a journey of exploration when he left Gorée, and proposed to the British government that they sponsor him to travel up the Gambia River. The lure was not so much geographical knowledge as commercial gains, and in particular the location of the goldmines that were believed to lie near the Gambia's banks. The idea was a good one, but was turned down because the government had other concerns at the time. It is not clear what happened to him in the five years between leaving Gorée and first approaching the African Association, but in 1790 Houghton had a wife, children and considerable debts. Like Ledyard, he hoped his mission to Africa would bring him fame and that fortune would not be far behind.

Houghton was not alone in submitting proposals to the Committee. Among the others, a Captain Mason was proposed by Samuel Whitbread, the brewer and a Member of Parliament, who had joined the African Association in 1789. Only one detail of Mason's

---

* Houghton addressed these letters to his wife 'at Mrs. Bengee's Boarding school, Soho Square', and therefore within sight of Banks' house.

proposal has survived, and that is the budget: he asked for the extravagant sum of £1200, of which Whitbread offered to pay two hundred. Houghton, on the other hand, estimated his total travelling costs at around £260. His proposal was accepted in July 1790.

This time, the Committee were sure, they had chosen the right man for the job. Houghton was a congenial and determined man in whom Beaufoy recognised 'a natural intrepidity of character, that seems inaccessible to fear, and an easy flow of constitutional good humour, that even the roughest accidents of life have no power to subdue'.[8] Equally useful was his ability to speak some Moroccan Arabic, a legacy of his embassy to the Emperor eighteen years before, and some Mandingo, which he had learned while stationed on Gorée. He was fit, used to the climate, conversant with some of the region's many languages and in need of a stroke of good luck.

Determined to avoid the mistakes they had made with Ledyard and Lucas, Banks and especially Beaufoy gave the Major a thorough briefing and detailed instructions that spelled out the aims of his mission: he was to sail to West Africa and proceed up the River Gambia. The river was known to be navigable as far as the Barra Kunda Falls, several hundred miles inland. From there he was to travel overland eastwards to Hausa, which Beaufoy could not locate with any certainty but which he described as being 'a considerable Empire . . . in the neighbourhood of the Niger'.[9] The rise, course and mouth of the Niger and the exact location of Timbuktu were also among his mission objectives. The route he would take on his return home was left up to him, though Beaufoy made it clear that the Committee would be pleased to have an account of the overland route across the Sahara to Cairo – Ledyard's intended route in reverse. It was a daunting mission, laced with dangers, packed with difficulties.

Towards the end of September, just before he sailed, Houghton went to visit Beaufoy in Great George Street. The Secretary again stressed the importance of collecting geographical information, particularly how many days it took to reach Hausa, the whereabouts of Timbuktu and the position of the setting sun, so that Rennell would be able to plot new information on his map. Beaufoy had devised fifty-four questions for his traveller to put to people who had been to Hausa. Grouped under headings such as Government, Regulations with respect to Property, Trade, Music ('What Instruments have they?') and Manners, these included a description of a typical day in the life of a Hausa merchant, the ruler's reputation for justice and the leading question of whether there was any gold to be found in the region.

Beaufoy had discovered that the ship on which Houghton had booked his passage to Africa was carrying a cargo of firearms commissioned by the 'Southern Foolies', one of the Fula or Fulani tribes who lived along the Atlantic coast near the Gambia River. He sniffed an opportunity, and briefed Houghton on how to take advantage of it:

> *As certain Messengers from the Foulees were expected to attend the arrival of the Ship for the purpose of receiving the said Fire Arms, Major Houghton should accompany the said Messengers on their return; should make a present to their King, and ask his permission to pass through his dominions, and under his safe conduct to the Empire of Houssa. – That he should state to the King, the important advantages to himself and to his People, that would result from a Treaty with the Sovereign of Great Britain.*[10]

Houghton's task had just become more difficult. As well as being a geographical missionary, with all the demands that made of an understanding of history, geography, sociology and a clutch of other sciences, he was now expected to be a political envoy. And although his mission had no official governmental sanction, it certainly aroused interest at the highest of levels: Banks was even able to arrange for the Irishman to have an audience with William Pitt, the Prime Minister, just before his departure. It was a change of fortune for the man who had suffered more than twenty years of hard graft and penury in the army.

Houghton's ship left England on 16 October and reached the mouth of the River Gambia three and a half weeks later. Stowed on board was some of the equipment Lucas had returned. Most of this was clothing, including the 'crimson cloth waistcoat Gold Laced lined with blue cotton, without sleeves', the 'Scarlet kerseymere long Shawl', the crimson skullcap and the crimson and blue sash. There would be no missing this man as he moved along the river or out across the desert. There was also a silver watch, pocket compass, thermometer and a quadrant – this was, after all, a scientific mission, and with these instruments it was hoped that Houghton would be able to plot an accurate chart of his progress and of the landscape of the interior. For his protection, he was also taking a pair of brass pistols.

Houghton's bill, sent to Beaufoy just before embarkation, included £50 for the quadrant and for 'various articles of private accommodation'. His passage to Africa had cost him thirty guineas and, as the Moor Ben Ali had suggested, he had with him some £200 worth of goods that he could trade for food, shelter and assistance along the way.

The mouth of the Gambia River is three miles wide and the land around it is flat. While the roaring Atlantic slowly eats away at the coastline, eroding the roots of palms and the foundations of seaside houses, the river brings rust-red mud from the interior and deposits it along its course. In the rainy season, the Gambia appears to bleed into the steely ocean. As in the eighteenth century, there is still neither bridge nor tunnel across any stretch of the river: if you want to cross it here or further upstream you must go by ferry. Not that there is any lack of passengers. The southern bank, where the river meets the ocean, is covered by the city of Banjul, the Gambian capital. Banjul's riverside waterfront is now a low-key, peeling place of warehouses, shipping offices and cheap hotels where sailors and stranded travellers wash up waiting for the next irregular

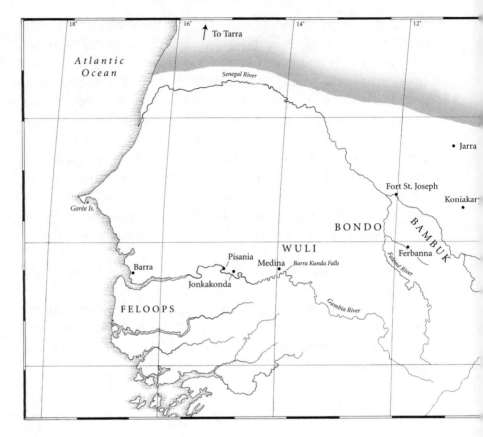

Major Houghton's progress in west Africa, 1790–91

ferry or for a passage into the Atlantic. A few blocks in from the river, the city is active by day, temporarily abandoned at night, an on–off existence that seems to reflect the job prospects of many Gambians as much as the irregular supply of electricity. There are no grand civic buildings, no imposing memorials to colonial power beyond the use of English and an unexpectedly long runway at the airport, paid for, so it is reported, by NASA, in return for the right to land the Space Shuttle here if necessary.

In 1790, when Houghton arrived, the site of Banjul was an island, flat, red and green, and dotted with fruit trees. Settlement was still

96

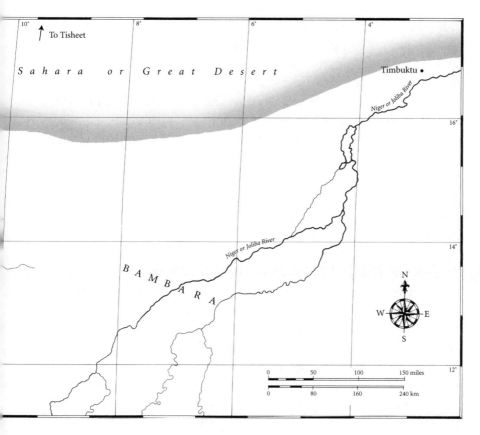

thirty-six years and a major policy shift away – the British built their first garrison there in 1816 to block the movement of slaves down the river.

The north bank today is less developed, with few houses, a bus station and taxi rank, offering transport over potholed roads to Dakar and the rest of Senegal. The north bank settlement is still called Barra, as it was in Houghton's time. The Major had visited the King of Barra in the early 1780s, when he led a timber-cutting expedition from Gorée Island. He had been well received there and elsewhere at the mouth of the river, where he had been protected

97

from attack by a patrolling French gunboat. In November 1790 he went to pay his compliments to the King, assuring a warm welcome by sending over presents worth around £20, or one tenth of the total value of his cargo.

He was fortunate with the weather: the rainy season had ended, the countryside was at its greenest and most beautiful, the sun was not too hot for a man who had already spent many years in the tropics, and Houghton was in high spirits. Then, just as had happened to Ledyard in Cairo, Houghton contracted what he described as a 'bilious fever'. His experience and acclimatisation helped him, and he was soon well enough to sail up the river.

The King of Barra was happy to offer his protection as far as it stretched, for which Houghton was grateful, but his mission was going to take him far beyond the frontiers of Barra. Where was he going? There is a good chance that he had a clear idea about the first steps of his journey, for by 1790 a considerable amount was known to Europeans about the Gambia River. Fifty-two years earlier, an English trader by the name of Francis Moore had sailed five hundred miles up the Gambia in search of goldmines and commercial opportunities. He had found trade, but no gold. Nor did he do much for the advancement of geography, admitting in his *Travels into the Inland Parts of Africa* that neither he nor anyone he knew was able to say 'whether the Nile divides, flowing part into the Mediterranean, and part into the Atlantic Sea, and whether the Gambia be one of the Branches of the Nile'. Moore's book was published in London in 1738 – Beaufoy had mentioned it while describing the pitiful state of African geography at the founding of the Association. In the intervening half-century, several trading posts and forts had been built on the banks of the Gambia, and British ships carrying merchants and adventurers had become a regular sight along the river. Few of them survived for long. One of the most notable exceptions was Dr John Laidley, who had established a successful base upriver at Pisania, from where he traded gold, ivory and slaves. Beaufoy makes no mention, in writing of Houghton, of the paradox of an Association that counted some of the leading anti-slavery campaigners among its members (Beaufoy himself was one of them, William Wilberforce, who had joined in 1789, another), yet relied on the help of slave traders to achieve its aims. It is a paradox that will become increasingly acute as the story continues.

In the town of Jonkakonda, sixteen miles from Pisania, Houghton met with his first adventure. He was about to leave for Medina, the capital of the Mandingo kingdom of Wuli, one of the key staging posts in West African trade. He had bought a good horse to ride and five asses to carry his trade goods, had hired a servant and interpreter and was on the point of setting out when something he overheard from one of the women of Jonkakonda brought him to a halt. Houghton's grasp of Mandinka, the local dialect of the West African Mandekan language, was far from perfect, but he understood enough of what was being said in the souks and alleys of Jonkakonda to realise that some people didn't want him to reach Medina or anywhere else along the river. 'The negro mistresses of the traders,' as Beaufoy later described them, 'feared that the Major's expedition portended the ruin of their commerce.'[11] Houghton recognised that it was not in the interests of the slave traders to allow his adventure to succeed.

The dry season was well advanced and the Gambia River was low. Realising that it would not be safe to take the common north-bank route from Jonkakonda, Houghton crossed the river with his horse and asses to follow the rougher south-bank track. The river provided some protection against the traders who wanted to stop him, but he continued across some demanding terrain towards Medina in a state of anxiety. Although nothing happened on the way, as soon as he reached the frontier of Wuli he sent a message to the King that he had come bearing gifts and that certain people were loath for him to arrive. The tactic worked and, before long, the youngest of the Wuli princes arrived with an armed escort to bring the traveller into town.

'I am now perfectly safe, and out of all danger, with the King of Woolli,' Houghton wrote to his wife on 10 March 1791.[12] He was also at the limit of European geographical certainties concerning the river, as he pointed out in a six-page letter he sent the Committee. When he wrote to his wife, he spared her the details, suggesting that she ask Beaufoy to let her see his letter. Unfortunately, the ship carrying Houghton's mail to England was wrecked and only the letter to his wife has survived. One thing the surviving letter clearly expresses is Houghton's sense of contentment:

> On my arrival here I was received in the most friendly manner by the King and all his people, who furnish me with every thing I want. I can go by myself on my horse to any part of his country in perfect security, the King having ordered every person to assist me in any thing I should require, and to furnish me provisions wherever I want.

It sounded like paradise, and after many years of ill fortune, Houghton was certainly enjoying the dream.

> They ardently wish my building a fort here, and I have accordingly found out a most agreeable and beautiful place on the river for that purpose, at Fattatenda, about twenty-six miles from Medina. I have been twice there to examine the place, which is most suitable, by a fine plain of meadow ground, plenty of grass, and water. I saw a great many deer on the plain, and some wild boars . . . Gold, ivory, wax, and slaves, may at all times be had here for the most trifling articles; and a trade, the profit of which would be upwards of eight hundred per cent, can be carried on at Fattatenda without the least trouble. You may live here almost for nothing: ten pounds a year would support a whole family with plenty of fowls, sheep, milk, eggs, butter, honey, bullocks, fish, and all sorts of game.[13]

It is maybe a sign of just how hard Houghton's life had been up to this point, as well as of his natural optimism, that he viewed the Gambia with such desire. Quite what Banks and Beaufoy made of this letter to his wife is not recorded, although the Secretary had this to say to the members: 'In this manner, he indulged in the dream of future prosperity, and with still more ample satisfaction contemplated the éclat of the discoveries for which he was preparing . . .'[14]

If the prospect of a future life in Wuli seemed idyllic, the present task of exploration did not seem too challenging to Houghton. Jatta, the sixty-year-old King of Wuli, had assured him that there was neither risk nor danger between Wuli and Timbuktu. His visitor believed him: 'I can travel with his people to Tombuctoo with only a stick in my hand,' he assured his wife.[15] Soon there was even better news: a *sharif* from Timbuktu, whom Houghton had met on his mission to Morocco in 1772, had arrived in Wuli. In May, the Major wrote to Dr Laidley downriver in Pisania, 'I have received the best intelligence of the places I design visiting . . . I find that, in the river I am going to explore, *they have decked vessels, with masts, with which they carry on trade from Tombuctoo eastward, to the centre of Africa*. I mean to embark on one of them from Genné in Bambara to Tombuctoo.'[16] Anyone who had been along the Niger between Djenne and Timbuktu – anyone who goes now – would immediately recognise in this description the great pirogues or pinasses of Mali, some of which continue, even in our technological age, to proceed by sail, wind and pole.

Contrary to his expectations, Houghton's run of bad luck had not ended, and while he enjoyed the hospitality of the cordial King of Wuli and prepared for the journey ahead, disaster struck in a way that seriously jeopardised his prospects. Medina was a town of around a thousand thatched huts, in one of which the Major was installed. Around noon on a bright day in March, a day of unusually strong winds, while Houghton was busy writing to Beaufoy, a fire broke out in a nearby hut. Within minutes the whole town had gone up like a tinderbox and houses were burning fiercely. Realising the seriousness of the blaze, Houghton grabbed whatever was to hand and ran to join the crush to get to the open ground beyond the town walls. He had brought out with him some razors, a compass, a bale of linen and a sack of beads, some shot and powder, the covering off his bed and his pillow. Clearly a man with an eye for detail and a weakness for drama, he also saved that fine blue frock-coat with which he was hoping to impress the Sultan of Timbuktu. But for all that he had salvaged, he had lost the rest of his bedding, his weapons, saddle, holsters, three ass saddles and most of his shot and ball, which melted in the intense flames. His scissors were lost, as was his mirror, a silver-mounted hanger and 'my broad beaver hat I bought at Beavan's to keep off the sun'.[17] The fire had also destroyed his compass, thermometer and quadrant, which meant that he was unable to take accurate readings of his position or to be sure of the direction in which he would travel. Whatever glory there might be in the discoveries he hoped to make, their scientific value would be considerably reduced. Major Houghton was not the sort to be deterred by such a setback and, assuming his estimate that 'ten pounds a year would support a whole family' was correct, he was still far from desperate. But the losses were significant, his circumstances were certainly reduced and, what's more, his misfortunes were far from over.

Shortly after the fire, he managed to buy a replacement firearm from a river trader. But it was of lesser quality than the one he had brought out from England and it, too, soon turned against him, exploding in his hands and wounding him badly in the face and arms. Soon after, the interpreter he had hired at Pisania, perhaps sensing that the Major's standing had been considerably reduced by his losses and injuries, ran off and took with him his master's horse and three of his asses.

Within the space of several days, therefore, Houghton had lost a significant part of his possessions, including many of the goods he had brought out to trade, the proceeds of which were supposed to support him on the journey. He had lost his firearms, been badly injured and had now lost both interpreter and transport. Ahead of him lay the sort of landscape that many people still prefer to avoid today, a sequence of forests that were home to dangerous animals, plains choked with dust, hills that were hard to climb, treacherous rivers and camel-killing deserts. To make matters worse, he had delayed so long that the dry season was well advanced, the country was dusty and food was scarce. Worse still, there was now the very real possibility that the rains would start while he was travelling, swelling rivers into floods and turning paths into slippery bogs. This was the time of year when malaria came marching at the head of a legion of diseases. And then, to cap off what must be judged a disastrous week by any measure, news reached Wuli and Barra Kunda of the war between the kings of Bondo and Bambuk, territories through which the Timbuktu 'road' passed.

A less determined traveller – Lucas springs to mind – would have looked ahead and concluded that it was unwise, foolhardy, perhaps even suicidal to continue. Yet although Houghton mentions these events, there is nothing in his letters to suggest that he was in any way daunted by his mission or the prospects of what was to come – Beaufoy was right when he identified his 'natural intrepidity of character, that seems inaccessible to fear'. In spite of the setbacks, he was happy to be on the River Gambia, the kingdom of Wuli looked as idyllic as ever, and he had had many reassurances from people who knew the way that the route from there to Timbuktu presented neither dangers nor problems. In the meantime, even the lack of accommodation created by the burning of Medina had been solved, for he had been invited to stay with the inhabitants of nearby Barra Kunda, a larger town of some two thousand houses a little upstream, beside the falls which marked the limit of the navigable stretch of the Gambia River. Here too he gives a sense of having fallen on his feet. 'I fare exceedingly well,' he wrote from his new hut, 'being daily supplied with rice, *couscous*, fowls, and milk, and often some honey, which cost me nothing.'[18]

Houghton had written home that the King of Wuli had offered to send some of his own men to escort him to Timbuktu, but something, perhaps the fire, perhaps a change of heart about opening the trade route to this foreigner, led to the offer being withdrawn. As the King was now either unable or unwilling to provide an escort, the Major made his own arrangements and agreed to join the caravan of a slave trader. He left the river on 8 May 1791, walking beside his two remaining asses and 'the wreck of his fortune'.[19]

The slaver had come from the land of the Feloops and Fulas in the south and was going to Timbuktu. On the way he intended to visit his family who lived on a farm on the border between the kingdoms of Bondo and Bambuk. With the hot season so far advanced, they travelled by night, which made the going easier, although it still took five days to reach the border of Bondo. Hough-ton's letters from this stage of his travels have not survived, so it is impossible to know whether he was aware of the significance of the journey. Beaufoy certainly was, and lost no opportunity, when writing his account of Houghton's journey in the Association's *Proceedings* the following year, to spell it out: 'He had now passed the former limit of European discovery.'[20]

European geographers were unable to place Bondo with any accuracy until this time, but thanks to a man by the name of Job ben Soliman, plenty of people in England knew of it. Banks and, we can be sure, Beaufoy were among them. Job ben Soliman was a Bondo prince captured by members of a rival tribe and sold to white slave traders. Shipped across the Atlantic, he was put to work on a plantation in Maryland. It soon became apparent that Job was unlike the majority of slaves. For one thing, he was devoted to Islam. For another, he managed to escape from the plantation. When he was recaptured, he was put in prison. But by then his behaviour had attracted the curiosity of some English traders, who asked to hear his story. Believing his claim to be a prince, they had him released and took him to England. In London, Job experienced a full reversal of ill fortune and was treated with the respect due to royalty. He was presented at court – where the Queen gave him a gold watch – and attended the Royal Society, where he translated Arabic manuscripts for the then President, Sir Hans Sloane. He was also welcomed by some of the most influential and wealthy people in the country, who encouraged him to publish his story, which appeared in 1734.

Several things about the Prince struck his new friends as remark-able, particularly that, although a devout Muslim, he was ready to discuss a range of religious matters without prejudice. 'How strange it must have seemed,' the historian Robin Hallett wrote, 'to find an African prince with the temperament and tastes of an English gentleman.'[21] Yet Job appears to have been seen as more than a mere curiosity; one person who met him described how 'in his natural temper there appeared a happy mixture of the grave and the cheerful, a gentle mildness guarded by a proper warmth, and a kind and compassionate disposition to all that were in distress'.[22] When he decided it was time to return to Bondo, Job received presents worth some £500 from his new friends to take to his homeland. After sailing back to the Gambia River, the remarkable Prince was visited on several occasions by English traders hoping to establish themselves on the river.

Houghton does not mention whether he knew of Job ben Soliman's story, nor, if he did, whether he heard any news of the man on his travels. Instead, 'he remarked, with pleasure, the numerous and extensive population of this unvisited country, [and] he observed, that the long black hair and copper complexion of the inhabitants announce their Arab original'.[23]

The next 150 miles were slow because the slaver stopped at every town they passed to conduct his business, but they did eventually reach the banks of the Falémé River. Houghton did not know that this was the largest of the River Senegal's tributaries, but what he did know was that it was the frontier of Bambuk, that it was dry and that its bed was composed of slate and gravel. His thoughts were soon turned from geology with the news that the war between Bondo and Bambuk had ended in victory for the King of Bondo, who had annexed a considerable amount of the Bambuk lowlands, where he was now installed. While the slaver visited his farm, Houghton went to pay his respects to the victorious King, taking with him the sort of gifts that had pleased the kings of Barra and Wuli. Unlike them, the King of Bondo was far from welcoming: he ordered the Irishman to leave his offerings, return to the border and wait there until he was sent for again.

Houghton was alarmed by the King's sullenness. At the house where he was staying, he hid 'a variety of items' as best he could. It was as well that he was cautious, for the next day he was visited by one of the King's sons, a man quite different in character and behaviour from Job ben Soliman. Arriving with an armed escort, the Prince demanded to see all of Houghton's trade goods. Knowing better than to argue when outnumbered by hostile men carrying weapons, the Irishman went into the house and brought out the bale of fabric, sack of beads and whatever else he had managed to collect. The Prince was obviously expecting to find better pickings, and now ordered the Major to bring out his own luggage and proceeded to help himself to whatever caught his eye. Houghton was devastated to report that this included the blue coat he had brought to wear during his triumphal entrance into the court of the Sultan of Timbuktu.

After being fleeced by the Prince, the Major sought refuge at the farm of the slave trader, where he slept on the roof, staying away from the trader's family and also enjoying some relief from the late dry-season heat. It was now obvious to him that the trader was going to stay longer at the farm than he had anticipated – a shortage of grain in the kingdom meant that the man was having difficulties ensuring that his family would have enough food while he was away. Houghton, on the other hand, was eager to be on the move and so decided to pay a visit to the defeated King of Bambuk at the town of Ferbanna, on the east bank of what Beaufoy calls 'the Serra Coles, or river of gold'.[24]

While the people of Bondo had 'long black hair and copper complexion', in Bambuk they had 'woolly hair and sable complexions'.[25] Houghton had entered a country that began with plains in the west, towards the ocean, and then rose up into hills in the east. People survived on agriculture, growing rice, raising cattle and goats, spinning and weaving cotton 'by a difficult and laborious process'.[26] They also produced honey, from which they distilled liquor that 'furnishes the means of those festive entertainments that constitute the principal luxury of the country of Bambouk'.[27] This was certainly the sort of information the Committee were hoping for, and they were glad for it. But there was one glaring omission from Houghton's report: there was no mention of goldfields.

As he had feared, the rainy season had started while he was still on the road. The going became so difficult that one wet, stormy day, as they passed through a forest in Bambuk, the guide lost sight of the track. They were still lost in the trees, trying to find their way back to the path, when the light failed, which left them with no choice but to make camp as best they could under a scant cover of branches. It was an uncomfortable night. The ground was sodden, the sky torn apart by lightning, the asses terrified and the men tormented by thoughts of all that crawls and slithers in the rich, vibrant African night.

The morning, however, was bright and the sun brought some relief, heating the travellers and drying out the land, but by then Houghton had developed a fever, which was made worse by the necessity of crossing the golden river, now swollen with rainwater. He made it across, but did so with difficulty, watched by a group of basking crocodiles. By the time they reached Ferbanna, Houghton was delirious. His guide took him to the house of some people he knew, who treated him well and nursed him until the fever had passed. The King of Bambuk, whom he met when he had recovered, was just as welcoming.

One of the reports Houghton managed to send back to London contained a detailed account of the recent war between Bondo and Bambuk. We only have the defeated King of Bambuk's word for what happened, and for obvious reasons he would not have wanted to point up any weakness in his own troops or tactics, but his explanation still sounds plausible. Bondo, being nearer the Gambia River, received its arms and ammunition from British traders. Bambuk, on the other hand, was nearer the Senegal River where the French traded: he bought his weapons from them. In this way, some sort of *status quo* was maintained. But recently, the King explained, the French had abandoned their trading post at Fort St Joseph on the Falémé and 'either from the dryness of the last season, or from other causes',[28] were not to be found on the Senegal River – presumably a consequence of the chaos in France following the revolution two years earlier. So while the King of Bondo was able to buy in fresh British-made arms and ammunition, the King of Bambuk could not, and had lost the war because he was unable to arm his warriors. 'Major Houghton availed himself of the opportunity which this conversation afforded,' Beaufoy assured his readers, 'to suggest to the king, the advantage of encouraging the English to open a trade by way of his dominions to the populous cities on the banks of the Niger.'[29] Once again, Beaufoy seems to have had no qualms about suggesting that British traders supply both sides of the conflict. Nor was he in the least bashful about describing to the Association's members the arms-dealing activities of their geographical missionary. The King of Bambuk, he assured them, warmly welcomed the suggestion and would do much to encourage British involvement in the Bambuk trade, presumably swapping guns for gold.

The rainy season heralded the start of a Bambuk festival at which presents were given to the King. This was 'followed by an intemperate festival of several successive days'.[30] Around this time, Houghton was approached by a trader called Madegammo, an old man well known in Bambuk. Madegammo had heard that the white man wanted to get to Timbuktu, and offered to take him for a fee of £125. Houghton explained that he was carrying very little in the way of money or goods: of his original £200 worth of merchandise, he had handed out three presents worth £20 and then lost a significant portion of his remaining goods in the fire at Wuli. So although he was happy to accept Madegammo's offer, it would have to be conditional on his reaching Pisania alive, where Laidley would pay off the debt. The trader agreed, the King approved – and gave him a parting gift of a purse of gold – and Houghton prepared for his departure.

From the Gambia River to Bambuk, Houghton had travelled slowly and often on foot, walking beside a caravan of packed asses and horses. The old man had other plans, so at Ferbanna the Major exchanged whatever was left of his cargo for gold dust and swapped his two asses for a horse. 'Such is the darkness of his complexion,' Beaufoy wrote of his traveller, 'that he scarcely differs in appearance from the Moors of Barbary, whose dress in travelling he intended to assume.' The Association's Secretary was upbeat in his assessment of Houghton's chances: 'From his poverty, which affords but little temptation for plunder, and from the obvious interest of his guide, whose profit depends on the faithful performance of the contract, he derives an assurance of success.' Houghton was just as optimistic. Mounted on a good horse, a purse of gold tucked in his belt, the King of Bambuk's blessings upon him and led by a man who was familiar both with the route and the people who lived along it, Houghton set out towards the end of July 1791 on the last stage of his journey. Timbuktu was little over a month away.

7

The Political Player

'Another Geographical discovery now offers the means of
effecting a revolution in the Mercantile Intercourse with the
Inland Countries of Africa.'
Minute Book of the Committee of the African Association, 6 March 1976

London, 1791

WHEN THE MEMBERS of the Saturday's Club passed the decanters
around the dinner table at the St Alban's Tavern and complained
about how little was known about Africa, they were well aware that
many people before them had tried to reveal the mysteries of the
interior, which had resulted in some remarkable journeys. In 1698,
for instance, ninety years before that dinner of consequence, a
resourceful, energetic Frenchman by the name of André Brue, commander of the French garrison on the island of St Louis, set off up
the Senegal River to see what he could do there. As it turned out,
the journey was more difficult than dangerous, and he eventually
reached a place called Dramanet, four hundred miles upriver on
the fringes of Bambuk territory. The town appeared to suit his
purposes perfectly. For one thing, it was independent but was at
the same time linked through a loose confederation to other settlements in the region. Just as important, most of Dramanet's four
thousand inhabitants were Mandingo traders, whom Brue valued
highly, describing them as 'a good Sort of People, honest, hospitable,

just to their Word, laborious, industrious, and very ready to learn Arts and Sciences . . . They carry on Commerce to all the neighbouring Kingdoms, and by this Means amass Riches, and propagate the Mohammedan Religion wherever they go.'[1] Ignoring the proselytising, they were something of a dream for a French administrator wanting to further his country's trade contacts in notoriously difficult West Africa. Most remarkable of all, 'they love Strangers either through Inclination or on Account of the Profit they gain by them'.[2] Brue recognised the opportunity they presented and persuaded them to let him create a French trading post in their town. Through this outpost, he was confident he could draw trade away from the British on the Gambia River and at the same time learn more about the route inland to the Niger and Timbuktu.

With the dry season well advanced and the river falling fast, Brue left Dramanet in a hurry. But the seed he had planted soon grew. In 1700 the French government built Fort St Joseph, and before long French traders were bringing European manufactures including guns upriver. Perhaps they were in too much of a hurry and pushed too far, or perhaps Brue's return home to France led to a shift in French attitudes, but whatever the provocation, the hitherto good-natured Mandingos of Dramanet lost faith in the foreigners. Many rumours spread around town, among them one that the French were in league with the Moroccans and would soon 'conquer the Country, carrying all those able to bear Arms into Slavery and oblige the Rest to work in the Mines'.[3] The people of Dramanet didn't wait to find out if this was true: they attacked and burned the fort and forced the French garrison to abandon their post.

Brue was back on the Senegal in 1714 and in his wake Frenchmen began travelling upriver again, notable among them a man called Sieur Compagnon, who spent eighteen months in and around Bambuk, leaving 'but a few Places unvisited . . . [and seeing] every Thing that had occurred with all the Exactness a Man of his Genius was capable of'.[4] The people of Bambuk were suspicious of the intruder, thinking that 'he must have some bad Design and wanted to steal their Gold, or conquer their Country after he had surveyed it'.[5] In spite of these suspicions, which left a considerable number of people in the region wanting to 'knock him on the Head', Compagnon managed to reach the fabled Bambuk goldfields and lived to tell the tale. 'It is not necessary to take the Trouble of digging,' he wrote, trying to explain the ease and abundance of the business. 'They need only scrape the Superficies of the Earth, wash it in a Bowl, and pour off the Water gently to find the Gold in Dust at the bottom, sometimes in large Grains.'[6]

At the same time as the French government was pushing inland up the Senegal River, British traders and adventurers were active a little further south. In 1689, an indomitable English sea captain by the name of Cornelius Hodges sailed up the Gambia River as far as the falls of Barra Kunda, which he was unable to sail beyond. Not one to be put off by a geographical obstacle, he loaded a significant amount of goods, lined up sixty-eight of his men and marched off inland in search of the Bambuk goldfields and trade. Like Compagnon, Hodges' arrival was a matter of great concern for local rulers, who were suspicious of his reasons for making the journey and worried that he was going to take over their trade. The accusation seemed plausible. Hodges was only able to start his journey 'after very strong disputes with ye Mandingo Chief and ye overcoming a vast many threats they put me too, upon their understanding of my Designe of travelling to ye gold-mines'.[7] His forcefulness met with disappointment, for by the time he reached the Bambuk goldmines, the country was in the grip of a famine. Without food there was no workforce, and without labour there was no gold.

But Hodges was not a man to go home empty-handed, and while he waited in Bambuk, he sent some men north to a place he calls Tarra,* then a major centre of the slave trade. Assuming the identification of Tarra with Atar is right, these men made an epic journey of more than five hundred miles as the crow flies. They described

* According to the historian Robin Hallett, ' "Tarra" seems likely to have been Atar, a town known to have existed in the seventeenth century and today one of the most important centres in Mauritania. The credibility of Hodges' narrative is confirmed by the fact that the Emperor Moulay Ismail (1672–1727) is known to have sent several expeditions south into Mauritania' (The Penetration of Africa, 83n).

Tarra as being 'very neare as bigg as ye Citty of London'. It was a lot less peaceful, for about this time Moulay Ismail, the great ruler of Morocco, laid siege to the town. Hodges' men, perhaps sensing which way the wind was blowing, joined the Moroccan Emperor's forces and were greatly admired for the way they used their fire-arms. After the fall of Tarra, Moulay Ismail sent the Englishmen back to their leader with a horse, two camels and an invitation to join him. Hodges was delighted, but this was too much for the people of Bambuk, who tried to prevent his leaving for the north, 'saying that since I was not satisfied with understanding ye Gold Trade, but I must make Inspection into ye Slave Trade, I should pay dearly for my experience'. Given the numbers ranged against him, Hodges saw no other choice but to turn south-west towards the Gambia, travelling through a land now completely ravaged by famine. 'I had lived 5 months on wild fruites, Roots,' he wrote at the end of the journey, 'such as I could gett in ye woods and never nearer starving in all my life. Some of my people dying of hunger and the natives daily!'[8] Hodges and the remainder of his men returned to Barra Kunda and the Gambia River a year after their departure.

Hodges, Brue and Compagnon were three of many Europeans with experience of travelling in the African interior, at least the part of it that was easily reached along its rivers. But while their stories delivered plenty of excitement, they revealed little of use to geographers or improvers in search of practical information. This was where the Association came in. But its goals were proving elusive. In April 1791, almost three years after the Saturday's Club dinner and some six months after Houghton's departure, Beaufoy admitted privately to Banks, 'That the rise of the Niger is we know not where, that its course is we know not what, and that it termin-ates we know not how are still the perplexing result of our African Researches.'[9] Houghton might have travelled further inland than either of the Association's previous geographical missionaries, but frustration at the slow rate of discovery soured every line of the Secretary's letter. In spite of some very 'suggestive' comments in Houghton's letters, including the news that, contrary to the beliefs of the ancients, the Niger flowed from west to east, that 'charge of ignorance' about the interior of Africa, which led to the creation of the Association, remained.

Three expeditions sent out, something in the region of £1000 spent and no geographical prizes; there was muttering in clubs and over dinner tables by some of the Association's now 109 members. All this weighed on Beaufoy, who took it out on Houghton, complaining to Banks: 'If the Major, in giving a list of the places that mark his intended rout [sic] to Tombuctoo, had mentioned their computed distances from each other, the value of his hearsay information would not have been lowly rated.'[10]

But not all was lost. The Major, looking increasingly like a Moor, was now riding inland, his gold dust securely stowed. His safety was guaranteed, to the extent that such a thing was possible, by the presence of the old trader Madegammo riding beside him. The Committee in London were confident that his route was the right one, and although the dangers were too easily imagined, the King of Wuli had given his royal assurance that a European could walk to Timbuktu with just a stick in hand. So while Houghton went off the map, his sponsors hoped and prayed that their man would feast his eyes on landscapes never before seen by people from beyond the shores of Africa and then return with tales, descriptions and, above all, locations of the Niger, Timbuktu and Hausaland.

One thing they did not worry too much about was the delivery of Houghton's letters. There was no official mail service between any part of Africa and England, so Banks and Beaufoy had instructed Houghton to write a note of credit on the back of his letters, promising to pay £5 to whoever delivered the letter to London. This had the effect of turning the letters into a commodity. Five pounds was a ridiculous sum to pay to have a letter delivered – it was, for instance, the amount the German Emperor paid his court musician, a thirty-four-year-old composer by the name of Wolfgang Amadeus Mozart, for ten days' work. Houghton reckoned that he and his family could feast every day for six months off it in the kingdom of Wuli. At the same time, you could send a letter from the Caribbean to London for little more than a shilling. But for the Committee, it was a small sum to ensure the safe delivery of their missionary's reports.

Houghton had followed this procedure in March 1791 when he wrote to his wife describing his journey to the kingdom of Wuli and his hopes for the future; the letter arrived in London some time late that summer even though the ship on which it was being carried was wrecked on the Atlantic coast. Houghton had ended that letter by warning his wife that 'I shall have no more opportunities of writing to you after I leave this, till I return to the river; so do not be uneasy if my silence appears long.'[11] Events proved him wrong, for on 30 December 1791 Beaufoy received a letter that was obviously more to his liking than anything he had received so far. 'A few hours after I had the pleasure of seeing you,' he wrote breathlessly to Banks, 'an African Merchant, Mr. Sharpless of Mile End, called upon me with the letters from Major Houghton . . . The first impression which the perusal of these dispatches made upon my mind was that of disappointment, for I did not imagine that a journey of 180 miles from Medina in the neighbourhood of Barra Kunda could have closed to 15 July the account of his actual progress. But a second perusal produced the more pleasing reflection that he passed the limit which former discovery had assigned to European knowledge – that the whole of his route from the Gambia to the Falene [sic], a journey of 150 miles, is a real acquisition to our African Geography, and that after having lost a considerable part of his goods by the knavery of his fellow Travellers and the rapacity of the Negro kings, betrayed and robbed by his Interpreter, and suffering by famine, floods and fire, he had still the resolution and apparently the means, to prosecute his journey to Tombuctoo.'

Nothing more was heard from Houghton before the Association's general meeting at the St Alban's Tavern in May 1792. But Beaufoy had enough new information to rouse members from their slumbers, and he assured them that, through his own experiences and from what he had heard on the way, Houghton had 'enlarged the limits of European discovery'.[12] He had provided the first reliable description of the kingdom of Bondo. There was also fresh information on the Niger, some of which contradicted what they had heard from Lucas and the Moors in London. 'The information he has obtained from the king of Bambouk, as well as from the native merchants with whom he conversed, has not only determined the course . . . of the Niger, but has furnished the names of the principal cities erected on its banks.' In an aside here Beaufoy added, 'The mistaken ideas which Ben Alli [sic] and the Shereef Imhammed entertained respecting the course of the Niger, appear to have arisen from their having judged of the direction of the stream by that of one of its reaches.'[13]

This was an exciting breakthrough, and if some of it was controversial, Beaufoy had fresh information from another source that seemed to corroborate the Major's report. Earlier that month he had received a letter from Perkins Magra, British Consul in Tunis. 'The account he has obtained of the Routs [sic] of the Caravans from Tunis to Tombuctoo, to Agadez and to Houssa, has enlarged our knowledge of the Desert, and the list of towns on the Niger from Tombuctoo to the place at which the River begins to be navigable, confirms in the strongest manner the account which Houghton has given of the rise of the Stream, and of its course from the West to the East.' Most important, as Beaufoy trumpeted, 'we have now an assurance that the Niger has its rise in a chain of mountains which bound the eastern side of the kingdom of Bambouk'.[14]

In May 1793, Major Rennell sat down to write *Elucidations of the African Geography* and to draw a new map. Although a work of undoubted geographical scholarship, it also serves as a reminder of how much of the interior remained to be discovered.

Rennell began with d'Anville's map of Africa and with another Frenchman, M. Delisle's, 1726 map of the Senegal and Gambia rivers, weighing up each claim and speculation and considering its viability. A serious man with a disciplined intellect, he was acutely aware of the flaws and problems associated with his methods. It had been hoped that Houghton's observations with compass and quadrant would provide detailed information, but that hope had gone up in smoke in the Wuli fire. Rennell had no alternative but to warn the Association's members that 'through the total want of observations by longitude, or of any accurate means of determining the distances between places that lie nearly east and west from each other, in the interior parts of Africa, we are compelled to rely on authorities that are much too vague to be adopted, but in cases of necessity'.[15] Just how vague was highlighted by Magra and Houghton, who reported distances in the number of travelling days or journeys. Several years earlier, Rennell had reported to the Royal Society that trade caravans covered an average of thirteen miles a day as the crow flew. 'But since the inquiry I have made into the rate of travelling of camels on the Arabian Desert, I find that fourteen miles may be allowed.' The difference may sound slight, just one extra mile a day, but it could lead to significant errors, as became clear when Rennell relocated Brue's old French trading post of Fort St Joseph some forty-two miles east of the position he had given it only three years earlier. And if Fort St Joseph or the start point of other caravan routes were wrong by as much as forty-two miles, then the end point at Timbuktu could be hundreds of miles too far to the east or west.

But Rennell was a stickler for detail, and he knew he was making advances. He now had accurate details of several routes to Timbuktu, while his general descriptions of places such as Djenne and Hausa will be recognisable to anyone who knows the region today. There were mistakes, of course: for instance, he confused Bambuk, the area between the Senegal and Falémé rivers, with Bambara, the kingdom that took in Bamako, Segu and Djenne. But there were also revelations. 'We are certain,' he now wrote, 'that the Joliba or Niger [he had realised that Joliba was the local name for the Niger] springs from a country, which has a part of its territory as far removed from Tombuctoo, as Bambouk is.'[16] Knowing that the source was in the hills of western Africa, Rennell then accepted that contrary to the accepted theory, the Niger was likely to flow from west to east.

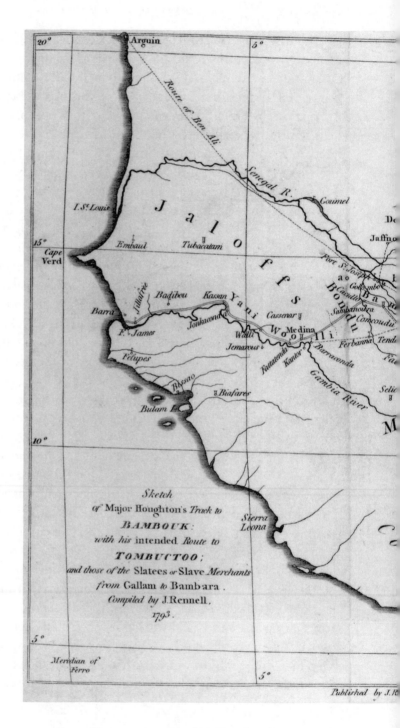

Rennell's 1793 map showing Houghton's route to Bambuk

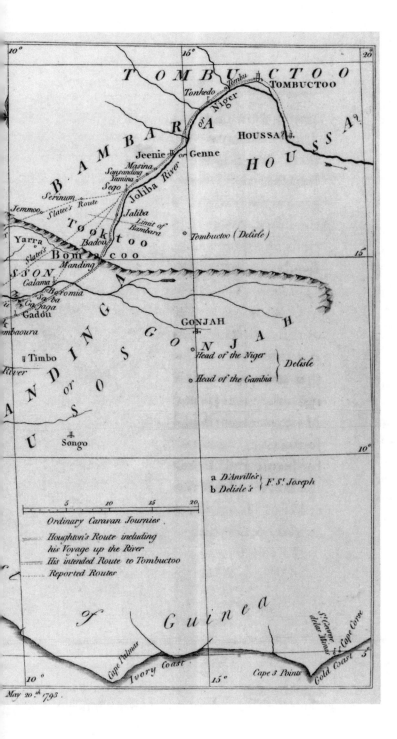

10°   15°   20°

T O M B U C T O O
                Tonkedo   Tombu   TOMBUCTOO
                          Niger
B A M B A R A   ᵒA
                              HOUSSA?
                  Jeenie or Genne   H O U S S A?
                 Masina   O U S S A
              Sansanding   H
              Yamina
        Sego   Joliba River
    Serinum
Temmoo   Slatee's Route   Jaliba
                        Limit of
T o o k t o o   Bambara   ᵒ Tombuctoo (Delisle)
Yarra   Badou
    Slatee's   B o m   c o o   15°
S S O N Manding
    Galama   Boromia
      Sarba
Ga Faga
Gadou   G O N J A H
mbaoura   GONJAH
                    o   N J A H
g Timbo   Head of the Niger   } Delisle
    River   o Head of the Gambia
                 U   o   S   S   O
                                        10°
    g Songo

                            a D'Anville's } F Sᵗ Joseph
                            b Delisle's

    5   10   15   20
    Ordinary Caravan Journies
    ------ Houghton's Route including
           his Voyage up the River
    ------ His intended Route to Tombuctoo
    ------ Reported Routes

        f   G u i n e a   Sᵗ George
                                    Delas Minas
                                    Cape Corso
    Cape Palmas   Ivory Coast   Gold Coast
10°   15°   Cape 3 Points   5°

May 20ᵗʰ 1793.

The end of the Niger was as much a mystery as ever: 'Major Houghton . . . almost flattered himself that he should find in this river, the remote source of the Nile.'[17] Rennell thought this 'improbable, in every respect', and for several reasons, one being that he knew that the Niger at Timbuktu and the Nile in Egypt both flooded in August. If they were the same river or were connected in some way, 'the waters of the Tombuctoo river, would require a full month to run from that country to Egypt'.[18] Beaufoy had summed up the options this way: 'the place of its final destination is still unknown; for whether it reaches the ocean; or is lost, as several of the rivers of Mount Atlas are, in the immensity of the Desert; or whether, like the Caspian, it terminates in a vast inland sea, are questions on which there still hangs an unpenetrated cloud'.[19] Rennell's own guess was that the Niger would be found to flow into a vast lake to the east of Timbuktu, and that perhaps the Nile would be found to flow eastwards out of the lake. But he admitted that the question of the river's course 'cannot be answered, from any documents that the Association is in possession of . . . For what the particulars of its course may be, through an interval of seven hundred miles, or more, it is impossible to guess . . .'[20] To this it was hoped that Houghton would provide an answer.

Prospects for their missionary, however, were looking grim. In an afterword to the *Elucidations*, Rennell made mention of a brief note Houghton had written in September 1791, a year and a half earlier. 'Major Houghton's compliments to Dr. Laidley, is in good health on his way to Tombuctoo, robbed of all his goods by Fenda Bucar's son.' The note was a puzzle and raised questions that neither Laidley, in Pisania, nor the Committee in London could answer. Who was Fenda Bucar's son? Why was Houghton carrying 'goods' when he had written months earlier to say that Madegammo, the old trader who was accompanying him to Timbuktu, had persuaded him to exchange his goods for gold? How far had the Major travelled into the interior? And what had happened since? These questions were met with silence. Dr Laidley, worried by the lack of further news, assumed the worst and sent word upriver that he would pay for the recovery of the Major's books and papers. He was confident that the offer of a reward would bring news. But nothing was found. It was as though Houghton had simply disappeared.

Houghton had written his note of 1 September in haste and in pencil. The name of the place at which it had been written had been rubbed so often that it was almost indistinguishable, but Dr Laidley thought it was Simbing. 'I cannot trace out any such place,' wrote a frustrated Rennell, 'either in the existing maps, or in any part of the intelligence communicated to the Association.' Unable to work with any certainties, he had no choice but to hazard a guess. He knew the route the Major had intended to take, but he did not know what might have happened on the journey, and neither did he know exactly where to locate Timbuktu. Yet he concluded that, 'At the distance of time at which it was written, from the date of the former dispatch, it may be supposed that the Major was far advanced on his way to Tombuctoo.'[21] Like many of his guesses, it was wrong.

As time passed, so optimism gave way to fears for Houghton's safety. And then in July 1793, two months after Rennell wrote his *Elucidations* and some twenty-one months after Houghton's note from Simbing reached Laidley, Banks received a letter from John Symmonds, a member of the Association who traded along the West African coast. 'I think it right to inform you,' Symmonds wrote, 'as the central point of general information, of whatever curious, or, interesting nature, that a letter was yesterday receiv'd from a young man . . . dated Gambia Jan.1, in which he says that the result of his enquiries respecting Major Houghton on that continent . . . has been uniformly unfavourable . . . He was understood to have penetrated beyond Tombut, and to have been killed by the orders of the sovereign of the adjoining kingdom.'[22] Another letter followed soon after, in which Symmonds reported 'that every account rec'd [received] on the coast seems to confirm that, before communicated, of Major Houghton's death in the Kingdom adjoining to Tombuto, by order of the Sovereign, who was led to consider him as a Spy, and, that his interpreter, that travelled with the Major to a very great distance, and afterwards return'd, assur'd the fact as a matter of perfect certainty.'[23]

So Houghton was dead.* The Committee were convinced, and Beaufoy, as Secretary, had the grim job of conveying their conviction to the Association's general meeting the following May, 1794. Having explained 'the reasons for their belief that such Reports were but too well founded', he went on to express 'in the strongest manner the Concern and regret of the Committee for the Loss of so valuable and zealous a Servant of the Association'.[24] Beaufoy later revised the estimate of Houghton's progress and claimed only that he was within a short distance of Timbuktu, 'no room to doubt'. 'It would seem,' he continued, 'that this unfortunate gentleman, notwithstanding the hospitable reception he had met with from the King of Bambouk, was no favourite of the natives in general. It was stated, on a former occasion, that he derived an assurance of safety *from his poverty*; but unhappily, he had no such security. Contrary to all the suggestions of prudence, and the remonstrances of his friends in England, the Major had encumbered himself with an assortment of bale goods, consisting of linens, scarlet cloth, cutlery, beads, amber and other merchandize, which presented to the ignorant Negroes such temptations as savage virtue could not resist.'[25]

Another couple of years passed before the Committee found out more about what had happened, though the full story will never be known. This much seems certain: from Bambuk and the Falémé River, Houghton travelled north-east, crossing the major stream of the Senegal River and reaching a place called Koniakary, where he was welcomed by the King and presented with a good white horse to help him on his way. It was another two weeks in the saddle from Koniakary across the kingdom of Kaarta to Simbing, a village set in a narrow pass between two rocky ranges of hills. By this time, for reasons that were not explained, Houghton had left Madegammo and hired native servants in his place. But at Simbing, the boundary between the southern lands ruled by black-skinned Negroes and the northern lands of the lighter-skinned Moors, five or six weeks after leaving Bambuk, these servants announced that

---

* Houghton's death left his wife and children in dire financial straits. The Association agreed to pay for the children's education and eventually persuaded King George III to provide Houghton's widow with a pension of £30 per annum.

it was not safe to go further. Houghton was not to be deterred and decided to go on alone; before he went he scribbled his note to Dr Laidley, reporting his good health and the loss of his goods to Fenda Bucar's son.

It was only a half-day's journey from Simbing, in modern-day Mali, to Jarra, then a town of 'considerable extent' whose houses were built of stone and clay, not wood and mud. Jarra's inhabitants were mostly Negroes, but they were ruled by Moors who treated them, in the words of a later traveller, 'with the utmost indignity and contempt'.[26] Here Houghton was told that the route to Timbuktu was not safe and that he would do better to travel to Tisheet,* ten days to the north. Tisheet was in the opposite direction to the Niger and Timbuktu, but it was an important caravan stop on the route between Morocco and the south – the Moors dug rock salt there, which they traded for gold. Houghton must have hoped that there would be caravans heading from the salt mines to Timbuktu.

He agreed to travel from Jarra to Tisheet in the company of some Moors, whom he paid with tobacco and his musket. Within a couple of days of leaving Jarra, he realised he had made a mistake. Convinced that these men were luring him into the desert to kill him, he refused to continue with them and insisted on returning to Jarra. They allowed him to go, but only after relieving him of all his possessions. Many people abandoned in the desert without food or water would have pleaded not to be left, or might have died once alone. But Houghton had already proved himself to be one of the most resourceful Europeans ever to set foot on the continent, and again showed his resilience by walking back towards the south. He made it as far as a watering hole by the name of Tarra,† where a party of Moors was camped. At this point the Major had not eaten for a couple of days; with nothing to trade for food, he attempted to beg a meal from them. Unfortunately their code of hospitality did not extend as far as feeding a white man. Hemmed in by the desert, without money, possessions or

---

* Often now spelled Tichitt.
† This is not the same Tarra that Captain Hodges' men had helped capture for the Moroccan Emperor in 1689, which was much further north.

food, unable to move on or to survive in that terrible place, Houghton starved to death. The Moors, so the story goes, then saved themselves the trouble of burying him by leaving his corpse to be eaten by scavengers.

Although the Association's charter stressed its geographical nature, with men such as Banks and Sinclair among the members, geography was always going to be put to practical use. Beaufoy suggested one way in which it could be used when he pointed out the 'important advantages to the Commercial Interests of the Kingdom'[27] that Houghton's discoveries offered. The idea that West Africa was of 'commercial interest' was hardly news: Europeans had been sailing south to trade for a couple of centuries. But the development of trade was retarded by a number of obstacles, one of them being the unexpected difficulties in establishing trading posts. Both the French and the British had tried settling along several stretches of the Gambia River. The most important of these posts occupied an island twenty miles upstream from the Atlantic. Known as James Island, it changed hands between the British, French and, bizarrely, a group of Welsh pirates, before the French put an end to the matter in 1778 by destroying it. James Island is now a picturesque ruin, washed by the river's tidal waters and regularly visited by tourists from the coast, its only surviving room being variously described by guides as a store either for food or for slaves.

More problematic even than international rivalry were the challenges posed by the climate. The lowest reaches of the Gambia River were particularly unhealthy, the mangrove swamps an ideal breeding ground for malarial mosquitoes. Almost every account of travel by Europeans to this part of Africa carries reports of a devastating number of deaths from fever: in 1782, for instance, two hundred British convicts were landed on the river to create a trial penal colony, but within a matter of months the climate had done its work and only fifty survived.[28]

Beaufoy was well aware of health problems along the Gambia, and was quick to recognise the value of Houghton's report on Fattatenda, the place where he had dreamed of settling. 'I find this part of the country much more wholesome than down the river,' the Major had written. 'It is a fine dry soil, and a good air; the king [of Wuli] says no white man ever died at Fattatenda.' In April 1792, the Secretary wrote to Banks, then laid up in bed suffering his first serious attack of gout: 'The dryness of the soil and the salubrity of the Air on the banks of the higher reaches of the Gambia, will obviate the chief objection to the establishment of a Factory in the Neighbourhood of Baraconda [Barra Kunda], and that from such a Factory, the merchandise of England may be conveyed on the Horses and Asses of the Country to the Cities of Tombuctoo and Houssa, for in this manner they are now transported by the native Traders to the inland states of Africa.'[29]

Houghton had been more specific, and recommended sending English soldiers to build a fort at Fattatenda. With that in place, he believed it would be possible for merchants – and it is clear that he wanted to be one of them – to dominate the trade of the goldfields and Timbuktu, operate regular boats along the Gambia River to meet ocean-going ships, thrive on good food and an ideal climate and make 800 per cent profit in the process. With this – and not geographical glory – in mind, in May 1792 members voted 'that the Committee be empowered to make, in the name of the Association, whatever application to Government they may think advisable for rendering the late discoveries of Major Houghton effectually serviceable to the Commercial Interests of the Empire'.[30]

Nothing came of this until spring 1793, by which time Britain and France were at war and the subsequent threat to British 'commercial interests' in West Africa convinced the Committee of the merits of sending a consul and a small force of soldiers – not to go as conquerors, but to establish a secure trading base up the Gambia River from which to promote British trade. In May, listening to a 'dull speech' on parliamentary reform, Beaufoy wrote Banks a hasty note introducing James Willis. Willis was thirty-something years of age, a governor of the Turkey Company, had a notable grasp of both classical and scientific knowledge and was, according to Beaufoy, 'of no ordinary Class'. He would, the Secretary suggested, make an excellent consul; as well as his own attainments, he had a powerful patron in Alexander Brodie, a wealthy Scottish MP who had close links to the Cabinet. As if that was not enough reason for Willis to be proposed, Beaufoy also pointed out that 'several merchants of great wealth in the City had offered to vest a large sum in the adventure'.[31]

At the annual general meeting of 25 May 1793, the formalities were observed: Brodie was voted into the Association and it was agreed that the scheme for a consul be proposed to Brodie's friend Henry Dundas, the Secretary of State for Foreign Affairs. Beaufoy laid out the Association's thoughts in a lengthy paper, which he began by pursuing neither geography nor politics, but by describing a trade whose extent was unknown but 'from the best information appears to be much under rated at a Million Sterling per annum'.[32] This figure was plucked from the air, but in the absence of facts there was plenty of room for dreams. Whatever the sums, the basic idea was sound, for even after crossing the Sahara and paying subsidies to the lawless Moroccans, Moorish traders were still able to make a handsome profit (although just how handsome no one was able to say). How much more might be earned by British traders travelling overland between the Gambia and Niger rivers, 'a Land-Carriage of 300 or 350 Miles . . . to reach the same Markets to which the Traders of the States of Barbary travel by a route of 1200 miles'?[33] 'On the first institution of the Society for promoting the discovery of the internal regions of Africa,' Beaufoy went on triumphantly, 'the course of the Niger was unexamined and un-known; nor were the ideas entertained of it, such as to suggest a belief, that it would prove of importance to the Inland Navigation of the Country.' Now it opened the possibility of what he called a 'complete revolution in the Mercantile Intercourse with the Inland countries of Africa'.

The statement is as remarkable in its vision as it is reckless in its assumptions. No one in Europe knew the extent of the Bambuk goldmines, although they were used to provoke the interest of

Foreign Secretary Dundas and Prime Minister Pitt. Nor had any European they knew of set eyes on the Niger – the Association's traveller had just been devoured by vultures or wild dogs in his attempt to do so. Yet Beaufoy concluded by insisting that 'if assurances of protection on the River Gambia (unquestionably a part of the British Dominions) could be given to the British Merchants, there is reason to believe that a Commercial intercourse from the Gambia to the Niger would be opened by Mercantile Houses of great character in London'.[34] This, and concerns that the French might step in before them, was enough to persuade the British government to give cautious approval to what Banks and Beaufoy called 'our African Expedition'. Beaufoy's use of Houghton's reports had turned the Association into a political player.

In April 1794, His Majesty's Government appointed Willis its Consul General in Senegambia. He was given a budget of £3000 to equip and run his expedition and told to get on with it. It was assumed he would arrive in Africa in October that year, at the end of the rainy season, but that was not to be. By the end of the following year he was still in England, had spent £5816, bought two ships and a considerable amount of other equipment, and was having to face government accusations that he had overspent. Banks and the lawyer Andrew Stuart, the only members of the Committee in London at the time, were given the task of scrutinising Willis' accounts, and though they could not find any hard evidence that they had been rigged, Banks seemed convinced that there had been sharp practice. He was also losing enthusiasm for the venture, perhaps in part because Secretary Dundas had suggested that the Association might make up any shortfall in Willis' budget. Banks was adamant that it could not do so. 'It appears,' he wrote in his report, 'that Mr. Dundas has not been sufficiently informed of the nature and object of the Institution of the Association for promoting the Discovery of the Interior parts of Africa . . . The Institution is supported entirely by the private Subscriptions of Individuals . . . to bear the expences [sic] of such proper persons as can be engaged to Travel into the unknown Regions of Africa, with a view to Geographical Discoveries of those Interior parts whereof no accurate knowledge has ever hitherto been obtained, and with a view of Discovering the natural or artificial Produce of these unknown Countries, and some knowledge of their Manners, Customs, and Political Institutions.'[35] While the debate continued, Willis' mission stalled.

Troubled by the Association's involvement in the Willis affair, Beaufoy, like Banks, now stressed the geographical goals, and not the commercial or political advantages, that might flow from the Association's discoveries. Great Britain and the people of the African interior might soon be united in one big commercial embrace, he suggested, and Britain might be involved in official matters up the Gambia River, but the African Association's thoughts were on higher ground. It was at this moment, while considering the advantages of greater familiarity between Britain and Africa, that he wrote, 'Much, undoubtedly, we shall have to communicate, and something we may have to learn.'[36] Few British politicians or businessmen over the coming century and a half of bloody communication between Europe and Africa would come out with such an extraordinary thought. There was more to come. Letting his imagination run wild, Beaufoy now showed just how enlightened and just how wrong he and his colleagues could be:

> That in some of the cities of these insulated empires the knowledge and language of ancient Egypt may still imperfectly survive, is not an unpleasing supposition: nor is it absolutely impossible that the Carthaginians, who do not appear to have perished with their cities, may have retired to the southern parts of Africa: and though lost to the world in the vast oblivion of the Desert, may have carried with them to the new regions they occupy, some portion of those arts and sciences, and of that commercial knowledge, for which the inhabitants of Carthage were once so eminently famed.[37]

Sons of the pharaohs alive and well and living along the Niger? The key to hieroglyphics, one of the many puzzles being teased out at the Royal Society, to be found south of the Sahara? The descendants of Hannibal doing deals in the dust? It is a great age indeed that places its hopes in such fantasies. A great Association too. Its members were convinced. And, what's more, with the appearance of an unusually talented and resourceful young man, they believed that their greatest day was about to dawn.

8

No Mean Talents

'It is a short expedition and will give me an opportunity of
Distinguishing myself.'

Mungo Park to his brother, 20 May 1794

London, 1794

IN THE EXTREMELY MOBILE but socially stratified society of
late-eighteenth-century London, it was not surprising that Sir
Joseph Banks and James Dickson met, but it was unusual that they
became friends. Where Banks had enjoyed a privileged childhood
and the finest education England could provide, Dickson was
self-educated. Banks' fortune exempted him from the necessity
of having to work, although he spent few idle days in his life.
Dickson, on the other hand, supported himself and his family by
working as a seedsman at London's Covent Garden market. Banks
had recognised Dickson's considerable botanical knowledge and
gave him access to his natural history collection and impressive
library at Soho Square. By February 1788 Dickson stood high
enough in Banks' esteem to have joined him and five other friends
at the Marlborough Coffee House to create the Linnaean Society,*

---

* Dickson was also one of seven people present at Hatchard's booksellers in Piccadilly on
7 March 1804 for the founding of the Horticultural Society.

Sir Joseph Banks, 'the godfather of exploration', painted by John Russell, R.A., in 1788, the year the African Association was founded. Banks is holding one of the first accurate depictions of the moon's surface, made possible by his friend Herschel's telescope. If he could look at the moon, how difficult could it be to reach the African interior?

Soho Square in 1812, by George Shepherd. Banks' house stood in the left-hand corner until it was demolished in 1936. Other residents of the square during his time included the map-maker Arrowsmith, the opium-eater Thomas de Quincey and the ladies of a noted brothel, Hooper's Hotel.

Frances Rawdon, the Earl of Moira, in 1789. Detail from one of the last portraits painted by Sir Joshua Reynolds, President of the Royal Academy. Rawdon commissioned the painting as a present for King George III's son, the Duke of York.

Left Bryan Edwards Esq. A paradoxical character, a Caribbean planter turned Southampton banker, a Fellow of the Royal Society who enjoyed dancing with 'Tinkers' wives and Blacksmiths' daughters'. Some credited him with making Mungo Park's *Travels* readable, others accused him of editing out Park's criticisms of the slave trade.

Below Major James Rennell, 'the father of British geography' and the Association's mapmaker, by John Opie. The Committee recognised Rennell's unique position in the Association by offering him an honorary membership.

Above John Ledyard, the first great American traveller. A portrait by the Swedish artist Breda was hung in the Royal Academy's 1788 Summer Exhibition, but has since been lost. This 'imaginative reconstruction' was made for a 1905 dinner of alumni from Ledyard's old school, Dartmouth College, Connecticut.

Right Sidi Hassan, the dashing late Bey of Tripoli. His successors provided both encouragement and obstacles to the Association's travellers.

SIDY HASSAN, LATE BEY OF TRIPOLI.

Murzuk in the Fezzan, now southern Libya. The Association's traveller was greeted with a scene 'as old perhaps, as the time of Saladin': the Sultan greeted him surrounded by slaves carrying swords, banners, lances and halberds.

Mungo Park, who more than any other Association traveller helped to open a 'gate into Africa'. He had left for Africa in good health and with a full head of hair, but this portrait, made by Thomas Rowlandson shortly before Park's second African journey, shows the toll travelling had taken. Still, as Park told Sir Walter Scott, he preferred to 'brave Africa and all its horrors' than stay at home.

Medina, the Wuli capital, nine hundred miles inland from the mouth of the Gambia River. The Association's traveller made plans to settle down there – 'ten pounds a year would support a whole family with plenty of fowls, sheep, milk, eggs, butter, honey, bullocks, fish, and all sorts of game' – until fire destroyed the town in the spring of 1791.

Mungo Park

The capital of Bondo, beyond the scope of European discovery in Africa until the Association's travellers arrived. A prince of Bondo, taken as a slave, had ended up being royally treated in London, but the Association's traveller received a less enthusiastic welcome here.

A View of Ali's Tent at the Camp of Benowm. Park was held captive on the edge of the Sahara because the King's wife was curious to see a white man. It was believed his mother had achieved the effect by dipping him in milk, holding him by his nose, which thus became large and pointed.

Lady C.S.H.del.

Lady E.F. Sculp.

Mungo Park having just reached the River Niger – the way it looked in London. Park received a hero's welcome in Britain: the Duchess of Devonshire composed a song in his honour, while Lady Elizabeth Foster made this engraving, which was included in the second edition of Park's *Travels*.

A view of Kamalia, in modern-day Mali, home of Karfa Taura. Many in London were outraged that Park befriended a slave trader, but he is unlikely to have survived without Karfa's help.

The Battle of Heliopolis by Leon Cogniet, *c.*1850, a romantic portrayal of a brutal clash between organised French troops and badly-led Egyptian forces. Napoleon's invasion of Egypt turned the African Association's Committee into political players and initiated a scramble for Africa.

named in honour of the Swedish naturalist Carl Linnaeus.*

Dickson and his wife, Margaret Park, were both children of the hilly Scottish borderlands, and in the summer of 1792 they had travelled north to visit their families. From the Borders, Dickson wanted to continue into the Highlands to do some botanising and had suggested that his twenty-one-year-old brother-in-law, Mungo, might like to accompany him. Mungo had just completed his studies in medicine at Edinburgh University and was happy to take up Dickson's proposal. Despite an age difference of almost thirty years, the two men found common ground, and when the botanist returned to London he invited Park to stay at his house near the British Museum. By the autumn, the young Scot was installed.

It was an age when who you knew was vitally important, and through Dickson, Mungo Park was introduced to Banks, who recognised his abilities and was happy to help him in whatever way he could. Park soon discovered the advantages of having a powerful patron. In February 1793,† six months after he had gone botanising with Dickson, he had been employed as an assistant surgeon by the East India Company and was sailing on the *Worcester* bound for Bencoolen in Sumatra.‡

Perhaps Banks proposed the journey as a test. If so, his young protégé rose to the challenge. No full account of Park's Sumatra voyage has survived, but it appears that the uneventful journey gave the young surgeon's mate plenty of time to read, while the twelve weeks the *Worcester* spent at Bencoolen loading pepper, senna and

---

* Linnaeus, whose system of classification for plants and animals is still in use today, had built a unique collection of nearly three thousand books, plants, minerals, insects and manuscripts, which was offered to Banks for a thousand guineas after the death of Linnaeus' son and heir. Banks didn't buy it, but was instrumental in persuading a young acquaintance of his, James Smith, to do so and then to create the Linnaean Society.
† Some historians have written that Park sailed for Sumatra in 1792, but the logbook of the *Worcester* states 1793. Hallett is unable to account for Park's movements in 1793 ('he seems to have stayed in London'), but the mystery of his 'lost' year appears now to be solved.
‡ This appointment may have come about through Banks' friend William Marsden, who had joined the Association in 1789. Described as 'one of the greatest Orientalists of the age', Marsden served in Bencoolen with the East India Company (1771–79) before setting up his own East Indian agency in London and writing the great *History of Sumatra* (1783). In 1795 he was appointed a Secretary at the Admiralty.

the aniseed-based spirit *arak* provided him with the opportunity to study local plants and fishes.

Park returned to London in May 1794. There had been great changes at home – his father had died while he was away – but an even greater one had taken place in the young man: on the voyage he had decided that his future lay not in medicine but in natural history. As soon as he returned to London he went to show Banks the specimens of plants he had collected and the watercolour sketches he had made of twenty species of fish. Banks was impressed, and Park's paper on *Eight small fishes from the coast of Sumatra* was duly read to the Linnaean Society.

There is a sense of inevitability about what followed. Late in May 1794, Park went home to Scotland to visit his family. There was something of a farewell about the visit, for he had already written to his brother Alexander that 'I have . . . got Sir Joseph's word that if I wish to travel he will apply to the African Association and I shall go out with their Consul to Fort St. Joseph on the river Gambia where I am to hire a trader to go with me to Tombuctoo and back again.'[1] While he was away, the Association held its annual meeting, at which Beaufoy stated the Committee's assumption that Houghton was dead and announced that an offer had been 'received from Mr Mungo Park to engage in the service of the Association as a Geographical Missionary'.* Park had already discussed the reports of Houghton's death with Banks and other members of the Association. From the little that was known of the circumstances, he concluded that the Major had either been worn down by the climate or killed by natives. For many people, this would have been reason enough not to follow Houghton into Africa, but not for Park. 'This intelligence, instead of deterring me from my purpose, animated me to persist in the offer of my services with the greater solicitude.'[2]

Whether wishful thinking or a sign of extraordinary courage, Park's response did at least acknowledge the risks involved in the

---

* It isn't known whether the Duke of Buccleuch, the first President of the Royal Society of Edinburgh and a member of the Association since 1789, was present at this meeting, but if so he would no doubt have taken pleasure from the knowledge that Park was one of 'his', for the Park family rented their farm from the Duke.

proposed journey. So why would a well qualified and extremely well connected young man who was just beginning to establish himself in London volunteer for such a dangerous journey? Money was part of the reason for Park, as it had been for Ledyard and Houghton. Before joining the *Worcester*, he had had to take an advance of £10 against his wages to clear debts and to equip himself for the journey. Financial concerns surfaced again soon after his return to England, and it was with a sense of relief that he wrote to his brother Alexander on 20 May that 'The Association pays for everything.'[3] If he succeeded in his mission, more money would be sure to follow. But it is wrong to conclude that money was his main motivation for wanting to travel. Much more important was the prospect of the glory that would be his if he became the first geographical missionary to reach the Niger and Timbuktu. 'It is a short expedition,' he wrote, 'and will give me an opportunity of Distinguishing myself.'[4] He longed for the challenge, an opportunity to prove himself, and he wanted to become a celebrity traveller. He made it sound so simple.

Two months later, on 23 July, Banks and Beaufoy met to discuss Park's offer at the Thatched House Tavern on Pall Mall.* Like Banks, Beaufoy had come to know the Scot well and was clearly impressed by his abilities, calling him 'a young man of no mean talents'.[5] This time, the Committee had even greater ambitions for the mission: they wanted Park to locate the Niger and Timbuktu, but they also wanted him to return with the sort of information Rennell craved. Here, too, Park was considered to be the right person. He had proved his ability to master new scientific skills on his Sumatran journey and Beaufoy commented that he was already 'sufficiently instructed in the use of Hadley's quadrant to make the

---

* By this time the St Alban's Tavern had closed; it was eventually pulled down as part of a redevelopment of the area.

necessary observations; geographer enough to trace out his path through the Wilderness, and not unacquainted with natural history'. As a bonus, his medical training ought to ensure that he would stay alive longer than most; at least he was unlikely to kill himself trying to cure an upset stomach, as Ledyard had done. Park differed in other ways from Ledyard: unlike the American, his only experience of long-distance travel was the journey to Sumatra, little preparation for the rigours to come. And unlike Lucas and Houghton, Park had no experience either of Africa or of its people. There were many young men then living in London who knew considerably more about Africans, and some, no doubt, would have welcomed an opportunity of employment with the Association, yet Banks had an instinct that Park was the man for them. He was selected.

The details of his employment were settled before Banks and Beaufoy left the Thatched House that day in July, and instructions were soon issued. The goals were the same as before – the Niger and Timbuktu were the main objectives, but Hausa, Britain's prospective trading partner, was also a priority:

> *The Committee having reason to believe that a considerable Empire distinguished by the name of Houssa has long been established in the neighbourhood of the Neel il Abeed (called by Europeans the Niger); and being desirous, for a variety of reasons, that a communication with the said Empire may be opened from the British possessions in the Gambia, Mr Park cannot more effectually fulfil the purpose of his Mission, than by travelling from the River Gambia, to the Capital of the said kingdom.*
>
> *The Committee being also anxious to be informed of the Rise, the Course, and the Termination of the <u>Niger</u>, as well as of the various Nations that inhabit its Borders, are in hopes that partly by Mr. Park's own Discoveries, and partly by the information he will be able to collect in the neighbourhood of the River, this object of his Mission may also be accomplished.*
>
> *The Accounts that have been sent to the Committee of the wealth and population of the City of <u>Tombuctoo</u> having*

engaged their earnest attention, they naturally entertain the hope that a visit to that place will be considered by Mr. Park as one of the principal objects of his journey.

The rout [sic] by which Mr. Park will return must be left to his own discretion, but the Committee feel the strongest solicitude to receive by every possible opportunity, an account of his Proceedings, and they are not without hopes that the various Caravans from Morocco, Godempsi (Ghedesmes) Fezzan and Cairo; as well as the communication of the slave dealers with Gambia and the Gulph of Guinea, may render the opportunities frequent, and that the expedient of drawing a Bill for Five Pounds on a part of each letter, may ensure the safety of the conveyance.

Whatever observations Mr. Park's Journey may enable him to make on the Animal, Vegetable or Mineral Productions of the Inland Countries of Africa, the Committee will be happy to receive.

Park was thrilled. 'I had a passionate desire to examine into the productions of a country so little known, and to become experimentally acquainted with the modes of life and character of the natives. I knew that I was able to bear fatigue; and I relied on my youth and the strength of my constitution to preserve me from the effects of the climate.'[6]

Several other things set this expedition apart from its predecessors. Most significant, Park was equipped with some sophisticated scientific instruments. British – and specifically London – manufacturers dominated the field of mathematical instruments towards the end of the eighteenth century. The workshops of men such as Jesse Ramsden, Peter Dolland and Edward Troughton were turning out instruments whose quality was unrivalled. Troughton, like Ramsden, was also a Fellow of the Royal Society and one of Banks' circle. From him, Park ordered some £15 worth of instruments, including a pocket sextant, a magnetic compass and a thermometer. A further £40 of unspecified equipment was also charged to the Association's account. With this, the would-be explorer was properly equipped to calculate his latitude and to make an accurate record of the direction in which he would be travelling. Houghton had been sent with the same sort of equipment, but his had been lost in the Wuli fire: Park's journey was to be the start of a new era in African discovery.

Park also had the satisfaction of being the first geographical missionary to be offered a salary by the Association. From 1 August 1794 he was to receive seven shillings and sixpence a day, just over two and a half pounds a week, about the same as he had earned in a month as an assistant surgeon on the journey to Sumatra, in addition to which there was also a generous allowance for equipment and his passage to Africa. Best of all, once he left the Gambia River and headed into the interior, his fee would double to fifteen shillings a day for up to two years. This presented him with an opportunity to significantly improve his circumstances. He would have little need or opportunity to spend his own money while away, so if he survived two years in the interior, he should have saved a considerable amount of money by the time he returned to London. Along with the settlement that was due to him under the terms of his father's will, some £400, he ought then to have the means to set himself up either in London or in his native Scotland.

The meeting ended with Park being told to prepare to sail for the Gambia with Consul Willis in September or October. As Willis' mission was repeatedly delayed, so Park remained stranded in London. Early in 1795, he complained to the Committee of 'being tired of leading what he called a Life useless to his Employers', but even so, it was not until April, with Beaufoy seriously ill, that Banks and Stuart convened a Committee meeting and decided that Park should wait no longer. He paid £15 for a place in the *Endeavour*, a small brig owned by Messrs Eden and Court, who traded English manufactured goods for beeswax and ivory. Here again Park had to be patient: the continuing conflict with France meant that there were tight controls on ships leaving the Thames, and the *Endeavour* was not allowed to leave British waters until 22 May. It was the start of a journey that Park hoped would make him as famous as Captain Cook.

His months in London had not been wasted. For one thing, he had had time to browse the shelves of the library at Soho Square and had read many accounts by earlier travellers in Africa, including that of Francis Moore, the English adventurer who had travelled up the Gambia River earlier in the century. Park had collected a great deal of information about social and political conditions in Africa, was familiar with the names of many of the small kingdoms along the coast and up the rivers, and now knew something of the manners and customs of their inhabitants. He also understood some of the threats posed to his safety. He knew he would make an attractive target for less scrupulous Africans, and was taking two fowling pieces, or shotguns, to make himself look less vulnerable. He also packed a magnificent blue frock-coat with yellow buttons – clearly an object of aspiration for late-eighteenth-century travellers in Africa, as Houghton had armed himself with a similar coat – and a good silver-topped cane. As a doctor, Park was well aware of some health risks and, although he did not have the benefit, as we do now, of inoculating himself against cholera and typhoid, yellow fever, hepatitis or meningitis, or of taking any effective protection against malaria, he did pack a medicine chest. Another benefit of his delayed departure was that he had had time to consider the geographical demands of his mission: Rennell had instructed him on what was needed for a new map of Africa to be drawn. The delay had been frustrating, but it turned out to the Association's advantage; by the time Park left England, he was as well-prepared a traveller as had ever set out on a solo voyage of exploration. After the regrettable failures of Ledyard, Lucas and Houghton, here at last was a man who could bring the Association the geographical glory it coveted. One of the great journeys of discovery was beginning.

9

Pity the White Man

'Go, White Man, go; – but with thee bear
The Negro's wish, the Negro's prayer;
Remembrance of the Negro's care.'
'A Negro Song', Georgiana, Duchess of Devonshire, 1798

The Gambia, 1795

IT WAS AN EASY PASSAGE down to Africa and, just a fortnight
after leaving Portsmouth, Mungo Park leaned over the railing of
the *Endeavour* and admired the high walls and whitewashed houses
of Mogador (Essaouira). Seventeen days later, on Midsummer's
Day 1795, he finally set foot on African soil for the first time, caught
that unique bouquet of new growth and old rot, saw the lush
monotony of the Gambia's greenery and, like a plant in new soil,
revealed himself as a man who had found his role in life.

The *Endeavour* anchored at Jillifree, a small, dusty north-bank
town of thatched huts near the remains of the British fort on James
Island. Park was in a hurry, and had no patience for these sights.
He wanted to be upriver already, wanted to be visiting Dr Laidley,
the British trader installed at Pisania, to whom Houghton had
addressed his last recorded words. But travelling upriver by trading
boat was a slow process and there were many stops to make along
the way: after Jillifree, the *Endeavour* stayed three days at a place

Park calls Vintain – more properly Bintang* – thirty miles inland from the ocean on the Gambia's south bank. Six days after leaving Bintang the boat reached Jonkakonda, where Houghton had heard he would be killed on his way inland. Park met with a friendlier reception, for Laidley arrived with an invitation for the traveller to stay with him in Pisania while he prepared for his trip. 'This invitation was too acceptable to be refused,'[1] Park noted. Laidley then sent a horse and guide, and on 5 July the geographical missionary was installed in the trader's home.

Pisania was a quiet cluster of a few houses in a clearing near the riverbank, a good place for Park to settle into the new continent. The biggest house belonged to Laidley – it was described as a mansion – while his neighbours were two English traders, the Ainslee brothers, and the many Africans whom they and Laidley employed. Their security was guaranteed by the nearby King of Yani, and they enjoyed whatever comforts could be had in the region – Park wrote glowingly of the slave trader and of his arrangements, no doubt to the mortification of the Abolitionist members of the Association.

While staying with Laidley, Park began to learn Mandingo, one of the region's more popular languages, without which, he was aware, he had little chance of collecting the sort of information he had been sent to find. His preparations went well, while at the same time he managed to avoid the sort of illnesses and fevers that had brought down so many Europeans in the region – Houghton, for instance, had contracted a fever as soon as he landed in West Africa. Park appeared to have no such problem. According to one theory current at the time, it would have been best for him to fall ill at the outset, because although they knew nothing about the immune system, some doctors believed that foreigners were not safe in Africa until they had gone through what was known as a 'seasoning sickness'. If they survived the first bout, so the theory went, they would be protected from further attacks. It wasn't entirely wrong.

---

* First settled by the British as early as 1651, Bintang had taken on a new lease of life in the ten years before Park's arrival when several British traders established new posts there. It is now a favourite day-trip destination for tourists from the Gambia's Atlantic beach resorts.

For a month Park settled in and continued his studies, congratulating himself on the strength of his constitution and on having
escaped the seasoning sickness. There was work to be done as well,
including an observation, on 31 July, of a lunar eclipse which he
hoped would allow him to calculate an exact longitude for Pisania.
It would serve as a start point for future calculations, and one he
knew Rennell would find helpful. That night, he stayed out late to
observe the moon, with dire consequences: 'the next day I found
myself attacked with a smart fever'.[2] Medical opinion at the time
was united around a theory that fevers were caused by exposure to
vapours, so as Park sank into delirium, he assumed it was caused
by the night vapours of Pisania. 'I imprudently exposed myself to
the night dew,'[3] he later wrote, although a more likely explanation
is that he had caught malaria. Luckily Laidley had seen enough
of it in his time along the river, and was on hand to look after
him.

For most of the next month, Park suffered the hell of malarial
fevers and headaches, the sweats, pains and cringing from light and
noise. Late-eighteenth-century cures for this sort of thing were
drastic, designed to force the body to expel the infection, commonly
through a series of bleedings, blisterings, purgings and sweatings,
none of which would have been very helpful. The only treatment
that would have made any difference with malaria was cinchona
bark, which fever patients at that time were often encouraged to
chew, or else which was served up to them as an infusion. Jesuit
missionaries in South America had stumbled upon this cure by
chance: cinchona bark contains quinine, now known to be effective
in the prevention and cure of malaria. Frustratingly, given that he
was a doctor, Park gives no more details either of his illness or the
cure, although he does make it clear that it went on for some
months and that he suffered a great deal.

'The care and attention of Dr. Laidley,' he later remembered,
'contributed greatly to alleviate my sufferings; his company and
conversation beguiled the tedious hours during that gloomy season,
when the rain falls in torrents; when suffocating heats oppress by
day, and when night is spent by the terrified traveller in listening

to the croaking of frogs, (of which the numbers are beyond imagination,) the shrill cry of the jackal, and the deep howling of the hyena.'[4] Even after the fever had passed, it took Park a long time to regain his strength and energy. But just as he had done in London while waiting for Consul Willis to leave for the Gambia, he made good use of this time, improving his grasp of the Mandingo language and writing up his observations of the people who lived along the Gambia River.

Park obviously liked many of the Mandingos he met around Pisania, whom he described as being 'of a mild, sociable, and obliging disposition'.[5] But he also found them something of a puzzle. 'Considering the use that is made of the [elephant] in the East Indies,' he wrote while watching the way they worked, 'it may be thought extraordinary that the natives of Africa have not, in any part of this immense continent, acquired the skill of taming this powerful and docile creature, and applying his strength and faculties to the service of man.'[6] He was just as enthusiastic about the neighbouring Jola, whom he found to be 'determined and faithful'.[7]

Park's words, with his attention to detail, the promise of exact scientific readings and his observations of the Mandingos near the river, would have been sweet music to the ears of his audience back in London. In fact, any word from him at this stage would have been welcome. In an undated letter, written some time during the winter of 1795–96, Banks complained that 'we have not been so fortunate as to hear from you since you saild [sic]', back in May 1795. 'By the time you receive this,' the great man continued, 'you will no doubt have returned from a perillous Journey if you have accomplishd the business of seeing Tamboucta [sic] you will deserve from the Association every thing they can do for you as I have no doubt you will be able to give a good account of what you have seen.' He ended, rather unrealistically, by expressing 'hearty hopes that we may see you at home very soon & congratulate you on having fulfilled an honourable & dangerous undertaking'.

We do not know whether Park ever received this letter – the

only surviving copy is in Banks' archive – though the presence of French privateers along the Gambia River was probably just as efficient at stopping mail coming in as it was at stopping most of Park's mail sailing out. But before Banks' letter could have reached West Africa, the explorer wrote to London to explain that he had been sick, was now better and was finally ready to set off into the interior. Dr Laidley had initially arranged for Park to travel with a *slatee*, an African slave trader who would leave for the interior during the dry season. But Park pointed out that 'the characters and dispositions of the *slatees*, and people that composed the caravan, were entirely unknown to me, and . . . they seemed rather adverse to my purpose'. He told Laidley he would prefer to travel without them, which showed sound judgement, though it was a scruple he found himself unable to afford later on his travels.

Laidley, ever the master of arrangements and perhaps also recognising in Park a good customer, now helped him set up his own expedition. He provided him with a horse ('To Bt. A Horse', as it appeared in the Association's accounts, '£7.8.0'[8]), which the explorer described as 'a small but very hardy and spirited beast',[9] and with everything a horseman might need ('To a saddle, Bridle, Holster, Pistols, and Spurs – all plated, £10.0.0'). To ease Park's way, he also hired a local man by the name of Johnson, an African who had spent seven years in service in England and would make an excellent interpreter ('To advanced your Linguist 12/-'), and a servant, Demba, a reliable young man who had worked in the trader's house and who spoke both Mandingo and 'the language of the Serawoollies'.[10] Although Park does not mention the fact directly, Demba was a slave. His loyalty was assured, so it was believed, by the promise that he would be given his freedom if he served Park well and if they returned safely to Pisania. These two men were provided with asses to ride ('To panelling for 2 asses, 3/-'). Among his luggage, Park packed some clothes, 'two fowling-pieces, two pairs of pistols, and some other small articles'. He was carrying enough food and water to keep the party moving for a couple of days, as well as 36.25 ounces (1 kilogram) of fine amber, ninety pounds (40.9 kg) of tobacco, twenty pounds (9.09 kg) of Jobaltic beads and just over £5 worth of Indian bafts and chintzes, all of which had been bought from Laidley for a total of almost £16. With these, he would be able to barter for food along the way; if things got desperate, he could also trade the pistols, the asses, his saddles, his horse ... Given that Houghton, a couple of years earlier, had reckoned that £10 would keep a family in food for a year, Park appeared to be well prepared. And then there was his scientific equipment, Troughton's pocket sextant, magnetic compass and thermometer that had survived the journey out from England. He also had his umbrella, useful against both rain and sun.

As Park and his two servants prepared to leave for the interior, other people asked to join them. In his last letter to the Association before setting off, Park mentions that Dr Laidley's blacksmith, a Muslim named Tami, and his son had asked to accompany him as far as their home town of Jumbo in Kaarta. He makes no mention in his letters of another man, Madiboo, who was on his way to Bambara, or of two Serawoolli slave traders going to Bondo, so perhaps theirs was a last-minute request to travel with him.

On 2 December 1795, almost five months after his arrival, Park finally turned away from the comforts of Pisania.* Dr Laidley, the two Messrs Ainslee and a number of servants came to see him off, riding alongside him for two days before returning to the river. Laidley, who had trade contacts in many towns between the Gambia and Niger rivers, knew the extent of the dangers for the first leg of his journey. But not even he knew what lay on the road to Hausa or on the way to the end of the Niger. 'I believe,' Park noted, 'they secretly thought they should never see me afterwards.' Given the experiences of earlier travellers, pessimism seems entirely reasonable. The only other expectation they had was that for as long as he survived, Park was going to have an adventure. Park, hamming it up for his audience back home, wrote, 'I had parted

---

* At Karantaba Tenda, twelve miles east of modern Georgetown, a memorial pillar marks the spot where Park left the river for the interior.

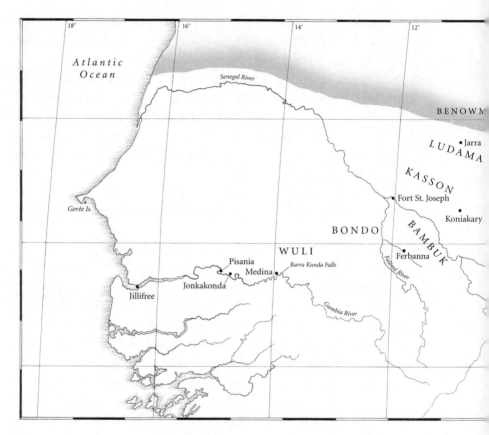

Mungo Park's first journey in west Africa, 1795–97

from the last European I might probably behold, and perhaps quitted for ever the comforts of Christian society.'[11] But who knew what lay ahead? Perhaps as he stepped off the known part of the map he would locate the great empire Beaufoy had imagined, and meet the descendants of the ancient Egyptians or Carthaginians, or the headless people written about by the ancient historians, or the elephants and savage beasts geographers had resorted to.

Two days later, Park arrived in Medina, the capital of Wuli. Houghton had been well received by the King, and now Park was

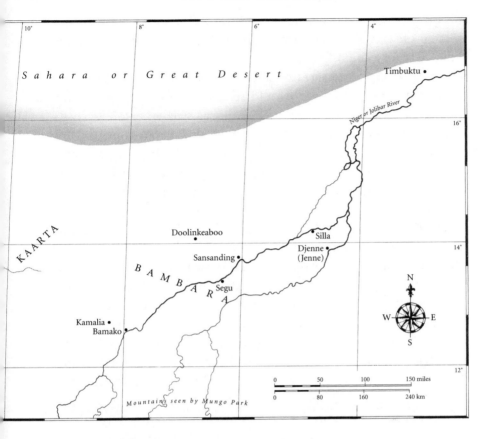

given a similarly warm welcome and was housed with one of the royal family. As soon as he was settled, he was summoned to meet the King. 'He was the same venerable old man of whom so favourable an account was transmitted by Major Houghton. I found him seated upon a mat before the door of his hut; a number of men and women were arranged on each side, who were singing and clapping their hands. I saluted him respectfully, and informed him of the purport of my visit.'[12]

Park was on easy ground here: he was in a kingdom that had regular contact with foreigners, where Laidley was known and where his predecessor had been treated with respect. King Jatta was happy to help the traveller on his way by providing a guide to the frontier of his territory and offering up a prayer for Park's safety. The King's customs officials had already extracted their dues, but Park now informed Jatta that Laidley would send him three gallons of rum in appreciation of his help. Before he allowed the foreigner to proceed, however, the King tried to talk him out of going, saying 'the people of the east had never seen a white man, and would certainly destroy me'.[13] Park laughed off these concerns, without recording whether the King thought his insistence a sign of bravery or stupidity.

On 6 December he left Wuli, and five days later reached the frontier of Bondo, where King Jatta's guide left him. Park now hired three local elephant-hunters as guides, showing his inexperience by paying them gold in advance. The extent of his mistake was made apparent the following morning when he discovered that one of them had run off. The surprise is that the other two had stayed. Four days later, the two Serawoolli slave traders left him, 'with many prayers for my safety'.[14] One of the things Park learned during these first two weeks away from Laidley's house was that the prospect of sharing a good pot of food in the evening encouraged plenty of people to accompany him during the day. So whenever there was good, cheap food to be bought, he laid in provisions – with notable results: on 19 December, for instance, near the Falémé River and some three hundred miles inland, twelve people joined him to eat a sheep and corn.

Across the Falémé River, Park entered the kingdom of Bondo and headed for Fatteconda, the capital. He was wary of meeting the King,* having heard that he was responsible for Houghton being robbed. Installed in the hut of a *slatee*, he prepared carefully for the coming interview. He decided to pre-empt theft by offering a generous present of gunpowder, amber and tobacco. To this he added the umbrella he had brought from London. But in case this

---

* In his book, Park calls the ruler King Almami, but Almami was a signifier for 'king', and the man's name was Isata.

ploy did not work, he took the precaution of hiding some of his valuables in the roof of the hut before leaving to meet the King. He also put on his new blue frock-coat with yellow buttons, which he was afraid might go missing in his absence. Together with his nankeen britches, his waistcoat, shirt and thick, broad-brimmed hat, he must have been an extraordinary sight in an African village, perhaps frightening, perhaps imposing to people who equated this sort of display with personal prestige, perhaps laughable.

King Isata greeted the traveller warmly, invited him to sit beside him and offered to trade gold or slaves. Park declined the offer: he had not come to trade. This refusal puzzled the King, who was only 'half-satisfied'. If the strange white man had not come to trade and was not going on pilgrimage or a raid, then what was he up to? 'The notion of travelling for curiosity was quite new to him. He thought it impossible, he said, that any man in his senses would undertake so dangerous a journey, merely to look at the country and its inhabitants.'[15] In this, it must be admitted, the King was not alone.

The expected trouble was not long in arriving. The King was pleased enough with the gunpowder, tobacco and amber, and was thrilled with the umbrella, but something else had caught his eye, and he was not used to having his whims or wishes denied. When Isata delivered 'an eulogium' on the glories of Park's blue coat, and in particular on its yellow buttons, the visitor was obliged to take it off and offer it as a present. Now the Almami was happy, so much so that he assured Park he would wear the coat on all state occasions and praise the generosity of the white man who had given him such a wonderful present. Having said which, he dismissed Park, perhaps because he was in a hurry to try on the coat without its former owner glaring at him.

The following day, the strange foreigner was presented to the many royal wives, to whom he was the subject of wonder and mockery. Surely, they claimed, no human could be born with skin so white and a nose so large? In which case, they concluded, as a child he must have been regularly dipped in milk and had his nose pinched and pulled each day until the present unnatural, unsightly deformation had been achieved. Park in reply praised the 'glossy jet' of their skin and the 'lovely depression' of their noses. His words clearly pleased the King's women, for that night they sent him a present of a jar of honey and a fish. The ease with which he talked to them and the pleasure they took in each other's company offered a welcome relief from the anxieties of his journey.

On 23 December, Park rode out of Bondo, without either his coat or umbrella, but with the King's consolatory present of gold tucked into his bag and with Johnson his interpreter, Demba his servant, Madiboo the fellow traveller on his way to Bambara and several other companions besides. The following day he entered the kingdom of Kajaaga, where the headman of a town of some two thousand people offered him protection for the night. The next morning, which happened to be Christmas Day, he was woken early by the arrival of twenty horsemen, sent by the King of Kajaaga. Madiboo, whose parents lived nearby, knew this meant trouble: Park was accused of entering the kingdom without first paying his dues. This was certainly something Park should have been aware of – he had paid his dues in Wuli, after all, and the people travelling with him should have known the customs. Recognising his mistake, he apologised and made amends by offering the gold he had been given by the King of Bondo. The men accepted this, but still wanted more, so forced him to open his bags and helped themselves to half of his goods. 'These proceedings dispirited my people, and our fortitude,' Park admitted dryly, 'was not strengthened by a very indifferent supper after a long fast. Madiboo begged me to turn back; Johnson laughed at the thoughts of proceeding without money.'[16] But the losses were not his only concern. He still had half of his property, which he had hidden from the horsemen, but he could not use it there because if word got out that he had bought food – and whatever he did, the horsemen would be sure to hear about it – they would come back. Here he had a stroke of luck: a nephew of Demba Sego Jalla, King of neighbouring Kasson, through whose territory Park wanted to pass, was in Kajaaga and had heard many stories about the white man. More out of curiosity than generosity, he came to see what all the fuss was about. When Park explained his dilemma, the Prince offered to escort him to his father's court.

By 29 December they had crossed the Senegal River and were in the country of Kasson, where, more recently, some of Africa's highest temperatures have been recorded. Park seems not to have understood the Prince's motive for offering his royal protection, but once they were on the Kasson side of the river, it became clear when the Prince announced it was time for the foreigner to offer him a present for services rendered. Seven 'bars' of amber and some tobacco were handed over. Some days later, having enjoyed the hospitality of Demba Sego Jalla for longer than anticipated (an enforced stay, it should be pointed out, as the Prince had ridden off on Park's horse), the traveller was invited to offer another present in thanks before leaving. Again amber and tobacco were handed over, and again half of all his goods were then taken from him by force.

The restrained tone of Park's description of his travels makes it difficult to be certain about his reactions to these 'unexpected propositions'. The people who helped themselves to his goods claimed that they were merely taking a tribute that was equal to the importance of his host, the King's brother. Park, on the other hand, is likely to have seen it as theft, and perhaps longed for the day when his own country's draconian laws could be imposed on the continent: under the British penal code, theft of anything to the value of more than thirty-nine shillings, just under £2, was considered a double felony and carried the death sentence. According to those rules, given that Park's goods were worth some £16 when he started inland and that he had been relieved, respectively, of a half and a quarter, both incidents would have ended the life of the culprit.

Does he lie in his hut at night and take his revenge, in his dreams at least, by imagining the King of Kajaaga's horsemen and the Kasson Prince swinging from a gallows? If he does, he never gives a hint of it in his journal. Instead, he writes about the generosity of some of the people he meets along the way and praises the companionship of his fellow travellers. When one of them, a black-smith, takes him to his family's village not far from where the Kasson Prince has lightened his load, Park watches in wonder as the man is cheered, songs sung in his honour and a feast prepared. He is most touched when the blacksmith's mother, an old woman, hobbles out supporting herself on a stick. 'Every one made way for her; and she stretched out her hand to bid her son welcome. Being totally blind, she stroked his hands, arms, and face with great care, and seemed highly delighted that her latter days were blessed by his return, and that her ears once more heard the music of his voice. From this interview I was fully convinced, that whatever difference there is between the Negro and European in the conformation of the nose and the colour of the skin, there is none in the genuine sympathies and characteristic feelings of our common nature.'[17] At a time when the debate about the morality and continuation of the slave trade was still raging, William Wilberforce and his anti-slavery readers will have relished the implications of these words. If there is no difference in sympathies and feelings between black and white, what justification can there be for slavery?

When he crossed into Kasson, Park was going, as far as geographical information was concerned, where only Houghton had been before; and of Houghton's experiences very little was known. But although he was stepping beyond the maps, the territory he wanted to travel through was already familiar to traders. So much so that there were people on whom he could call if he needed some service. One of them was a *slatee* by the name of Salim Daucari, one of Laidley's business contacts who lived in a village not far from the court of King Demba Sego Jalla. Daucari proved to be a godsend, for he owed Laidley the value of five slaves, which Park was authorised to collect in goods or gold. For another thing, Daucari's position in Kasson ensured the traveller a good reception. It also meant that

when word got out that the foreigner had just acquired a considerable amount of gold and the Prince arrived to demand half of it
for the King and more for himself, Daucari was able to negotiate
the 'tax' down to some European merchandise, powder and ball to
the value of £2.

Powder and ball would have been most welcome, for Park had
been told by Demba Sego Jalla that war was about to break out
between himself and the King of Kajaaga, provoked by a dispute
over cattle. This was bad news for the traveller, as was the expectation that the two kingdoms he intended to pass through next –
Kaarta and Bambara – would also be involved. With the help of
some diplomatic leverage on the part of Demba Sego Jalla and
travelling under royal protection, Park set off. On 8 February he
stood at the border between Kasson and Kaarta, watching hundreds
of people crossing westwards, fleeing the oncoming war. For the
next four days he travelled east through rich fields and lush stands
of fruit trees, as yet untouched by war. This welcome scene of
abundance was rounded off by an equally warm welcome in the
Kaarta capital Kemmoo.

At the court of King Daisy Koorabarri, Park found the sort of
reception he must have wished for all along the way. The King,
sitting on a leopard skin with his warriors to his right, women and
children to his left, was courteous and keen to attend to his visitor's
needs. A sheep was sent to his hut for supper, the people were
curious but respectful, and his stay would have been rewarding had
it not been interrupted by news of the advance on the capital of
the Bambara army. King Daisy suggested that Park return west to
Kasson and wait a few months for the wars to end. Park later
admitted that the King's advice was well meant, and that he was
perhaps at fault for not accepting it. He could be forgiven for not
wanting to return to a place where he had been fleeced and where
he knew he would have to deal with constant demands for presents
and tribute. But he was also concerned about the weather. Summer
was fast approaching, and after it would come the rains, the season
of fevers: 'I dreaded the thoughts of spending the rainy season in
the interior of Africa.'[18] But whatever else happened, he was not

going back to the coast until he had made what he called 'greater progress in discovery'. The Niger and Timbuktu were ahead of him, and he resolved not to let a little local feuding stand in his way.

It was a disastrous error of judgement. Whatever he had suffered before at the hands of local chiefs, who were justifiably suspicious of his motives and covetous of his possessions, whatever fear he had experienced passing through woods at night or crossing rivers by day, were nothing compared to what lay ahead.

War broke out across the region between the Senegal and Niger rivers, and once on his way and having made up his mind not to turn back, Park found himself obliged to travel further north, away from the Niger and towards the Sahara. It is difficult to plot his course precisely, but at some point before this northerly diversion he was perhaps as little as 150 miles from the river he had risked so much to find. But it was 150 miles of war-ravaged countryside. Needing to avoid it, he was forced north into the land of the Moors, the people who controlled the trans-Saharan trade and whose attitude towards strangers made the Fulanis, Serawoollis, Mandingos and all other black Africans he had met seem positively cordial.

On the afternoon of 16 February 1796, Park was asleep on a cowhide bed in a town called Funingkedy, when he was woken by the screams of women. Climbing onto the roof of his hut, he watched five Moors on horseback round up a large herd of the town's bullocks, choose the best sixteen of them and drive them away. What struck him most about this was not the audaciousness of the theft but the fact that the five hundred inhabitants of Funing-kedy simply watched it happen. Only one of the villagers, a herder, made a move to stop the theft and he was shot in the leg by the Moors. As a doctor, Park was later asked to examine the young herder. The shot had passed through both bones below his knee

and there was substantial loss of blood. Park recommended amputa-
tion at the knee, but the villagers were horrified: 'they evidently
considered me as some sort of cannibal for proposing so cruel and
unheard of an operation'.[19] Instead, they prayed over the wound
and the victim died.

On the eighteenth Park passed Simbing. 'From this village,' he
recalled, 'Major Houghton wrote his last letter with a pencil to Dr.
Laidley.'[20] Whatever the achievements of Houghton's dramatic and
fateful journey, Rennell had found it difficult to plot his exact course
and therefore to give him the credit he undoubtedly deserved. Park
was determined that his own journey would be of use, and had
already taken twenty readings between Pisania and Kemmoo, recording how long each journey had taken, his compass bearing, and
the nature of the country he was passing through. On four occasions
– at Pisania in Yani, Kolor in Wuli, Koorkoorany in Bondo and in
Kemmoo – he had also taken a reading of his latitude. Since leaving
the Gambia River, he had moved from 13° 35' to 14° 25'.

As he passed the place where Houghton wrote his last note, Park
would have done well to have remembered what happened to his
predecessor. Later he remarked that Houghton was 'deserted by his
Negro servants, who refused to help him into the Moorish country
... This brave but unfortunate man, having surmounted many
difficulties, had taken a northerly direction, and endeavoured to
pass through Ludamar.'[21]

Later on 18 February, Park arrived in Jarra, where Houghton had
met the Moors who lured him north into the desert to rob him.
Park had a very different experience in Jarra, where he met another
Gambian trader, Damon Jumma, who owed money to Laidley.
From him Park collected the value of two slaves and traded whatever
beads and amber he had left for gold, 'more portable ... and more
easily concealed from the Moors'.[22]

At this point, like Houghton before him, Park found his men

unwilling to follow him any further. However prepared he was for the journey, this should have caused him concern. 'The difficulties we had already encountered, the unsettled state of the country, and, above all, the savage and overbearing deportment of the Moors, had so completely frightened my attendants, that they declared they would rather relinquish every claim to reward, than proceed one step farther to the eastward.'[23] Park admits that he could not blame them for their fears, since there was a genuine risk that they would be taken by the Moors and sold as slaves.

Through Damon Jumma, Park sent a messenger to Ali, the sovereign of Ludamar, the Moorish lands to the north, asking for permission to travel across his kingdom. While he waited for a reply he prepared for his departure, leaving Johnson, his translator, with a copy of his notes and asking Damon Jumma to look after his surplus clothes and equipment: he now knew that possessions were only going to cause him trouble. He also appears to have asked Jumma to inform Laidley of his plans, because on 1 August the trader wrote to Willis, the prospective British Consul to the Senegambia, still trying to get his mission underway, that Park had 'reached the residence of an Arabian king, situated to the northward, and considerably to the eastward of Sego [sic]'.[24]

He was not there yet. Three days later, travelling north with Demba, 'my faithful boy', believing himself to be under the Emir Ali's protection, Park was insulted and spat upon by a group of Moors. He did not respond, suspecting that these men were looking for a pretext to fight and then confiscate his belongings, and recognising that he was outnumbered. A week later he met with very different behaviour in a Negro village where the headman was so honoured to have a white man stay that he killed a sheep, begged Park to stay long and, when he insisted on leaving, offered to lead him himself to the next village. The afternoon passed in conversation, the telling of stories and the drinking of corn beer.

'In the midst of this harmless festivity I flattered myself that all danger from the Moors was over. Fancy had already placed me on the banks of the Niger, and presented to my imagination a thousand delightful scenes in my future progress, when a party of Moors unexpectedly entered the hut, and dispelled the golden dream.'[25] These were Ali's men, sent to drag him before their leader. And why? Because he hadn't paid his dues? Because they had heard he was carrying gold? No. 'Their visit was occasioned by the curiosity of Ali's wife, *Fatima*, who had heard so much about Christians, that she was very anxious to see one.'[26]

Park was clearly badly treated by the Moors, and was probably right in guessing the reasons why: 'I was a stranger, I was unprotected, and I was Christian; each of these circumstances is sufficient to drive every spark of humanity from the heart of a Moor; but when all of them, as in my case, were combined in the same person, and a suspicion prevailed withal, that I had come as a spy into the country, the reader will easily imagine that, in such a situation, I had every thing to fear.' His anger towards them (hatred may be too strong a term) colours his narrative: as he tells it, they were without exception ruthless, thieving, murderous and immoral. His portrait of the ruler is no happier: 'Ali was sitting upon a black leather cushion, clipping a few hairs from his upper lip; a female attendant holding up a looking glass before him. He appeared to be an old man, of the Arab cast, with a long white beard; and he had a sullen and indignant aspect.'[27]

By this stage Ali had both captured Johnson and recovered the excess baggage Park had left with Damon Jumma, though not the copy of his papers. When he failed to find gold in the baggage, Ali sent men to search his body, where they found gold, amber, his watch and a compass.

The compass became a talking point. 'Ali was very desirous to be informed why that small piece of iron, the needle, always pointed to the Great Desert.' Park told him that it pointed to the direction of his mother, so he would always be able to find his way home. Ali handed it back to him, not wanting to keep anything with such magic attached to it. It was a rare moment of triumph for the explorer, a triumph brought about by his knowledge both of science and of Ali's superstitious nature. A victory of sorts, but a very small one in the face of what was to follow.

Park was captured on 7 March, but it was not until 3 May that he finally met Ali's queen, Fatima. He described her as having the facial features and long black hair of an Arab woman and being extremely fat. She was clearly shocked by the way he looked and was uneasy about having him nearby. But speaking through a boy who could speak both Mandingo and Arabic, he won her round and was allowed to stay. When the meeting ended the Queen offered him a bowl of milk, 'which I considered as a very favourable omen', though it is possible that she would have done the same to a pet goat.[28]

Ali had explained to Park that he was being held because Fatima was curious to see him, but months had passed since the meeting and he was still unable to leave Ludamar. He was, however, allowed more freedom of movement. By then the wars had spilled over into the north, and when news reached them that Daisy of Kaarta was moving their way, Ali broke camp, sending Park and his interpreter Johnson, who had been captured and was still with him, to Jarra. Demba, Park's Mandingo-speaking boy servant, who was to have helped him through the Bambara countries and later been freed, had already been taken as a slave despite Park's protests that Demba was a freeman, had done nothing wrong and did not deserve such treatment. Ali warned him to be quiet or risk being enslaved himself. 'There is something in the frown of a tyrant,' Park wrote as a result of this exchange, 'which rouzes [sic] the most secret emotions of the heart: I could not suppress my feelings; and for once entertained an indignant wish to rid the world of such a monster.'[29]

For several days towards the end of June, the chaos of war spilled over into Ludamar. In the confusion, Park and Johnson seemed to have slipped away from Ali's men and were moving east away from Jarra towards Queira, when Ali's chief slave and four Moors caught up with them. That day, Johnson overheard the men debating whether to take Park's horse to stop him escaping – they decided it was so lame, he would not be able to ride very far.

'I dreaded nothing so much as confinement again among the Moors,' Park wrote, preferring the risk of travelling east to Bambara. Johnson by this stage had had enough, and insisted he would rather forfeit his pay than continue. In that case, Park insisted, he would go on alone.

That night, while Johnson listened to the Moors, Park assembled his belongings. Ali had confiscated all his scientific instruments except the compass, and Park had left most of his baggage in Jarra. So with two shirts, two pairs of trousers, two handkerchiefs, an upper- and an under-waistcoat, a pair of half-boots, a cloak and the hat in which he had hidden his notebooks, he prepared to make his escape. It was almost dawn before Johnson came to tell him that the Moors were finally asleep. 'The awful crisis was now arrived, when I was again either to taste freedom, or languish out my days in captivity.'[30] Park hesitated for a moment, flushed with cold sweat, and then said goodbye to Johnson, stepped over the sleeping bodies and escaped from Queira.

He had only ridden a mile or two before he came upon some shepherds. This was the first time he had been alone in Africa, and the encounter was discouraging: the shepherds threw stones at him. A little while later, three Moors came storming up, brandishing their double-barrel guns. Park's horse was in no condition to outride them, so he turned its head to face them. The men had come to take him back to Ali. 'When the human mind has for some time been fluctuating between hope and despair, tortured with anxiety, and hurried from one extreme to another,' Park noted stoically, 'it affords a sort of gloomy relief to know the worst that can possibly happen: such was my situation.'[31]

There were more twists of fortune ahead. Before they had gone too far, after the Moors had had some sort of debate, they obviously decided they would rather rob him than return him to Ali. At gunpoint, they forced him to open his bundle. The only item of any value was the cloak – 'it served to cover me from the rains in the day, and to protect me from the musketoes in the night'[32] – which they took, and then rode off, leaving him to continue alone, eastwards, in the vague direction of the Niger.

'It is impossible to describe the joy that arose in my mind, when I looked around and concluded that I was out of danger. I felt like one recovered from sickness; I breathed freer; I found unusual lightness in my limbs; even the Desert looked pleasant.' Three days later he was in newly-conquered Bambara territory.

Bambara was a kingdom of pleasures after Ludamar. The land was rich and the villagers friendly, although some were a little too curious for Park's comfort: one headman cropped one side of his head, convinced a white man's hair must have magical properties. He made good progress, too, usually after a full meal and a good night's rest. By 18 July he knew he was getting close to Segu, the Bambara capital, because things were becoming a little more difficult for him: 'owing to the great concourse of people daily going to and returning from Sego, the inhabitants are less hospitable to strangers'.[33] Among the people travelling the Segu road were a group of seventy slaves, 'tied together by their necks with thongs of a bullock's hide, twisted like a rope; seven slaves upon a thong, and a man with a musket between every seven'. They belonged to some twenty Moors who came riding along after them, following their cargo up into Ludamar, across the Sahara to the slave markets of Morocco.

On the night of 19 July, Park arrived, exhausted, at a village called Doolinkeaboo, where the headman offered him water but refused to provide food. It rained that night, so he slept badly. The following morning things appeared to have taken a turn for the worse when even the village slaves refused him food. The explanation came later when he realised they thought he was a Moor. If he was a Moor he was a poor one, for by now his horse was so exhausted that he had to walk behind it for much of the day, encouraging it along.

Another village meal, a night troubled by mosquitoes and the threat of lion, and then he was riding in the company of some people from Kaarta. It was market day in Segu, so the road became increasingly busy as they got closer. Then the ground grew marshy. Difficult to ride over, but it meant that water was near. Park started peering anxiously from one side to another, looking for the river, when one of the Kaartans pointed ahead, up the road, and said, 'Geo affili, see the water.'[34] There, across the red earth, beyond a few trees, 'I saw with infinite pleasure the great object of my mission,' the Niger, long sought and majestic, 'glittering to the morning sun, as broad as the Thames at Westminster, and flowing slowly *to the eastward*'.[35] Park hurried to the bank and knelt down to drink from the river he had risked so much to find. And then, the first recorded European to have reached the Niger, the first unquestionably successful African Association missionary, he offered up a prayer of thanks to 'the Great Ruler of all things' who had allowed such a thing to happen.

Segu Koro, old Segu, sits on the south bank of the Niger River and looks much like many Malian villages you can see today. Several mosques, their minarets pierced with wooden batons, stand out above a maze of mudbrick houses in solid Sudanic style. A clearing under a big shade tree serves as the place where women trade food, news and gossip. Nearby, in a fenced-off cemetery, lie the remains of Biton Koulibaly, the man who founded the Bambara kingdom of Segu before being buried there in 1755, forty years before Park's arrival. Today, visitors coming from the modern town of Segu, several miles upriver, are first taken to the village chief, himself a Koulibaly and descended from the original King, who requires payment in much the same way that his ancestors did centuries ago, before a visitor may enter.

Mungo Park approached Segu from the north bank. Three ferries operated from various landings along the bank, but so many people were trying to cross that he decided to sit and wait for the crowds to ease. Two hours later, he was still waiting when a courtier arrived with a message from the King, Mansong: why had the strange man with the sad horse come to Segu? What was his business? Until the King was satisfied with his answer, he was forbidden to cross the river and was sent off to stay in a nearby village. Here too he must have looked suspicious, for no one would take him into their houses or feed him. Not knowing what else to do, Park sat under a tree. It threatened to rain, and then dusk fell. Knowing there were lions and other wild animals in the neighbourhood, he was considering climbing the tree and sleeping in one of its branches, when a woman returning from her fields offered to look after him. She took him to her family compound, cooked him a very fine fish for dinner and then offered him a bed. Later, as he was trying to sleep, one of the women of the family extemporised a plaintive song in his honour:

> *The winds roared, and the rains fell.*
> *The poor white man, faint and weary, came and sat under our*
> * tree.*
> *He has no mother to bring him milk; no wife to grind his corn.*

There then followed a chorus in which all the women joined:

> *Let us pity the white man; no mother has he . . .*

Park was so moved that the following morning he cut two of the four remaining brass buttons from his waistcoat and gave them as a present to his saviour.

Two days later, Mansong, Koulibaly's descendant, sent another messenger to ask if the European had by any chance brought him any gifts. In reply, Park gave a brief version of his adventures. Experience, all those bitter, depleting experiences, should have taught him that this would not be acceptable. It probably had done, in which case he would have been expecting what came next. The following day another courtier arrived to tell him that Mansong had decreed the white man could not cross the river. But as proof that the King cared about the fate of strangers in his dominions, if the European wished to continue on his way downstream towards Djenne, he could do so. However, the King would provide protection as far as Sansanding, thirty miles away.

Park was not being offered a choice; this was not part of a discussion or a diplomatic negotiation. He understood that much quite clearly, just as he understood why the King had sent a bag of five thousand cowrie shells* 'to relieve a white man in distress'.[36]

---

* Cowrie shells, originally found in the Maldive Islands, had spread across Africa's slave routes and become accepted as a currency. These five thousand shells were worth the equivalent, at

The shells were intended to ensure that the white man would go away, that the white man would not die on his doorstep and haunt his kingdom.

Park was obviously disappointed at not being allowed to enter the city and meet the King. Yet, given his treatment in Ludamar, he must have been delighted to have been sent a present. He called Mansong a 'benevolent prince' and declared himself happy to believe what he later heard from his guide, that the King was reluctant to admit the stranger because he was unable to guarantee his safety at court due to the presence of hostile Moors. Park suspected there was another motive: 'The circumstances under which I made my appearance at Sego, were undoubtedly such as might create in the mind of the king a well-warranted suspicion that I wished to conceal the true object of my journey.' He said he had come to see the river. Were there no rivers to look at in his own country?

Six days further east along the great, shimmering, Thames-like, eastward-flowing Niger, Park found himself in a large south-bank town called Silla. The rains had started in earnest, his fever had returned with a vengeance and he was beginning to have serious doubts about the wisdom and viability of continuing in his present state. He knew Timbuktu was tantalisingly close, only fourteen days' journey by land, he had been told. With the start of the rains, the land route would soon be impassable, so he would have to go by boat. But it was unlikely he would find anyone willing to carry him, or that he would be able to pay his passage. And even if he did make his way there, he had been warned that if the Moors in Djenne did not kill him, the people of Timbuktu would. And even if he did make it in and out of Timbuktu, he then faced the prospect of continuing along a river that, he had been told, 'runs to the world's end'. Should he go on and risk dying in Djenne, or Timbuktu, or somewhere else along the way – as Houghton had done – and in the process deprive the Association of his achievements and himself

that time, of £1. A more useful measure is found in Park's comment that he could support himself and his horse on one hundred of them a day. Mansong had provided him with just enough money to keep himself alive for seven weeks, plenty of time to leave the country.

of the rewards? Or should he get home with the information he had in his head and the notes bundled up inside his hat? That night he lay in the damp hut racked with fever and indecision. The following morning, 30 July 1796, he crossed the river, *his* river, and began the long journey back to England.

10

The Golden Harvest

'I am in great expectation that our Traveller will conquer the difficulties of the Bambara Country.'

Rennell to Banks, October 1796[1]

London, 1797

EARLY ON CHRISTMAS MORNING, James Dickson was doing one of the things he loved best, attending to the gardens of the British Museum. At that time on that day he expected to have them to himself, so when someone entered, he looked up. He blanched and shuddered, believing that he was seeing a ghost. It was his brother-in-law, Mungo Park.

Park could hardly contain his delight at being in London. It was almost a year and five months since he had spent that feverish, defining night beside the Niger in the village of Silla, the rain running off the thatched roof, his chances of reaching Timbuktu and Hausa also draining away. The journey back was packed with almost as many difficulties, dangers, pains and adventures as the journey out had been, but there was a difference; by now he was seasoned in the ways and means of travel in West Africa. And cutting such a miserable figure in his worn, torn clothes, he made a far less attractive target. Not that he wasn't robbed, but by this point it was obvious to everyone, even to prospective thieves and extortionists, that he was a very poor catch. Even though he was

163

reduced to a single change of clothes and those precious notes, stored in the inner band of his hat, he was still held up. Eventually he was robbed of the only thing left to him, his clothes and boots, leaving him naked in the dirt. Happily, on that occasion his assailants then decided to return his trousers and the more ragged of his two shirts. Even more happily for posterity, at the last minute they also threw back his hat; they had seen his notes tucked inside it and feared that they contained some sort of spell. They knew better than to tamper with a white man's magic.

Swimming rain-swollen rivers, trekking through fly-ridden forests, crossing foot-ripping hills, threatened by man and beast, by bandits and lions, sun and rain, snake and mosquito, Park crossed more than six hundred miles of scrub, forest and pasture. For food and shelter, he relied on the charity of villagers, occasionally earning his keep by writing charms or allowing a little more of his hair to be cropped. The irony of this exchange cannot have been lost on him: he, the all-too-frequent victim of robbers and extortionists, a man without money or clothes, was writing magic charms designed to protect the bearer from harm and to guarantee him considerable wealth. Often he wished he really did possess the power villagers ascribed to him.

Despite the hazards and hardships and his own persistent fever, he continued moving westwards through what is now the state of Mali, passing the present capital Bamako. Two months after leaving Silla, racked with fever and slowed by the flooded countryside, he arrived at Kamalia, a village in the hilly woodlands west of Bamako. Here, in need of food and shelter, he was taken to the house of the only man who could provide it, a successful Muslim slave trader called Karfa Taura. Karfa greeted him with warmth and civility, and assured him that it would be impossible to continue to the coast in his condition and during the rainy season. 'When a caravan of natives could not travel through the country,' Karfa assured him, 'it was idle for a single white man to attempt it.'² Houghton might have gone on regardless, but experience had taught Park to accept local advice. He decided to stay, and reached an agreement with the slaver: Karfa, for his part, would care for the stranger, provide him with a hut, a mat and water jar. 'Karfa now looked at me with great earnestness,' Park remembered fondly, 'and inquired if I could eat the common victuals of the country – assuring me he had never before seen a white man.'[3] When Park explained that there had been days when he had been happy to beg for the 'common victuals of the country', the matter was settled. Come the dry season, Karfa would take his guest along with him when he went to the Gambia to deliver a shipment of slaves. In return, Park promised to give the trader the price of a slave – some £20 – when they reached the river. But when they did eventually reach Dr Laidley's house, Park was so happy with the generous treatment he had received that he decided to pay the slaver £40. 'Karfa,' Park recorded, 'was overpowered by this unexpected token of my gratitude.'[4] Dickson and Mungo's sister were equally overpowered by his appearance in London that Christmas Day.

From Dickson's house, Park went to pay his respects to his patrons. Henry Beaufoy had died in May 1795, just a week before Park left England, although it is not clear whether the traveller knew about this before he sailed. At the end of that year, just before he left Laidley's house, Park had received a letter in which Banks explained, with his usual erratic punctuation, 'I have undertaken the Office of Secretary [as well as Treasurer] for a time but I shall soon give it up I have so many things to do that in truth I should not have done it now if it had not been that I had such expectations from you & was unwilling that your affairs should be conducted by any one else I will take care when I give it up to see every thing concerning you properly managd [sic].'[5] And so he had.

Park hurried round to Soho Square with his notes, which he had worked on during the long sea passage from Africa via the Caribbean, and also some of the botanical specimens he had collected. Banks was delighted, and hailed the return of the explorer as a double victory: he was the first Association missionary to reach the interior and live to tell the tale, and he had seen the Niger. Here was the long-awaited success, the geographical breakthrough. Park had proved that it was possible to travel from the Gambia to the Niger, had proved the direction of the river's flow, and been just a boat ride away from reaching the geographical grail of golden Timbuktu. This was an achievement that could be understood by even the most uninterested of people, and Banks wasted no time in making capital out of it. On 4 January 1798, both the *London Chronicle* and the *St. James' Chronicle or British Evening Post* carried a mention of Park's having travelled further into Africa than any of his predecessors. Three weeks later, the *True Briton* and *The Times* ran bigger stories about the Scot's discoveries, *The Times* allowing its enthusiasm to get the better of the facts and reporting that he had located the great city of Hausa on the Niger near Timbuktu, that it was twice the size of London and that great interest had been shown in his English manufactures. Just a couple of weeks after returning to England, Park emerged blinking into the new year of 1798 to find that he was a celebrity.

His return could not have been better timed. The war against France was going badly and the nation needed diverting from the gloom over Europe. In 1796 Spain had sided with Napoleon, further strengthening Bonaparte's hand. Fifteen thousand French troops had then attempted a landing in Ireland, clearly a prelude to a move against mainland Britain. The French army was defeated by bad weather, but a smaller force comprising six hundred mostly French convicts, led by an elderly American called William Tate, did manage to get ashore on the Welsh coast near Fishguard in February 1797. They were soon rounded up, and surrendered in the Royal Oak pub.* But however unlikely, the possibility of French republican soldiers fighting their way towards London, Bath or Brighton was keenly felt, particularly by the wealthy and the aristocratic, sensitive to the guillotined fate of the French nobility. Banks obviously thought the threat was real enough, for he mentioned it in a letter to his old friend Sir William Hamilton, the British Minister in Naples and, it should be added, a Fellow of the Royal Society: 'We are here threatened with an invasion which every well informed person really believes will soon be undertaken and yet we eat and drink and sleep

---

* The Royal Oak in Fishguard still displays memorabilia of the last invasion of Britain. Among the local stories is that of Jemima Nicholas, said to have frightened a dozen Frenchmen into submission with her pitchfork.

I think as comfortably as I ever remember us to have done. As danger approaches . . . domestic harmony increases.'[6] Since then the French had defeated the Austrian army, and in the year of Park's return the unthinkable had happened: some of the Royal Navy's 114,000 sailors had mutinied, blocking the Thames to add weight to their demands for better pay and conditions and the retirement of less capable officers. Into this gloom Park's return was seen as a ray of sunshine. 'The man who had found the Niger' was living proof that Britons were capable of great and meaningful achievements.

Park was propelled into London society by Banks and Earl Spencer, an active member of the African Association for the past five years (he was to become its chairman in 1823) and brother of the notorious Georgiana, Duchess of Devonshire. The Scot was not cut out for London's shifting allegiances, rivalries and extravagances. The great age of social madness, when Georgiana and her confidante, Lady Elizabeth Foster, earned their reputations for wild living and even wilder debts, was over, but wit and artifice were still essential skills for a *mondaine* and gambling still a social accomplishment. A crofter's son turned doctor, turned botanist, turned explorer was not naturally endowed to flourish in this environment. The demands were continuous and specific: hostesses wanted to be transported to the tropics, while their husbands hoped to hear first-hand his tales of the slave trade and the prospects for 'improvements', of adventure and outrage and, given the sexual licence of some members of the *beau monde*, certainly also of his amorous adventures (Banks, after all, had had plenty to tell on that score on his return from Cook's second voyage).

For a while, Park's story stirred the imagination of many in Britain, perhaps none more so than the Duchess of Devonshire. Georgiana was particularly struck by the events on the night of his arrival at the Niger, when he had been left out in a storm, rescued by a village woman and invited to her home. The Duchess, who had already shown her literary skills by publishing a dire novel, now turned her hand to poetry and reworked the chant of the Niger women. From the original verse, which had started 'The winds roared and the rains fell . . .', she now conjured 'A Negro Song':

The loud wind roar'd, the rain fell fast;
The White Man yielded to the blast:
He sat him down, beneath our tree;
For weary, sad, and faint was he;
And ah, no wife, or mother's care,
For him, the milk or corn prepare.
(Chorus)
The White Man, shall our pity share;
Alas, no wife or mother's care,
For him the milk or corn prepare.

The storm is o'er; the tempest past;
And Mercy's voice had hush'd the blast.
The wind is heard in whispers low;
The White Man far away must go;–
But ever in his heart will bear
Remembrance of the Negro's care.
(Chorus)
Go, White Man, go; – but with thee bear
The Negro's wish, the Negro's prayer;
*Remembrance of the Negro's care.**

Park was flattered and included the Duchess' literary present in the first edition of his *Travels*, ascribing it to 'a Lady, who is not more distinguished for her rank, than for her beauty and her accomplishments'.[7] He also included the music to which the Italian composer G.G. Ferrari set the song. To this, Lady Elizabeth Foster added an engraving showing Park slumped under a palm, with several Africans encouraging him towards a nearby hut.

* The poet Coleridge seemed to approve of the Duchess' poetic efforts, for he wrote:
  'O lady, nursed in pomp and pleasure,
  Whence learned you that heroic measure?'

However much Park enjoyed the attention, he found it hard to perform. After all he had gone through along the Niger, he had more recently spent months being tossed and turned on the Atlantic, first on his way to Antigua and then to Falmouth. And as he had shown in Africa, humour and a lightness of touch were not his most prominent qualities. It was not long before the sheen wore off and London's fascination with his novelty and celebrity gave way to vitriol. Lady Holland was not alone when she confided this to her journal and posterity: 'A person who was sent about two years ago to explore the interior parts of Africa is just returned. He is a Scotchman of the name of M. Park, very much protected by Sir Joseph Banks, and esteemed a man of veracity. He has neither fancy or genius, and if he does fib it is dully.'[8] Another, more generous observer described him as having 'the manners and dignities of his Niger kings', certainly meant as a backhanded compliment. Another commentator described him as 'quite unspoilt and without vanity or affectation; indeed, strangers who looked to him for animation and lively conversation found instead considerable coldness and reserve'. Whether it was the shock of his return, the effects of his illnesses or some other cause, Park, the man who had confessed to his brother before leaving for Africa his ambition to distinguish himself, seems to have found little pleasure in being lionised in London. Within months the flow of invitations to balls, breakfasts and soirées had dried up, which was just as well, for he had some writing to do.

Park had made detailed notes in Africa whenever it was safe for him to do so, and had made use of the long journey home by getting them into better shape and order. But there was still a great deal of work to be done before they could be shown to the public. Rennell also had work to do on the quadrant and compass readings Park had made as far as Jarra and the notes he had kept thereafter, especially since Banks was keen to make some of this material available to members at the Association's next annual meeting late in May. The pressure was on. Banks' many other responsibilities meant that he had less time to devote to the Association, especially after 1797, when he was appointed to the Privy Council, the King's inner circle.* Happily help was at hand in the shape of the Association's new Secretary, Bryan Edwards, himself a talented author.

It is typical of the nature of the Association that the new Secretary would come from within its ranks, but given the strong Abolitionist tendencies of many of the members – and remembering Beaufoy's own thundering damnation of the slave trade in Parliament nine years earlier – Bryan Edwards was a curious choice.

Edwards was the same age as Banks, fifty-five in 1798, and like Banks his father had died young, but that is where similarities end, because Edwards' father left his family destitute. Yet by the time he was thirty he was living in Jamaica and had inherited two estates. Over the next decade he made enough of a fortune to return to England, and in 1792 he set up house in London's Upper Wimpole Street and opened a bank in Southampton. It is not clear when he first met Banks, but in 1794, after the publication of his well-received *History of the British West Indies*, which the *Gentleman's Magazine* described as 'a monument more lasting than marble',[9] he was elected a Fellow of the Royal Society. By then he was also calling himself the Deputy Secretary of the Association, a post he appears to have taken seriously, insisting that 'negligence and inattention shall not be justly imputed to me'.[10] He also seems to have shared with Banks an appetite for enjoyment that sometimes went against the image of an Academician and historian: in June 1794, for instance, he wrote to Banks that he had just arrived at his house in Southampton from the most distant parts of Cornwall and that he needed to rest before going up to London, because he was both tired and disordered by 'the very becoming amusement at my time of life of dancing with Tinkers' wives and Blacksmiths' daughters on the wet

---

* Banks' appointment drew a stinging response from the satirist John Wolcot, who wrote this attack under the name of Peter Pindar:

> 'After a butterfly to scamper,
> And with a net his captive hamper,
> Sir Joseph is expert, and must delight;
> But as for politics!–O Heav'n!
> The Board must very hard be driv'n,
> To choose a swearing Tadpole Knight!'

(quoted in Lyte, p.211)

grass'.[11] But on one key issue, Edwards differed with Banks and many other members of the Association: the issue of abolition.

In the same letter of 14 June, Edwards complained to Banks about the Association's apparent anti-slaving attitude.

> *Hitherto the motives and labours of the Association have been considered by the Merchants and Masters of Ships trading from Liverpool to Africa* as hostile to the slave trade; *and under this idea, they are accused (by Major Houghton particularly) of obstructing every attempt to reach the interior country. Surely it is not necessary to make these men our enemies! Many of the slave captains are known to me personally; and I am persuaded I can prevail upon some of the most intelligent among them to co-operate with and materially promote the views of the Society.*[12]

Banks' reply is not on record, but, however conciliatory, it must surely have pointed out that the Association and a considerable section of the British public were hostile to the slave trade. Edwards' position was complicated. He may not have liked the slave trade, but he was against abolition for two reasons: he could see no other way of maintaining the Caribbean plantations (his and others'), and he believed that freed slaves would have problems finding work and supporting themselves, as had already proved to be the case in parts of England.

Unlike Banks, Edwards had political ambitions and had secured a seat in Parliament. The Speaker of the House of Commons, who clearly did not like the newcomer, described him as 'a heavy-looking man' whose speech was 'very awkward and inelegant'.[13] Whatever his lack of graces, by 1797 Edwards was Acting Secretary to the Association, and the following year had assumed responsibility for working on Park's notes.

There were to be two accounts of Park's voyage. The first was 'an epitome or abstract of his principal discoveries', as the Association called it, mostly to be written by Edwards and published privately for members of the Association. The second would be a more complete version that Park would write and offer for sale to the public. Wanting to get away from London society, Park went to stay with Edwards in Southampton to write the 'epitome'. Progress was slow, and Edwards found it frustrating to work with Park. But by the end of February 1798 the Secretary was able to write to Banks, 'The Papers came safe, and I have made as many corrections as I can ... I have likewise added some curious anecdotes with which Park furnished me – but I know not if the rules of Decorum will allow me to retain them all. One of them relates to the Holy Water, which he received, in consequence of a Moorish Wedding, as a Nuptial benediction from the Bride. He will tell you the story and it is a choice one.'[14]* A month later the Committee had met and approved the *Abstract*, as it was now called, for the printer.

While Park's African adventures were easily dressed up for the members' entertainment, assessing the geographical significance of his journey presented more problems. Banks seemed oblivious to this when he wrote again to his friend Hamilton in Naples, this time in March 1798:

> *We have just now received a missionary from Africa who has made most interesting discoveries. He has penetrated into Africa by way of the Gambia near a thousand miles in a strait [sic] line from Cap Verde so that his Tour has been about equal to what we call the Tour of the South of Europe. He has discovered a river taking its source in the same mountains as the Senegal and Gambia but running eastward. This river he has traced for more than 300 miles from the point where it first became navigable till it was larger than the Thames at London. His adventures are interesting in a degree he will publish them soon and I will send you the book.*[15]

The task of explaining the intricacies of Park's contribution to geography, beyond comparing them to a Riviera tour, fell to James Rennell. 'I rejoice to hear that Parks is safe,' Rennell had written to Banks towards the end of 1797, 'altho' he can tell us nothing about Tombuctoo.' Then he added with a sense of resignation,

---

* Park may have told the story to Banks, but it was not included in the *Travels*.

'There seems to be a spell upon that road.'[16] It was not until well into the new year that Rennell saw the details of Park's journey and the second-hand information he had collected on Timbuktu, Hausa and the course of the Niger. In February Park paid him a visit at his home in Brighton. His work must have been well underway by then because, as with the *Abstract*, Rennell's *Geographical Illustrations of Mr. Park's Journey* needed to be printed in time for the Association's meeting late in May.

'The inland geography of that vast continent ... had been less invisible to the Arabian Moors than to any other nation.' So wrote the great historian of the age, Edward Gibbon. Gibbon had taken an interest in African geography towards the end of his life and along with his patron, Lord Sheffield, had become an early member of the Association. Gibbon died in 1794, before the age he had done so much to enlighten was able to emulate the geographical achievements of the ancients and correct the mistakes of the Arabs and Moors. Rennell opens his *Geographical Illustrations*, the longest of the essays he wrote for the Association, by singing Park's praises: 'The late journey of Mr. Park, into the interior of Western Africa, has brought to our knowledge more important facts respecting its geography (both *moral* and *physical*), than have been collected by any former traveller.'[17] But where Edwards could talk up the explorer's bravery and fortitude and boast about 'choice' stories, Rennell had to admit to gaps in knowledge. Park had confirmed the existence and direction of the Niger, but he had failed to discover its end and had not reached Timbuktu or what the Committee had called the 'considerable Empire distinguished by the name of Houssa'.[18] 'It must be acknowledged,' Rennell goes on to point out, 'that the absolute extent of Mr. Park's progress in Africa, compared with the amazing size of that continent, appears but small, although it be nearly 1100 British miles in a direct line ... But it affords a triumph to the learned, in that it confirms some points of fact, both of geography and natural history, which have appeared in ancient authors, but to which our want of knowledge has denied credit.'[19]

The medieval geographers Abul Feda and al-Idrissi, among

others, had described the Niger flowing westwards into the Atlantic. Even Leo Africanus, who had seen the river, described it as rising out of 'a certain desert to the east, called Seu, or springeth out of a lake, and after a long race, falleth at length into the western Ocean'.[20] Now Park had confirmed the opinion of the ancients, of Herodotus, Pliny and Ptolemy: the Niger flowed eastwards into the interior.

Rennell then aimed a few arrows at more recent geographers, particularly the great Frenchman, d'Anville. 'Concerning the errors of former geographers,' he confessed, 'they are more easily detected than the *causes* for them.'[21] He then went on to make more mistakes of his own, although in his defence it must be pointed out that he was not helped in his task by the extraordinary amount of incorrect second-hand information the Association had accumulated over the previous ten years. To this was added the confusion over the similarity of names: there are several Medinas, for instance, and the names of Ghana, Ginny and Ginea were understood to be interchangeable, even though, as Ghana, Djenne and Guinea they are many hundreds of miles apart. So when Rennell stated the 'fact' that Ginny, which he understood to be Ghana but was meant to be the Malian city of Djenne, was forty days' travelling from Timbuktu, he was literally heading in the wrong direction.

The most significant claims in Rennell's 160-page work concern the two great rivers, the Niger and the Nile. The question of the rise and course of the Niger, 'the prince of the western rivers of Africa', had been answered 'by ocular demonstration'.[22] But that of its end had not. Rennell weighed up the options. Did it flow into the centre of the continent and there join the Nile, as some Arab authors had claimed? Did it run into a great salt lake in the middle of the continent? Or did it turn south and run out into the Atlantic? The occasion called for a judgement, and he was better placed than anyone else to make it.

Park and others made mention of a range of mountains that could be seen running east–west on the horizon to the south of the Niger. To these had been given the name the Mountains of Kong. Rennell showed them as running from the Gambia River to the centre of the continent. With these in place he then argued that with such an impenetrable barrier, the Niger could not turn south and flow into the ocean. Also, his knowledge of the different altitudes of the Niger at Segu and the Nile in Abyssinia convinced him that, unless water could flow uphill, these two streams could not be connected. And so, quoting the reports that Park had brought home, the testimony of the Moor Ben Ali and references to earlier writings, Rennell concluded that, 'on the whole, it can scarcely be doubted that the Joliba or Niger terminates in lakes in the eastern quarter of Africa'.[23]

This less than emphatic statement reveals his unease at having to state an opinion on a subject about which he was still ambivalent. Explaining that the Niger's end in the African lakes could 'scarcely be doubted' left open the possibility that doubts could occur, especially since the existence of the lakes had yet to be proved by 'ocular demonstration'. But one thing Rennell's *Map shewing the Progress of Discovery & Improvement in the Geography of North Africa* did unequivocally was to show the advances that had been made in understanding the relations between the Gambia, Senegal and Niger rivers and the southernmost extent of the Sahara, at least as far as Timbuktu. The boundaries of a number of nations – Kasson, Kaarta, Ludamar among others – could now also be drawn with some certainty. With plenty to feel proud about, Rennell's work was approved along with Edwards' *Abstract* and sent off to the printers.

There is a strangely subdued note to the minutes of the general meeting of 1798. Even more strangely, there is no mention of Park being present, although an advertisement in *The Times* on 25 May announced that he would be there. At the Star and Garter Tavern in Pall Mall on Saturday, 26 May, members resolved 'that Mr. Park has obeyed his Instructions as far as was practicable, and executed the purposes of his Mission with a degree of Industry, perseverance and ability that entitle him to the warm approbation of the Association'.[24] Given his achievements, it is hard to imagine more mean-spirited praise. But members then made up for any lack of generosity in the wording of their resolution by agreeing to continue paying Park's salary of 7/6 a day for the following year while he wrote the fuller account of his journey. They also agreed to allow him to publish the book 'for his own emolument, under the Sanction and Patronage of this Association'.[25] Wanting to show support for a man whose friendship he clearly valued, Banks then came forward to open a list of subscribers to Park's work, writing his own name down for one of the first copies.

In the middle of May, Banks turned Park's attention to another part of the world and asked for his opinion of a plan to explore New Holland, now known as Australia. It was a decade since the First Fleet had gone out to create the prison colony in New South Wales, time enough for it to have become painfully clear that nothing the colony produced and nothing the colonists had found around them was worthy of being exported to Britain. Banks was convinced, as he wrote to John King, Under-Secretary of State at the Home Office, that further exploration would change all that. He was equally sure that 'such a body of land, as large as all Europe' would have 'vast rivers, capable of being navigated into the interior'.[26] Having at hand a man who had just made a similar sort of journey, Banks asked him for his thoughts on the proposal. It is not clear whether he wanted Park to volunteer for the job, but that is precisely what he did. On 15 May, Banks wrote to Under-Secretary King suggesting Park as the ideal man for the mission. Perhaps remembering the enormous amount of government money squandered on Willis' failed mission as Consul to Senegambia, and knowing that cost was a key factor at this time of war, he added, 'He [Park] is very moderate in his terms, contented with 10s. a day and his rations *and happy if his pay is settled at 12s.* The amount of his outfit for Instruments, arms, presents, etc., will not I think exceed £100.'[27] At its meeting of 26 May, the African Association had voted to recommend their explorer for the New Holland expedition, and by June, when he left for Scotland, Park must have been confident that he would soon be on his way south.

He was back in London at the end of the summer, and on 9 September was at the Home Office in Whitehall to meet Secretary King and discuss the expedition. The Lieutenant-Governor of the New South Wales colony was also present; it was hoped that Park would sail with him in ten days' time. Apparently King was unable to find Banks' letter, so when they came to the subject of remuneration, he suggested a salary of not twelve but ten shillings a day, and omitted to mention any funds for equipment.

Park did not express any doubts to King about the viability of the expedition or the possibility of his involvement, but he soon wrote to Banks explaining that he had decided not to go. Banks was furious, pointed out that 'till your absense [sic] from London you always appeared to solicit [the appointment] with eagerness'[28] and summoned Park to Spring Grove, his house in Heston, outside London, to explain himself. Banks' humour cannot have been helped by the fact that he was suffering from an acute attack of gout – for the first time in his adult life he had not been well enough to make his annual visit to his Derbyshire estate. At Spring Grove, with James Dickson present, Park aired his grievance over pay – ten shillings a day was less than the African Association had paid while he was in Africa. Did his achievements and experience count for nothing? Banks made it clear that bureaucratic bungling, not deception, was behind the mistake. When the explorer left, Banks clearly thought the matter settled. One can therefore imagine his annoyance when Park admitted to him on 20 September that 'those triffling [sic] misunderstandings have considerably dampened that enthusiasm, which prompts to, and is necessary to ensure the success of such an enterprise'.[29] He was not going on the expedition.

Banks, still tormented by gout, replied the next day. 'In all my former Transactions with you, I never noticed you to be more than properly attentive to pecuniary considerations. I am astonished to find your Enthusiasm dampt by the small difference between the pay you had taught yourself to expect and that really offer'd to you, because real Enthusiasm, which you certainly possess, is very little sway'd by pecuniary motives.'[30] But Banks, who had signed himself 'your friend and well wisher', was not to give up so easily: that same day he wrote to ask King for more money, and two days later was able to reassure Park that the government would pay him 12s.6d. a day and guarantee that he would be properly equipped. Park waited three days before replying. 'Pecuniary concerns, however contemptible in themselves, serve as a good criterion by which to estimate the importance or inutility of any office or pursuit; and, tho' my fancy had painted this as a Voyage of some Importance, I found that Government considered it in a very different light . . .'[31] He had a good point, but money was not the only thing keeping him from this latest adventure: during the months in Scotland he had fallen in love and was now engaged to be married. An absence of several years was out of the question, and the dangers he was likely to face had to be avoided at all costs. Also, given his continuing desire for a place in history, it would be extremely rash to take on the risks of a new expedition before he had written the full account of his last one.

Park never mentioned the romance to his patron, who heard about it from his trusty friend Dickson. 'I have found out from his sister, which is my wife,' the seedsman wrote from his business in Covent Garden, 'that there is some private connection, a love affair in Scotland, but no money in it (what a pity it is men should be such fools that might be of use to their country), that is the cause of it; and, should such a thing take place, he is burying himself and his talents, a thing which both his sister and me disapproves much of.'[32]

It might have been an explanation, but to a man of Banks' mind it was definitely not an excuse, especially since it left him having to write an apologetic letter to the Home Office. Banks was quick to condemn the young man, explained that his protégé would not travel and expressed his regret at 'having put my confidence in this fickle Scotsman'.[33]

Edwards offered Banks his sympathy. 'I grieve exceedingly to hear that your health is so poorly,' he wrote from Southampton, 'and am mortified and surprised that Park should add to the vexation of your illness by his fickle and perverse conduct. I have been hard at work for him for the last six weeks. I have corrected and newly arranged all the papers he put in my hands, and, after transcribing the whole with my own pen, I have employed a clerk to make a fair copy. What I have done constitutes, however, but a small part of the work. I have yet brought him no further than Jarra [at the entry to Ludamar]. His imprisonment among the Moors, his discoveries to the Eastward and his return along the Niger remain yet to be described, and this will constitute the most interesting part of the Book and the pleasantest also to the transcriber.'[34] Edwards then aired his own frustration with Park, writing, 'It is not my fault that I have not done more, for have exhausted all the original MSS and have written without effect to Park to furnish me with the remainder.'[35]

Once the issue of the Australian expedition was settled, Park went back to work on his African story. Edwards clearly had a very poor opinion of Park's literary abilities, writing in October to tell Banks that he was working on the narrative up to the point that the explorer was taken by the Moors, 'after which, his story becomes sufficiently interesting and he cannot spoil it in the telling. Previous to his captivity, there is such a sameness in the Negro manners, and the occurrences which he relates are so unimportant, that it requires some skill in composition and arrangement.'[36] A month later, not only was the air cleared, but Park seems to have discovered a previously unsuspected talent, for Edwards describes his account of his captivity as 'extremely well done. I have only divided it into chapters of the same size as those that are gone to the press; and corrected a few verbal inaccuracies.'[37]

By October, Park had written half his story, and by late January 1799 he was on the homeward stretch. Edwards, realising the end was in sight, was clearly relieved. 'Park goes on triumphantly. He improves in his style so much by practice that his journal now requires but little correction; and some parts, which he has lately sent me, are equal to anything in the English Language.'[38] Park himself was more sanguine, insisting that his book 'has nothing to recommend it but *truth*. It is,' he went on, 'a plain unvarnished tale, without pretensions of any kind, except that it claims to enlarge, in some degree, the circle of African geography.'[39] Whatever its literary merits – and Park certainly did not have the talent of later African travellers such as Richard Burton or Wilfred Thesiger – the book-buying public expressed their approval of *Travels into the Interior of Africa* in the only way they could, with their money. Four hundred people or institutions had subscribed to the first edition, the King's Library among them, but when the *Travels* was published in April 1799, the entire print run of fifteen hundred copies was sold in a week. It is a figure that some travel writers in our own time fail to match with their first books, while Park's royalties are likely to have them wishing they too had been writing at the end of the eighteenth century: gross receipts from the first edition were £2363, of which Park pocketed £1050, or almost 45 per cent. Two subsequent editions appeared and were sold before the end of the year, to which was added a French translation, something that Banks, while openly championing the free exchange of ideas and scientific information between Britain and France during the Napoleonic wars, watched with alarm.

The *Gentleman's Magazine* made no exaggeration when it observed that 'Few books of Voyages and Travels have been more favourably received.'[40] Mention was made of the book's authenticity, its simplicity of style and the excitement of its story. The magazine also listed Park's achievements: the settling of the direction of the Niger (and proving, in the process, the authority of Herodotus), the confirmation of trans-Saharan caravan routes, and the presence of Jews in Timbuktu and Muslims throughout the region. And while his story confirmed the ferocity of the Moors, it also showed that 'the Negroes of these districts are not to be considered an uncivilized race; they have religion, established governments, laws, schools, commerce, manufactures, *wars*! The mode of supporting foreigners among them does great honour both to their humanity and to their police.'[41] And if there was any doubt as to the accuracy of Park's speculations, the magazine assured its readers that 'The labours of the African Association will verify, we doubt not, many of the author's conjectures.'

In his *Travels*, Park remembered that the slave trader Karfa Taura, having saved his life, had asked him 'with great seriousness, what could possibly induce me, who was no trader, to think of exploring so miserable a country as Africa'. Park had given his own reason for travelling at the beginning of the narrative: 'I had a passionate desire to examine into the productions of a country so little known, and to become experimentally acquainted with the modes of life and character of the natives.'[42] It would have been just as truthful, more so perhaps, to have mentioned that he was also driven by a desire for glory and the need for money, that he had seized the chance to make something of himself. As for why the Association wanted to send him, a succinct explanation was provided by the *Quarterly Review*: 'Park is employed by a small but select society of literary characters, at their own expense, to ascertain a geographical fact, which had divided the opinions of the western world for more than two thousand years.'[43] Reasons for their wanting to ascertain that fact emerged at the next general meeting of the Association, on 25 May 1799.

It was expected that Edwards, as Secretary, would spell out the Association's progress in African exploration, while Banks would sum up their financial situation and prospects. But two weeks before the meeting Edwards wrote to Banks from his London house with bad news.

> *My health which has been very precarious all this winter, is now so exceedingly bad that I find myself under the absolute necessity of leaving town immediately. I shall stay at South-ampton a few weeks to try the Salt water, and from thence proceed to Bath. You have no idea of what I suffer from nervous headaches. I sometimes think that my time is nearly come and that I have soon a much longer Journey to undertake than poor Park's. At all events, I shall not forget, while I have memory, your friendship towards me.*[44]

In spite of the fatalistic tone, he hoped to be back in London for the meeting, although, given the apparent seriousness of his illness, it seemed doubtful he would make it. As the month went on, Banks prepared his own speech for the members.

Banks no longer viewed the world in the same way as he had when he looked at the map of Africa in 1788 and dreamed of what might be found in the interior. The world order had been torn apart first by the consequences of American independence and then by the French Revolution. French armies now seemed unstoppable, as Napoleon took control of central Europe and a large part of Italy, including the Vatican. Diplomacy had won over the Dutch, while impotence had forced the Spaniards into a treaty. A year earlier, Bonaparte had led his army on a successful invasion of Egypt, removing for the moment the threat of the invasion of Britain, but raising the spectre of France controlling the shortest route to India and the Far East, and being in a position to strike into the heart of Africa. That threat had begun to recede in July 1798 when Nelson destroyed the French fleet off the Egyptian coast at the Battle of the Nile, but the French were still the major power in Europe. The shadow cast by French domination loomed over Banks as he rose to address members at the tavern in Pall Mall on a Saturday late in May 1799.

He started by giving the latest news of Park, making it clear that their argument over the Australian expedition was behind them, for, having expressed his disappointment in Ledyard, Lucas and Houghton, he called Park a credit both to himself and the Association. He heaped praise on his 'Strength to make exertions; constitution to endure fatigue; temper to conciliate; patience under insult; courage to undertake hazardous enterprises, when practicable; and judgment to set limits to his adventure'.[45] These were not the words of an angry or bitter man.

Banks then turned to the Association's achievements. 'We have already by Mr. Park's means opened a Gate into the Interior of Africa, into which it is easy for every Nation to enter and to extend its commerce and Discovery from the West to the Eastern side of that immense continent. The passage by Land, from the Navigable waters of the Gambia to those of the Joliba is not more than . . . days march.' Curiously, the number of days was left blank on Banks' pages, but it is easy to imagine Rennell leaning forward to help him out with a rough figure. Banks may have paused, but he was still in his stride, and he now outlined his plan for a Gambia–Niger link. 'A detachment of 500 chosen Troops would soon make that Road easy, and would Build Embarkations upon the Joliba – if 200 of these were to embark with Field pieces they would be able to overcome the whole Forces which Africa could bring against them.'[46]

There is no record of any response from the members that day, neither gasps, nor mutterings of 'Hear! Hear!', but from where we stand it is an extraordinary statement and a measure of how much the ambitions of the Association had changed since its founding. Ten years earlier it had called for the interior of Africa to be explored because it was concerned that Greek and Roman geographers knew more about the continent than they and their contemporaries. Five years later, in 1793, Houghton's report on the King of Wuli encouraged the Association to call for a British consul to be installed on the Gambia River, 'unquestionably a part of the British dominions',[47] to encourage and protect British traders travelling on the 'road' to Timbuktu. Now, six years later, with the country bruised by its war, Banks was calling for five hundred British troops to blast their way along 'Park's river' into central Africa. This was a turning point for the African Association and a crucial moment in British and African history. Ideas about what they should do when they got there had also progressed.

In 1793 the Association had suggested controlling for 'Great Britain the trade which is now carried on by the Barbary States to the Inland Nations of the Continent',[48] calculating it to be worth more than the trade along the entire West African coast. By 1799 it had put a figure to that speculation: 'The Trade which the Moors carry on . . . to the Towns Situated on or near the River,' Banks confidently assured his friends and colleagues that day, 'is said to produce an annual Return of about a Million Sterling – much of it in Gold.'[49]

Here again was that utopian dream of El Dorado, spawned by the memory of the generosity of the great Malian King, Mansa Musa, who had flooded Cairo with gold in the fourteenth century. Banks now hitched that dream to his favourite doctrine, Improvement:

> *The Rivers that empty themselves into the Mother Stream [Niger] generally abound in this Metal [gold], and the natives are well experienced in the art of collecting it, in the form of Dust, near their mouths.*
>
> *If Science should teach these ignorant Savages, that the Gold which is Dust at the mouth of a river must be in the form of Sand at a high part of the Current, of Gravel in a still more elevated Situation, or of Pebbles when near the place from whence it was originally washed, as was the case at Wicklow where Gold was found at the Summit of a Mountain, many pieces being of more than an Ounce weight and one of more than a pound, is it not probable that the Golden harvest they are already in the habit of gathering might be encreased [sic] an hundred fold?[50]*

It was all speculation, of course, although perhaps not entirely unfounded: Banks' wild estimate of the value of trade along the Niger happened to match exactly the gross income British slave traders were earning from the sale of slaves in America,[51] a fact that cannot have been lost on the Abolitionists, nor on Edwards' personal contacts, the slave captains. In contrast to the prospects for the slave trade, which looked increasingly unattractive given the growing move against the trade in both Britain and France, Banks saw a rosy, healthy, profitable future for the Niger trade under British control.

On 29 May 1799, four days after the general meeting, Banks and the Earl of Moira put these thoughts into a memorandum, which Banks then sent to his old friend the Earl of Liverpool, a Cabinet member and President of the Board of Trade. Banks, as a Privy Councillor, knew how pressed the government were in this time of war and crisis: 'It is scarce possible to gain a moment's audience on any subject but those which stand foremost in their minds,'[52] he complained to the Governor of the New South Wales colony. Perhaps because of this, in his letter to Lord Liverpool Banks went further than he had done at the Association's meeting: 'The first step of Government must be to secure to the British throne, either by Conquest or by Treaty the whole of the Coast of Africa from Arguin [Cap Blanco in present-day Mauritania] to Sierra Leone; or at least to procure the cession of the River Senegal, as that River will always afford an easy passage to any rival nation who means to molest the Countries on the banks of the Joliba.'[53] The shift in the Association's intentions, from scientific enquiry to military intervention and colonisation, was drastic, but the advantages were obvious to Banks: benign government for Africans, the gradual spread of the 'mild morality' of Christianity, the blocking of the slave trade, the application of Science to exploit West Africa's gold reserves and the boosting both of Britain's international trade and its home-based factories. All this was a far cry from the fortified trading post called for six years earlier. It was also a most fertile seed, which sprouted roots and was to develop, late in the next century, into an urge among European powers to colonise Africa. Banks also knew that many Africans would reject European intervention; five years earlier he had heard from John Symmonds, a fellow Saturday's Club member, that Africans in Sierra Leone had told him, 'this is not white man's country, this belong to black man, who will not suffer white man to be master here, as he is in the East, and West Indies'.[54]

History is full of 'if's, full of speculations about what might have happened if events had taken a different turn, leaders made other decisions, or people behaved otherwise. Banks' speech suggests another one: if there had been no war with France, he would not have been so troubled by French intentions, and there may not have been this urge to colonise Africa. But there was a war, and it was clearly the French Banks was referring to when he warned that,

'If this Country delays much longer to possess themselves of the Treasures laid open to them by the exertions of this Association, some Rival Nation will take possession of the Banks of the Joliba, and assert by arms her right of Prior possession, should we afterwards attempt to participate in the benefits of this New Trade, or in the honor [sic] of exploring Nations which are yet unknown to Europe.'[55]

Banks knew of several reasons to fear French intentions in Africa. As the anonymous author of *A Historical and Philosophical Sketch of the Discoveries and Settlements of the Europeans in Northern & Western Africa at the close of the Eighteenth Century*, published in Edinburgh at this time, pointed out, the French occupation of Egypt 'must inevitably attract the gold-trade of the interior regions of Africa, which was probably, at the most ancient periods, the principal source of the power of the Egyptians'. If this wasn't serious enough, there were more specific French threats to British ambitions in Africa. Through M. Jean Charretié, the French Commissioner in London, Banks had received copies of papers read at the Institut National in Paris. Among them was one from the brilliant Foreign Minister Talleyrand. Entitled *The advantage to be gained from new colonies in the present circumstances* and read before the Institut in July 1797, it called for, among other things, the creation of a new colony near the Gambia River.[56] In 1798, Talleyrand, encouraging Bonaparte in his expedition against Egypt, had predicted that 'we will penetrate into every part of the immense continent of Africa and discover there the rivers of the interior, the mountains and the mines of iron and of gold in which that country abounds'.[57]

It was as blunt a declaration of intent as could be made, and it was one that had shaken Banks. But by then, he had the reassurance of knowing that the Association already had a brilliant explorer travelling the road that Talleyrand coveted.

11

The Göttingen Connection

'At no period of time has the spirit of enterprise been more active than the present, nor at any time has the eagerness for discoveries been more amply rewarded.'

European Magazine, June 1799

London, 1796

THE AFRICAN ASSOCIATION'S new traveller was a German by the name of Frederick Hornemann. To understand how he came to Banks' attention, we must go back several years and consider Banks' relationship with another German, a brilliant scientist called Johann Blumenbach.

'I certainly wish that my Country men should make discoveries of all kinds in preference to the inhabitants of other Kingdoms,'[1] Banks wrote to the French Geographer-Royal Buache de la Neuville in November 1788. But over the next ten years only one Englishman was employed by the Association, and he was the courtier Simon Lucas, who had distinguished neither himself nor his nation. As well as the Englishman there had been an American (Ledyard), an Irishman (Houghton) and a Scot (Park). Then, in 1794, the former diplomat and enthusiastic supporter of the Association, Sir John Stepney, suggested they employ a Frenchman. That summer Stepney wrote to Banks introducing an escapee from the revolution across the Channel, a man he thought was born to be an explorer. Banks was not amused. 'With every possible admiration for Emigrant Virtue and every possible compassion for Emigrant distress,' he wrote with inimitable long-windedness, 'I have my doubts as to the propriety and still more as to the Policy of our sending out in the Capacity of an African Association a French Gentleman as a Traveller. Were we to do so it would bear the appearance or at least be subjected to the interpretation of our not being able to find in our Island a Person fitted for that business and was a Frenchman to succeed even moderately in the investigation on which he might be employed, are we not sure that his Countrymen would give the whole merit of the adventure to the National Character of a Frenchman?'[2] Frenchmen were out. Germans, it seems, were not.

Johann Blumenbach, Professor of Medicine at the German University of Göttingen, shared many of Joseph Banks' passions and talents, to which he added one that Banks would never match: he was a brilliant public speaker, said to be able to draw 'the natural sciences out of the narrow circle of books and museums into the cheerful stream of life'.[3] The son of a schoolmaster, he was appointed to the Chair of Medicine at Göttingen at the age of twenty-six and remained there for sixty-two years, devoting his life to the sciences, inspiring men such as Alexander von Humboldt and becoming one of the founding fathers of ethnology. Blumenbach's interests led him to look out to the wider world, particularly those parts of it that were being newly visited by European travellers and which might provide fresh information to further his research. In Germany, he now became linked to exploration: he was, for instance, the obvious choice to write an introduction to the German edition of James Bruce's long-awaited *Travels to Discover the Source of the Nile*. During the winter of 1791 he spent more than three months in London, and saw a great deal of Banks, who shared his passion for ethnology and antiquities – Blumenbach opened three Egyptian mummies in front of Banks and other Fellows of the Royal Society that winter. Among other topics, the two men discussed the African Association – Banks was hoping at the time for news of Houghton's journey into the interior. The German was clearly impressed, because he spoke about the Association and its goals to his colleagues and students in Göttingen. Four years later, in 1795, he wrote to Banks to inform him that he had found the Association a new traveller. Frederick Hornemann was the son of a Lutheran priest from the Lower Saxon town of Hildesheim, and was studying theology at Göttingen when he first heard about the Association. He had long wanted to travel, and presumably met Blumenbach while looking for books to satisfy his curiosity about Africa.* The young student left the university for a teaching post elsewhere in 1794, but he was back at Blumenbach's door the following year, explaining that he had made up his mind to become an explorer and asking for an introduction to Banks. The timing was fortuitous.

Although Mungo Park was just then sailing south towards the Gambia, the Association was already looking for another African traveller, and since Beaufoy's recent death the task had fallen entirely to Banks. He had already approached another Englishman, one of his long-time correspondents, the trader James Jackson, based in Morocco at Mogador (Essaouira). Jackson had met Banks through his friend Willis, the man involved in the abortive project to send a consul to Senegambia. Although Jackson's letters reveal him to be an irritating and arrogant pedant, Banks must have recognised in him the qualities necessary for a traveller. In reply to an offer of employment from the Association, Jackson assured Banks that while it was an honour to be asked, he was 'sorry to be obliged to decline a journey of the kind as he does not conceive how the benefit to be derived from the journey which Sir Joseph suggested could be adequate to the enterprise. Whenever Mr. J sees any probability of a great national or commercial object to be gained most willingly will he undertake any journey of the kind. No difficulties or dangers will ever impede him from promoting the manifest interests of his King and country.'⁴ In other words, as a trader, Jackson did not think the rewards justified the risks.

---

* The Professor had by this stage built up what the poet Coleridge, who visited him in 1799, called 'a complete little Library of his own collecting, consisting of books written entirely by African Blacks' (Hallett, *The Penetration of Africa*, p.190).

It was at this moment that Banks received Hornemann's offer. He was interested, but he was also becoming more selective in his choice of traveller and asked Blumenbach to find out more about the young volunteer. It was not until the following spring, in May 1796, that a packet was delivered to Soho Square containing the Professor's reply and a proposal from the would-be explorer. 'As soon as I received your Letter,' Blumenbach reported, 'I enquired for the most particular information about his character, Talents, circumstances, &c. and now after all what I have learned I may say, that there will be hardly a Man better qualified for the purpose in question than he is.'[5] The Professor thought it particularly worth mentioning Hornemann's physical features. 'He is a young robust man of an athletic bodily constitution, infatigable [sic], but always taking great care and good precaution for preserving his health.'

Hornemann seems to have understood what was wanted of him. With Park already on his way to the Gambia, Hornemann suggested reverting to the Association's original plan and taking the route Ledyard had been sent to travel, from Cairo to Murzuq and then across the Sahara to Timbuktu. On 3 June 1796, Banks and his fellow Committee member, the parliamentarian Andrew Stuart, met and approved the proposal.

Blumenbach wrote again, this time to suggest that he prepare Hornemann in Göttingen before his departure for Africa. Not long before this, Banks received an approach from another would-be traveller, an academic by the name of Professor Abraham James Penzel, a man who liked to flaunt his classical learning and who addressed Banks as '*viro clarissimo Josepho Banks, Equiti*'. Banks declined Penzel's offer, explaining that, 'For the first journey a young strong man of adventurous spirit, fertile in resources and capable of enduring hunger, fatigue and ill usage will be a better Missionary than the most learned professor in all the universities of Europe,' but also making the point that, 'after the first journey has been made and the practicability of making a second is ascertained it will be in my opinion the proper time for a man of education to be employed'.[6]

In Hornemann, Banks had found someone who was both 'a

young strong man' and 'a man of education', for he was already a university graduate and had a considerable knowledge of African manners, history and geography. Blumenbach, however, thought that before he was sent on his way, Hornemann should be put through a period of wide-ranging, though specialised study.

Mungo Park's expedition had been intended as a groundbreaking scientific journey, and although neither Banks nor Blumenbach could have known it at this time, he had succeeded in taking readings of his position up until his encounter with Ali of Ludamar. In Blumenbach's mind, this idea now took root: his explorer would be trained and equipped specifically to carry forward scientific investigations. While Banks had been content to send botanists and other scientists in the wake of explorers – just as he himself had travelled as a scientist alongside Cook – Blumenbach wanted the Association's next geographical missionary to be both explorer and scientist.

The Professor explained his plan in a letter to Banks. Hornemann should receive instruction in the classics from one of the most eminent historians of the time, Professor C.G. Heyre, a Fellow of the Royal Society and therefore already known to Banks. Among the texts they would study were the ancient writers such as Herodotus and Pliny who had written about Africa. 'I,' Blumenbach went on, outlining his plan for the ultimate explorer, 'will furnish Mr Hornemann with such notices of natural history, which may make his expedition the more useful. But besides this he would spend his time principally with our Orientalists for the Arabian language and with our mathematicians and astronomers, &c. In the meantime he will also acquire some necessary practical knowledge of domestic medicine and surgery, and employ a part of his time for perfectionating himself still more in drawing &c.'[7]

The Professor thought it would take a few months to prepare Hornemann at Göttingen, during which time the usual letters of introduction and credit could be prepared and equipment collected. It was a very optimistic assessment, and in September 1796, more than three months later, he wrote again to explain that he 'thought it in dutio very prudent, if he [Hornemann] procured himself likewise some practical astronomical knowledge, as it would be of the highest advantage for his Geographical Researches, in case that he would contrive it in such a way to wear with him a Timekeeper or a pocket Hadley's Sextant: which seems from one side at least not quite impossible, and from the other so very important for the views of the Association'.[8] Another three months on, Hornemann was still in Germany. On 7 December he wrote his first letter to Banks, thanking him 'for enabling me to satisfy my desire to travel in unknown regions of the globe, which ever increased with growing age'.[9]

The original plan was for Hornemann to travel directly from Germany to North Africa, but Banks changed his mind and on 6 January 1797 asked him to come first to London, 'now the French are Masters of the Mediterranean'.[10] In the end, it was not until 19 February that Blumenbach sent his pupil on his way, penning this formal letter to his friend in London:

> Sir,
> Here I have the honour to introduce to you my good friend, Mr. Hornemann; for really so I call him and so I reckon him, having now had opportunity enough to study his character and to convince me of his talents and application for his great purpose.
> It will make me very happy if the Association, but particularly yourself find to your satisfaction that I have been right in this my judgement.[11]

Banks had made arrangements for Hornemann, finding him rooms at half a guinea a week with a Mr Paas off Throgmorton Street, just around the corner from the Bank of England. According to his calling card,* Hornemann was in attendance in his rooms at No. 2, Shorter's Court from 11 till 3 on Mondays and Thursdays.[12] The rest of the time there were meetings, preparations and dinners to attend. Then on 20 March the Committee met at Lord Rawdon's house to issue its instructions. Rawdon and Banks were there, as

---

* The name on this card is spelled HORNEMAN, but elsewhere it is spelled Hornemann, the spelling I have used, assuming the other is due to a printer's error.

always, as was the lawyer Andrew Stuart, who was helping to fill the gap left by Beaufoy's death, and another of the Association's founding members, Richard Watson, the Bishop of Llandaff.

Hornemann's instructions were as unlike those of the Association's earlier travellers as he was from men such as Ledyard and Houghton. He was to proceed to Cairo and find himself lodgings in a monastery; he was going to be in the Egyptian capital for as long as it took him to become fluent in Arabic 'and of such others [languages] as he may think likely to be of use to him in his Travels'.[13] This done, he was to look out for 'Strangers from the Interior'. The plan was for him to become friendly with foreigners passing through the city with the caravans. When he found a group he thought he could trust who were going deep into the interior, he was to find a way of travelling with them to their country. The aim of this journey, the ultimate goal, was not to arrive at Timbuktu. Park, it was assumed, was already there (though at the beginning of June 1797 he was almost back at the Gambia River with Karfa Taura and his slave coffle). Hornemann's area of interest was marked out to the east of Timbuktu, according to Rennell's calculations right in the heart of the continent, in particular the 'extensive empire of Cashna [Katsina]'. Much had been heard of this empire, which, together with neighbouring Borno and the Bambuk kingdoms around Djenne and Timbuktu, had been marked out by Rennell as the great centres of population and power in the interior.

Leo Africanus had clearly not enjoyed his time among the people of Katsina – he dismissed them for living 'in most forlorn and base cottages . . . and beside their base estate they are mightily oppressed with famine'.[14] But the Association had heard from Lucas, the Moor Ben Ali and others that the place had since become more significant. As a centre of learning, it was now as reputable as Timbuktu and Djenne. There were also reports of an enlightened monarchy – Muslim, of course – and of trade in salt, gold, ostrich feathers, horses, slaves and civet ('obtained,' Beaufoy had noted in the *Proceedings* of 1790, 'from a species of wild cat, that is common in the woods of Bornou, and of Cashna'[15]). Here, as Park was finding further west, the currency was gold or cowrie shells.

Beside these descriptions of Katsina, the Association had also been provided with an account of the route from the Fezzan: the caravan always left in October, and had to cover thirty-three days of rough terrain – desert, low mountains and empty 'heaths' – before reaching 'a delightful country, as fertile as it is numerously peopled; and while the exhilarating sight of Indian corn and of frequent herds of cattle accompanies and chears [sic] their passage, the eighth day introduces them to the large and populous city of Agadez ... the most commercial of all the towns of Cashna'.[16] If there were significant markets and millions of willing consumers at the heart of Africa, this was where the Association hoped to find them.

It sounded so simple, but obstacles nearer to home needed to be overcome first, such as the crossing of hostile France. The minutes of the 20 March Committee meeting mention that Banks agreed to approach the French government for a passport, so that Hornemann could safely cross France and sail from one of its Mediterranean ports to Egypt. In spite of the reservations he had expressed about French involvement in their African project and the fact that the two countries were at war, Banks was happy to do so. This might appear to be a contradiction, given that his African plan was in part motivated by a desire to take control of the Niger trade before the French did. Yet Banks had always insisted that Science should be above petty national rivalry, that there should be, as he put it, 'during the horrors of a war unprecedented in the mutual im-placability of the parties engaged, an unconditional armistice for science'.[17] And while this did not extend as far as employing French travellers on Association missions, it did include cooperation between scientists on both sides of the Channel.

Banks was hopeful that his request for a *laissez-passer* for Hornemann would be granted in Paris, in spite of the hostilities between the two countries, if only in thanks for past services: when the ship of the French botanist Jacques-Julien de Labillardière was captured in Java in 1796, Banks had used his access to government to ensure that both the botanist and his collection were returned to France. He even covered the transport costs himself. In return, he had received help the previous December. The *Robert*, a British ship travelling back from the Gambia, had put in to Cadiz harbour soon after Britain and France had gone to war, and found herself seized by French sailors. This was nothing new: ships on both sides were being held at ports around the world. But the *Robert* happened to be carrying letters from 'my correspondents in Africa respecting the person employed in exploring the interior of that Country', Banks wrote to Jean Charretié, the French Commissioner in London. 'I should esteem myself infinitely obliged to your Government,' he went on, 'if they would order such letters directed to me as may be found on board this vessel and relate wholly to Science and discovery in Africa, to be returned to me.'[18]

Banks now wrote to Charretié regarding Hornemann. 'Encouraged by the friendly civilities I have repeatedly received from you, and the uniform protection given by your nation to all attempts for the increase of human knowledge, I have no hesitation in making the following request.'[19] Other Englishmen would have hesitated, and Banks was to be severely criticised later on for his flattering overtures to the enemy at a time of war. But whatever was to come, five weeks later Charretié was pleased to inform Banks that the Directoire in Paris had agreed to issue papers to his traveller.

In the meantime, Hornemann went about his final preparations. This was the worst time of all for a traveller, keen to be gone before foreboding began to overwhelm him, but held back by the need to complete his arrangements. Hornemann busied himself in preparing his equipment. Both he and the Committee were convinced that the less he took with him, the less of a target he would be for bandits in the desert or greedy rulers across the Sahara. But a certain basic kit was needed if he was to provide Rennell with the readings he required to map towns, villages, wells and other geographical points, as well as for the accurate logging of journey times. On 5 April he had taken delivery of a consignment of instruments from Jesse Ramsden, the 'Mathematical, Optical and Philosophical Instrument-Maker at the Golden Spectacles' off Sackville Street, Piccadilly: Ramsden was the inventor of a dividing machine that had revolutionised the manufacture of portable scientific instruments by providing previously unimaginable accuracy.* Included in the order were a pocket compass (£1.5.0), a military telescope and stand in a mahogany box (£8.8.0), a pocket thermometer (£1.1.0), a complete hand sextant with a silver arch (£12.12.0) and an artificial horizon (£2.12.6). To this Hornemann added 'a few necessary books'[20] and a memo book with ivory-coloured pages.

On 23 June he was at Banks' house, with Sir Joseph and the Association's Secretary, Bryan Edwards, to receive his passport and final instructions. He was to leave as soon as possible, pass through Paris and then make for Marseilles. When he reached Cairo, he should head for a monastery – the one belonging to the Fathers of the Propaganda† was recommended – where he would live until he was ready to join a caravan for the interior. Banks and Edwards had not heard from Park at this time, but from Houghton's last report and some other information collected, they thought it likely that the Niger flowed west to east and ran into a great lake in the centre of the continent. As well as reporting on Katsina, the Committee stressed that it was 'a matter of extreme importance'[21] for Hornemann to collect as much information as possible on the course of the Niger. They were also clearly concerned that other people should not know what he was up to. His instructions included the clear injunction that when in Cairo he should 'live there quietly, without divulging his intentions of travelling to the English Resident, or to any other European'.[22] Nor was he to pass on any information he might obtain to his friends in Germany. The reason for this, he was told, was to protect any publication that might follow his expedition, but it is more likely that Banks had not told the French the full nature of Hornemann's journey.

On 26 June, still in London, Hornemann expressed some of his

* Ramsden's invention of the dividing machine had been rewarded by a prize from the Board of Longitude, on which Banks sat. During the previous decade, he had made some of Europe's finest scientific instruments. His theodolite marked the beginning of serious geodetic work, while his zenith sector was accurate to 0.1 second.

† The Monks of the Propaganda were properly called the Sacra Congregatio Christiano Nomini Propaganda. They were proselytising Catholics who had charge of ecclesiastical matters in Egypt.

frustration when he wrote to his classics tutor, Professor Arnold Heeren, in Göttingen, 'The naked Majesty of an African state will certainly have more interest for me than Great Britain in all its glory.' His letters of credit were ready by the end of the month. Banks had given him £60 for the journey to Alexandria, Charretié had provided some *louis d'ors* and letters of credit that he could exchange in Paris, while the Secretary of State had been asked to instruct George Baldwin, the 'English Resident' (British Consul) at Alexandria, to provide Hornemann with credit against the Association. With his instruments packed, his will made (in the event of his death, whatever money was due him should be paid to his mother and sisters), the emotion began to show. 'I wish, Sir,' he wrote to Banks on departure, 'I could explain to you my feelings on this last time I am in London.'[23]

By 12 July he was in Paris. The Channel crossing had been easy and surprisingly quick – three hours – there was a space as far as Abbeville in a coach with some French prisoners of war, and from there he had taken the public coach, two days and nights, to the capital, where the Ministry of Police had accepted his papers. His host in Paris was the astronomer Jérôme Lalande, who presented him at the Institut National and introduced him to a range of people. One of them was Muhammad D'Ghies,[24] a Turkish-born Tripolitan of great influence who offered to provide letters of recommendation to Tripoli and to a friend of his in Cairo. Lalande was a curious choice of host for Hornemann, because, as Banks well knew, two years earlier he had published his *Mémoire de l'Afrique*, in which he had written: '*Le trajet depuis le Sénégal jusqu'à la Mer rouge, depuis Tunis jusque au bord de l'Océan, à travers l'Afrique, est le voyage le plus curieux de tous ceux que l'on peut faire actuellement sur la surface de la terre* . . . '* This was a belief he shared with Banks. But he had gone on to claim: '*Il serait plus facile aux Français qu'à aucune Nation, de pénétrer dans l'intérieur de ce riche et curieux pays, et d'apprendre à toute l'Europe des choses toutes*

---

* 'The journey from Senegal to the Red Sea, from Tunis to the ocean, across Africa, is the most interesting of all those that one can make at this time in the world.'

nouvelles . . . '* This would have stoked Sir Joseph's anxiety about the French claiming the prize on which he had set his heart, especially since this extract was used as a preface to the French translation of the combined journals of Houghton and Park. The other claim of note that Lalande makes in his *Mémoire* is that the Niger flowed from east to west. Before Hornemann left his house in Paris, the astronomer gave him several copies of his book to give to whomever he should meet on the way who might be interested. The young traveller was off to a good start, and his letter to Banks bubbles over with enthusiasm.

James Jackson, the Mogador trader who had turned down Banks' offer to travel for the Association, had by this time changed his mind. Hearing that a German had been employed, he wrote to warn Banks of possible dangers: 'May Mr. J. be allowed to observe, that if a foreigner crosses the continent of Africa the honor [sic] will not be derived to this country but to a foreign one.'[25] But Banks was not to be put off, at least not by Jackson. He had liked what he had seen of the sharp, reserved German theology scholar in the months he had spent in London. 'I confess,' he wrote to Blumenbach, 'I have great hopes that this young man will succeed: he seems to have been born for some enterprise of Travel that will do him honor in the eyes of his contemporaries, and to have had his mind fix'd, ever since his reason ripen'd, upon the means of carrying into execution the purpose for which he was originally destin'd by providence. I hope I am right in this conjecture.'[26]

* 'It would be easier for the French than any other nation, to penetrate into the interior of this rich and fascinating country, and to teach all Europe things completely new.'

12

Juset ben Abdallah

'To have accomplished so great a journey across so vast and unexplored a region without a companion to support him was one of the great achievements in the history of geographical discovery.'

E.W. Bovill, *Missions to the Niger*, I, p.38

Cairo, 1797

WITHIN A FEW HOURS of arriving in Cairo, Hornemann had disobeyed his instructions. And with this unpromising start began one of the great African journeys.

The crossing of the Mediterranean proved troublesome. At Marseilles there were ships for Livorno, Cyprus, Smyrna even, but nothing for Alexandria. The young explorer waited, and then began to fret. 'I think very often,' he complained, watching boats sail for other ports on the Mediterranean, 'that it perhaps may be easier for me to go in the Interior of Africa than to Egypt.'[1] Little did he know of what was to come.

On 11 August he gave up hope of finding a direct passage and booked a berth on a ship bound for Larnaca in Cyprus and from there to Egypt, which he finally reached on 9 September. He had good reason to be frustrated: Ledyard, ten years earlier, had travelled the whole way from Paris to Alexandria in the time Hornemann had taken to cross the Mediterranean. But there were good reasons for the disruption of sea traffic between France and Egypt, which he was soon to discover.

In Alexandria the new geographical missionary made contact with George Baldwin, the British Consul in Egypt. The Committee had advised him to take a room in one of Alexandria's convents and had instructed him on no account to discuss his mission with Europeans, not even with 'the English Resident', Baldwin. But a week after arriving in the Egyptian port, Hornemann wrote to London that Baldwin 'shewd [sic] me the greatest civility, and invited me to live with him. I sayd [sic] that I had the intention to stay in a convent, but he invited me again, and because I think to set off for Cairo after morrow, I accepted his invitation, and I don't repent it.'

There is a surprising naivety about the letter. 'Is it by my conduct, or is it in his character?' he wonders regarding Baldwin's hospitality. 'He has shewd me so many services, and given me so many advises, as I could ever ask of him, if he was a member of your Association.'[2] But Baldwin was not a member of the Association, nor, in spite of his many fine qualities, was he simply a good man. Alexandria, where much of Cairo's elite settled for the summer to escape the heat of the capital, was awash with rumours, among them an expectation of imminent foreign intervention. Two years earlier, Baldwin had sent London news of a Frenchman named Tinville who had arrived 'to inveigle the Beys of Egypt into the designs of the French, and particularly to obtain consent to their project of passing an army through Egypt, to the East Indies [India], by the Red Sea, in order ... finally to annihilate the British Dominion in the East Indies'.[3]

Survival in this political climate, as Baldwin well knew, depended on the quality of one's information; he was a master in these circumstances, however, a subtle manipulator who made it his business to know what was going on. He was also a trader – he had only been appointed to his diplomatic position because he had promised the British government that he could secure a renewal of the agreement James Bruce had reached to allow British ships to sail up the Red Sea, in spite of the Turkish ban. He never did manage to obtain official consent, but he did receive an unofficial nod and became the agent for caravans passing between East and West. On one occasion, as he memorably recorded, 'we composed our bowl of the Ganges, the Thames, and the Nile, and from the top of the pyramid drank prosperity to England'.[4] From what he knew of the Association, he seems to have assumed that its interest in the interior was not purely geographical. Perhaps he thought Hornemann would be more likely to reveal his secrets if he was his guest, and so, by inviting him to stay, to some extent Baldwin was flirting with the emissary of his imagined rival. 'At all events,' Hornemann wrote that same October day to Bryan Edwards, 'I mean to lodge at Cairo in a Convent.'[5]

A month later, installed in the capital, he wrote again to London. 'I had requested Mr Baldwin to recommend me to Mr. Rosetti [sic], but at the same time to inform him, that I meant to lodge at a Convent,' he started encouragingly. 'Mr. Rosetti however invited me in so obliging a manner to stay at his house that I could not refuse. He represented that the Convents were at present filld [sic] with Travellers, and that he could not immediately fix upon any house convenient for my reception but his own . . .'[6]

'Perhaps in reading this letter,' the German continued, 'you are led in your mind to advert to the first article in my instructions. When I was at Alexandria, I mentiond [sic] nothing of the aim of my journey to any one but to Mr Baldwin's family, requesting him and his people not to divulge it, to which they have faithfully kept. As to the other Europeans, both there and probably here, they seem so little interested in it, that I am convinced they would take me for a fool, if I were to speak of it in any other than a slight cursory manner. I have sometimes conversed with the Monks of the Propaganda at Alexandria, about the interior of Africa, the best mode of penetrating into it &c., but they always directed me to Mr. Rosetti. When I arrived at Cairo, I soon perceived that all the Monks here were in a manner dependent upon this man, and that he possessed great influence. I found likewise that his opinion of the African Association was, that they were connected merely by commercial interests. On this account I deemed it the more necessary to form a closer connection with him, which however must never exceed the bounds dictated by prudence.'

This letter, written in October 1797, arrived in London on 10 January 1798 and had Banks, Edwards and the rest of the Committee wondering whether they had made a mistake in their choice of traveller, for Hornemann was clearly a victim of intrigue. Besides being British Chargé d'Affaires and Venetian Consul in Cairo, the Italian Carlo Rossetti also ran a business trading with the interior: Venetian glass beads, highly prized in Africa, were his speciality. Like Baldwin, therefore, he would have regarded the Association as a possible commercial rival, and although outwardly helpful, it simply was not in his interests to allow Hornemann to succeed.

Within a month of his arrival in Africa and in spite of the first article of his injunctions, Hornemann had discussed his mission both in Alexandria and Cairo. He must have known how Banks would react: the reply was not long in coming. On 16 January, Banks informed him that the Committee 'do not complain of your having forgot the advice you so frequently receivd [sic], against connecting yourself in any shape with Baldwin or Rosetti [sic]; but they are seriously sorry you have done so. The only advice I ever gave to you in strong language was to avoid by all means suffering either of those Gentlemen to know your intention of Travelling. I cannot, however, but feel gratitude to them for the hospitality they have shewn to you; tho' no part of their motive is in any shape attributable to my interest with them.'[7]

Hornemann had also mentioned that caravans had arrived or were expected in Cairo from Sennar, Darfur, Siwa, Ghadames and the Fezzan. Unfortunately, no one seemed to know anything about caravans from Katsina or Borno, the Saharan kingdoms he hoped to visit. The delay was as well, for he clearly was not ready to leave the city. 'My chief employ at present is the study of the Arabic language, for which I have hird [sic] a Greek Roman Catholic . . .'[8]

This, at least, was good news. Two weeks before Banks wrote to Cairo, Mungo Park had made his Christmas morning appearance in the gardens of the British Museum. When writing of this to Hornemann, Banks shared the encouraging news that Park had reached the Niger, had seen that it flowed from west to east and had travelled to within two weeks of Timbuktu. He also mentioned that Park

> *might have entered that Town could he have passed for a Mahometan; but he desisted from the attempt on being told by all the persons he met that the Mahometans, who have the Rule of the Town, would certainly put him to death as a Christian, if he enterd* [sic] *it . . . He was uniformly well treated by the Pagan Negroes, whose hospitality never failed to relieve him; not ill treated by the Mahometan Negroes, but they seem'd to hate him for being a Christian; and he was always very ill received and twice taken prisoner and plundered by the Arabs, who spar'd his life, but took all he possess'd even his instruments.*

Banks then formulated the Association's new thinking about how their travellers should proceed. 'The Committee,' he concluded, 'wish you to remain quietly where you are, and by no means to move, till you have attained a fluency in the Arabic Language and a competent knowledge of the Customs of the Mograbins &c. They are well aware that a detention, even of considerable length in the place where you now are, is likely to facilitate very much the ultimate object of your Mission.'[9] Disguise would open the ways that were otherwise closed to outsiders.

The Cairo in which Hornemann found himself was ruled by a Turkish-appointed governor and a council of leading *beys* or nobles, most of whom also came from across the Mediterranean, their rule enforced by Mamluks, a class of soldiers the majority of whom had come from the slave markets of Circassia and Istanbul. It was into this hive of activity and intrigue, stirred by the arrival of caravans from Arabia and Sudan, from Fezzan in the west and Europe to the north, troubled by rumours of invasion, that Hornemann now settled. The Committee had told him to lie low and live quietly in one of the convents to the south of the city, built on the ruins of the Roman settlement. They must have assumed he had finally got the message, because for ten months they heard nothing more. But rather than living quietly, he was surviving one of the most dramatic months Egypt had seen in many centuries.

He had started out quietly enough, followed his instructions and moved to a convent, where he continued his language lessons. In October 1797 he took on an interpreter, another German by the name of Joseph Frendenburgh. Ten or twelve years earlier, in circumstances that were never explained, Frendenburgh had been taken as a Mamluk and forced to convert to Islam. Hornemann found him an excellent guide into the manners and customs both of Egyptians and of African travellers, many of whom Frendenburgh had met on the three pilgrimages he had made to Mecca. Encouraged by the progress he was making and by his countryman's compliments, by April 1798 the missionary felt he was sufficiently prepared to think of joining a caravan for the Fezzan. Negotiations took a while, and just as he persuaded the Fezzani *shaykh* to allow him to travel with his caravan there was an outbreak of the plague in the city and everyone went into hiding.

The plague obliged him to stay in Cairo for several more weeks and brought with it new expenses, so that by the time he was ready to travel again he had another problem: he did not have sufficient funds for the journey. Banks had made arrangements for Baldwin to advance him money, but Baldwin was now in Alexandria and Hornemann was leaving from Cairo. Banks had approached Baldwin through his friends in the Foreign Office, but as a security – in case Baldwin was away or something happened to him – he had also made arrangements with the Smyrna office of Lee & Partners, a London trading house. According to the Association's accounts of 25 May 1797, £600 was 'lodged with Messrs Richard William Lees to be credit of Mr. Hornemann part of which he has already drawn out'.[10] But although this was the regular way of arranging finances – an early form of travellers' cheques – no one in Cairo was prepared to advance Hornemann money against the letters for Baldwin or Lee. Perhaps here we see the hand of either Baldwin or Rossetti at work to frustrate his mission. As a result, it took the traveller until the beginning of July 1798 to raise the money he needed, helped in the end by a French commercial house in Cairo 'on whom I had no letters of credit or other claim to confidence, but what arose from private friendship and esteem'. In the first days of July everything seemed to have been arranged – Hornemann had negotiated with another caravan heading for the Fezzan – when news reached him that a French army had invaded Egypt. Alexandria had already fallen and rumour had it that this victorious army, headed by Napoleon himself, was moving rapidly up the Nile towards the capital.

There was panic in Cairo. Bonaparte had landed his printing presses soon after the army and, in words that could have come from a twenty-first-century American president, was issuing decrees in Arabic and Greek as well as French, assuring Egyptians that his fight was not with them but with the corrupt Mamluks who ruled over them. But Cairo had seen enough conquerors for its inhabitants to know that the wary, the cautious and particularly the unseen tended to live longer and prosper: many people fled. Those who stayed in the city began throwing up defences, men were conscripted, an enormous chain was pulled across the Nile to stop an attack from the water, the price of gunpowder shot up, and abandoned houses were looted in the search for weapons and anything else that could be used in the city's defence. By Tuesday, 17 July, French and Egyptian forces were facing each other on the west side of the Nile at Imbaba. On that day, Shaykh Abd al-Rahman al-Jabarti, a Cairene magistrate, wrote: 'The streets were deserted. One only found women, who stayed in their houses with their children. Men who were too weak to move elsewhere also stayed home with their women. The souks were reduced to nothing. The streets were dirty, neither swept nor watered.'[11]

This climate of fear was quickly translated into anger towards foreigners. Christians, whether Syrian, Copt, Egyptian or European, were also a target, and their houses were looted for arms and what al-Jabarti loosely calls 'other things': 'The people burned with a desire to massacre Christians and Jews. The authorities forbade them. Without this ban, the people would certainly have massacred them.'[12] To ensure their safety – and perhaps also to stop them from making trouble – Cairo's European residents were placed under arrest in their homes or locked up in the stronghold of the Citadel. Hornemann went to the Citadel, which he saw 'more as a place of refuge from the indignation and fanaticism of the populace, than as a prison'.[13] And there he remained while extraordinary events happened beyond the walls.

Also in the Citadel, it appears, was Carlo Rossetti, because it was from here that Murad Bey, the Mamluk commander of the Egyptian army, summoned the Italian to his house to find out what he knew of the infidel invaders.[14] Rossetti knew enough about the superiority of French discipline, tactics and weapons to recognise the dangers, but Murad would not listen; his 'eyes became red and fire devoured his entrails'.[15] While the other Mamluk *beys* on the ruling council were in favour of flight – and at least one of them, Ibrahim Bey, made preparations for a quick escape* – Murad was spoiling for a fight, pride having convinced him that no infidel could stand up to an army that fought under the green banner of Islam.

On 21 July, Napoleon drew up twenty-five thousand troops in front of a significantly smaller number of Mamluks and reminded his men that history was looking on them. The ensuing fight, known as the Battle of the Pyramids though it took place nearer the Nile at Imbaba, was brief and bloody. The Mamluk cavalry began with a charge, their magnificent silk robes flying behind them, reins gripped in their teeth, carbines fired at full gallop, pistols emptied, javelins tossed, scimitars drawn for close combat. The French formed into tight squares and waited for them to come closer before opening fire. It was not a battle, according to Baron Vivant Denon, one of the artists accompanying Bonaparte, 'it was a massacre'.[16] Al-Jabarti was more detailed in his description: 'The dust thickened and the world became dark from the smoke of the gunpowder . . .

---

* Some Egyptians went to great lengths to protect the foreigners in their country. Charles Norry, an architect attached to the French expedition, noted that Ibrahim's 'lawful wife had taken under her protection twenty-seven Frenchmen who had been apprehended at Cairo on the news of the invasion. She had placed them in her house. When she left them to join her husband, she left them provisions and arms, recommending them to be on their guard even against her own servants. This virtuous and humane woman departed with her husband. No accident happened to the twenty-seven Frenchmen, who left their place of concealment after the success of the battle.'

Men became deafened from the constant firing, and it seemed to them the earth was shaking and the heavens falling.'[17] The main fight lasted little more than forty-five minutes. As the gunsmoke cleared, it revealed a thousand Mamluks dead on the ground, twenty-nine French soldiers beside them.

The rout left Cairo unprotected. However unsettled the city had been before the battle, it was now in a state of complete anarchy. Murad Bey and the other ruling Mamluks fled as soon as defeat was inevitable, and many Cairenes tried to follow their example, burying valuables or loading them onto camels and donkeys and crowding through the city's gates, where gangs of bandits waited for them. Inside the walls, the city was looted, houses burned, atrocities committed. 'Never was there a crueller night,' al-Jabarti declared. 'The ear heard the tale of deeds of which the eye would not have been able to support the vision.'[18] *The Times* later quoted 'German journals' in reporting that 'the Beys ... enraged at being defeated ... committed the greatest cruelties on the European Christians in Egypt'.[19] Throughout all this, Hornemann was safely locked in the Citadel, guarded by soldiers who were aware that the French, when they came, would be thankful that the lives of Europeans had been spared.

Bonaparte entered Cairo on 25 July and within days an eerie calm, a veneer of normality, settled over the city as Cairenes discovered that these latest conquerors had come not to kill or burn but to wander the streets unarmed. They were playful and full of laughter and, most strange, paid top prices. Among these apparently amiable foreigners were the mathematician Gaspard Monge and the chemist Claude Berthollet, whom Hornemann had met a year earlier at the Institut National in Paris. When they heard about the young German's plight, they arranged his release from the Citadel and had him brought to the large house on the square of Ezbekieh where Napoleon had set up headquarters.

In his interview with Bonaparte, Hornemann again disobeyed his instructions and described his mission. Despite the suspicions of Banks and others in London regarding French activity in Africa, Bonaparte displayed a surprising lack of concern at what

Hornemann had to tell him. 'His regard for science, and esteem of learned men are too well known to render it necessary for me to expatiate on these high qualities,'[20] Hornemann wrote glowingly of the conqueror. Bonaparte's love of science is well documented – he once told Banks' friend Sir John Sinclair, one of the Association's founders, 'that he did not make war against education or literature'.[21] The order he issued only a week after entering Cairo, creating the Institut d'Egypte, testifies to this. But had the interview happened in August, rather than July, Napoleon may not have been so well disposed towards the British-sponsored traveller, because on the first of that month a British squadron under Admiral Horatio Nelson destroyed the French fleet off Alexandria. The loss of those ships changed the balance of power in the Mediterranean, ended Bonaparte's plan to strike at British interests in the East, and significantly reduced French ability to move further into Africa. The artist Denon summed up this change when he wrote, 'On the morning of 31 July 1798, the French were masters of Egypt, Corfu and Malta; thirty vessels of the line united these possessions with France.' By the end of 1 August, 'the Army of the East was imprisoned in its own conquest'.[22]

The news of the naval disaster did not reach Bonaparte in Cairo for several days, by which time Hornemann had had his interview and the French leader had 'promised me protection, he offered me money or whatever was requisite to my undertaking, and he directed the necessary passports to be made out to me'.[23] Magnanimous indeed. As Hornemann made his way out of Ezbekieh and back to the convent where he was staying, he believed all obstacles to his crossing of the desert had finally been removed.

By the middle of August trade caravans had begun to regroup, and the foreigners planned their departure from Cairo. Hornemann reported three caravans around the city, one heading for Sennar, one for Darfur and another for Fezzan. Perhaps because of the interrupted movement across the region, he described those heading for Sennar and Fezzan as being composed of several caravans. 'Fezzan,' he wrote, 'is the true point, whence one must start for the interior, but one must approach that district from Tripoli, the journey from there not being so difficult as from here [Cairo] to Fezzan,' as Simon Lucas had found out in 1789. 'There is,' Hornemann informed London, 'every three months an opportunity of going, as they tell me.'[24]

On 31 August he wrote to Banks that after two weeks of preparation the Fezzan caravan was ready to leave Cairo and that he was going to travel with it. He wrote several other letters to London during those last two days, which will have cheered Banks and Edwards, who had had no news since the previous winter – though the manner of their arrival will have raised a few eyebrows in London, since they were carried by command of Napoleon Bonaparte and arrived in Soho Square bearing his seal. Anticipating the Committee's response, the traveller quickly explained that as their letters had not reached him in Cairo and as he could see no other way of being certain of getting his to them, he had accepted Bonaparte's offer to deliver them, although it had been on the condition that he write them in French. He agreed to this because in his opinion the letters contained nothing secret.

No secrets, perhaps, but good news for the Committee:

> I will be travelling as a Mohamedan, as a trader of the Caravan, and I find this disguise the most helpful for me in my mission. When one knows a little of the Arabic language, when one knows how to behave with everyday matters, when one knows the manners of these people and their ceremonies, it is not difficult to travel as a Mohamedan, because the caravan has been to Mecca and knows very well that there are Mohamedans who have different manners and language.[25]

So convinced was Hornemann of the viability of disguise that he pointed out that Park would have travelled further along the Niger had he been dressed as a Muslim, rather than wearing the breeches, boots, thick coat and hat of a European. 'I hope to do better than him,'[26] he concluded, displaying a touch of arrogance.

Hornemann also sent to London a rough timetable for the journey. He hoped to be in Fezzan by the beginning of November and to reach Agades and Katsina some time in 1799. He reckoned it would take him ten months to explore the region, and that he would then be able to make it home via either Senegambia or Mecca. 'I hope,' he continued, 'to have the honour of speaking to you in person in two and a half or three years.'[27] In the meantime, he asked that letters of credit for £100 or £150 be sent to Tripoli. There was also a warning: 'Pray write, and direct the English Consul at Tripoly [sic], or elsewhere, never to make enquiry after me of the traders from Fezzan, and particularly when conveying any thing from me consigned to you. These people are of a very jealous and inquisitive temper, and any inquiries made after me by a Christian, might raise a thousand suspicions, and prove even of fatal consequence to me.'[28] Just how suspicious the caravan traders could be, he was to find out soon enough.

With a great sense of relief, not to mention elation, Hornemann left Cairo on 5 September 1799. Dressed as a Levantine trader, going by the name of Juset ben Abdallah,[29] he rode out on horseback, accompanied by a train of camels carrying his merchandise in the care of his German friend, the Mamluk Joseph Frendenburgh. 'I regard the day of my departure as a day of big celebration because I have overcome in these past six months more obstacles than I care to mention.'[30] The difficulties of his stay in Cairo – and he had survived some terrifying moments – were now behind him.

All around the outskirts of Cairo small groups of traders from Tripoli and the Fezzan, from kingdoms along the Niger and others even further towards the Atlantic were meeting up, banding together according to tribe and standing, each group ruled over by a *shaykh*. Hornemann had arranged to travel with traders from the Libyan oasis of Awjila, returning home after making a pilgrimage to Mecca. They met at the village of Kerdassah* and

---

* Because of its position at the start of one of the routes across the desert to Siwa oasis, Kerdassah became a centre of cotton weaving. One of its most distinctive products was a blue patterned fabric used as a veil by Siwan women. Even though new highways have passed it by and there is no longer a direct link between village and oasis, Kerdassah contines to make this fabric and the women of Siwa continue to wear it.

then travelled north along the fringe of the desert until they met the main body of the trans-Saharan caravan at the village beneath the ruined pyramid of Abu Ruash, on the border between agricultural land and desert. 'We halted at some little distance from the pilgrims,' the German wrote, 'and encamped until the next morning; when the monotonous kettle-drum of our Sheik [sic] awakened us before rise of the sun, with summons to proceed on our journey.'[31]

Travelling by caravan was unlike anything Hornemann had experienced before, and he was acutely aware of the need to observe protocol, particularly on those first days when his fellow travellers were most curious about him and when his claim to be a Muslim was most severely tested. This first full day's journey exposed his inexperience. 'We had travelled from day-break till noon, and no indication appeared of halt or refreshment, when I observed the principal and richest merchants gnawing a dry biscuit and some onions, as they went on; and was then, for the first time, informed, that it was not customary to unload the camels for regular repast, or to stop during the daytime.'[32] He was saved from a day without eating by the generosity of some Arabs in his group, who shared some of their own food.

That night, he again betrayed his ignorance of caravan etiquette. At sundown they stopped in the desert and made camp on a bleak, flat, rocky plateau. Hornemann was watching Frendenburgh prepare their dinner, musing on the fact that even in Europe his assistant would have passed for a good cook, when an old Arab from Awjila noticed him. 'Thou art young,' the old man said pointedly (curiously, his Arabic was turned into Biblical English by the Association's traveller), 'and yet thou dost not assist in preparing the meal of which thou art to partake: such, perhaps, may be a custom in the land of the infidels, but is not so with us, and especially on a journey . . .'[33] Hornemann was stung by the criticism, but the old man had not finished. 'Thou oughtest to learn every thing that the meanest Arab performs, that thou mayest be enabled to assist others in cases of necessity; otherwise, thou wilt be less esteemed, as being of less value than a mere woman: and many will think they may

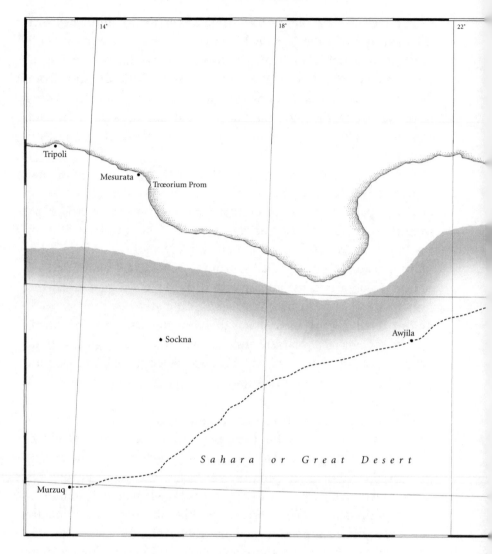

Hornemann's route from Cairo to Murzuq, 1799

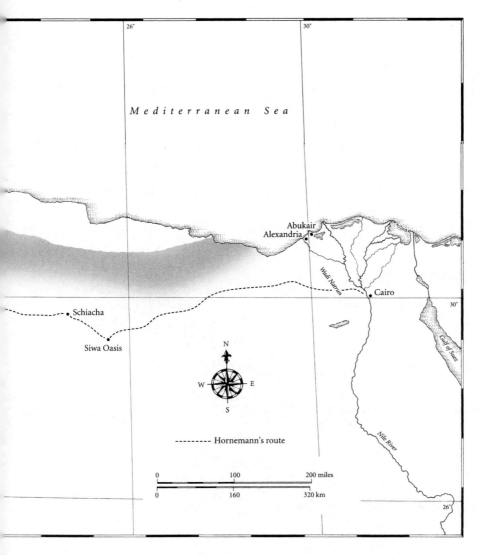

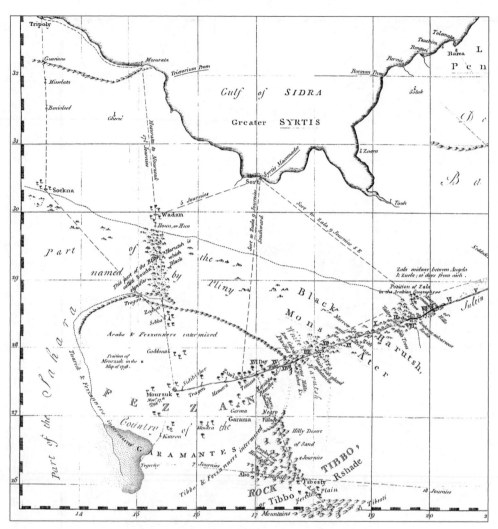

Detail from Rennell's 1802 map of Hornemann's journey

justly deprive thee of every thing in thy possession, as being unworthy to possess any thing.' He then added mischievously, 'Perhaps thou art carrying a large sum of money, and payest those men well.'[34] The criticism was not lost on the eager traveller, and he was soon able to report that he 'was no longer considered as a weak and useless idler in their troop'.[35]

The workings of the caravan fascinated Hornemann. Frustrated by the long delays in starting the journey, by not finding a boat from France and the months spent studying in Cairo, by the lack of regular caravans and the French invasion, he was at long last on his way, and clearly relishing the journey. 'Circumstances light and trivial often delineate manners, and characterize nations,'[36] he wrote during one of his more philosophical moments, but the camp routine of most caravan travellers seemed much the same. They travelled with flour, couscous, onions, mutton suet, oil or butter and water, which they stored in goat skins, 'stripped from the animal as entire as possible; those made at Soudan are the strongest and best; water may be preserved in them for five days, without acquiring any bad taste'.[37] Rich travellers also tended to lay in some biscuit and 'dried flesh'. At sunset, when the caravan halted for the night, the bags were unloaded, the camels hobbled and a search made for firewood and three stones. A hole was then dug in the sand, a fire started and a cooking pot placed on the stones. Some nights, however, they could not make fires: on their second night, for instance, near the Coptic monasteries of Wadi Natrun, they spotted a group of Bedouin watching their movements, so the *shaykh* thought it best to carry on. They quickly reloaded the camels and rode for another four hours, until 'about eight in the evening [when we] reached the foot of a sand-hill, and encamped in great disorder, created by the late alarm:– making no fires, and using every precaution to avoid notice or discovery of our retreat'.[38] The ruse worked, the Bedu were not seen again and after what Hornemann later called 'an indefatigable travel, by a great Desert of 13 days' they reached the legendary oasis of Siwa, where further tribulations awaited him.

Hornemann was not the first European to visit Siwa. That prize had been claimed six years earlier by a young Englishman, W.G. Browne. Banks had made some mention of Browne while writing out Hornemann's instructions, referring to his claim that Siwa was the seat of the famous ancient oracle, the one Alexander the Great had risked his life to visit. Browne had also risked his life, but saw no temple in the town before 'the discovery of his being a Christian rendered it . . . necessary for him to make a precipitate retreat from the Country'.[39] How much more Browne had achieved was not known until he returned to London in the autumn of 1798, just as Hornemann was leaving Cairo for Siwa.

Browne's story deserves a longer telling than I can give it here, but like James Bruce a generation earlier he had shown how much a single and single-minded traveller could achieve through intelligent perseverance. Like Beaufoy and Lucas, Browne was the son of a wine merchant. He had taken a degree at Oxford and was studying law in London when his father's death left him financially secure. In 1791, twenty-three years old, stirred by the French Revolution, inspired by James Bruce's account of his travels and fascinated by the plan of the African Association, whose first report had been published the previous year, he decided to see what he could do as an African traveller. Naturally enough, he called on both Banks and Beaufoy before leaving London, but found neither of them at home. It was their loss more than his, for they would have liked to have claimed his achievements for the Association.

Browne was convinced that Bruce was wrong when he claimed that the river he had seen in Ethiopia was the main stream of the Nile. According to Browne, it would be found further inland; and to prove the point he decided to go and find it. In Alexandria in January 1792 he decided to gain a little exploratory experience by looking for the famed ancient oracle of Jupiter Ammon at Siwa. It took him six weeks to locate the long-lost oasis – he is the first European known to have visited it since antiquity – and once there, he set about inspecting the subsidiary temple that lies outside the town. In doing so, he aroused the suspicions of the Siwans, who believed that good Muslims had no interest in the works of pagans. Although he was dressed as a Muslim trader, the Siwans began to suspect that he was an infidel and chased him out of the oasis before he could look for the temple of the oracle.

Back in Cairo, Browne prepared for his journey to the south by learning Arabic. Disguised as a merchant, he travelled the Forty Days' Road to Darfur with a caravan, crossing the hostile Libyan Desert during June and July, the hottest months of the year, only to run into trouble once he reached Darfur: an argument with the man he had employed as his agent and suspicions about his note-taking led to him being arrested by Abd ar-Rahman, the King of Darfur. It was a reminder of how vulnerable travellers were to reversals of fortune and the whims of foreign rulers.

Browne took two years to secure his freedom from the King. During that time he collected information, made repeated demands for compensation for the goods the King had impounded, and managed to tame a lion cub. Darfur, he discovered, was a dead-end, surrounded by tribes who were even more hostile to non-Muslims. He also heard tell of a big river that rose in the mountains to the south and that flowed north towards Egypt; not, it turned out, the White Nile, but the Bahr al-Gazal, one of its tributaries.

In 1798, Browne reappeared in London. He had been away for six years, was now thirty years old and was aware that he was completely unsuited to life in England, as he made clear in his *Travels*. In a chapter entitled 'Comparative View of Life and Happiness in the East and in Europe', he went against fashionable opinion by extolling the virtues of the East, talked up the 'gravity and patience' of Orientals and concluded that, 'The Greeks and ourselves have indeed stigmatised them with the name of barbarians, but impartial inquiry pronounces that they are susceptible of all that is admired in a polished people.'[40]*

---

* By 1800 Browne was back in the Middle East, this time in touch with Banks, who was urging him to continue south. Browne was reluctant. Writing from Cairo in September 1801, he explained that, 'My warm wishes to promote the discovery of the interior of Africa would infallibly reconduct me to that country, were it not for the existence of some impediments which I cannot discover the means to surmount' (DTC, 12, pp.258–62). He never explained what those impediments were, but instead returned to England where he lived as a virtual recluse. In 1811 he set off east again, this time heading for the heartlands of the Turkic people, only to be murdered by robbers in Persia. The year was 1813 and he was just forty-five years old.

Hornemann, the second European at Siwa, was determined to solve the mystery of Alexander the Great and the Ammonian oracle, but the Siwans took one look at him and Frendenburgh and 'from our fairer complexion, from our gait and manners, and from our Turkish-dresses'[41] concluded that they were Christians. Instead of lying low and staying with the rest of the Awjila caravan, Hornemann aroused the Siwans' suspicions by going to look for the temple Browne had described. Now known as the Temple of Amun or, more colloquially, Umm Obaydah, it stands below the old town of Aghurmi, surrounded by palms and fruit trees, near a well that had fascinated Herodotus for its ability to bubble at regular intervals.

Over a couple of days Hornemann made three visits. On the first two occasions he attracted such a large crowd of suspicious villagers that he was physically unable to get a clear view of the temple's decorations. On the third visit, another crowd formed and this time he was challenged. 'Thou undoubtedly art a Christian in thy heart,' one of the villagers challenged him, 'else why come so often to visit these works of the Infidels?'[42] Knowing it would be dangerous to continue his researches – he had wanted to measure and sketch the building – he was obliged to rely on his general observations and memories. His description was vague, referring to 'these rude heaps, and mouldered and disjointed walls',[43] but that did not stop him from conjecturing that 'they *may be* remains of the *Temple of Jupiter Ammon*'.[44] They were, but the main temple of Ammon, also known as the Temple of the Oracle, lay a few hundred metres away, in the middle of the old settlement of Aghurmi.

Perhaps because of the suspicions they had (rightly) held of him, Hornemann left a damning account of the people of Siwa, describing them as 'obtrusive and thievish'. You can feel him breathe a sigh of relief when, after eight days of bartering Kerdassah cloth and other fabrics for Siwan dates and olives, the *shaykh* of the caravan concluded business by having his big drum banged to announce their imminent departure.

Even when they were well on their way into the desert, Hornemann's trials were far from over. Four days out of Siwa they camped for the night in what he described as the fruitful valley of Schiacha. Around eight o'clock, the camp was disturbed by the arrival of some Siwans, who came to warn them that a thousand Bedouin from Fayoum were lying in wait for them the next day. Later that night as many as a hundred Siwans rode up on asses, camped nearby and explained to the *shaykh* of the caravan that they had come to fight with them against the Bedu. At sunrise the *shaykh* held a council, to which Hornemann sent Frendenburgh. The interpreter soon returned in panic. It wasn't the Bedu that the Siwans had come for, it was the Europeans. 'We are both of us unavoidably lost men,' Frendenburgh wailed at the missionary. 'They take us for Christians and spies, and will assuredly put us to death.'[45] The German Mamluk panicked, arming himself with a double-barrelled shotgun and 'two brace of pistols', but Hornemann now revealed some of the strength of character that Banks had recognised, but that had been little in evidence so far on this journey.

He marched over to the meeting 'with a firm and manly step' and greeted the hostile crowd.

'You are of the new Christians from Cairo,' he was told, by which they meant that he was a French spy, 'and are come to explore our country.'[46]

'Tell me, brother,' Hornemann replied, deciding it was best not to offer a direct reply, 'hast thou ever before known 300 armed men take a journey of three days, in pursuit of two men who dwelt in their midst for ten days, and who had eaten and drank with them as friends?' He and Frendenburgh were not two of those invading Christians, he assured them. On the contrary, they were making this journey in an attempt to get away from them.

His confidence earned him a few admirers and for a moment he felt that things might go his way, but then someone mentioned that they knew he was travelling with papers from these new Christians who had done so much damage along the Nile: Frendenburgh, Hornemann discovered, had told them of the passport Bonaparte had issued.

Without waiting for the Siwans to demand it, he went to his tent to fetch the paper, which he handed to the chief of the Siwans. Frendenburgh was with him now, calmer, more collected, sensing that there might be a way out. 'Can anyone read this?' the Siwan asked. Hornemann smiled and shook his head. He could not read it, he told them, but he had been told it would allow him to leave Cairo without being bothered by those new Christians.

At this point Frendenburgh interrupted them, waving his Koran. 'This is the book which I understand,'[47] he shouted, and proceeded to recite a long *sura* by heart. Hornemann then took paper and pen and wrote out a few lines he knew from the holy book, a feat of learning far beyond the capabilities of anyone else in the crowd. All this produced the desired effect, and the *shaykh* of the caravan now declared himself satisfied, as did many of the Siwans. 'The security of my future voyage is thus assured,'[48] the traveller assured his masters in London. But there was a price to pay: while Hornemann was facing down the elders, Frendenburgh in his panic had taken anything that might be incriminating – 'my remains of mummies, my specimens of mineralogy, my more detailed remarks, made on my way from Cairo to Schiacha, and generally my books'[49] – and hurriedly sent a slave to go and bury them. Which he did, so thoroughly that they were never seen again. When the caravan went on its way, it left in the sand the prospect of a tantalising find for a future desert archaeologist.

They were now six rough days from Awjila, the most tiring and unpleasant Hornemann experienced, but the arrival there made up for the hardships. This was home for many of Hornemann's fellow travellers. One hundred and fifty miles from the Mediterranean coast, Awjila was also the base of the Bey of Benghazi, the Pasha of Tripoli's Viceregent. Before they reached the town, some twenty Arab customs officers arrived to assess the caravan and decide the amount of tax to be levied. 'These Arabs then ranged themselves, and formed a right wing of our caravan,' Hornemann wrote, his prose finally reflecting some of the passion of his journey, 'drawn up for procession. The merchants who had horses [he among them] formed the left, and the pilgrims and ordinary Arabs formed the centre, headed by the Sheik preceded by a green flag. The pilgrims marched in singing; and the Arabs made their horses prance and curvet.'[50]

Their departure from Awjila several days later was as exciting as their arrival. Some of Hornemann's fellow travellers were remaining in Awjila, but new travellers had joined his part of the caravan, so they were now 120 men. The German, who was up near the front, saw many people ride out of Awjila to wish them a safe journey, honouring them with a *fantasia* of prancing horses and shooting off their muskets. No sooner had they left than a large body of horsemen were reported closing in on the caravan. They would be no match for a Bedouin raiding party, but all the same, the *shaykh* took defensive action, ordering the boys to drive the laden camels to high ground. Anyone with a gun was required to stand and fight, including Hornemann. They watched and waited with growing tension, until some of the men from Awjila recognised their comrades: the horsemen had been sent by the Bey of Benghazi, who had been alarmed by the sound of the villagers' gunfire.

They now faced another tough journey, this time of sixteen days to the borders of Fezzan, many of them over the waterless plateau of Haruj. But however hard the going was for Hornemann, he was aware that it was tougher for others, particularly some of the pilgrims, among them an old man from Fez, well beyond his sixtieth birthday, returning home from his third pilgrimage to Mecca, travelling without food, water or money. Once in the kingdom of Fezzan, the caravan was fêted at each village it passed. Hornemann spoke particularly well of the holy town of Zawilah, known as the Bilad as-Sharif, the Country of the Sharifs, and formerly the capital of the region. Here more horsemen and gunfire welcomed them, the trading was good and at night the Sharif sent slaves carrying meat, broth and ten small loaves of bread to each tent. 'This most ancient custom the Sheik of the Sultan keeps up and strictly adheres to on arrival of each caravan.'[51]

Whatever greetings they had had before, the most significant was still to come. On 17 November, ten and a half weeks after leaving Cairo, they reached Murzuq, and the traveller found himself in a scene from the Arabian Nights. To acknowledge the arrival of the caravan, the Sultan had set himself up on a small hill, sitting on a worn, green-and-red-striped armchair, wearing a silver-embroidered *gallabiya*. On either side of him, Mamluk and black slaves stood with sabres drawn, while others behind him held banners, lances and halberds, 'of a fashion as old perhaps, as the time of Saladin'.[52] According to tradition, anyone of any importance now went to greet the Sultan. One by one the merchants advanced, until it was the German's turn. Removing his slippers, he crept forward until he was close enough to bend and kiss the 'imperial' hand. The Sultan was unaware of it, but he was greeting the first European we know of to reach the Fezzan.

When the ceremony was over, the Sultan returned to his palace followed by his soldiers, slaves, drummers and a crowd of onlookers. The caravan disbanded and Hornemann went to his lodging in the fortified town, where he immediately heard of a caravan of Hausa merchants preparing to cross the Sahara to Borno, in what is now northern Nigeria. Much as he was tempted to join them, he also heard rumours that Tuaregs to the south were preparing to attack it. Concerned that the Hausa traders were not of sufficient significance to guarantee his safety in the interior, and knowing that a large caravan was expected to arrive any time from Borno, he decided to wait. He had another reason for wanting to stay in town a little longer, for by now he was showing signs of 'the country fevers'. Weakened by the rigours of the journey, soon after their arrival both he and Frendenburgh went down with malaria. Through the windy days and icy nights of the Fezzani winter, the two travellers burned with fever, for which they took regular doses of 'Kina' (cinchona bark, which contains quinine). The cure worked on Hornemann, who soon began to mend, but Frendenburgh continued to suffer and was dead within a few days, leaving his friend distraught and angry – in a letter to his mother, Hornemann blamed the death on Frendenburgh's having been 'led astray by wine and women'.[53]

Sadness at the loss of his companion may explain in part why Hornemann found nothing complimentary to report of the capital of the Fezzan. Once the caravans had left, he thought it was 'the most disinteresting Town I ever saw',[54] although there was much that was new for him, including the local delicacy of locusts and grasshoppers. 'When eaten,' he explained, 'the legs and wings are broken off and the inner part is scooped out, and what remains has a flavour similar to that of red herrings, but more delicious.'[55] There was also a drink called *lugibi*, the fresh juice of a date palm, sweet enough and good to taste, 'but apt to produce flatulencies and diarrhoea'.[56] He was made welcome at the house of the Sultan's brother, one Sidi Mintesser, with whom he spent evenings drinking *busa*.* Some evenings, the Sidi called for dancing girls, known in the Fezzan as *kadanka*. They were as notorious as the *ghawazi* of Cairo, whom Edward Lane, a few years later, described as dressed in 'nothing but the shintiyán (or trousers) and a tób (or very full shirt or gown) of semi-transparent, coloured gauze, open nearly half-way down the front. To extinguish the least spark of modesty which they may yet sometimes affect to retain, they are plentifully supplied with brandy or some other intoxicating liquor. The scenes which ensue cannot be described. I need scarcely add, that these women are the most abandoned courtesans of Egypt. Many of them are extremely handsome; and most of them are richly dressed. Upon the whole, I think they are the finest women in Egypt.'[57]

Hornemann's experience would not have surprised Lane; the traveller relates an evening spent in the company of the Sidi and a dancer during which the Sidi disappeared with another girl soon after her arrival. 'On her return,' Hornemann wrote soberly to London, 'she was asked with a significant smile where she had been.

---

* *Busa* is a date liquor still found throughout the region. I have been served it in small Egyptian villages on the occasion of the local saint's festival. Thick and frothy, it tastes like rotten cider.

She immediately took up her instrument [a *rhababa*], played upon it, and sung, in the Arabian language, "Sweet is Sidi Mintesser, as the waters of the Nile, but yet sweeter is he in his embraces; how could I resist?" [58] Hornemann doesn't relate whether he too enjoyed the pleasures of the *kadanka*, though he does refer to 'the great freedoms allowed to the sex' in Murzuq, and gives detailed information of common Fezzani venereal diseases and their cures. Given how far the former theology student had travelled, it would be surprising if he had not sought out some pleasure.

Whatever pleasures he found there, Murzuq depressed him. The men were often drunk, the Sultan a tyrant, the people lacking in energy of mind and body, their produce of little interest – 'I could not find one single artificer in any trade or work' [59] – the houses miserably built and the climate 'at no season temperate or agreeable'. [60] As soon as he recovered his strength, he decided to head for the fresh air and relatively refined company on offer up at the coast in Tripoli, justifying the journey by his need to ensure the safe despatch of his letters and journal; their arrival in London in some way vindicated him. Anyway, he argued, there was no reason to stay in Murzuq during the blistering summer when the long-awaited Borno caravan had again been delayed.

So, in the middle of June, Hornemann headed for the coast. Slowed by the heat, it took him two months to cover the less than five hundred miles to Tripoli, but in August he was able to write to Banks and Edwards while feasting his eyes on the soothing azure of the Mediterranean.

The British Consulate in Tripoli was housed in a building half a century old, the former residence of the founder of the ruling Karamanli dynasty and now the home of one of the Association's first missionaries, Simon Lucas. If his North African journey had produced few rewards for Banks and the Committee, it had provided the Oriental Interpreter with a leg up the diplomatic ladder.

Having reported on the difficulties, financial and social, faced by his predecessor, Consul Tully, Lucas had persuaded the British government's mandarins that he was the right man for the job. Given that he had refused to cross the desert between Tripoli and Murzuq during the summer on account of the heat, and that Hornemann had just made such a journey, there was bound to be some antagonism between the two men. Happily, Lucas was away on leave when the Association's man reached Tripoli in September 1799.

Lucas had left Dr Bryan McDonogh to perform his duties in his absence. McDonogh was the consulate's medical officer and the Chargé d'Affaires for the Portuguese Consulate General. Whatever his conflicting allegiances, he was happy to approach the Pasha for a *laissez-passer* for Hornemann, which the geographical missionary knew was essential for his safety 'in this country, because every stranger is taken a spy of the French'.[61] McDonogh also offered to forward the traveller's letters to London for a small fee. Hornemann valued the doctor's help very highly. 'He is liked by the present Basha, & can give me assistance more than any Turk in town: he is a literate man, & knows to esteem the undertakings of the Society, & is acquainted with many members of it. I arrived here considered ... as a man of doubtful character; but he puts me now by his assistance & credit in a very good situation.'[62]

Helped by McDonogh, Hornemann stayed several months on the coast, working up his notes and preparing for his journey into the interior, though he made a point of finishing his business before Lucas returned, writing acidly to London, 'I don't know if the Committee believes his excuses for returning to England, or if they give them so little credit as I do.'[63] He then headed for the Arab part of town and took a room in a caravanserai, avoiding Lucas' company. Later, with McDonogh away, he was obliged to ask the Consul's help in negotiating a draft, which was denied, although Lucas turned out to have a more generous nature when he wrote to Banks after Hornemann's departure, 'From my knowledge of his person and abilities during his short residence here, I perceived that you could not have fixed upon a more proper person for such an undertaking and I doubt not if God spares his health he will prove himself worthy the choice of your respectable Society.'[64] Perhaps he had recognised Hornemann's talents, as Banks had, and wanted to be seen to have helped him towards achieving his goals.

On Lucas' return, McDonogh sailed from Tripoli to the Sicilian capital Palermo, taking Hornemann's letters for London, which he hoped to be able to forward from there. As it turned out he found the most secure of messengers in Palermo in the person of Lord Nelson, who was conducting his famous romance with Emma, the wife of Banks' good friend Sir William Hamilton. Sir William was also present on the island and wrote to Banks that 'Lord Nelson received from the Vice-Consul of Tripoli yesterday the packet enclosed and directed to you. We agreed it should be opened, and that we should take a copy, in case Mr. Horneman [sic] should die, or the original not get to you, but, seeing this Letter of no great Consequence, we send it to you without having taken a copy. I hope the man explains himself better by word of mouth than he does by writing; however, some allowance must be made for his being a Foreigner.'[65] Indeed it should, and happily the Association did just that.

Hornemann meanwhile had rediscovered Muhammad D'Ghies, the Tripolitan Turk to whom he had been introduced by Jérôme Lalande in Paris. That chance meeting now turned to Hornemann's advantage, for D'Ghies was still one of the Pasha's advisers and was happy to use his influence in his favour. Nelson's proximity also helped Hornemann's cause, for Tripoli relied for its prosperity on the free movement of goods across the Mediterranean, and since the defeat of the French fleet off Alexandria the previous year, the sea was undisputedly controlled by the British Navy. This, and the fact that Hornemann was recommended by some of the most powerful people in England, helped ensure that he left Tripoli in November 1799 with letters of recommendation from the Pasha, in which 'he calls me by my adopted Turkish name – calls me one of his men he liked chiefly ... he beg'd me to go where I should like'.[66]

But where would he like to go? He had already completed a journey of considerable importance. He might not have been the first European to reach the Fezzan – Italian mercenaries in the Pasha's army were said to have been there before him – but he was the first to arrive with the intention of plotting its location on a map and of collecting political and commercial information. Now the interior of Africa seemed to be within his reach, and he wrote to Banks to explain his plan to travel from Murzuq to Agadez, Kashna, Kebbi, Nupe and on to Timbuktu.

'I am now returning to Fezzan,' he explained to Banks on 29 November, while still living among some sixty Turks and Arabs in a grimy, cramped Tripolitan *funduk*.

The Camel which carries some little Merchandize, as looking glasses, red cloth, knives, &c. for me, is gone. I myself shall follow tomorrow with my other camel, serving me to carry my baggage, arms, victuals, books, instruments, water, &c, plenty of articles, but very few things on the whole. Then pray, Sir, do not look on me as an European, but as a real African. My victuals e.g. from here to Mursuck consists of 40lb Cuscasu [couscous], 15lb meal, and 10lb Linses [lentils], with the necessary Oil and Butter. My baggage is two Tripolinian dressings, because I shall take again the Sudan dressing as soon as I am arrived at Fezzan. My books I turn'd overboard, excepting 3, but replaced them by an Alcoran [Koran], and some other holy books of that kind.

My instruments are yet altogether well, except the Thermometer. It is true I could during my Travel until Fezzan not make great use of them, but from here departing I shall have more occasion for to use them.

I look upon my Travels done, as upon the work of an apprentice. Now I think I have the experience at least of a young Master. It is a new plan to travel as a Mahomedan in these Countries, dangerous between these superstitious people leaded by fanaticism and intolerancy, but dangerous only for the beginning. Afterwards it is safer and better.

> *I am very far to think to advise the Committee of the*
> *African Association, composed of Gentlemen like respectable*
> *by their knowledge as by their character; but after having lived*
> *two years in these Countries, and having heard so much of*
> *the more remote Countries, I think it very proper the Society*
> *might expect my return, before they send out another Traveller*
> *for the Northern Africa. I cannot determine the month in*
> *which I shall be returning to Europe; but I suppose that will*
> *be about 1802.*[67]

After a seven-week journey, on 20 January 1800 Hornemann was back in the wind-swept alleys of Murzuq. At the beginning of March a large caravan arrived and would have allowed him to travel alongside, but he decided not to join it, for once again rumours reached him that it was going to be attacked. It was a fortuitous decision, because while waiting in Murzuq, Hornemann met a *sharif* from Borno. The letter of introduction from the Pasha of Tripoli helped here, for it earned him the *sharif*'s confidence; he would soon be returning to his homeland and he would be happy to escort this man whom the Pasha 'liked chiefly'. On 6 April, Hornemann wrote again to Sir Joseph in his neat, exact handwriting, mentioning new observations on the smallpox and venereal diseases, passing on information about the rivers – he had been told 'the communication of the Niger & Nile was not to be doubted' – and noting that in Borno as in ancient Egypt, a girl was sacrificed each year to the rising river. It was a hurried note:

> *Our Caravan is in the moment of setting off for Bornou, I*
> *myself shall join it in the evening. Being very healthsom [sic]*
> *& perfectly acclimated to this Country, sufficiently acquainted*
> *with the manners of my fellow travellers, speaking the Arabian*
> *language & somewhat the Bornou tongue & being well armed*
> *& not without courage under the protection of two great*
> *Sheriffs, I hope a good success of my undertaking . . . I consider*
> *this letter as the last for this year, or perhaps as the last before*
> *my arriving at one of the Coasts of Africa.*[68]

Then, recommending himself to Banks' remembrance, he signed himself 'Your most obedient servant' and stepped off the map into the Sahara, bound for the heart of Africa.

13

Many Deaths

'Thunder, Death and Lightening:– the Devil to pay.'
Lieutenant Martyn to his wife, Niger River, November 1805

London, 1802

WHEN MUNGO PARK visited the Île de Gorée off the Senegalese
coast, he had noted that it would make a perfect base from which
to launch further voyages into the interior. In May 1799, Banks had
spoken of the Association's missionaries having opened a gate into
the African interior and suggested that British redcoats be marched
through it to take control of the Niger and its trade for Britain.
Somewhere between Park's comment and Banks' proposal, a significant shift had occurred in the Association's intentions, forcing
gentlemanly scholarship to compete with national aspirations. It
would be an exaggeration to suggest that a comment or a proposal
could have been the direct or sole cause of what happened, but it
certainly had an influence. Banks had sent a copy of the Association's plan to his friend and mentor Lord Liverpool, and Liverpool,
as President of the Board of Trade, had presented it to the Cabinet.
In April 1800 British troops landed on Gorée, forcing the French
garrison off the island (they put up little resistance) and claiming
it for King George.

Whatever excitement the capture of Gorée caused in Soho Square,

230

the British government took no further action in West Africa. At the time, it needed to concentrate its resources elsewhere in the struggle against revolutionary France. But when the Peace of Amiens was agreed in 1802, Banks was hopeful that the government's attention could be turned to the equally glorious activity of exploration. What's more, he now had more than just the recommendations of his missionaries with which to persuade Cabinet ministers.

That summer, he received from Paris a book entitled *Fragment d'un Voyage en Afrique*, written by Sylvain de Golbéry. Golbéry was no newcomer to Africa, having served in the 1780s as aide-de-camp to the French Governor of Senegal. Recognising Bonaparte's new world order and the mood of the moment, he now urged that French arms be directed towards the control of the African coast from Senegal to Liberia. 'Let there be conceived a plan of operations in this part of Africa,' he wrote, 'let there be a well-organised land-force and a very active maritime one. These will concur to give us an importance in Africa.'[1] Banks sounded the alarm over this latest and greatest example of French designs on what he clearly regarded as his area of influence, and repeated the dire warning he had issued to the Cabinet several years earlier. And in case Golbéry was dismissed as an inconsequential voice in the French corridors of power, other evidence emerged of France's colonial intentions in Africa.

In the second half of 1802, taking advantage of the new *entente* created by the peace treaty, the Association presented Bonaparte with a copy of Hornemann's journal in thanks for the help he had offered their traveller after the invasion of Egypt. Bonaparte seems to have recognised the significance of the work, for he ordered it to be translated into French. Louis-Matthieu Langlès, France's foremost Orientalist and a member of the Institut National, had the honour of editing the French edition. In his introduction, Langlès highlighted the achievements of the African Association, which he thought deserved 'the attention of our government, and of every Frenchman who is a friend to his country, and to science: may a noble spirit of emulation, induce us to form an *African Society in*

France'.[2] No sooner said than done: la Société de l'Afrique intérieure et de Découvertes was immediately founded.

The Société was not necessarily going to mount a serious challenge to British interests, but Banks recognised that its creation could add weight to his argument that if Britain delayed in West Africa, the French would not hesitate to take advantage. On the other hand, immediate action would bring central and West African trade under British control at a time when the national economy was struggling to pay for the costs of war. Delay would hand the trade and its profit to the French and might later oblige Britain to fight a war in Africa.

In spite of his outspoken attacks on French ambitions in Africa, Banks was happy to help Frenchmen elsewhere in the world, particularly if they were scientists. The many volumes of his correspondence are filled with ongoing discussions with scholars and scientists throughout Europe. 'The science of two Nations may be at Peace,' he assured one of his correspondents, outlining his belief in the universal nature of science, 'while their Politics are at War.'[3] During the war years, he had used his prestige and the influence of his friends – Nelson among them – to the benefit of several French scientists. He went to great lengths to help Déodat de Dolomieu, the French geologist shipwrecked in the Mediterranean, who was held in appalling conditions with the connivance if not on the orders of the King of Naples. In July 1801, after Dolomieu was freed, Banks assured him that 'I took every measure in my power, and used every argument I could suggest, to interest these my friends to sollicit [sic] your release.'[4]

His efforts did not go unnoticed on either side of the Channel. In Paris, French intellectuals were quick to reward his efforts on their behalf, and as soon as the preliminaries for peace were concluded, the Institut National elected him its first Associate Member. The honour clearly pleased him, for in his letter of acceptance he described it as 'the highest and most enviable literary distinction which I would possibly attain'. He went on to call France 'the empire of virtue, of justice, and of honour'.[5] No one would question the achievements of the Institut, nor that Banks was worthy of the honour it was showing him. But for many of his compatriots, the savagery of the Revolution and the horrors of the war were just too fresh for such fraternising. Retribution was not long in coming: Banks was attacked in the London press, most savagely by a Fellow of the Royal Society. Writing anonymously under the *nom de plume* 'Misogallus',* the Fellow addressed a vitriolic letter to the 6 November issue of *Cobbett's Weekly Register* accusing Banks of servility, disloyalty and falsehood, and his 'respectable brothers' of the French Institute of plundering 'libraries and cabinets with as much alacrity, and as little scruple, as he [Bonaparte] displayed in treasuries and in churches'.[6] The letter ended by calling on Fellows to strip Banks of the Royal Society's presidency at a meeting to be held on 30 November. Banks weathered the storm, as he had done earlier ones, by not replying. Nor was he unseated at the Royal Society.

It is ironic that some in Britain doubted where his sympathies lay, because beyond the realm of science Banks was as wary of the French as anyone in England, his natural prejudice heightened by what he perceived as the madness of the Revolution. 'We in England, Sir,' he wrote to Dolomieu, after the geologist had been freed, 'are as firmly attached to Regal Government as you can be to Republican.'[7] And in spite of his efforts to encourage a free exchange of scientific ideas and discoveries, he still wanted science to benefit Britain more than any other country, and he still wanted British scholars and British explorers to win the glory of discovery, just as he wanted British trade to benefit from overseas involvement.

Spurred on by the foundation of the Société de l'Afrique and by Golbéry's suggested plan of operations, Banks now spelled out to the British government the dangers posed by French ambitions, particularly their claim to the whole of Senegambia, with its extensive goldfields: 'I am clear,' he wrote to John Sullivan, the Under-Secretary of State at the newly-created Colonial Office on 1 August 1802, 'that His Majesties [sic] Ministers should be aware of the contents [of Golbéry's book], and hold in mind what will happen, which

---

* Charles Lyte, one of Banks' biographers, suggests that Misogallus may have been Dr Samuel Horsley, a Cambridge prelate and dissenting former member of the Royal Society's Council.

is that whoever Colonizes in that part of Africa with Spirit will Clearly be able to sell Colonial Products of all kinds in the European market at a Cheaper price than any part of the West Indies can afford it.'[8]

Sullivan recognised both the danger and the opportunity, but he was a careful man, loath to be rushed into action. Before making a decision, he canvassed opinions from people with intimate knowledge of the issues and the place, including Zachary Macaulay, the former Governor of the fledgling settlement at Sierra Leone, Philip Beaver, the hero of an ill-fated attempt to settle an island off the West African coast eight years earlier, and the geographer Rennell. All three understood the need for action as well as the difficulties posed by the terrain and climate, yet it was Rennell, who had no first-hand experience of Africa, who was the most specific in his recommendations, following the Association's line by calling for a Resident or Consul to be established in Bambuk.[9] Macaulay and Beaver were more cautious, but crucially could provide no compelling reasons not to follow the course advocated by Rennell and Banks. Convinced by the experts, Sullivan recommended to the Cabinet that the James Island fort be rebuilt and used to protect a new trading post to be established higher up the river, perhaps at Fattatenda, the place that had so pleased Daniel Houghton. Whatever the Cabinet's decision, no action was taken until the following year. But by October 1803 the peace treaty had been abandoned, Bonaparte had sent a hundred thousand troops to Boulogne in preparation for an invasion of Britain (he also put the Bayeux Tapestry on show to make his intentions clear), half a million Londoners turned out to cheer King George III as he reviewed war volunteers in Hyde Park, and Sir Joseph Banks had written the following surprisingly formal lines to his former protégé, Mr Mungo Park, in Peeblesshire.

> I am requested by Lord Hobart* to desire your attendance immediately at his Lordship's office in Downing Street.

---

* Lord Hobart was Sullivan's superior at the Colonial Office; like Sullivan, he clearly recognised Banks' value as the government's unofficial scientific adviser. In October 1793 he had written to Banks that 'wide as the world is, traces of you are to be found in every corner'.

After his earlier disagreement with Banks and the government over the terms of a mission to explore the interior of Australia, Park had followed his heart and returned to Scotland, where he had married and settled down to life as a Lowland doctor; his wife Alison gave birth to three children – a fourth was on the way. Yet for all the harmony and the income from a good medical practice, Park complained to friends about the difficulty of making a living. The difficulty was perhaps not so much financial as that of settling for the Scottish Lowlands after the interior of Africa, for the ride round his practice after a journey to the Niger, for anonymous domestic contentment after the adulation heaped on him in London. One of his friends, the novelist Sir Walter Scott, pointed to this when he wrote that Park had confessed he 'would rather brave Africa and all its horrors than wear out his life in long and toilsome rides over cold and lonely heaths and gloomy hills, assailed by the wintry tempest, for which the remuneration was hardly enough to keep body and soul together'.[10] If that was a true reflection of Park's state of mind, then the letter that came from Banks will have been doubly welcome, for it assured him that the business to which he was being called 'will suit your wishes, and that proper terms of engagement will be offered to you'.[11]

The plan under discussion was no longer merely the reoccupation of Fort James. It seems that Banks' concern that French troops and traders might occupy West Africa had been taken seriously: the British government had decided to get there first. The crux of Banks' commercial argument rested on the Moors, who acted as go-betweens, selling European goods south of the Sahara and African produce to Europeans in the north. Even taking into account the costs and difficulties of crossing the Sahara, they were still able to make a healthy profit. How much more, the great improver wondered, might be made if British merchants, making a shorter and easier journey from the Gambia River, were able to trade directly with the markets along the Niger? The obvious conclusion was that enormous profits were waiting to be taken. To make this possible, the British government had decided to build a string of forts between Bambuk and the main cities along the Niger, wherever they may be. Park was now to travel not as the missionary of the geographically-inclined African Association but as the ambassador of His Most Britannic Majesty, King George III, to persuade the rulers of Segu, Timbuktu and Hausa – and anyone else of note – that they would be better off trading with British merchants than with the Moors. To protect Park, and as a visible proof of British power, an armed boat and a detachment of soldiers were also being sent: gunboat diplomacy was about to arrive on the Niger.

We can only speculate on the turn that history might have taken had Park succeeded in this mission, because in the spring of 1804 the Niger kingdoms were spared the blessings of British arms by the fall of Henry Addington as British Prime Minister. Nothing could be done until the new administration under William Pitt the Younger was in place. Park, who was in London and expecting to leave for Africa, found himself travelling north once more, this time in the company of his government-paid Arabic tutor, a man by the name of Sidi Omback Boubi, a Moor whose habits included abstinence from alcohol and slaughtering animals with his own knife, and who was soon to become the talking point of the borderlands.

By September 1804 Pitt's new government was installed, with Lord Camden as the Secretary of State for War and the Colonies. Once again there was talk of sending Park to Africa, only now the plan had changed. Military goals were out, and there was no more talk of establishing fortified trading posts. In their place Camden stressed the more modest aims of exploration and diplomacy. He had also had a change of mind as to who should run the expedition, and wrote to Banks that 'this undertaking ... bears so much the description of a Journey of Enquiry without any military attendance upon it, that it seems to me more fit that Mr. Park should be instructed as to his Enquiries and Researches by those who have turned their Mind to this subject as much as you have done than by me'.[12] The government would fund the expedition, and Camden was 'happy to cooperate in whatever way be useful'; but Banks, scientific adviser to the new government as he had been to its predecessors, and his African Association were to be the organisers.

Park arrived from Scotland championing a new theory regarding the course of the Niger. No one along the North African coast had any idea where the river ended, so it was unlikely to run into the desert. Having talked the matter over with several people who had lived along the West African coast, he was now certain that the Niger did not run into lakes in the middle of Africa, or into the Nile either. Instead, he believed, it flowed into the Congo, and from there into the ocean. To prove it, he suggested retracing his steps inland from the Gambia with thirty soldiers and six carpenters, building boats and sailing down the river to settle the matter of its ending.

Rennell was against the plan. The 'facts' as he knew them proved that the theory was flawed, and he 'earnestly dissuaded Park from engaging on so hazardous an enterprise'.[13] Banks disagreed with his geographer, and was sure the Niger would prove to be the Congo, or at least run into it. It ended, he was sure, and in spite of what Rennell claimed, in the ocean, not in a lake somewhere in the interior. He was aware, too, of the dangers, but he thought them worth the possible rewards. Perhaps he was reminded of the risks he had taken when sailing around the world with Captain Cook when he wrote that, 'Mr. Park's expedition is one of the most hazardous a man can undertake; but I cannot agree with those who think it too hazardous to be attempted: it is by similar hazards of human life alone that we can hope to penetrate the obscurity of the internal face of Africa: we are really wholly ignorant of the country between the Niger and the Congo, and can explore it only incurring the most frightful hazards.'[14]

Now that they had government approval for the plan and, more important, the money, there was a hurry to get Park out to Africa before the rains broke. On 18 December 1804, Banks had an interview with Camden at the Ministry at which they worked out a timetable: if Park left England early in January he would have six months to reach the Niger, which, according to Banks' calculations, would be ample time: two months to reach Fattatenda high up the Gambia River, two months to make the overland crossing to the Niger and another two 'for building the Boats, Felling Trees, Sawing Planks etc. etc.'[15] What Banks had not counted on was the speed at which the Ministry would move: it took a month to issue Park's instructions even though, as John Barrow, Secretary at the Admiralty and therefore a man who understood the workings of a ministry, later pointed out, they were 'grounded upon his [Park's] own memoir, in the shape of a letter, which could not have employed half an hour in writing'.[16] In the end Park did not sail out of Portsmouth until the morning of 31 January 1805, accompanied by his brother-in-law Alexander Anderson but without his Moorish language teacher Sidi Omback Boubi.* Lord Camden's official instructions reminded Park that 'His Majesty has selected you to discover and ascertain whether any, and what commercial intercourse can be opened, with the interior.'[17]

On Cape Verde Island they bought donkeys, and from the British garrison on Gorée they recruited their soldiers – three officers and thirty-three privates. The lure was the offer of double pay and, for the privates, many of whom were convicts or the victims of press-gangs, the promise of freedom from future service – 'they jumped into the boats', Park reported, 'in the highest spirits, and bade adieu to Goree with repeated huzzas'.[18] But all of this took time, considerably more time than Banks had allowed, and it was not until 4 May, two months late according to the timetable, that Park led his party of forty-three Europeans into the bush beyond Mr Ainslee's house at Pisania and headed for the Niger River.

Banks had calculated the timetable for Park's trip using the explorer's own account of his journey back to the Gambia River. Having already fallen behind schedule, Park now discovered there

---

* It appears that Omback Boubi was not invited to join Park, for on 15 February 1805 the Sidi wrote to Banks protesting 'that my character has suffered much ... from my having denied what has been reported to them, that *you* had offered me or knew of your own knowledge that I had been offered £500- to go with Mr. Mungo Park'.

was a great difference between travelling alone or with a coffle of slaves, and travelling with heavily-laden donkeys and inexperienced European soldiers. Each day they dropped a little further behind time. The season was already more advanced than they wanted, and temperatures were rising rapidly; they found themselves walking through the bush in temperatures over 100°F (38°C) in the shade. The going was tough and slow and there were few moments of relief, though on 4 June they did find time to pause to honour King George's birthday, slaughtering a bullock and a calf and toasting the King's health with water. Park hoped the day's rest would prove a turning point, but instead of improving conditions, it was, as Park confessed to his journal, 'the beginning of sorrow'.[19] That night, right on cue according to Banks' timetable, they were forced to huddle under whatever shelter they could find or improvise as the sky clouded over and they were hit by 'a squall with thunder and rain'. The rainy season had started.

There is a nightmarish quality to Park's writing once the rains start. Each day the going becomes more difficult, the rivers swollen, the paths more slippery, both men and animals worn down by the rain and the diseases, particularly the malaria and dysentery that came with the season. Many die or are left to be cared for in villages along the way. And as the caravan becomes weaker and less able to defend itself, so the villagers make heavier demands and the bandits raid with greater daring. It isn't until 19 August that the remnants of the party finally reach the Niger at Bamako.

The going had been bad, the toll even worse. 'I reflected,' Park confided to his journal, 'that three-fourths of the soldiers had died on their march, and that in addition to our weakly state we had no carpenters to build the boats in which we proposed to prosecute our discoveries; the prospect appeared somewhat gloomy.'[20]

At this point, others might have thought of abandoning the project, or sitting out the rains. 'Every reasonable man,' Barrow later commented, 'would not only have pronounced his justification, but applauded his resolution,' had he done so. But Park was a determined optimist; he was not going to give in, and he took comfort wherever it could be found; he was cheered, for instance, by the

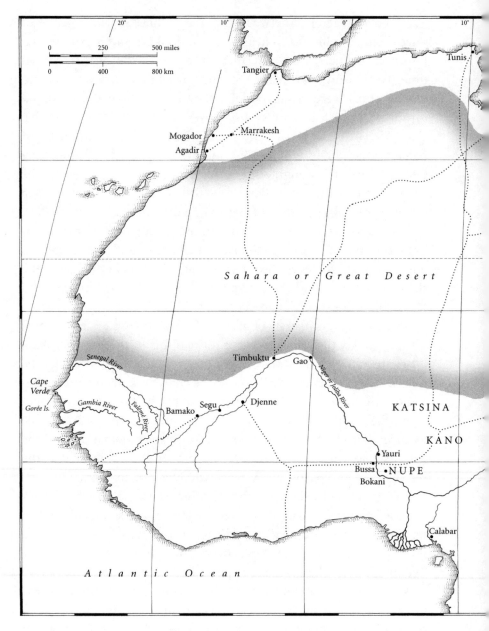

Key locations for Park's journey to Bussa and Hornemann's to Bokani

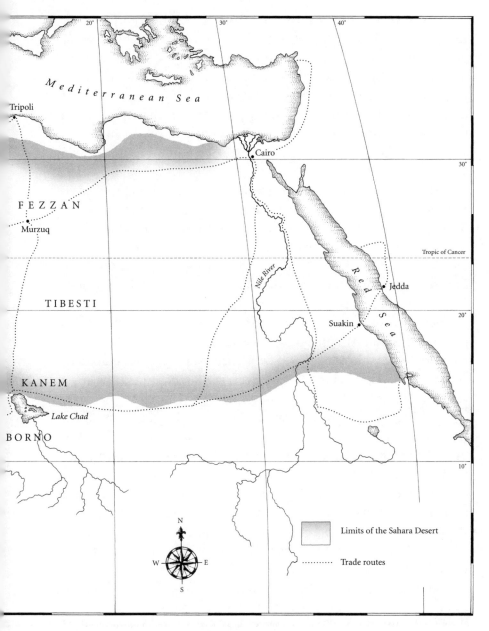

Limits of the Sahara Desert

·········· Trade routes

fact that they had trekked overland from the Gambia to the Niger River without having to fight. 'In fact,' he went on, 'this journey plainly demonstrates, first, that with common prudence any quantity of merchandise may be transported from the Gambia to the Niger, without danger of being robbed by the natives; secondly, that if this journey be performed in the dry season, one may calculate on losing not more than three or at most four men out of fifty.'[21] In spite of his certainty, Park's assessment was nothing more than speculation.

Park and the remaining one-quarter of his expedition floated in canoes much of the way from Bamako to Segu, pulling in to the bank for frequent halts. The ten men were now in such a weak condition that even the wolves were a threat, carrying off one of the dead before he could be buried. Finally they reached Segu, capital of Mansong, the King who had helped Park on his previous visit by providing enough cowrie shells for him to continue his journey. During the past nine years Mansong had tightened his grip over his Bambara kingdom while at the same time adding new territory to it. Park knew that if he wished, Mansong could guarantee the foreigners' safety, at least as far as Timbuktu, so the royal audience was crucial to his mission's success.

The King showed his habitual caution by sending his First Minister, Modibinne, to find out why the white men had come and to inspect the gifts they had brought. Park displayed the presents and then levelled with the Minister, explaining his mission. The people of Segu bought goods made in Europe, on which the Moors, the traders of Timbuktu and of Djenne were making a profit. 'Now,' Park told him, 'the king of the white people wishes to find out a way by which we may bring our own merchandise to you, and sell everything at a much cheaper rate.'[22]

Both the Minister and the King had suffered at the hands of the Moors and they liked the sound of Park's proposition. For the first time in many months, the geographical missionary was confident of success – but he was ignoring one significant factor: Mansong was afraid of white men. He was not afraid of their violence or their intentions – at this stage, he did not know enough about them to worry – but he was clearly scared of the bad magic they seemed to bring, which explains why he refused, even now, to meet the white traveller. Park sent an African to the King to offer his greetings and hand over the presents. When the man returned, he reported that the King was still afraid, and that when the white men were mentioned, Mansong 'immediately began to make squares and triangles in the sand before him with his finger'.[23]

Eager to help the Europeans leave his kingdom, the King offered to provide canoes for their journey, but as the days passed and the river dropped, no canoes arrived. Park made use of the time by shedding his excess baggage and earning local currency – the cowrie shell. On 8 October he reported that he had 'opened shop in great style, and exhibited a choice assortment of European articles to be sold in wholesale or retail . . . I found my shop every day more and more crowded with customers; and such was my run of business, that I was sometimes forced to employ *three tellers at once* to count my cash. I turned one market day twenty-five thousand seven hundred and fifty-six pieces of money (cowries).'[24] According to Park's earlier calculations, this was equal to more than £5, enough for a man to buy food to support himself and his horse for more than eight months. But to put it in context, it was nothing compared to the slave trade: a prime male slave, according to Park's account, fetched forty thousand cowries in the market, while a prime female could go for as much as one hundred thousand.

Park felt that his market days provided ample proof of the viability of British trade with the Niger, but there were sceptics back in England. John Whishaw, who wrote the biographical sketch that appeared alongside Park's *Journal* in 1815, pointed out that he was only making 100 per cent profit on the English prices of his goods. This might have seemed good business in the heat and dust of Segu's marketplace, but it was not going to be nearly enough to cover the costs and compensate hardened British merchants for the considerable risks the venture entailed, among them the possibility of death. It seems likely that Park was heavily undercharging for his goods, perhaps to prove the point he had made to Modibinne, the King's Minister, that European goods would cost less if British traders were able to open a direct communication between the Niger and the Atlantic via the Gambia River. Local traders were naturally unhappy with the *toubab*, the white man, undercutting them in their own markets. Refusing to see their livelihood disappear without a fight, 'the Jinnie [Djenne] people, the Moors, and the merchants here joined with those of the same descriptions at Sego, and offered to give Mansong a quantity of merchandise of greater value than all the presents I had made him, if he would seize our baggage, and either kill us, or send us back again out of Bambarra'.[25]

Mansong did neither. Instead he sent along a pair of rotten canoes, which Park and the other survivors managed to refit into one riverworthy sailing craft. Forty feet long according to Lieutenant Martyn, who sailed on it, six feet wide, with five-foot-high sides, it was a large, patched-up shell of a craft that did not live up to the grandeur of its name, His Majesty's Schooner *Joliba*. Park's brother-in-law and confidant Anderson had succumbed to his fevers and joined the long list of fatalities while they were waiting, so, as Park wrote to Lord Camden from the *Joliba* on 17 November 1805, 'I am sorry to say that of forty-four Europeans, who left the Gambia in perfect health, five only are at present alive; namely, three soldiers, (one deranged in his mind,) Lieutenant Martyn, and myself.'[26]

He ended by suggesting that, 'If I succeed in the object of my journey I expect to be in England in the month of May or June.'[27] What were his chances? The rains had ended and what he calls the healthy season begun. He was more than seven hundred miles inland from the coast, was in good health and enjoyed King Mansong's protection. This seems not to have extended as far as Timbuktu, because the King now sent him a message to leave as soon as he could, before the Moors of Timbuktu heard about him and made trouble for both of them. Park had money, arms and trade goods, a shallow boat that, with a little luck, would be strong enough to carry them down the dropping river, and a guide, Amadi Fatouma. Fatouma assured him that the Niger turned south after Katsina. Although he was not sure where the river was going to end or whether it would run into the Congo, Park was still certain, as he assured Lord Camden, 'that it can end nowhere but in the sea',[28] by which he meant the Atlantic Ocean. Lieutenant Martyn, writing to his wife, noted that 'Captain Park has made every enquiry concerning the River Niger, and from what he can learn there seems no doubt but that it is the Congo.'[29] Martyn also noted – 'Thunder, Death and Lightening:- the Devil to pay'[30] – that Park had not been himself since leaving Gorée.

In his last letter to his wife before leaving Mansong's kingdom, Park wrote that he had no intention of stopping or landing anywhere until he reached the ocean, and this appears to have been what happened. 'I have still a sufficient force to protect me from any insult in sailing down the river to the sea,'[31] he wrote home, just before setting sail. When it was necessary to pay tribute or to buy fresh food, Fatouma would go ashore with sacks of cowrie shells and buy whatever was needed. We can only guess Park's motives for refusing to land – memories of how badly the Moorish King Ali of Ludamar had treated him on his previous expedition seem the most obvious motivation. Mansong's warning about the Moors of Timbuktu will not have helped.

Not surprisingly, they attracted suspicion wherever they went. Their boat was unusual on two counts: because it was equipped with guns and hide screens, to protect the passengers from attack; and because so few passengers were rarely seen travelling in so large a boat. Fatouma thought it could easily have held 120 passengers. Their behaviour was as provocative as their appearance. In a region where it was customary to stop and talk, or palaver, at just about every settlement of any size, Park steered the *Joliba* down the middle of the stream and avoided pulling in to the bank. Even when he reached the port of the much-longed-for Timbuktu, the grail of African travellers for past centuries, he sailed straight past rather than stop and risk his life in another bid for glory. But then Lieutenant Martyn had pointed out that Park was 'not himself' – by this stage he was in the grip of a madness, a touch of fever perhaps, so that when faced with anxious or even angry men in canoes, he opened fire rather than offering explanations. At Sibbe beyond Djenne, at Timbuktu and many other places he blazed a trail of blood along the river. Once embarked on that course, the outcome was inevitable.

The end, when it came, was due more to a misunderstanding of local politics than to open hostility. The *Joliba* had passed Timbuktu and Gao, traversed the great Niger bend and was heading due south – that, in itself, would have been achievement enough to guarantee Park's fame. By now he must have realised that the river was running into the ocean, although he is unlikely to have had an idea of just how close they were, less than 350 miles, from the ocean. At a place called Yauri, in what is now western Nigeria, the Hausa Emir came close to the water to greet the foreigners and to point out the difficulty of the river ahead – some reports mentioned rapids, others hostile natives. The *Joliba* was pulled in to the bank at this point, because this was as far as Amadi Fatouma had contracted to travel with them.

The Emir suggested that if they wanted to get to the ocean, they would be wise to travel overland. He offered one of his own guides and an escort to protect them. Park was clearly suspicious, perhaps thinking this was an attempt to lure him away from the safety of the boat only to attack him in the bush. He declined the offer. What happened next will always remain a matter of confusion.

The *Joliba* slipped away with Park and his surviving companions on board, carrying sacks of cowries, the remains of their trade goods and equipment, and a considerable armoury. What they did not have with them was any knowledge of the water or an ability to speak to people along the way. From this point on, nothing is certain. Some reports suggest they were attacked from the rocks – perhaps they had upset a local ruler by not stopping to offer presents or pay their respects. Another suggested that they hit the rapids of Bussa that the Hausa Emir had mentioned. Whether killed by arrows or drowned, some time around the end of 1805 or early in 1806 Mungo Park, one of the world's great travellers and the African Association's brightest hope, finally came to rest at the bottom of the dark river that he had done so much to illuminate.

'Should you yourselves not hear of me these three years, make no inquiry,' the German traveller Frederick Hornemann had written to Banks from southern Libya before disappearing into the Sahara. More than five years had passed since his departure from Murzuq, and two years since an unsubstantiated report appeared in the German *Altona Gazette*, quoting a Fezzani trader who claimed that 'Jussuph [Hornemann's assumed name] was gone to Gondasch, with the view of thence proceeding to the coast, and returning to Europe.'[32] No one, not even the encyclopaedic Rennell, had any idea where Gondasch may be located. Frustratingly, the *Altona Gazette* also offered no clue as to where the Fezzani trader had last seen Hornemann, but the London-based *Philosophical Magazine*, which also ran the story in its April issue, seemed to think that this had been at Buran. 'Buran too,' the Association's Secretary noted ruefully, 'is unnoticed on our maps.'

At the Association's general meeting of May 1805 Sir William Young, writer and politician and now the Association's Secretary, announced that something had, at last, been heard of the traveller. Over dinner at Banks' house the previous December, he had met Dr McDonogh, the medical officer and acting Consul who had helped Hornemann in Tripoli and delivered his journal to Lord Nelson on Sicily. McDonogh had told Young that he had it on good authority from 'a respectable Moorish merchant' that Hornemann had been in Katsina in June 1803, that he was well and that the people of Katsina regarded him as a *Marabout* or holy man. 'Scarcely two years have elapsed,' Young told his audience in 1805, 'and we must not yet forgo the hopes of receiving from himself, an account of the interesting tract of country which he had then reached, and of his observations made, successively at Cas'na, at Houssa, and at Tombuctoo.'[33] But news was frustratingly slow to seep out of the interior and find its way back to London.

While Park and Hornemann were still in the field, Banks had written to Johann Blumenbach in Göttingen that he was 'inclined to an attempt from Calabar, or some other point on the coast of Guinea to visit Gana near the Lake of Wangara, which was, when the Portuguese made their discovery, the Capital to which the Gold and Ivory Coasts etc were subject'.[34] Wangara was also one of the inland places Rennell had earmarked as a likely end for the Niger River. Blumenbach replied by recommending several young men whom he thought would make promising missionaries. Whatever qualities these men possessed, the French had effectively cut Göttingen off from England and made interview and selection impossible. So, for the moment at least, the field was open for two would-be British travellers. Mr Thomas Fitzgerald volunteered to travel east from the Cape of Good Hope, a fascinating expedition no doubt, but of no immediate interest to the Committee. At the same time, Mr Henry Nicholls made it clear that he would be happy to go wherever the Association wanted to send him, and therefore found himself commissioned to travel to Old Calabar, a port along the coast of present-day Nigeria and not far, as we now know, and as the Committee had not even suspected, from the several mouths of the Niger River.

On 9 June 1804, Nicholls was at Soho Square to face the Association's Committee. Depleted by deaths and absences, it had recently been boosted by the election of several new members, among them the Reverend Dr Anthony Hamilton, the sixty-year-old vicar of the church of St Martin-in-the-Fields, in what has since become Trafalgar Square, Sir Edward Winnington, a serving Member of Parliament, and Roger Wilbraham, a noted collector of books and paintings. All three were Fellows of the Royal Society and obviously enjoyed Banks' support. Young and Rennell were also present as Nicholls was told to go away, read Park's *Travels* and whatever else he could find on the interior of West Africa, and 'bestow serious consideration on the dangers and difficulties of the enterprise'.[35]

Two weeks later the would-be explorer was back in front of the Committee, having done his reading and concluded that the mission was 'suited to the temper of his mind and ardour for curious research'. He had also done his sums: he wanted 10s.6d. a day while in London and £500 a year from the day he sailed for Africa. The Committee accepted him, but, suffering a shortage of funds, cut his African fee to a guinea a day (£382 p.a.) and put a condition on it: they would only pay him for a year in Africa, and only if he managed to travel more than five hundred miles inland. It might seem an unlikely clause, but something about Nicholls seems to have reminded Banks of Simon Lucas; there were concerns that he might be more interested in setting himself up as a West African trader than in making his name as one of the Association's geographical missionaries. Perhaps there were also concerns that, like Hornemann, he might end up spending a year or two in Africa before making a move towards the interior.

Banks and Young now used their contacts to approach traders with experience of the coast around the Bight of Benin, in the hope that their information might be of help to Nicholls. By August the plan was clear: sixty miles up the 'River Calaba' there lay a settlement called Newtown. This was the home of three important *slatees*, traders in slaves, ivory and gold dust. Nicholls was to base himself in Calabar for some months, collect whatever information he could on the interior and then make contact with the Newtown *slatees* who, it was hoped, would provide him with a way into the interior, as Karfa Taura had provided Park with a way out of it. His passage booked on the *Aurora*, due to sail from Liverpool for Old Calabar on 31 October, Nicholls prepared himself for departure by running up an impressive bill of £295 at Messrs Brancher & Co., outfitters, and smaller but still significant bills at the tinman, gunmaker, hardwareman, cutler, swordcutler, optician, bookseller and at Read & Co., a cane and umbrella store.

On 10 August 1805, nine months after his departure and almost six months after its author had put quill to paper, the first of Nicholls' letters reached London. He had arrived in Old Calabar on 17 January, just before Park sailed from England, and had immediately found himself in as tricky a diplomatic situation as Park would ever have had to face. As soon as his ship anchored off Calabar, which was some way upriver from the ocean, he went ashore to pay his respects to the principal chief and trader, the evocatively named Egbo Young Eyambo. 'To my great mortification,' Nicholls wrote to London in February 1805, '[I] found myself very badly received. He wished to know my reasons for coming to his country; if I came to build a fort the same as on the Gold Coast, or if I came from Mr. Wilberforce.'³⁶ William Wilberforce, the leader of the anti-slavery movement and an active member of the Association for the past sixteen years, had in some way been involved in making Nicholls' mission possible, but the Englishman assured Eyambo 'that I had been sent by some great men in my country to endeavour to find out dye-woods and other things, to increase their trade, and do good for Calabar',³⁷ though the next day he was a little more candid and explained that he had come to look at the country, 'to describe the beasts, birds, fishes, and plants, and to write a large book about it'.³⁸ This answer pleased Eyambo beyond Nicholls' wildest expectations, for it turned out that the ruler owned a volume of Captain Cook's *Voyages*. The idea of the Englishman producing as important a work about Calabar appealed to the ruler's vanity. 'He promised me every assistance to go all over his territory and the neighbouring kings, and to forward me with safety as far towards the interior as his people dare go.'³⁹

These 'neighbouring kings' were scattered along the river, almost within sight of each other. There was Duke Ephraim, 'another chief, and by far the greatest trader', an elegant young man whom Nicholls decided to befriend; Antera Duke, whom he found malignant; the gloriously named Ego Honesty, King of Ebongo; and King Aqua of Aqua Town, who spoke a little English, presumably picked up in his dealings with English traders. Nicholls' problem was that all of these kings wanted to help him, and several were very keen for him to live with them before he made his journey into the interior. How to spread himself around, how indeed to find the information he was after, without offending them? In the end, he agreed to stay an equal length of time with each king, although he was soon set up in a house of his own in Duke Town, one of the quarters of Old Calabar.

Nicholls had clearly set himself up well, and was living in a house that had been shipped out in pieces from Liverpool in 1785 by a trader named Patrick Fairweather. Three storeys high, sixty feet long and thirty high, it was significantly larger than anything Park had encountered on his journey. Nicholls' own room was about forty feet by twenty-five. 'As the contents of it, I am sure, will amuse you,' he wrote to Young, 'I shall particularly describe it; it sometimes puts me in mind of a drawing room in England.' He then went on to list three sofas, twelve chairs, two desks, six tables, a marble sideboard, 'an immense quantity of glasses, china, and earthen ware; six paintings, and twenty large engravings, five clocks, and two musical ditto: and a pretty jumble of furniture it is'.[40]

There was certainly no doubting Nicholls' talent for observing detail. Given the friendly welcome he had received from the local rulers and his comment that 'the climate agrees with me very well', there were high hopes that he would make it in and out of the interior with a tale worth telling.

Eleven months after Nicholls' first letter reached London, while the British Parliament was debating an increase in maintenance payments for the young royal princes, with Vesuvius spewing out a four-mile lava flow and the late Admiral Lord Nelson's will being published, leaving Lady Hamilton 'as a legacy to my King and Country', Mungo Park's death was announced. On 10 July 1806, *The Times* revealed that 'a letter, it is said, has been received from the River Gambia, stating, that Mr. MUNGO PARKE [sic], the traveller, and his retinue (two or three excepted) have been murdered by the natives of the interior of that country. This story is stated to have been verified by the arrival of the persons who escaped the massacre, at Widah.'[41]

Over the next decades, reports concerning Park's death continued to leak out of Africa and find their way to London. On 1 September 1806, *The Times* reported that 'Mr. Park and the few of his companions who remained, had been murdered by order of the King of Sego, who considered them as spies'.[42] Three weeks later, James Jackson wrote to Banks: he had just returned from Morocco, where he had heard a report that Park had been in Timbuktu in March. In December that year, Banks received a letter from another English trader in Morocco, who had heard from a Moor that Park had been attacked by Tuaregs. Four years later, the same trader had news that Park's party had been met on the Niger in the summer of 1808. As the years passed, so the connections became ever more extended: in June 1813, Banks heard from a Cambridgeshire clergyman, who had heard from his brother, a Bombay merchant, who had heard from a captain sent to Abyssinia, who had heard from a Muslim trader from Gondar that a strange white man, fifty years old, with a red beard, had been seen in the interior of Africa.

And so it went on. Sightings were reported, ghosts appeared, and another life was lost when Park's second son Thomas went out to discover the truth about his father's death.* Even as late as 1858, Park's fate was a matter of national interest. In July of that year, *The Times* carried the following report:

> *Lieutenant Glover, one of the officers under the command of Captain Baikie, has stumbled upon a valuable relic of Mungo Park, and has of course secured it. Passing through a native village near the scene of Park's melancholy death, an old man accosted the lieutenant, and showed him a book which had for years been in his possession. It was a volume of logarithms, with Mungo Park's name, and autobiographic notes and memoranda. The possessor offered it to Mr. Glover for 200,000 cowries. Inestimable as the prize was, the price demanded was enormous, and it was impossible to pay it. After some consideration the lieutenant took from his pocket a clasp knife,*

---

* The British government granted Park's family £4000 (£200,000 today) after the explorer's death.

and asked the native what he thought of that. This was too
tempting a bait to be refused, the native joyfully took the knife,
and the lieutenant still more joyfully secured this valuable
memento of the distinguished African traveller.[43]

Another death quickly followed Park's: on 3 May 1807, members
gathered in the Thatched House heard that a letter had been received
from George Case, a Liverpool trader, in which he informed the
Committee that Henry Nicholls had died of a fever a couple of
months after his arrival in Calabar. There was worse to follow: the
captain with whom Nicholls had sailed had also died. In the absence
of anyone else with whom he had a connection, 'not one paper of
Mr. Nicholls had been brought home & nothing more than a few
of his cloths a Watch & a Fowling Piece worth only 8 or 9 pounds
in the whole': the rest of the £300-worth of equipment he had taken
out with him was lost.[44] The three letters he had sent back were
then read out to the meeting, not, it was explained rather disconso-
lately, 'with a view of communicating any very material information
on the great objects of his enquiry, as to shew the habits and modes
of life prevalent amongst the inhabitants of the coast'.[45] The letters
were charming and informative, but Nicholls' first mission, like
Park's last, had added nothing to the geography of Africa, and had
done some harm to the Association's reputation.

In almost twenty years, they had sent out six explorers: Ledyard
had died without making progress, Lucas had returned without
making progress, Houghton had made advances in West Africa but
had then been murdered, Park had found glory and then death on
the Niger, and now Nicholls had died before even leaving the Atlantic coast. Of Hornemann, nothing had been heard for seven years.

Another year, another general meeting: in 1808, it fell to the lot
of Lord Moira to say something about Hornemann. 'It may be
thought proper,' the Earl began, 'and probably is expected, that
your Committee should say something with regard to the situation
of your highly esteemed traveller, Mr. Hornemann; the Committee
wish that it was in their power to give any satisfactory information
on that interesting subject.'[46] All they knew for sure was that when

he left Murzuq, seven years earlier, Hornemann had been in good health and high spirits. The Earl then added that 'your Committee is not without some gleam of hope, founded on some uncertain reports, that he may still be in safety, and at some future time may be able to return to his anxious employers'.

The following year he spoke again on the subject, this time adopting a gloomier note. 'Some few circumstances relating to your traveller, Mr. Hornemann, have been laid before your Committee, but of so vague and uncertain a nature as to afford no great hope of a successful termination of his important undertaking, but at the same time not so absolutely unfavourable as to extinguish every hope of his return to his friends and to his country.'[47] No record of these 'few circumstances' has survived, so we can have no idea on what Moira based his comments. Whatever it was, it was the last that was heard of Hornemann for many years, and the Association was left to conclude that if he was still alive, he was either unwilling or unable to make his way home. The most they dared to hope for was that the traveller's journals and belongings might one day emerge out of the interior and somehow reach London.

Nothing more was heard of Hornemann for the next eight years, but then in July 1817 the *Quarterly Review* reported that 'a communication' had just been received from Commander W.H. Smyth, a Royal Navy officer who had been surveying the North African coast.* In Tripoli, Smyth had met the Bashaw of Tripoli and the Bey of Fezzan, who told him that Hornemann had made the desert crossing and then 'fell ill at Houssor [Hausa], in the dwelling of a Tripoline merchant established there, and resuming his travels before he was perfectly recovered, relapsed, and died at Tombuctoo'.[48]

There was soon confirmation of this story from two other sources. In 1818, the energetic explorer Captain George Lyon met a man in the Fezzan who claimed to have travelled from Murzuq with the German, and presumably also the Bey. Five years later, another Scottish explorer, Captain Hugh Clapperton, heard a similar story

---

* Smyth was also collecting Roman antiquities for the Prince Regent. He was to have a key role to play in later African exploration.

from two Fezzani merchants he met in Kano (northern Nigeria), who were with Hornemann when he died. From these accounts, it is possible to piece together an account of what happened to the traveller.

On 6 April 1800, as he had written to Banks, Hornemann was optimistic about his chances of success. That night he left Murzuq to join the large caravan heading across the desert to Borno, a journey he made in the company of the Fezzani Captain Lyon later met and of Hat Salah and Benderachmani, as reported by Clapperton. The Fezzani left Hornemann at Borno, where he stayed for several months, but the men met again when they joined the same caravan travelling west to the Hausa city of Katsina, where they stayed for a while before moving on with a caravan to Nupe. The people of Nupe were animists, but there were many Muslim Fulanis resident in their towns and villages. It was with one of these, a man by the name of Ali or Yussuf, in a village called Bokani, that Hornemann stayed. When his Fezzani fellow traveller left him, he was 'in good health and spirits, and had not experienced any difficulties',[49] but when he reached Kashna, just several days away, he heard that the European had died of dysentery. Hat Salah and Benderachmani, who were with him at the end, also remembered that he died of dysentery after a six-day illness.

From these corroborating accounts, it was safe to assume that Hornemann had made it across the central Sahara, and that in the eight or nine months after his departure from Murzuq he had seen and heard much that would have been of value to the Association. But the Committee waited in vain for his journal to be delivered to Soho Square: this time, in spite of the Pasha of Tripoli's assurance that 'Moors never destroy papers',[50] the £5 reward was not enough to guarantee its safe return. For some time mystery surrounded the fate of the papers, particularly after 1818, when Consul Hanmer Warrington announced that, 'Respecting Mr. Horneman's Papers Instruments &c. they were delivered by the Minister and Mourad Reis to Mr. Mc Donough a Gentleman attached to the British Consulate.'[51] This, it seems, was a reference not to his trans-Saharan journal but to material Hornemann had sent from Murzuq before leaving Fezzan. It was not until Captain Clapperton reached the southern courses of the Niger that a credible answer emerged. Even though several years had passed since the explorer's death, Clapperton sent a messenger to Bokani to see whether any of Hornemann's effects survived. The messenger returned empty-handed, but with a story: 'Jussuf Felatah, a learned man of the country, with whom Mr. Hornemann lodged, had been burned in his own house, together with all of Mr. Hornemann's papers, by the negro rabble, from a superstitious dread of his holding inter-course with evil spirits.'

Hornemann's death was a tragedy not just for himself and his family, but also for the Association and the cause of African geogra-phy. When he arrived in Bokani he was just one day's walk from the Niger and the town of Rabba, a major trading post that had regular trading links to Timbuktu.* There is every reason to assume that with his knowledge of the customs of the caravan and of northern Africa, and with his ability to speak the languages of the region, he would have reached Timbuktu if his health had held up, and would therefore have opened up the trans-Saharan and Niger 'roads'. As it is, his crossing from Cairo to Bokani still stands as one of the great journeys of the period, and also one of the most significant: without his journals, the Association were no wiser about central Africa than they were before his departure, but with this journey they had just opened the field of desert exploration. Yet by the time the facts of his death emerged, Hornemann was forgotten by all but a few, and the Association, which had published his journal to Murzuq back in 1799, was neither capable of nor interested in blowing his trumpet.

But if Hornemann's magnificent achievement was destined to be forgotten and his journal and belongings reduced to ashes in a hut a few miles from the Niger, he did manage to pass on one last, valuable lesson. In 1818, Captain Lyon heard from the Fezzani who had travelled with the German that, 'The people became greatly

---

* Bokani was also little more than fifty miles from Bussa, where Mungo Park met his death five years after Hornemann.

attached to Horneman, on account of his amiable deportment and skill in medicine; and he was generally considered as a Maraboot.'[52] As Hornemann had explained in a letter to Banks, 'When one knows a little of the Arabic language, when one knows how to behave with everyday matters, when one knows the manners of these people and their ceremonies, it is not difficult to travel as a Mahomedan, because the caravan has been to Mecca and knows very well that there are Mahomedans who have different manners and language.'[53] His journey had proved this to be true. Mungo Park had packed a frock-coat and black hat for his attempt on Timbuktu, but the Association's next traveller was going to travel disguised as a native.

14

The Swiss Gentleman

'The dangers that await me are not so innumerable as the
name Africa may perhaps already seem to you to imply . . .
The legends about wild cannibal tribes are absolute lies.'

Jean Louis Burckhardt, 1809

London, 1806

IN 1806, on his sixty-third birthday, Sir Joseph Banks could look
back on a life of exceptional achievement. He had, as he wrote to
the Court of Directors of the East India Company, 'voluntarily
Exchanged my prospects [of] Parliamentary consequence & possibility of high office'[1] for the opportunity of pursuing a love of
botany and other sciences. His botanising had spread his name
throughout the world, but he had achieved much more than
renown. The settlement he had pushed for, advised upon and helped
to organise in New South Wales had taken root, his emissaries were
collecting plants and seeds around the world, and his house in Soho
Square was still one of the city's social and intellectual hubs: it
buzzed with the activities of his loving wife and sister, his librarian
and the enthusiasms of a large number of distinguished guests. His
friends occupied the highest of places – the government of Lord
Grenville, the so-called 'Ministry of Talents' which passed the law
abolishing slavery, relied upon his expertise on many troublesome
questions. And even the King in his moments of lucidity continued

The Pyramids and Giza Plateau, by Henry Salt. Salt must have installed himself in the Citadel, one of the Pasha's residences, to paint this view of the southernmost cemetery, the snaking aqueduct, the Nile and the Giza pyramids.

Henry Salt, talented artist, Abyssinian traveller, Egyptian antiquity collector and British Consul General in Cairo from 1816 until his death in 1827. The portrait is by Joseph Bonomi, who trained at the Royal Academy, London.

Jean Louis Burckhardt, Swiss gentleman. Before leaving for Africa he was sent to Cambridge University to study Arabic under Professor Edward Clarke. This etching was made by Clarke's daughter Angelica, after a portrait by Salter.

Below The transition is complete: Burckhardt as he appeared in 1817, after eight years of rough travelling in the Levant, Arabia and North Africa. Henry Salt, who made this portrait, called him 'the perfect Arab'.

Abu Simbel, Ramses II's great temple complex as it looked when rediscovered by Jean Louis Burckhardt in 1813. The sketch was made several years later by another Association traveller, Linant de Bellefonds.

William Martin
Leake, Secretary
of the Association
from 1822 and a
founder of the Royal
Geographical Society.
A topographer and
antiquarian, Leake
was known for his
work on classical
Greece.

John Barrow,
Second Secretary
at the British
Admiralty, Banks'
protégé and the
principal motor
for British
exploration after
1815. By 1830, with
Banks and Rennell
dead, he was the
obvious person to
lead the new Royal
Geographical
Society.

Right Major Alexander Gordon Laing. His military abilities were said to be as bad as his poetry and he lost his heart to a consul's daughter, but he believed it was his destiny to reach Timbuktu.

Below Réné Caillié, inspired to look for Timbuktu by the exploits of the African Association's travellers, and by the French Société Géographique's offer of ten thousand francs. His compatriots called him the first Western traveller into Timbuktu, a claim hotly disputed by the Association.

Overleaf Timbuktu as it was during the age of the African Association, no longer the golden capital of a rich and powerful king. Laing wrote that it had met his expectations, but Caillié's description of a 'mass of mud houses, surrounded by arid plains of jaundiced white sand' was nearer the truth.

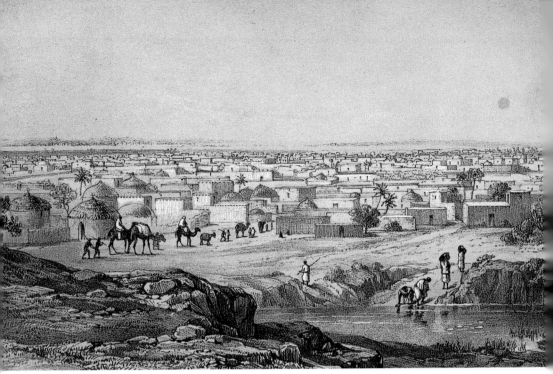

Kano, one of the Hausa cities, a city of such sophistication and colour that
Lieutenant Hugh Clapperton's naval dress uniform failed to turn heads.

Camel Riders in Nubia, by Linant de Bellefonds. The bearded rider in the centre may
be a self-portrait of the artist-explorer, who became loath to part with his work.

to depend on Banks' guidance in scientific matters, particularly regarding Kew Gardens. (George III, keen to reward Banks for his service, had made him a Knight of the Order of the Bath in June 1795,* citing in particular the way he had encouraged landowners to raise militias against a possible French invasion.) So much achieved, and yet still so much to do.

Not that everything in his life was blessed. His health was increasingly a problem, and the attacks of gout became regular and confined him to bed, sometimes for months on end. But in his usual indomitable way, Banks used discipline, diet and exercise to help him remain mobile when many sufferers would have been confined to their chairs. 'I have of late taken much to riding,' he wrote to his old friend Lord Liverpool soon after his birthday in 1806. 'I find vast benefit from the exercise the only one I am capable of taking your Lordship accuses me of imprudently proceeding unattended through the Streets I wonder you should think me Capable of so absurd a measure I have always a Servant walking on the Pavement within a few yards of me who carries my Stick without which I Could not go up my neighbors Stairs when I visit them.'[2]

Banks' African adventure was proving to be as painful and troublesome as his gout. Six years into the new century and the African Association was looking suspiciously, uncomfortably, unavoidably, a failure. True, Park and Hornemann were still believed to be out in the field, their return eagerly awaited. And two letters had been received from Nicholls in Calabar. But in truth they were all most likely already dead. Even if they had returned, real achievements, such as geographical facts, trade treaties with African rulers, progress on locating the West African goldfields or filling in the blanks on Rennell's map were notably absent. Sir William Hamilton had realised this when he described Hornemann's journal as a 'Letter of no great Consequence', unworthy of the effort of handing to a copyist. It received a more

---

* Banks' initiation into the Order of the Bath didn't take place until May 1803. The ball at Ranelagh, paid for by the new knights, was a suitably impressive affair – supper was laid for 1870 covers at a cost of £1450, plus another £1000 for wines, £450 for lamps and £300 for police and flowers. Banks was seated beside Lord Keith (later Elphinstone) and opposite Nelson.

enthusiastic reception from the Committee and members in London: Rennell had set to work on another of his *Geographical Elucidations* and Sir William Young had written a long and pompous introduction. It was this that seems to have bothered the anonymous critic of the *Edinburgh Review*, who attacked the Secretary's 'most oppressive stiffness of style, perpetual affectation of depth, and ludicrous attempt at abstraction'.[3] Of Hornemann's travels – at least as they are represented in his journal to Murzuq – 'we can scarcely allow, that his discoveries have been so important, as to justify the vaunting style of the Secretary; or that he has hitherto done more, than give a very fair promise of succeeding in the subsequent part of his expedition. Neither are we extremely sanguine in our expectations of the commercial advantages that may result from the part of his labours which is already terminated.'[4]

Banks was furious at this attack on his traveller and wrote to one of his many friends, Lord Brougham, who was connected to the magazine and who knew the review's author. Brougham agreed with Banks that 'if the slightest disrespect was meant to the celebrated body under whose patronage Mr. Horneman [sic] pursues his adventures, the article deserved suppression'.[5] At this point, a motive for the attack became clear: the author was not objecting to the Association or to Hornemann but to Young, who as a landholder in the Caribbean was known to support the slave trade. 'The Secretary of the Association,' the reviewer wrote, 'when he boasts of the benefits which its labours are to confer upon Africa, would do well to consider, how unavailing are his efforts, in this capacity, to promote the civilization of those vast regions, while his zeal, in another place [i.e. Jamaica], is devoted to perpetuate their barbarism.'[6]

The Association's lack of success was followed at the beginning of the nineteenth century by a fall in membership numbers. In 1799, riding a wave of enthusiasm after Mungo Park's victorious return from the Niger, Banks had counted 143 subscribers. Of these, he had reckoned only fifty-three were what he called still 'efficient', the rest having died, withdrawn or just not paid their subscriptions.

Thirty-five new members had been admitted between 1799 and 1802, but Banks still complained to his friend Matra in Tangier that 'We have lost many subscribers on account of the vast increase in personal taxes on the rich.'[7] Without subscribers there could be no missions; and without missions there was no future for the Association.

Given this limitation on the Association's possibilities, many people in Banks' position might have distanced themselves from it. There must have been some suspicion that this was exactly what he was doing when, in 1804, he resigned as Treasurer, handing over the post he had held for sixteen years to the Reverend Dr Anthony Hamilton. But the Association's minutes noted that Banks was retiring because of 'the infirm state of his health which prevented his engaging in active business & correspondence as formerly'.[8] So gout, not disillusionment, was the reason for his quitting the post; and yet, in spite of frail health, he remained the most active member of the Committee – it was he who had organised Mungo Park's second expedition in 1804, and he who prepared Nicholls for his journey to Calabar. Banks was still, as the adventurer John Gray had called him ten years earlier, 'the Father of research, the advocate for enquiry, and the friend of the adventurous Traveller',[9] and whatever else he might have given up, he still controlled the selection of the Association's missionaries.

Nothing about the young Swiss gentleman who arrived in Soho Square in July 1806 suggested that he would become an explorer. Jean Louis Burckhardt* had come to visit Banks in the hope of introductions, not employment. But Professor Blumenbach, his tutor in Göttingen and one of humanity's great scrutinisers, had recognised his potential, and perhaps on that summer day Banks

---

* Reflecting his native Switzerland's bilingual status, writers variously refer to Burckhardt as Jean Louis and Johann Ludwig (and John Lewis). In his letters, Burckhardt used the Francophone spelling and signs himself Louis. I have followed his lead.

also saw in him the qualities he knew would make a great traveller.

Louis was the eighth child of one of Basle's most distinguished families. The Burckhardts were wealthy, cultured merchants who played a key role in the city's cultural life and took pride in the fact that they had entertained the likes of Goethe and Gibbon. Louis' life might have been very different had a revolutionary French army not occupied Switzerland in 1798, and had his father, Rudolph Burckhardt, not been so vehemently anti-republican. Rudolph survived the occupation, but the family lost much of its fortune and Louis grew up knowing that he would have to make his own way. For a young man with a deep-rooted hatred of France, England increasingly came to epitomise all that was just and honest in the world.

Burckhardt was a serious, scholarly teenager, and in 1800, at sixteen, he went up to study at Leipzig University. Three years later he moved to Göttingen, where he spent a year studying the sciences with Johann Blumenbach. But while at Leipzig he had also shown another side to his character, and spent what he described as a 'far from frugal' winter: like many students then and now, he had had some fun and run up considerable debts. Not wanting to burden his parents, he pleaded for financial help from his elder half-brother, Johann, who was now running the family business. Johann let their parents know about the debt, and in the process made Louis look both extravagant and deceitful. The crisis passed, but rather than expect his family to support him, when his year at Göttingen was over Louis was determined to find work. His cousin, Christoph Burckhardt, who was serving with the English forces, suggested that Louis go with him to London, where they would be sure to find career openings.

Before he left Switzerland, Louis was offered a diplomatic post by one of the royal German courts, but turned it down because he wanted nothing to do with an ally of France. In the summer of 1806, accompanied by his cousin and armed with various introductions, among them a letter from Blumenbach to Sir Joseph Banks, Louis arrived in London in search of an opening in the Foreign Service. Progress was slow, but he did make some headway, and in 1807 was introduced to George Canning, the new Foreign Secretary. Nothing came of that contact, however, nor of the wide range of people he met during the following year. Outside the meetings he passed his time studying English and reading avidly in the Soho Square library. But however fruitful this existence promised to be, he could not afford to remain unemployed: as the small allowance he received from his family began to run out, he found himself obliged 'to mingle with the great in the daytime, and buy in the evening, secretly in a back street, provisions for a few days'. Ever eager to prove himself to his parents, he wrote that he was at least learning the value of economy and of prayer. He was also learning a great deal about North Africa and the Middle East, for among the people he met at this time were Henry Salt, W.G. Browne, the first European to visit Siwa oasis in Egypt, and George Renouard. Salt, a twenty-seven-year-old artist, had recently returned from more than four years travelling in India, Abyssinia and Egypt as secretary and draughtsman to a wealthy and well-connected aristocrat, Viscount Valentia. He was now working on journals and illustrations that were to be included in Valentia's 1809 *Voyages and Travels*. The Reverend George Renouard, also in his twenties, had served for two years as chaplain to the British Embassy in Constantinople. From these and others who moved in and out of Soho Square, Burckhardt heard fresh and stirring stories of travel in the Near East and North Africa. As his efforts to find employment failed, as his meagre resources became ever more stretched and provisions bought in the evenings had to be made to last ever longer, so his thoughts turned to travel.

At the African Association's general meeting of 3 May 1807, members learned, with a sense of inevitability, of the death of Henry Nicholls. They were also told that they had £1605 on deposit with Messrs Coutts & Co., more than enough to mount another expedition, given that Park's first journey, their most expensive to date, had cost them £1307. Hornemann, who was to be the model for the next traveller, had spent less than £650. Nine months later, on Valentine's Day 1808, Burckhardt mentioned in a letter to his parents that it was 'not quite impossible'[10] that he might find employment as an explorer with the African Association, and the following month he made a formal offer of his services to a Committee meeting in Soho Square.

Burckhardt's initial plan was to sail to Malta, where he would stay for as long as it took him to become familiar with the region and to perfect his disguise as a 'Moorish merchant'. From there he would sail to Tripoli and follow Hornemann's route through Murzuq to Katsina, the Niger and Timbuktu. 'From Mr. Burckhardts [sic] conversation and habits of Life & the recommendation of him by Mr. Professor Blumenbach of Gottingen in a Letter to Sir Joseph Banks the Committee is of opinion that Mr. Burckhardt should be employed in the Service of the Association.'[11] Terms had been worked out by the time the Committee met again the following month, and Burckhardt was offered the same deal that had been offered to Nicholls: half a guinea a day until he reached Cairo, and a guinea a day from then on. The Association would also provide £120 for equipment and transport, and he would be able to draw another £150 in Cairo to buy camels, trade goods and whatever else he might need for the desert crossing.

Burckhardt was pleased with the offer. Familiar with frugality, he reckoned he could live off considerably less than his daily allowance once he was on his way, particularly for the journey beyond Cairo. Together with royalties from the publication of his journals, he hoped to have saved some £2000 by the time he returned to London.

A sketch of Burckhardt from this time in London shows him with his black hair swept forward, a full, curling beard and moustache. He has a long, straight nose, fine eyebrows and dark, direct eyes. There is an unmistakable air of resolve and determination about him. This was something the Rev. Dr Hamilton, the Association's Treasurer, noticed when he took the precaution of talking through the dangers of the mission with him, in case they were not sufficiently obvious. Hamilton found Burckhardt 'admirably adapted to the undertaking by his natural and acquired talents, as well as by the vigour of his constitution'.[12] The risks seemed to increase as rumours of the murder of Park and his men were added to the news of Nicholls' death. But in a letter to his parents that spring, Burckhardt showed the sort of insight that was later to set him apart from the majority of travellers. 'The dangers that await me,' he explained, 'are not so innumerable as the name Africa may perhaps already seem to you to imply. With countries which are only half known, which have for centuries been almost completely unknown, simply because no one has felt the urge or dared to make the attempt to penetrate them, with countries such as these it could not possibly have happened otherwise: they have been and still are the subject of many stories. The legends about wild cannibal tribes are absolute lies; unfortunately it is just rumours of this sort, listened to from childhood on, that have rooted themselves so deeply in our imagination.'[13] To people who knew nothing of Africa, this may have sounded a remarkably clear-headed assessment of what lay ahead. But it came from a man whose experience of the world was confined to the road between Basle and London, and it was simply not true: given the example of the travellers who had gone before him, it was about as unrealistic as it could possibly be.

The Committee had their own views on what should happen next. Previously they had sent adventurers, a courtier, army officers, a former religious student and a naval surgeon, but now they were engaging a well-bred and educated young gentleman who was their social equal. This, together with their experiences with previous explorers, accounts for the unusually thorough preparation the Committee now decided upon: Burckhardt was to become their model geographical missionary.

Hornemann's route was to be followed, as was his mode of travel; the German's experiences between Cairo and Fezzan had convinced the Committee that only in disguise would their travellers reach the interior. As William Leake, a future Secretary of the Association, explained some years later, 'The Association having had the good fortune to obtain the services of a person of Mr. Burckhardt's education and talents, resolved to spare neither time nor expense in enabling him to acquire the language and manners of an Arabian Musulman in such a degree of perfection, as should render the detection of his real character in the interior of Africa extremely difficult.'[14]

Once his terms of engagement had been agreed, Burckhardt went to Cambridge to study under Professor Edward Clarke. Clarke was not part of Banks' circle and never became a member of the Association or a Fellow of the Royal Society, but like Banks he cherished a love of travel and a dedication to the sciences. In his late thirties, Clarke was a mineralogist, a subject in which he later became Professor at Cambridge. He had travelled widely across Europe and was fortunate to have been in Egypt in 1801, when the British were deciding which antiquities to take from the French as part of their terms of surrender; among them was the Rosetta Stone.* All these experiences were to come into play as he prepared the young traveller for his mission.

Under Clarke's guidance, Burckhardt added Arabic to the five languages he already spoke, and attended lectures on 'chemistry, astronomy, mineralogy, medicine and surgery',[15] all subjects Clarke thought might be useful on the journey. Burckhardt quickly became a familiar figure around the campus, made noticeable by his decision to grow a beard and adopt Oriental clothes – the job ahead called as much for a talent to disguise as it did to observe. He also began to prepare himself physically. The summer of 1808 turned out to be unusually hot, which he recognised as an opportunity to test himself against the elements; he began making 'long journies [sic] on foot, bare headed, in the heat of the sun, sleeping upon the ground, and living upon vegetables and water'.[16] With such a Bohemian appearance, Burckhardt could have passed for a Romantic disciple of the poet Wordsworth, who six years earlier had spoken of 'a spontaneous overflow of powerful feelings'[17] in the face of nature. In temperament, however, both he and the mission he had been entrusted with belonged to the rationalistic Enlightenment.

* 'I was at Cairo when the capitulation began. There I learned from the Imperial consul, that the famous inscription which is to explain the Hieroglyphics, was still at Alexandria. I then intended to write to General Hutchinson and Lord Keith on that subject, to beg that it might be obtained for the University of Cambridge, or the British Museum, as I know full well, we have better Orientalists than the French, and a knowledge of eastern languages may be necessary in some degree towards the development of these inscriptions' (Otter/Clarke, p.494).

During these Cambridge days, Burckhardt had plenty of time to consider what lay ahead. He had read reports of the Association's previous missionaries and the published works of many other travellers in the Middle East and Africa, and he had had long talks with Clarke and W.G. Browne. He had also become friends with William Hamilton, son of the Association's current Treasurer, who had just served seven years as a diplomat in Turkey; in Egypt at the same time as Clarke, Hamilton was well aware of the needs and dangers of travel in the region. From all that he had read and heard, Burckhardt knew that his journey would be considerably rougher than anything he had experienced in Europe. The challenge seems only to have strengthened his resolve. 'I want to be of some use in this world,' he wrote to his parents. 'I have not taken on this task, God knows, in order to be gaped at and pointed at on my return' (the reception Mungo Park had received in London must have been in his mind when he wrote that), 'but because in an age like this, when whole nations – my own among them – have given themselves up to a wretched, selfish, sensual absorption in the affairs of the moment, reeling round in circles of utterly unprincipled corruption, I can take heart in treading the same path as those who still think about and believe in the future.'[18] If this sounds pompous and overblown, he was more modest in another letter home to Switzerland: 'I have at last achieved what I have been craving for during eight years – a definite sphere of activity. I have at last found a goal. And I shall spare neither industry nor effort. I have some intelligence and I shall use it now. But do not overestimate yourself, you might say. I won't. This journey, and what I shall observe while I travel, requires not genius but a straightforward, clear mind and some ability.'[19] That may have been true, but the fact that he was to bring genius to his journey made what followed all the more extraordinary.

Burckhardt sailed from England for Malta on 2 March 1809, disguised as an Indian Muslim and calling himself Shaykh Ibrahim ibn Abdallah. He had changed his plan since his first proposal to the Association. According to his instructions, which he himself had drawn up and which Banks and Hamilton senior, now acting as both Treasurer and Secretary, had signed on 20 January, 'It is absolutely necessary that you should be intimately acquainted with the language and manners of the Arabs, individuals of that nation will be your constant fellow-Travellers from the confines of Syria to that of the Negro Countries. It is by being able fluently to converse with them in their own idiom, that you may hope to conciliate their good will and to obtain an accurate knowledge of their Tribes and the Country they inhabit.'[20] So instead of moving on from Malta to Tripoli, Burckhardt was going to spend two years in Syria perfecting his Arabic and his knowledge of the customs of the region.

There were good reasons why he should not stay too long on Malta. For one thing, several traders from Tripoli regularly went there to do business. Burckhardt intended to pass through Tripoli later in his travels, and wanted to avoid the risk of being compromised by these traders if he met them in their home port. So while on Malta he kept contact with Tripolitenes to a minimum, offering no more than a *Salaam aleikum* (peace be with you) as they passed in the street. More immediately troubling was the presence of a Swiss regiment on the island, because Burckhardt knew many of the officers from home. 'This,' he wrote to Banks on 22 May 1809, 'has made me very cautious in going abroad, and now, after a seven weeks residence, I have the satisfaction to find that I have succeeded in passing unknown, and unnoticed.'[21]

The Committee had chosen Syria for Burckhardt's 'schooling' because it was sufficiently far from Africa for whatever indiscretions he might make while learning the language and perfecting his disguise not to filter further south. So imagine his astonishment, as he sailed from Malta in June, to find himself sharing the boat with three Tripolitenes. Here again the young traveller rose to the challenge. He introduced himself as an Indian merchant, a Muslim who had long been resident in England and was now on his way home, and was sufficiently convincing for the Africans to invite him to eat with them. It took a fair amount of bluff to get him through the days that followed. When asked to speak some Hindi, he showed a talent for improvisation by answering in what he described as 'the worst dialect of the Swiss-German, almost unintel-ligible to a German, and which, in its guttural sounds, may fairly rival the harshest utterance of Arabic. Every evening we assembled upon deck to enjoy the cooling sea breeze, and to smoke our pipes. While one of the sailors was amusing his companions with story-telling, I was called upon to relate to my companions the wonders of the farthest east; of the Grand Mogul, and the riches of his court: of the widows in Hindostan burning themselves: of the Chinese, their wall and great porcelane [sic] tower, &c. &c.'[22] The days spent reading in Banks' library came in handy, too: Burck-hardt recognised Herodotus being quoted back to him when one of the wealthy Tripolitene merchants told stories of the Sudan, 'of one nation which is in continual warfare with their neighbours, of a nation of speaking sheep, of another of necromancers . . .'[23]

Ten years had passed since Bonaparte had invaded Egypt. His suc-cessful Battle of the Pyramids had been followed by a series of conflicts and campaigns – the Battle of the Nile in 1799, the Siege of Acre and so on – that had left the region tense and its people with no great love for Europeans, or Franks, as they called them. Landing off the Syrian coast, Burckhardt travelled to Antioch, where he felt the full force of this climate of suspicion: the Aga or chief sent his *dragoman* (interpreter) to talk to the foreigner, hoping that he might turn out to be an infidel and could therefore be forced to pay a higher tax. Burckhardt took an immediate dislike to the *dragoman*, 'a wretched Frank, who pretended to be a Frenchman, but whom I would rather suppose to be a Piedmontese. I pretended complete ignorance of the French language, he therefore asked me

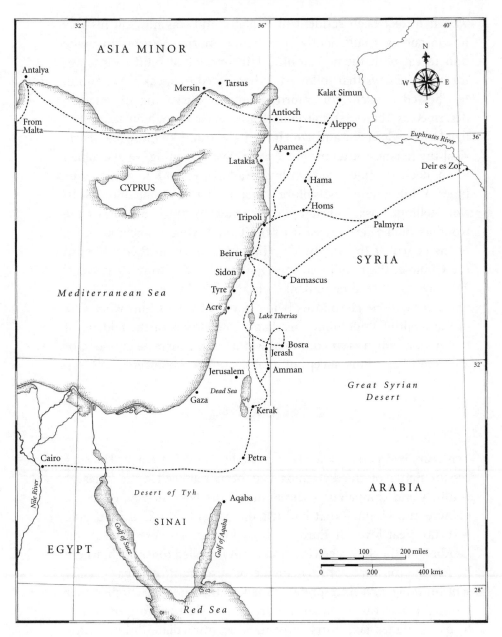

Burckhardt's route to Cairo, 1809–12

in Italian minutely about my affairs ... When the man saw that nothing in my manners betrayed my Frank origin, he made a last trial, and pulling my beard a little with his hand, asked me familiarly "why I had let such a thing grow?" I answered him with a blow upon his face, to convince the bystanding Turks how deeply I resented the received insult; the laugh now turned against the poor dragoman, who did not trouble me any further.'[24]

All this must have reassured the Committee that their traveller would produce results. But he had much to learn before he could begin his African journey. No one was more aware of this than Burckhardt himself, as he confessed in a long letter to the Committee describing his journey to Antioch with an Aleppo-bound caravan: 'I am at a loss to state how far I succeeded in sustaining my assumed character; I thought that the major part of the caravan people were gained over to my side, but the town's people were constant in their imprecations against me.'[25] Worse was to come.

Nothing in his behaviour could be called unusual, but there was obviously something about Burckhardt – his build, the way he moved, a light in his eyes – that roused suspicions in other travellers with the Aleppo caravan, because one night when he went to relieve himself, two members of the caravan followed him and later reported that they had 'observed some irregularities in the ablutions necessary to be performed on such occasions'.[26] Perhaps they had seen him using his right hand when only the left should be used, the right being kept clean for eating. Perhaps also they had realised that he was uncircumcised, and therefore could not be a Muslim. For whatever reason, Burckhardt was branded *haram*, forbidden, and was isolated. To this he responded by doing what any self-respecting Arab would do, insisting 'that I would rather eat nothing and starve, than have any further friendly dealings with men who professed themselves my friends one day, and proved my enemies the next'.[27] His genius for acting had carried him through again, but the incident was a reminder that however convincing his disguise of Shaykh Ibrahim, it had to be lived to the full, twenty-four hours a day.

In Aleppo, Burckhardt received confirmation of news he had heard from the Tripolitans on the passage from Malta: the Wahabis, a radical, reformist sect of Sunni Muslims, had taken control of Mecca and Medina. Troops from moderate, Sunni Egypt had been sent to safeguard the Holy Cities from what the rulers in Cairo regarded as the Wahabi heresy. While these two groups fought for control of Mecca, the caravan trade to Timbuktu and the interior had come to a halt. Even in Aleppo traders were suffering the consequences of the Wahabi uprising: the Syrian caravan had not left on pilgrimage for the past three years. He would have to hope that this conflict between rival Islamic doctrines was over by the time he was ready to make the desert crossing to central Africa.

Burckhardt wanted to be able to move freely between the native and European parts of Aleppo, so although he continued to be addressed as Ibrahim and still wore his 'Turkish dress', he was known as an Englishman. 'It frequently happens,' he wrote by way of explanation to Banks, 'that people coming into the Levant change their names.'[28] He also made friends with John Barker, the English Consul, whom he described as 'a most worthy and amiable man, of true English blood (which is scarce enough in the Levant), and possessed of much more talents than are necessary to fulfil the duties of his situation'.[29] With Barker's help, he rented a house, took on a servant, bought a good horse and found an old Maronite Christian who turned out to be an excellent Arabic teacher. The young traveller was inquisitive, quick to learn and eager to cross over from his own culture into that of Islam. One of the exercises he set himself during the winter of 1809 was what he called 'the metamorphosis of the well known novel of Robinson Crusoe into an Arabian tale, adapted to Eastern taste and manners'.[30] This 'travestied Robinson'[31] he called *Dur al Bahr*, the Pearl of the Seas, and sent to London.* Sadly there is no record of the response of Banks or any of his London friends to Burckhardt's present.

* The manuscript is listed as 'an abridged Arabic version of Robinson Crusoe, written by Ibrahim b. Abd Allah al-Inglizi, who came to Aleppo in AD 1810, and entitled durr al-buhur ...'

Sitting at the junction of the Near East and the fringes of Asia, Aleppo is the most cosmopolitan city between Cairo and Istanbul; even today its souks are packed with Armenians and Kurds, Russians and Turks wanting to do business with Syrians, Lebanese, Iraqis and Palestinians. Burckhardt clearly enjoyed the place. 'I find great pleasure,' he wrote to Clarke in Cambridge, 'in the study of Arabic, and confess that the oriental amusements of riding, bathing, and smoking, are likewise much to my taste.'[32] Between Arabic lessons, he rode out of town, visited the hammam and haunted the souks, learning tricks of the trade that might be of use when he got into Africa.

He also enjoyed the life of the European enclave and became good friends with Consul Barker, who often included him in his parties to hunt partridge, bustard, teal and a range of other birds, or that took salukis to course hare and gazelle across the plains beyond the city. Through Barker, Burckhardt got to meet most of the more notable European travellers passing through the area. He also met the Dutch Consul, van Masseyk, who had 'intimate knowledge of the Turks, their language and manners'.[33] The Dutchman became his regular riding partner, and taught him to ride Turkish style, another embellishment for his disguise. 'Summing up the history of my private life in Syria,' Burckhardt wrote to Clarke, 'I have passed as many pleasant hours in this country as I might have expected to enjoy in any other.'[34]

He was beginning to travel, too. In the spring of 1810 he made several journeys beyond Aleppo, visiting places that touring Europeans either did not or could not get to. The first took him into the tents of a tribe of Reyhanli Turkomen, where he passed several weeks in the guise of a physician looking for medicinal herbs. Early in the summer he was off again, this time with a Bedouin *shaykh* whose tribe was camped beyond the ruined oasis town of Palmyra – Burckhardt was hoping to use the journey as an opportunity to visit the ruins. In spite of his promises, the *shaykh* proved unable to protect him and he was robbed by a band of Mawali Arabs and left 'stripped literally to the skin'.[35] When he did finally reach Palmyra, the *shaykh* 'in consideration of my empty purse'[36] relieved him of the saddle on his horse. By August he was installed in Damascus, staying in the house of a Jewish banker, held up by the insecurity of the region after the Pasha of Damascus was overthrown. In September he left again, this time for Lebanon, and then in November he set off on what he considered to be his first groundbreaking trip, to the Jebel Druse, the barren, mountainous region south of Damascus that was home to the Druse.

'I assumed the dress of the Haouran people,' he wrote in his report to the Committee, 'with a Keffie, and a large sheep-skin over my shoulders: in my saddle bag I put one spare shirt, one pound of coffee beans, two pounds of tobacco, and a day's provender of barley for my horse.'[37] He had eighty piastres (£4 then) hidden in his waistband and a few more in his pocket, a watch and compass, notebook, pencil and knife and his tobacco pouch. He had rented an ass from a man who was travelling in his direction, a smart move as he knew that 'the owner of the ass necessarily becomes the companion and protector of him who hires it'.[38] He was also armed with letters of recommendation from the Pasha of Damascus and the Greek Patriarch.

'Whatever you resolve upon,' the Committee had warned Burckhardt before he left London, 'let neither rashness nor timid caution influence your conduct . . . Be as Rigidly exact in noting down your observations as you possibly can consistant [sic] with prudence.' Prudence was relative. In the summer of 1810, the Jebel Druse had been overrun by six thousand camel-mounted Wahabis, but by the end of the year, when Burckhardt was on the road, they had turned back south into the desert. His greatest difficulty, perhaps, was acquiring the knack of keeping a journal and recording place names and compass bearings without attracting the suspicion of his travelling companions, although the Christians were considerably less suspicious than others in the region: as well as a physician looking for medicinal plants, he was also introduced to villagers as a lay brother sent by the Patriarch, and a foreigner curious to see the country. None of these characters seemed to bother the villagers.

Before leaving for the Jebel Druse, Burckhardt had written to

London asking permission to stay in Syria for six months beyond the original two years. Now, on his return, he found himself 'under the disagreeable necessity of telling you that notwithstanding every economy in expense I have spent my last farthing', and this in spite of the fact that he had travelled in what he called 'the garb of a pauper'.[39] The facts support his claim, for in the nineteen months since leaving Malta he had spent less than £10 a month, £170 in all – in the three and a half weeks spent touring in the Jebel Druse, he had spent a mere £4. The Committee could hardly complain of his extravagance. But even if they had, the quality of his reports would have more than justified the expense – unlike Hornemann's description of his journey to the Fezzan, Burckhardt's journals are meticulously detailed, filled with the names of every village and town he passed through, with travelling times between places and with details of notable sites, ancient ruins, medieval churches, the number of mosques and natural features. He was just what the Association needed, an observant, intelligent and dedicated traveller with the necessary physique, talents and knowledge to succeed in his mission.

Some of Burckhardt's report from Syria was groundbreaking work, the first descriptions of the region to reach Europe since the age of the Crusaders. What's more, his journal contained intriguing observations, most useful of which (with hindsight) was his description of the town of Hama on the Orontes River, where he spotted a stone 'in the corner of a house in the Bazar with a number of small figures and signs, which appears to be a kind of hieroglyphical writing, though it does not resemble that of Egypt'.[40] Some years later, this stone provided one of the keys that led to the decipherment of Hittite writing.

Another year and a half passed before the Association's geographical missionary was ready to move south towards Egypt. On 7 June 1812, more than three years after his departure from England, and as Napoleon massed his armies and prepared to invade Russia, Burckhardt wrote to Banks from Damascus that he had obtained the last letter of introduction he needed for his journey south; he hoped to be in Cairo within eight weeks.

He left on 18 June. The regular route to Egypt ran through Jerusalem and Gaza, but ever on the lookout for fresh information, Burckhardt had decided to make a detour along the almost unknown eastern shore of the Dead Sea and down into Arabia Petraea. This, he wanted to make clear to his employers, was 'sufficiently laborious and hazardous, not to be mistaken for tours of pleasure'. And in case the Committee were in any doubt on that count, he added, 'That which I am now entering upon is certainly subjected to almost as many difficulties as any African travels can be. In performing it, I hope to complete my preliminary exercises, and at the same time to obtain some information upon the geography of an unknown region.'[41]

As before, Burckhardt travelled under his assumed name of Shaykh Ibrahim ibn Abdallah, an Indian Muslim brought up in England. His means were slight and his mode of travelling harsh: 'I put up every time in the dirtiest caravanserai, take my cloak for a blanket, the earth for a mattress, eat with camel drivers, groom my own horse – but see and hear many things those who travel in comfort will never know.'[42] The wisdom of travelling humbly became apparent on 22 August. He had already passed through Palestine, skirted Lake Tiberias, run down the Jordan valley with a small caravan of 'petty merchants', passed south of the Dead Sea and been held up for a month by the Shaykh of Kerak, when he heard 'the country people' speak about wonderful antiquities in the Wadi Musa. He had some difficulty finding a guide who would take him by that route, rather than the direct road to Aqaba. 'I therefore pretended to have made a vow to slaughter a goat in honour of Haroun [Aaron], whose tomb I knew was situated at the extremity of the valley [Wadi Musa], and by this stratagem I thought that I should have the means of seeing the valley in my way to the tomb. To this,' he wrote with obvious satisfaction, 'my guide had nothing to oppose; the dread of drawing upon himself, by resistance, the wrath of Haroun, completely silenced him.'[43]

Burckhardt, his guide and the sacrificial goat made their way through wooded valleys, passing the odd spring and the remains of walls and paved roads. After five and a half hours they came to a place where the dome of Aaron's tomb could be seen in the distance. Many Arabs who had taken vows to make a sacrifice to Aaron were happy enough to fulfil it there, still some way from the actual site: a number of small cairns were evidence of this. 'Here my guide pressed me to slaughter the goat . . . but I pretended that I had vowed to immolate it at the tomb itself.'[44]

It seems likely that the guide wanted the sacrifice made there because he was not able to take Burckhardt any closer to the mountain, which fell under the control of another tribe. But Burckhardt was adamant, and hired a guide from Eldjy, the main village of Wadi Musa. With the new guide carrying the goat and the traveller slinging a skin of water over his shoulders, the two men set off for the mountain. Before long, they came to a large vaulted tomb cut into the rock, which Burckhardt observed as they passed. Further on they entered a steep, narrowing passage known as the Siq, where the rocks towered overhead and the path dropped sudden and steep into a deep valley. A little way into the Siq, they passed under a bridge 'thrown over the top of the chasm'. Here Burckhardt realised his guide's weakness: he was superstitious, and declared that no one had ever been able to climb up to the bridge, which must be the work of the *djinn*, the genies.

One of the world's great surprises lay in store for Burckhardt at the bottom of the Siq, as the path opened onto a magnificent, temple-like mausoleum cut into the rock and fronted by a colonnade and pediment some sixty feet high. He described it as 'one of the most elegant remains of antiquity existing in Syria; its state of preservation resembles that of a building recently finished . . .'[45] Further on they came to a row of these extraordinary monuments, many of their façades shaped like truncated pyramids. What was this place he had stumbled upon? 'Great must have been the opulence of a city,' he deduced, 'which could dedicate such monuments to the memory of its rulers.'[46] Nearby there was another indication of the opulence of the lost city: a theatre, also cut out of the rock, capable, he guessed, of holding three thousand spectators.

However great his genius for impersonation and disguise,

Burckhardt found it hard to contain his excitement at finding himself in this great antique city. As the two men and the goat made their way through the broadening valley towards Aaron's hilltop tomb, the traveller finally gave way to his curiosity and stopped to enter some of the great monuments. When they reached the western end of the *wadi*, he veered off towards another of the ancient buildings, the Qasr Bint Faraon (Castle of the Pharaoh's Daughter). At this point his guide aired his suspicions: 'I see now,' he said fiercely, 'that you are an infidel, who have some particular business amongst the ruins of the city of your forefathers; but depend upon it that we shall not suffer you to take out a single para [coin] of all the treasures hidden therein.'[47] Burckhardt assured him that his only purpose in going there was to make the sacrifice, but that these strange monuments had provoked his curiosity. 'He was not easily persuaded,' he wrote back to London, 'and I did not think it prudent to irritate him by too close an inspection of the palace, as it might have led him to declare, on our return, his belief that I had found treasures, which might have led to a search of my person and to the detection of my journal, which would most certainly have been taken from me, as a book of magic.'[48] Elsewhere he explained that he had not dared to make detailed notes of his discoveries: 'I knew well the character of the people around me; I was without protection in the midst of a desert where no traveller had ever before been seen; and a close examination of these works of the infidels, as they are called, would have excited suspicions.'[49]

So what had he found? 'In the red sand stone of which the valley is composed,' he wrote to Banks, 'are upwards of two hundred and fifty sepulchres entirely cut out of the rock, the greater part of them with Grecian ornaments. There is a mausoleum in the shape of a temple, of colossal dimensions, likewise cut out of the rock, with all its apartments, its vestibule, peristyle, &c. It is a most beautiful specimen of Grecian architecture, and in perfect preservation. There are other mausolea with obelisks, apparently in the Egyptian style, a whole amphitheatre cut out of the rock with the remains of a palace and of several temples.'[50] A lost city worthy of an early Indiana Jones. It was, Burckhardt believed, the lost Nabataean capital of Petra, and although he was humble enough to defer to Greek scholars, history has proved him right.*

Banks was delighted, not just for the attention the discovery brought to the Association, but also because in his description of the site, glimpsed briefly and under great duress, Burckhardt had proved himself a skilled observer. None of the earlier travellers, not even the great Park, could have delivered such a detailed report under such difficult circumstances. It boded well for what was to come.

In the end, there was not enough daylight left for the traveller and his guide to reach Aaron's tomb, so the goat had its throat cut out on the plain, looking up to the tomb, the guide including in his incantations, 'O Haroun, be content with our good intentions, for it is but a lean goat!'[51] They let the blood run into a pool which they covered with stones, as was the tradition, and then trimmed off the best of the meat, doing no more than searing it over the fire, afraid that the flames might attract robbers to their camp. In the morning the two men hurried out of the *wadi*, and the following day they heard of a caravan taking camels to Cairo.

Eleven days later, on 4 September 1812, Burckhardt entered the Egyptian capital, concluding his journey, 'by the blessing of God, without either loss of health, or exposure to any imminent danger'.[52] The British Consul, Colonel Ernest Missett, was at that time in Alexandria, but Barker in Aleppo had warned him of Burckhardt's arrival, and Aziz, the English Agent there, had been told to look out for the Swiss traveller. Things, however, did not go as planned. In the words of Thomas Legh, a British Member of Parliament on a tour through Egypt, 'He [Burckhardt] presented himself in the guise of an Arab shepherd at the residence of the English agent at Cairo. He remained in the outer court of the house for some time, and it was with some difficulty he obtained an interview with M.

---

* To Clarke he described 'several hundred large and elegant sepulchres cut out in the rock on the wady's side, with some beautiful and colossal mausoleums, in which the Grecian and Egyptian styles of architecture seem to meet. The ruins of temples and palaces, an aquaduct, an amphitheatre cut entirely out of the rock, and other antiquities, render this spot of great interest to history as well as to the fine arts' (Otter/Clarke, p.602).

Aziz, whose astonishment may easily be imagined when he heard a person of such appearance address him in French.'[53] If an Egyptian used to spending time with Europeans had not seen through Burck-hardt's disguise, then the transformation was complete: the Swiss gentleman had become the Muslim *shaykh*, or, as one of the residents of Cairo was to call him, 'a perfect Arab'.

15

Shaykh Ibrahim ibn Abdallah

'He has contributed very much towards the elucidation of
History, Antiquities, Geography, and the State of Societies . . .'
Major Rennell to Sir Joseph Banks, 1813

Cairo, 1812

CAIRO HAD BEEN transformed in the dozen years since Frederick
Hornemann spent his months there. Where Hornemann had witnessed intrigue and fear as the ruling Mamluk *beys* fought among
each other and then collapsed in the face of a superior French army,
Burckhardt found a thriving city whose prosperity was centred on
its bustling markets.

The hasty departure of the English and French seven years earlier
had left Egypt without an effective ruler, a vacuum that was quickly
filled by an opportunistic Albanian officer, Muhammad Ali. In 1805
the Albanian had such a grip on the country that the Turkish Sultan
had no alternative but to recognise him as his Viceroy in Egypt. In
1807 the new Pasha defeated a British force sent to unseat him, and
in 1811 he secured his throne by eliminating the *beys*, the ruling
aristocracy, and their Mamluk soldiers. This latter deed was accomplished at a banquet in honour of Muhammad Ali's son Tousson.
According to the account of an Englishman present in Cairo at the
time, as many as five hundred Mamluks were murdered that night,
although legend, ever the romancer, has it that one fine horseman

managed to ride over the castle walls and escape. Whatever the truth of events that night, not all the Mamluks were killed, because many of them were absent from the feast. Some of these absentees fled south, eventually beyond Aswan, where they were later to create problems for Burckhardt. Others who stayed were dealt with: as Burckhardt informed London in 1815, 'what secures to the Pasha the possession of Egypt more than anything else, is the death of three or four thousand soldiers, the most rebellious and fiercest of his troops, whom he constantly placed as vanguards against the Wahabi, and of whom very few returned'.[1]

The new Pasha, who never learned to speak Arabic, was as merciless towards the *fellahin*, the peasants of Egypt, as he was towards troublesome soldiers: thousands were pressed into working as slave labour on his new projects, particularly digging canals. But Muhammad Ali was also a revelation to people long used to lame, exploitative rule by self-serving governors appointed from Constantinople. Energetic and powerful, autocratic and ambitious – and unexpectedly mild-mannered, according to Europeans who were granted audiences – he wanted to be the absolute ruler of Egypt (in that, no one was likely to stop him), and he wanted his country to thrive. He was also a moderniser. He had seen enough of Europeans and their ways to know that they could help drag Egypt into the nineteenth century. As trade picked up, as harvests improved and the now secure 'overland route' between Europe and the East via Cairo and Suez flourished, so Muhammad Ali found himself with funds to pay for their expertise. Burckhardt's letters to London make many references to the growing European presence in Egypt – an Italian running a gunpowder factory that employed two hundred people, an Englishman setting up a large-scale rum distillery, a Frenchman reorganising the army . . .

In September 1812, when the African Association's missionary arrived in Cairo, the one thing that was not running as usual was the caravan trade. Cairo, as ever, was the crossing point of two major trade routes: pilgrim caravans moved east–west between central, north and western Africa and Mecca, while others brought slaves, ivory, ostrich feathers and other exotic goods from Nubia and the south. In 1812, the east–west trade was still disturbed by the Wahabi uprising, while trade along the Nile was interrupted because of insecurity over Mamluks active around Dongola, in what is now Sudan. So when Burckhardt reached Cairo on 4 September and discovered that a caravan would be leaving for Fezzan in three weeks' time, some people pressed him to join it. But Burckhardt was adamant. 'It would not have been advisable for me to have made any attempt to accompany [the Awjila caravan],' he wrote to London in November, after its departure. 'I should hardly have had time to prepare for setting out with them; I knew no body to whom to address myself for introduction to the caravan; I had no funds to equip myself; and I was as yet too little acquainted with the Egyptian and African world to suppose that I should be able to take my measures in such a way as to remain undiscovered. I am moreover extremely averse to any hasty steps; they are the ruin of the traveller's health as well as of his plans.'[2]

Four years after his departure from London, Burckhardt's aversion to haste was perfectly clear, but the Committee seemed to approve of his caution as much as Rennell was delighted by the results of his travels in the Holy Land. 'I don't know how far the African Association, collectively, may approve of the mode in which Burckhardt has employed his time since he landed in Syria,' the geographer wrote to Banks in 1813, 'but for my own part, I feel that he has contributed very much towards the elucidation of History, Antiquities, Geography, and the State of Societies, in Countries infinitely more interesting to us, than Africa ever can be, and, even in this last expedition in Africa, has given us notices, respecting a country that we know as little of, as of London. Had he at first dived into Africa at large, we possibly should have heard no more of him. I regard his journey from Damascus to Egypt, as containing more of what we want, than nine tenths of the late published Tours.'[3] Rennell no doubt was equally approving of Burckhardt's next step. As the next Fezzan caravan was not expected to leave Cairo until the following June, he decided to be 'profitable to African geography'[4] by travelling up the Nile between the first and third cataracts, a journey of some five months through country that had not been recorded by Europeans.*

He was travelling this time with a man named Shaharti from Assuit, his 'trusty servant' who had worked for him since he first arrived in Cairo. Both men were mounted on asses, which also carried what little they had in the way of luggage: Burckhardt was a minimalist on the move, a man who believed in travelling light, insisting that 'the less the traveller spends while on his march, and the less money he carries with him, the less likely are his plans to miscarry'.⁵ We have a rare glimpse of him as he moves south, for on two occasions he met Legh, the parliamentarian, cruising on the Nile. In Assuit, Legh had seen him 'extremely well dressed after the Turkish fashion, and in good health and condition',⁶ though when they met again further south, near Derr, the traveller 'had all the exterior of a common Arab, was very thin, and upon the whole his appearance was miserable enough. He told us he had been living for many days with the Shekhs [sic] of the villages through which he had passed, on lentils, bread, salt and water, and when he came on board, could not contain his joy at the prospect of being regaled with animal food.† The day before we had bought a lean and miserable sheep . . . and our friend contributed to our repast some excellent white bread which he had brought from Essouan. We smoked our pipes, congratulating each other on our good fortune in having met.'⁷

The further south Burckhardt travelled, the greater the problems. The local *shaykhs* were mistrustful, even though he carried letters of introduction from several people, including the Pasha Muhammad Ali. The situation was made more difficult by the poverty of

---

* On the map that accompanies Burckhardt's travels in Nubia, the route of two Frenchmen, Poncet and Duroule, is marked, south along the Nile to its division near modern-day Khartoum. The story of these two Frenchmen, who made embassies to the Negus of Abyssinia around the end of the seventeenth century, has been vividly captured in Jean-Christophe Rufin's historical novel *The Abyssinian* (Picador, 1999).

† Burckhardt may well have been happy to eat Legh's meat, but he had eaten more than bread and vegetables in Nubia. Listing the local birdlife, he mentions 'a small species of partridge, with red legs, which sometimes afforded me a welcome supper' (*Travels in Nubia*, p.22).

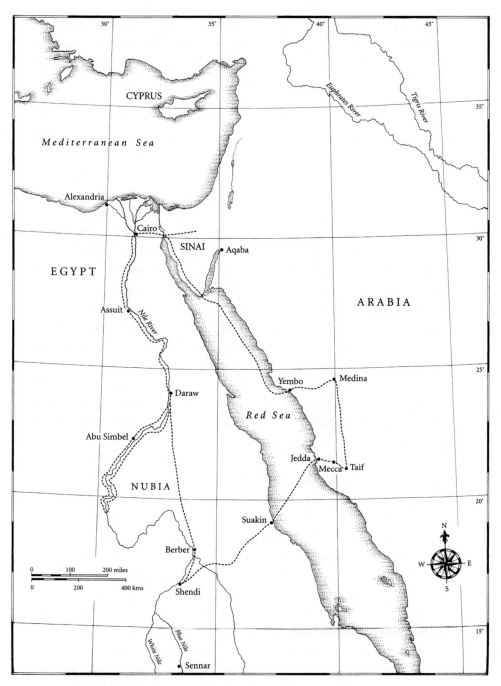

Burckhardt's travels in Africa and Arabia, 1812–17

Nubian villagers: even if they had wanted to help, they had little to share with him. And beyond Nubia, in the Dongola country, the remainder of the Mamluks were still a danger, although Burckhardt presents a pathetic image of them, transposed from their native Balkans and the borders of Central Asia to tropical Africa: 'Unable to bear the heat in their thick woollen dresses, which they still continue to wear, they constructed a number of rafts, on board of which they passed the whole of the summer, under awnings of mats, kept continually wet by their slaves.'[8] Not entirely unlike the manner in which foreign visitors continue to survive the Egyptian and Nubian summer.

Burckhardt's journal of his travels in Nubia is a masterpiece of observation and comprehension. He had travelled further up the Nile than any other curious European since antiquity, reaching what appeared to be the southernmost limit of safe travel on the river, his way blocked by the lawless Mamluks. While there, he heard from an Arab that Borno, one of the intended goals of his journey, was a tantalising twenty-five to thirty days' travel distant, but that there was almost no water along the way.

Although Burckhardt learned little about the route across the desert towards Timbuktu, he gave a vivid impression of life along the great river. There are lists of the wildlife and agriculture, careful noting of towns and villages, their names in English and Arabic script, descriptions of the manners and customs of the people, the local rulers and the people they owed allegiance to, lists of words in English, the Kensy and Nouba languages and, perhaps most unexpected given that another decade was to pass before there was a breakthrough in deciphering hieroglyphs, a thorough and convincing description of the many ancient Egyptian buildings he saw along the river. And just seven months after he had walked through Wadi Musa and become the first European since the Crusaders to see the remains of Petra, there was another magnificent archaeological rediscovery.

Burckhardt had heard from many people of an ancient temple that dominated the river between the first and second cataracts, but on the way upriver had had no glimpse of it. On the morning of 22 March 1813, a month after leaving Aswan, he left his camel and his guide on a mountain he called Ebsambal and climbed alone down a sheer sandbank, a steep and arduous descent, though he made no mention of the difficulty because at the bottom he found a massive rock-cut temple fronted by six monumental carved figures, several chambers within, the remains of the ancient Egyptian cult figures in the sanctuary. This discovery would have repaid the efforts he had made to find it, but there was more to come.

> *Having, as I supposed, seen all the antiquities of Ebsambal, I was about to ascend the sandy side of the mountain by the same way I had descended; when having luckily turned more to the southward, I fell in with what is yet visible of four immense colossal statues cut out of the rock ... The entire head, and part of the breast and arms of one of the statues are yet above the surface [of the sand]; of the one next to it scarcely any part is visible, the head being broken off, and the body covered with sand to above the shoulders; of the other two, only the bonnets appear ... The head which is above the surface has a most expressive, youthful countenance, approaching nearer to the Grecian model of beauty, than any ancient Egyptian figure I have seen.*[9]

He was right in thinking that these figures 'belong to the finest period of Egyptian sculpture'. They formed part of the façade of Ramses II's masterpiece, his great temple at Abu Simbel, and Burckhardt had just become the first known European to see these glories since antiquity. Later that day, unable to go south alone, he decided to return to Esna and wait there for the Sennar caravan to depart.

Seven months later, a tall, bearded, dark-haired trader appeared at the camel market in Daraw. Then as now, Daraw was the meeting place of Sudani camel traders, the end-point of the fabled Forty

Days' Road by which camels continue to be brought into Egypt. The camel-drivers gather in a camp just outside this quiet, dusty, palm-fringed town on the narrow wedge between the Nile and the eastern desert. The newcomer among them was not Egyptian, but then foreigners were a common sight around the market – he could, perhaps, have been a Levantine or a man from the East, though he was dressed according to the local custom, in white linen shirt and trousers and a loose brown wool cloak, a white woollen cap and turban on his head. In his pocket he had a small journal, a pencil, compass, penknife, tobacco pouch and a steel for striking a light. His two hundredweight of baggage and provisions included sugar, soap, nutmeg, razors and steels and some wooden beads. To support himself he had packed what any modest Egyptian would take for a long journey: some flour, biscuit, dates, lentils, butter, salt, rice, coffee, tobacco, pepper and onions. His cooking utensils included a coffee pot, cooking pot, copper plate, knife, spoon and a wooden drinking bowl. A spare shirt, a comb, a carpet to sit on and a rough Magrebi cloth to sleep under were the extent of his comforts. This was Burckhardt's latest mode of travelling, and it contributed to a convincing performance: if there was anything unusual among his baggage it was the Damascus Koran, the spare journal, inkwell and some loose sheets of paper for writing charms. He carried a gun, a pistol and a metal-tipped stick in case the charms did not offer sufficient protection, while his purse, tucked into his girdle, hidden under his cloak, contained fifty Spanish dollars. He had also hidden in there two firmans or letters of recommendation, one from Muhammad Ali, the other from his son, the general, Ibrahim Pasha.

Burckhardt would not be needing the dollars just yet, for he had sold his camel to a local trader, and part of the deal was that the new owner would carry his baggage as far as Sennar. Once business was concluded, provisions laid in, evil spirits purged by the bluish flames of salt thrown onto coals by Bedouin women, the caravan set off for the south. Burckhardt was delighted. 'I am almost dying of boredom,' he had written to his parents during the months of inactivity. 'Not wishing to be known, I kept as little company as possible, dressed myself in the poorest dress of an inhabitant of Egypt and spent as little money as I possibly could.'[10]

In a letter to Banks written at the same time, he sent assurance that 'if I supposed that this journey presented great risks I should not undertake it; for I wish to expose myself to hazards only on the western side of Africa'.[11] And yet there were difficulties ahead, made more so by his having dismissed his servant. He was convinced he was right to do so, believing that 'those who have no other motive in performing difficult and dangerous travels, but that of gaining their monthly pay, are averse to incur any perils, and stagger at the smallest difficulties'.[12] At the start of his journey, the pay may have been Burckhardt's big motivator, but time and experience had changed all that and he was now so absorbed by the life of a traveller, so fascinated by the lands he had travelled through, so curious about what lay ahead, that it is clear he would have gone just for the pleasure of going.

The difficulty this time lay not only in the route, across desert and barren hills, but also in the method of travel. He had introduced himself as a poor trader in search of a brother who had gone missing with the bulk of his fortune. This left him exposed and vulnerable, and it was not long before others in the caravan began to take advantage of him. First came the man who had bought Burckhardt's camel: in his greed he had overloaded the beast, which collapsed and died a couple of days out into the desert, forcing Burckhardt to find someone else to carry his baggage. By the time they reached Berber in Sudan, his standing had sunk so low that some of his fellow travellers were even stealing his water; no one wanted to be associated with a man who could not afford to pay someone to make tea or draw water from the wells. He had to wait to have his revenge, which he found in print when he wrote that 'The traveller in this part of the world ... must consider himself as surrounded by some of the most worthless of the human race, among whom he must think himself fortunate, if he can discover any less depraved than the rest, whom he can place some degree of confidence in ...'[13] He also pointed to the difficulty of taking notes. 'The expression here [in Sudan], and also in Egypt, when any traveller is seen taking notes, is, "he writes down the country".'[14]* On the move, he was able to ride ahead of the caravan on his ass and pull out his journal under his cloak, hiding it again before the others caught him up. But in Berber and elsewhere there were no moments of privacy, especially as he was sharing accommodation with the Daraw traders. He could have rented a room by himself, but he knew that would be an invitation to thieves and extortionists. 'I was not sorry to leave Berber,' he wrote of his departure on 7 April, just over a month out of Daraw, 'for the character of the inhabitants is such, that a stranger can never consider himself safe for a moment amongst them.'[15]

On 17 April the caravan reached Shendi, a place of some thousand houses on the sandy plain half an hour's walk from the Nile. It was ruled over by a *mek* or chieftain called Nimr, a proud, cunning man referred to as 'the Leopard'. The Association's missionary was clearly glad to be there, his relief at his safe arrival apparent in his description of the gentleness of the people and the wonders of the country, which included elephants and prancing horses which 'surpassed in beauty any other horse I ever remember to have seen'.[16] He was at one of the Sudan's major crossroads, a trading town made prosperous, as far as Burckhardt could find out, by the fact that Mek Nimr levied no taxes on passing trade. Burckhardt set up stall in the great marketplace, buried by the crowds, surrounded by bundles of tobacco, sandalwood from India, fenugreek from Egypt, tanned leather, rocks of salt from deep in the desert, cloves, pepper, cardamom, gold from the south (no one would tell him where), slaves from Nouba and Abyssinia, ivory and rhino horn and a range of other goods. 'The market is so crowded, and the dust and the heat are so great, during the mid-day hours, which is the favourite time for transacting business, that I was unable to remain in the market-place many hours together.'[17]

He sent a long report back to London on the trade in Shendi,

---

* I have experienced a similar suspicion in Egypt on several occasions during the past ten years – along the Suez Canal I was even handed over to the police for scribbling in my notebook.

the origins and values of whatever was on sale, the nationality of traders, the routes they followed and profits made. German steel and Venetian glass were the most noteworthy European goods on sale, and there was little from western Africa and the Niger – only some slaves brought from Borno. This might not have thrown much light on Burckhardt's mission, but it was the most complete report to date of Sudani trade. Two of his observations were bound to be cause for discussion in the salons of Soho Square.

The first was that however successful Europe, and at this stage particularly Britain, might be at stopping the slave trade in West Africa, the Caribbean and America, slavery would continue in East Africa for as long as there were Muslims.

> It is not from foreign nations that the Blacks can hope for deliverance; this great work must be effected by themselves, and can be the result only of successful resistance. The European governments . . . may contribute to it by commerce, and by the introduction among the Negroes of arts and industry, which must ultimately lead them to a superiority over the Mussulmans in war. Europe, therefore, will have done but little for the Blacks, if the abolition of the Atlantic slave-trade . . . is not followed up by some wise and grand plan, tending to the civilization of the continent. None presents a fairer prospect than the education of the sons of Africa in their own country, and by their own countrymen.[18]

What hope was there that this would come about? Little, in Burckhardt's opinion: knowing how little European governments did for their own poor, he realised that they were unlikely to exert themselves for Africans.

Burckhardt's other observation related to firearms, which he had not seen on sale in Shendi market. He had been obliged to hand over his own gun to the Mek of Shendi in exchange for four dollars and a good meal. The few other guns he had seen in town all looked unusable, although they were still brandished by Mek Nimr's slaves, and to great effect. One reason for the lack of weapons was that traders were loath to carry them for a reason that will have become only too obvious to Burckhardt: local rulers had a habit of borrowing them and not giving them back. It set the Swiss traveller thinking. Musing on the fear with which people in the region regarded firearms, even ones that he recognised posed more of a danger to their owners than to anyone they might want to shoot, he believed that a small party of armed European soldiers would be unstoppable in the region: 'If 250 miserable Mamlouks [sic] conquered and kept possession of Dóngola, a body of experienced Europeans could not have much to fear . . .'[19] This, he believed, had a bearing on the future exploration of the African interior. 'Single individuals attempting to make discoveries in the interior of this continent, through districts unfrequented by northern [by which he meant Egyptian or Tripolitan] traders, will, I fear, always fall victims to their zeal and honourable ambition; and if the sources of the Bahr el Abyadh [the White Nile] are ever to be discovered, it must be by armed force. England has, by her different voyages of discovery, and her missions to explore distant countries, far surpassed all the nations of Europe: and a successful expedition through the interior of the African continent is alone wanting to render her triumphs complete.'[20] You can almost hear the self-congratulations emanating from Soho Square.

From Shendi, Burckhardt had three options: he could return to Egypt, move up the Blue Nile into Abyssinia, or join the Suakin caravan to the Red Sea coast. Ethiopia was attractive, but both the Frenchman Poncet and Scottish Bruce had been that way before, while there were no records of a European crossing the Nubian Desert between the Nile and the Red Sea this far south. The desert journey was full of dangers and difficulties, but it offered the possibility of reaching Mecca in time for the annual *hajj*. 'I was then, as I still am, fully convinced that the title of Hadji would afford me the most powerful recommendation and protection in any future journey through the interior countries of Africa.'[21]

The caravan's departure was inauspicious: on the first of forty foot-slogging days to cross to Suakin, one of the Mek's slaves attempted to force Burckhardt to hand over his remaining gun.

Two days later, the traveller's large waterskin burst. These would have been serious calamities on the crossing from Egypt, given the bad feeling towards him. But in Shendi he had bought a slave to accompany him, and on this journey others in the caravan turned out to be happy to help – the Mek's slave was scared off and Burckhardt and his slave were offered water from other skins.

The caravan made a majestic sight, some two hundred laden camels, 150 traders, three hundred slaves, thirty horses and another thirty-odd camels carrying the richest of the traders. This large group was divided into several smaller allegiances: Burckhardt travelled alongside a group of five traders, three of whom had come, many years before, from West Africa. Their chief, the Hajj Ali al Bournawi (from Borno), was a well-travelled man who had spent time in Constantinople and Damascus but was now based in Kordofan. He was making his fourth pilgrimage to Mecca. This fact and his constant, obsessive reading of the Koran gave him an air of sanctity and earned him the respect of the *meks* and other chiefs of the places they passed through. Yet Burckhardt found him to be 'a complete bon vivant, whose sole object was sensual enjoyment. The profits on his small capital . . . were spent entirely in the gratification of his desires.'[22] He had brought along his favourite female slave to keep him company, but rather than have her walk like other slaves, she was seated on a camel so as not to tire her unnecessarily, while his saddlebags were stuffed with whatever delicacies the Shendi souk could provide: he and the slave of his dreams ate better than anyone else in the caravan. 'One might have supposed he knew vice only by name',[23] yet there was a sinister side to him, as Burckhardt learned along the way. The previous year the Bournawi had been surprised to meet his cousin in Mecca; she had come via Cairo to make the pilgrimage. According to Borno tribal customs, under these circumstances and given that she was not attached to anyone else, a man may claim his cousin. This Hajj Ali proceeded to do: he married her there and then. But by the time they reached Medina he had had a reversal of fortune and his money was running out. It was unfortunate for him, but worse for his cousin because he then sold her as a slave to some Egyptian traders and she, unable to prove that she was a free woman, had no choice but to go with them.

It was the beginning of June, and with the sun withering at midday, they began the day's march early, slept through the heat and then carried on late. Burckhardt allowed his slave to ride on the camel for the first four or five hours of the day, much to the astonishment of the Suakin traders, and then rode the rest of the day himself. Whenever the caravan stopped, he wandered around whatever village or town might be nearby to do some research.

My appearance excited an universal shriek of surprise and horror, especially among the women, who were not a little terrified at seeing such an outcast of nature, as they consider a white man to be, peeping into their huts, and asking for a little water or milk. The chief feeling which my appearance inspired, I could easily perceive to be disgust, for the Negroes are all firmly persuaded that the whiteness of the skin is the effect of disease, and a sign of weakness; and there is not the least doubt, that a white man is looked upon by them as a being greatly inferior to themselves.[24]

Things were no better when he finally reached Suakin towards the end of June. By then, as he admits, his already humble dress was reduced to rags and he looked like a beggar. He was also easy prey for the Aga or ruler, a Turk by the name of Yemak, who was sufficiently skilled as an extortionist to recognise an opportunity to confiscate what few goods the traveller might be carrying. He began by accusing Burckhardt of being a Mamluk spy, which provided a pretext for seizing his camel, which had been much admired on the march for its strength and speed. When Burckhardt refused, the confrontation soon escalated. '"Not only thy camel," [the Aga] demanded, "but the whole of thy baggage must be taken and searched."'

Burckhardt protested, more humble than ever. He was just an unfortunate merchant who had suffered greatly along the way and did not deserve such misfortunes. The Aga was unmoved and called for the *wali* or policeman to seize the foreigner. At this point Burckhardt played his trump card, the firmans he had brought from Egypt. No one could have failed to be impressed: the one from Muhammad Ali was an imposing sheet of paper, two and a half feet long and a foot wide, written in Turkish and carrying the Pasha's great seal. The second, from Muhammad Ali's son Ibrahim, was smaller and written in Arabic. These documents had the desired effect: people around the Aga were amazed, the Aga himself stupefied and appalled. Not knowing Turkish, he read only Ibrahim Pasha's firman, but it told him enough, referring to Burckhardt as *Radjilna Ibrahim es-Shamy*, Our Man Ibrahim the Syrian. The Aga kissed both firmans and pressed them to his forehead as a sign of acquiescence. From that moment on, his behaviour towards Burckhardt was transformed. Fear was the motive. Hoping that he could persuade the foreigner not to mention his indiscretions when he returned to Cairo, Yemak could not do enough for him, offering him a slave and a new robe as presents, both of which the traveller refused. The food, however, he was glad to accept.

The Aga was humiliated by the extent to which he had to crawl to pacify Burckhardt, who continued to wear his ragged clothes. 'The people of the town laughed at seeing this man's pride humbled by the attentions he thought it incumbent on him to shew to a beggar like me. My object was to find protection in his company, recruit my strength by his good fare, and to save expense, for by this time I had only two dollars in my purse.'[25] Ten days later, Burckhardt put the Aga out of his misery by boarding a boat to Jedda – as a final gift or bribe, Yemak arranged a free passage and had food sent on board.

The boat was packed with slaves, traders, pilgrims and sailors, eighty-nine people sharing a forty-foot open boat for twelve days. When he saw the conditions on board, Burckhardt considered waiting for another sailing, but was told every other boat would be as full until the end of the pilgrimage in November. Food was scarce, the crossing was rough, drinking water ran out, but Burckhardt suffered these discomforts in the knowledge that they would end in Jedda, where he could draw money on one of the Association's letters of credit, and that they would open the way to Mecca and the final step of his preparation for his journey across Africa.

'I think that the discovery of the interior parts of Nubia is well worth a year's labour and the expense attending it,' Burckhardt had written to Banks before leaving Egypt in March 1814. 'My journey through Arabia may probably qualify me better than any thing else, to future perilous travels in the Mohammedan world, nor will it, I hope, be devoid of some advantages to science.'[26] Burckhardt was not the first European to make the pilgrimage to Mecca. In recent years a Spaniard, Domingo Badia, had set out for the city under the name of Ali Bey al Abbassi, though at this stage nothing more had been heard of him. Then in 1809 another of Professor Blumenbach's students from Göttingen, Ulrich Seetzen, had performed the *hajj* and then continued to Yemen. But Seetzen's account of his travels never reached Europe: as Burckhardt later heard from one of the East India Company's employees at Mocha in Yemen, Seetzen was poisoned by order of the Imam of Yemen and all his belongings taken to Sanaa. So although the Hejaz was not untrodden territory and other Europeans had performed the pilgrimage to Mecca, the way was still open to Burckhardt to write the first complete account.

He begins his *Travels in Arabia* with an announcement of 'unfavourable circumstances'. The person in Jedda to whom his letter of credit was addressed refused to advance him money, claiming the letter was out of date. The way the traveller looked cannot have helped matters: 'It must be confessed also that my torn clothes did not speak much in my favour.'[27] Things got worse a couple of days later when he went down with a violent fever, caused perhaps by eating too much fruit from Jedda market after a year of meagre diet. Whatever the reason, the fever became worse, until help arrived in the form of what Burckhardt calls 'a barber, or country physician',[28] who suggested a remedy of ginger, nutmeg and cinnamon. The traveller had other ideas and insisted on being bled. Whether this helped or the fever passed by itself is not clear, but two weeks later he was on his feet again.

His lack of finance proved more difficult to remedy. The man on whom he was supposed to draw money continued to refuse his letter of credit. The only asset now left to him was the slave he had bought in Sudan; not having any option, he now sold the young man in Jedda's slave market. Burckhardt had paid sixteen dollars for him in Shendi and sold him for forty-eight, a significant profit. But while the Association will have approved of his boosting his funds, they would have been extremely embarrassed by the method.

With the money from the slave, Burckhardt was able to pay his bills and buy some new clothes, what he called 'the dress of a reduced Egyptian gentleman'.[29] Being now well enough to go out, he learned that Muhammad Ali, the Pasha of Egypt, was in the Hejaz to put down the Wahabi uprising. The Pasha was installed at Taif, eighty miles inland from Jedda, where Burckhardt now sent a letter addressed to Bosari, the Pasha's Armenian physician, whom he knew from Cairo, asking for a loan. Before Bosari had time to reply, news of Burckhardt's presence in Jedda reached another physician whom he knew from Cairo, a man named Yahya Effendi, who immediately ended his financial worries.

The letter to Bosari produced another reaction: when Muhammad Ali heard that Shaykh Ibrahim, the celebrated traveller whom he had met in Cairo and who was becoming something of a legend in the region, was wandering the streets of Jedda in rags, he sent a messenger with two camels, fresh clothes, enough money to cover his expenses and an order, not a request, that he should travel to Taif.

The fasting month of Ramadan was well underway when Burckhardt reached the hills, but whatever inconveniences fasting may have brought were far outweighed by the relief of the cooler mountain air after the blistering heat and sapping humidity of the coast. Soon after his arrival, Bosari appeared with orders to bring Burckhardt – Shaykh Ibrahim – to an audience with the Pasha. Also present would be the Qadi of Mecca, one of Islam's most revered spiritual authorities. In front of this man, according to Bosari, the Pasha had expressed doubts about Shaykh Ibrahim's religion, saying, 'It is not the beard alone which proves a man to be a true Moslem.'[30]

Burckhardt never clarified the matter of his religion. He had certainly been raised a Christian, but for several years he had been living as a Muslim, and in the Hejaz he told several people that he had converted. We will never know whether this was merely part of his disguise or whether he had indeed done so. To the Pasha, that night in Taif, he replied, 'That I certainly should not go to the Pasha's public audience, if he would not receive me as a Turk,' by which he meant a Muslim. The Pasha teasingly replied that he was welcome, whatever he was. Burckhardt went, expecting to be put to the test, but instead found himself being questioned about the exile of Bonaparte on Elba, which had just been announced, and the possibility, now that the French were dealt with, of England invading Egypt.

The next day, 29 August, he went to visit the Qadi, Sadik Effendi, a man from Istanbul and 'a true eastern courtier, of very engaging manners and address'. The Qadi began to question him on his travels and his reading of the Koran and its commentaries, something Burckhardt knew better than many Muslims. Things improved considerably later on: after the day's fast ended and they prepared to eat, the two men said their prayers together, 'when I took great care to chaunt [sic] as long a chapter of the Koran as my memory furnished at the moment'.[31] It is not clear whether the Pasha or his Qadi were convinced. Burckhardt had clearly done enough to satisfy appearances, though back in Cairo Muhammad Ali told the English Consul that he knew Burckhardt was an English Christian.* In Taif, Burckhardt suspected that he was seen as an aristocratic English spy, although were that the case it is unlikely that Muhammad Ali would have allowed him to leave Taif for Mecca, as he did on 7 September; it is more likely that he thought him eccentric.

In Mecca, he announced himself as 'a reduced member of the Mamelouk [sic] corps of Egypt',[32] bought himself another slave and

---

* Richard Burton seemed convinced that Burckhardt had converted to Islam.

rented rooms in a quiet part of town, overlooking trees – 'more exhilarating than the finest landscape could have been under different circumstances'.[33] He reported different reactions to the place to different people. In his *Travels* he wrote that, 'During all my journies in the East, I never enjoyed such perfect ease as at Mekka.'[34] To Dr Clarke he described it as 'a dirty town of almost thirty thousand inhabitants, situated in a complete desert'.[35] At the same time he complained of being sick for much of his stay, mostly with diarrhoea, which he blamed on the city's brackish water. In spite of this, on 25 November he was well enough to perform the pilgrimage in the company of some eighty thousand people, in the process earning the right to be addressed as *hajji*.

The Arabian journey convinced Burckhardt, for he saw it with his own eyes, that there were no caravans from Borno or elsewhere in West Africa. He also saw the success of Muhammad Ali's campaign against the Wahabis: on 11 January 1815, the Pasha's army faced them at a village called Byssel. Seven thousand Wahabis died in the battle, while five hundred taken prisoner were soon impaled in Mecca and Jedda. Whatever Burckhardt's feelings about the severity of the Pasha's actions, he was pleased with the result, because the Wahabis were the reason the West Africans had stayed away. Now that they were out of the way, the trans-Saharan caravans were expected to resume.

'Of the prosecution of my travels into the interior of Africa,' Burckhardt wrote from Cairo to William Hamilton, Secretary of the Association, 'I shall say nothing at present.'[36] In the meantime, however, there was much to say about Arabia. In January 1815 he had travelled from Mecca to Medina, the burial place of the Prophet Muhammad and a town unknown to Europeans. The new geographical information this produced was gained at great cost, because while there he contracted dysentery and was laid up for three months. Too weak to pursue his original plan of travelling overland to Egypt via Aqaba, he headed for Yembo, hoping to cross the Red Sea by boat. Yembo – 'that abode of death',[37] he later called it – was not a great choice for convalescence, for there was an outbreak of plague. The sea crossing, when he managed to find a space in another dangerously overcrowded boat, was hellish and his account makes many references to sickness, vomiting and the death of two passengers. When he finally touched ground again, on the southern tip of Sinai, he heard that the plague had broken out in Cairo as well, so he headed for the desert hills, where he stayed in a Bedouin village. At the beginning of June, recognising the opportunity of crossing the desert in safety, he travelled to Suez and joined Muhammad Ali's wife and her caravan – six hundred camels and a significant guard to transport them home – and two weeks later he was back in Cairo, having been away two and a half years and having completed one of the great journeys of the age.

In February 1816, Burckhardt sent one of his journals to London. 'It has been ready for some time,' he wrote to Banks, unlike the trans-Saharan caravans, of which there were no news. In the middle of April he wrote a hasty note announcing that there was plague in Cairo, that he expected it to spread along the Nile and had decided to return to Sinai and from there travel the length of the eastern coast of the Sinai peninsula, which had not been seen by any European he was aware of. When he returned to Egypt in the summer of 1816, there was a change at the English Consulate. Colonel Missett had been replaced by one of Burckhardt's young friends from London, the artist and Abyssinian traveller Henry Salt.

Early in 1809, just before Burckhardt had left England for Malta and Syria, Salt had been sent back to Abyssinia on an embassy from the British government to thank the *Ras* for his expressions of friendship and to see whether trade could be encouraged between the two kingdoms. Salt took with him presents, including artillery, worth the considerable sum of £1906. This was intended to 'impress the present monarch with a favourable idea of the power and riches of his new ally'.[38] On 26 December 1806, just before he left London, Salt visited Soho Square to attend a Committee meeting of the African Association. Dr Hamilton, the Earl of Moira and Joseph

Wyndham, a wealthy scholar and antiquary and the newest member of the Committee, had joined Banks in commissioning Salt to procure 'usefull [sic] and curious information, relative to the interior of Africa'.[39] The huge sum of £500 was put at his disposal, part of it intended for the possible mission into the interior of Nathaniel Pearce, a British sailor who had 'turned Turk' and whom Salt had left in Abyssinia during his first visit.

Salt's embassy to Abyssinia was less of a diplomatic success than was hoped and very little new information emerged for the Association, but for Salt it was a great triumph, and on his return to London he found himself fêted in society – even the Prince of Wales extended an invitation. Perhaps in gratitude for Salt waiving his claim to any sort of fee for his limited services, the African Association caught the mood of the moment and elected him an honorary member. He even earned £1000 from the publication of his *Travels*. But most important, when word reached Salt that Colonel Missett had resigned as English Consul in Cairo due to poor health, Salt's previous experiences in the region made him the front-runner for the post. His patron Lord Valentia recommended him to the Foreign Secretary and Banks seconded him, adding, 'from an intimate acquaintance with Mr. Salt I consider him as more capable than any other person I know to execute with ability and integrity the Duties of that office and able as well to promote the interests of Science wheresoever it may be his privilege to be stationed'.[40] This was the man who now appeared in Cairo.

The two Association men met again as soon as the famous Swiss *hajj* returned to the capital; Salt said Burckhardt looked as 'black as a negro'.[41] The two men lived very different lives, Salt the official life of court and consulate, duty and intrigue, Shaykh Ibrahim his beloved city life of souk and hammam, and yet they soon developed a close understanding and mutual admiration. Missett had moved the Consulate to Alexandria, so Salt had had to find and decorate a suitable house in Cairo, settling near what became the heart of the foreign community, at Ezbekieh. He described the house to Valentia as having 'two large salles and my own bedroom, or rather library, looking on really a respectably-sized garden, and plenty of other rooms for my secretary and the strangers who occasionally visit us'.[42] The halls were paved with marble, the ceilings painted in the 'Constantinopolitan style'. To run the establishment there was a secretary, a *dragoman*, grooms for three horses, two guards, a steward, a cook, two footmen, a gardener and a laundress. Burckhardt, on the other hand, lived the life of a modest Cairene in a small stone house near the Bab al Hadid, which he shared with his servants, an unusual Scot who had been captured during the war against the English, forced to convert and now known as Osmyn, Shaharti from Assuit and two slaves, one of them an Abyssinian woman whom he hoped would teach him her language.*

Soon after Salt's arrival, Burckhardt came to the Consulate with a proposition. William Hamilton, the Association's Secretary and the government's Under-Secretary of State for Foreign Affairs, who had toured Egypt in 1801 with Colonel William Leake,† had described a fallen stone bust at the West Bank temple known as the Memnonian as 'the most beautiful and perfect piece of Egyptian sculpture that can be seen throughout the whole country'.[43] On his visit to Luxor, Burckhardt had made a point of looking up this sculpture and he too was struck by its beauty. He later enthused about the bust to Byron's friend W.J. Bankes, who had taken 'a proper rope with pullies and machinery'[44] with him when he sailed up the Nile, but had been unable to move it. Burckhardt, in one of his interviews with Muhammad Ali, had suggested that the Pasha might like to offer it as a present to England, but clearly the Pasha did not like to: as another foreigner in Cairo at the time remarked, 'it must have appeared to a Turk too trifling an article to send to so great a personage'.[45] These were the words of an extraordinary Italian by the name of Giovanni Belzoni, a Paduan of great height – perhaps as much as six feet eight inches – immense strength and even greater character. A former circus strongman who had appeared at London's Sadler's Wells as a giant, slain by Jack, he had been lured to Cairo by the Pasha's growing reputation as a moderniser. Since

* *The Times*, ten years later, reported that Burckhardt's wife still lived in this house. It referred to her 'lively and animated manners and her lack of beauty'.
† Leake was also a member of the African Club and later became the Association's Secretary.

leaving the stage, the Italian had acquired some knowledge of hydraulics, but not enough to impress Muhammad Ali. Burckhardt, on the other hand, was won over and found him 'as enterprising as he is intelligent, high-minded and disinterested'.[46] He also recognised that Belzoni was the man to move the head of Memnon.

Some time earlier he had written to his friend Clarke in Cambridge complaining that 'every thing of antiques is exceedingly dear; medals may be had cheaper in Covent Garden streets than among the peasants of the Thebaide'.[47] Now that Salt was in Cairo Burckhardt was confident that they could persuade Muhammad Ali to donate the bust of Memnon in Luxor, and that the Association's two men could share the cost of having Belzoni drag it to the banks of the Nile and ship it to London. On 1 July 1816, Burckhardt wrote to Hamilton in London that 'Mr. Salt and myself have made a common purse to defray the expenses of the land and water carriage.'[48] The deal was done.

Throughout the summer and autumn of 1816, while Belzoni, his wife, several other foreign helpers and as many as 130 Egyptians were dragging the head of Memnon (actually Ramses II) to the Nile and then excavating 'Burckhardt's' Great Temple at Abu Simbel, the Swiss *shaykh* stayed in Cairo and wrote up his Arabian and Sinai journals. 'The repeated notices I have transmitted concerning the Bedouins of Arabia,' he wrote to Hamilton in London on 15 October, 'will show how much I am interested in them. I believe that very little of their real state is known in Europe, either because travellers have not sufficiently distinguished Bedouins from Arabs in general, or because they have attempted to describe them without having had the advantage of seeing them at leisure in their own tents, in the interior of the desert.'[49] His study of the Bedouin was another first, one that was greatly appreciated by the more bookish of the Association's members.

In spite of the work on his journals and the time spent collecting Arabic manuscripts in Cairo, the delay in the arrival of a trans-Saharan caravan and the lack of progress on his mission weighed heavily on Burckhardt. He complained that Cairo lacked interest. 'Were I in Syria, or Arabia, I should not be so impatient, as I have friends there of greater interest. Here I have neither the one nor the other, and if I could not pass the time studying my Arabic manuscripts, I should scarcely be able to stay quiet.'[50] To London, he once again sent apologies: 'I feel the greatest regret, in being obliged to inform you ... that I have no well founded hopes of being able to leave Egypt before next spring. It would be tedious to enter into all the disappointments I have experienced, by the non-arrival of the western caravan.'[51]

One disappointment hit harder than the rest. When Burckhardt left London he had intended to make a name – and some money – for himself by achieving something in African exploration. After all, he had only to look at Mungo Park to see what could be done. True, while travelling he had become so enamoured of the people and landscape that he was in no hurry for his mission to end – time was not a factor. But equally, had a Fezzani caravan arrived that day, he would have gone with it. In the meantime, he had the satisfaction of anticipating the stir that his account of his pilgrimage to Mecca would cause. Now, however, he had the misfortune to be handed a copy of the *Quarterly Review*, in which he learned of the publication of Ali Bey's* *Travels in Morocco, Tripoli, Cyprus, Egypt, Arabia, Syria and Turkey*, which contained a description of the *hajj*. 'I have lately had an opportunity of perusing his work,' Burckhardt wrote to reassure London. While he could not fault much of what Ali Bey had written, 'I hope to be able to give some information in addition to his.'[52] In the event, Burckhardt's descriptions and observations were infinitely more valuable.

More worrying for him were reports of other missions setting out for the interior. Perhaps worst of all, the *Quarterly Review* also carried the spectacular story of Robert Adams, an American sailor who claimed to have been shipwrecked off the African coast in 1810 and taken as a slave to Timbuktu. Burckhardt devotes several pages

* Don't be misled by the name: Ali Bey was a Spaniard, Domingo Badia, who although not an official African Association missionary, travelled to London to see Banks before starting for Africa. His original plan seems to have been to cause a revolution in Morocco. When that failed, he decided to make the pilgrimage to Mecca. In 1817, after the publication of his *Travels*, he set off, with French backing, to cross Africa from east to west, but died the following year in Syria.

of a letter to dismissing some of Adams' claims, most significantly that he had crossed the Sahara – 'some of his statements', he assured his employers, 'convinced me of his want of veracity', adding that 'they can be contradicted only by the few who have actually crossed the deserts'.[53] However, the Committee in London found it harder to dismiss Adams' account, particularly as Sir Joseph Banks himself had had an opportunity to interview the poor man. Adams had been a sailor on the *Charles*, a 280-ton ship that left New York in June 1810 and was wrecked off the West African coast in October. He claimed that he and the other ten members of the crew all made it to shore. Some of them were then captured by Moors and taken to Timbuktu, where he remained for several months until ransomed by the French agent in Mogador, Joseph Dupuis.

In October 1815 Adams reached London, having worked for a time for an English trader in Cadiz. Before long, word of a man 'having been a long time in slavery in the interior of Africa, and having resided several months in Tombuctoo'[54] spread around the city. One of London's African traders discovered him 'in very ill plight both from hunger and nakedness. Scarcely recovered from a fit of sickness, he had, in that condition, begged his way from Holyhead to London, for the purpose of obtaining through the American Consul, a passage to his native country; and he had already passed several nights in the open streets amongst the many other distressed seamen, with whom the metropolis was at that period unfortunately crowded.'[55]

As Adams could neither read nor write, his story was taken down and edited by a trader called Samuel Cock. Cock goes to some lengths to offer proof of the veracity of Adams' story, pointing out that Adams himself was loath to tell it, having at that time received an offer of a passage to America from his Consul. Cock and his associates provided Adams with food, shelter and clothing and promised to pay for his passage across the Atlantic if he would tell his story in full. This he agreed to do, and over the course of several weeks went several times over the details, never contradicting himself, as Cock is quick to point out. It was then that he was examined by Sir Joseph Banks and John Barrow, a Secretary at the

Admiralty. Cock admits that 'Adams had the misfortune, at his first interview with these gentlemen ... to excite some doubts in their minds by his account of Tombuctoo, and by his mistakes on some subjects of natural history.'[56] Whatever his reservations, Banks would have taken in Adams' comments on Timbuktu, which the sailor described as being as large as Lisbon, and on the trade conducted there: Adams had seen tobacco, tar, gunpowder, cloth and jars being traded for gold dust, ivory, gum, ostrich feathers, cowrie shells and goat skins. He had also seen the King of Timbuktu dressed in a blue frock-coat, 'decorated with gold, having gold epaulettes, and a broad wristband of the same metal', which invites the delicious speculation that this could have been the blue frock-coat that Houghton had had taken by the Prince of Bondo or perhaps the one Park had been obliged to take off and hand over to the King of Bondo.

Whether true or false, Adams' account of Timbuktu contained little information of use to Rennell and his maps. The American could not locate the town with any accuracy, had not been able to plot his journeys, and hadn't even seen the nearby Niger. In geographical terms, at least, it did not really matter whether he had made the journey or not. In this way, Burckhardt was able to brush aside Adams' *Narrative*: when the Swiss traveller reached Timbuktu, the world would at last have a detailed and reliable account of where it was and what went on there. One thing he could not ignore, either with Adams or Ali Bey, was that a race was now on to be the first geographically aware traveller to Timbuktu.

With the final defeat of Bonaparte at Waterloo in June 1815, the month Burckhardt returned to Cairo from Mecca, European governments found they had both the time and the resources – particularly the manpower – to launch missions of exploration. Burckhardt had heard of two planned British missions, one to travel up the Congo River by boat, the other to look for the sources of the Niger. Burckhardt mentioned them in a letter to his mother, blithely commenting, 'It would be pleasant if we could meet in Central Africa,' then adding ominously, 'if I could leave very soon it might be possible. But there are still delays, and I cannot fix the date when I shall be able to leave Egypt. To remain here begins to depress me.'[57] When his mother expressed anxiety at the idea of someone else reaching Central Africa before him, he wrote to reassure her: 'People have some sense of justice, and will be able to differentiate between an expedition by a corps of soldiers, and a single person who travels without any escort.'[58]

By the spring of 1817, there was still no way forward for him. Belzoni had managed to ship the head of Ramses II as far as Alexandria, so Burckhardt was confident that the gift he and Salt had offered would arrive at the British Museum. All his notes and journals from his various travels had been written up and sent to London, along with the manuscript of his *Arabic Proverbs*, a collection of vulgar expressions common in Cairo at the time. He had spent two years in Cairo, not daring to travel elsewhere in case a caravan passed through the city in his absence. By September, his patience appeared to have paid off: Fezzani traders arrived on their way to Mecca. They would return through Cairo towards the end of the year.

Which they did; only by then, Burckhardt was unable to join them. At the beginning of October, he went down with a slight attack of dysentery. On the fourth, with the symptoms getting worse, he went to consult Dr Richardson, a physician staying at the Consulate as a guest of Salt. Richardson prescribed some medicines, expecting to hear no more of the problem. But on the evening of the tenth, he returned from a visit to the Pyramids to find several notes from the sick traveller waiting for him at Salt's house, asking him to visit him urgently. On the fifteenth, the patient even asked Consul Salt to come to his house, something Salt had not done before, given that Burckhardt – Shaykh Ibrahim – lived in the Turkish quarter.

'I went over immediately,' Salt later remembered, 'and cannot describe how shocked I was, to see the change which had taken place in so short a time.'[59] It was clear to all of them that Burckhardt was dying. He asked Salt to write down his will, in which he settled considerable amounts of money on Osmyn and Shaharti, made a donation to the poor of Zürich and left his collection of Arabic manuscripts, the finest outside the Arab world, to Cambridge

University, with the stipulation that his old friend Dr Clarke look after it. 'I was starting,' he dictated to Salt, 'in two months time with the caravan returning from Mekka, and going to Fezzan, thence to Tombuctou, but it is otherwise disposed . . . The Turks will take my body, I know it, perhaps you had better let them.'[60] When the document was signed and witnessed, he shook Salt's hand and asked him to leave.

Dr Richardson arrived back at the Consulate late that night with the news that the great traveller was dead. Salt recognised the significance of Burckhardt's death, which he called 'a terrible blow to the African Association, which had built all its hopes and with justice upon him; he was enterprising, yet cool and prudent, had been ten years preparing himself, had become the perfect Arab, and in two months intended to set out . . . God has otherwise disposed it.'[61]

The following morning, as Burckhardt had predicted, the Turks – the city's Muslims – 'took him'. Wrapped in a winding sheet, accompanied by a respectful crowd, he was carried through the city's great Bab an-Nasr, Gate of Victory, and lowered into a simple grave where he is still revered as al-Hajj as-Shaykh Ibrahim ibn Abdallah al Lausani.

16

A New World Order

'Long may this patron of science [Banks] live to distribute his bounty and his benefits, and to assist unprotected genius! for we are not afraid to say, that we know not where to find the man who could worthily replace him.'

Quarterly Review, October 1814

London, 1817

BY THE AGE OF SEVENTY-FOUR, Sir Joseph Banks was so over-whelmed by gout that he was unable to use his legs, but this did nothing to dim his appetite for all things scientific. Queen Charlotte, who had visited him on several occasions at Spring Grove, his house conveniently placed between Windsor and London, had described him several years earlier as being 'in excellent spirits, looking like Ivory, free from Pain, but quite helpless in point of legs'.[1] Banks was a little more blunt when he referred to himself as 'a Foundered horse lame when I go out, unsound when I come in'.[2] His 'helpless-ness' of legs made travelling increasingly difficult, and in October 1817 he made his last journey north to his estate at Revesby in Derbyshire. His eyesight had begun to fail as well, which made letter-writing a chore. But his mind was still clear, and although his movements were curtailed he was still able to serve wines to his Queen and her party, still entertained at breakfasts and soirées, sat in the President's chair at the Royal Society and encouraged anyone with a scientific quest to use his Soho Square library. In 1817 he even took on new work, agreeing to chair a government committee examining weights and measures and holding the eternal debate on whether Britain should adopt the metric system. He held that position for the next two years. He also made a point of attending meetings of the many other societies and organisations to which he had lent his patronage and prestige, among them the African Association.

Of the Association's dozen founding members, only Banks was still active. The Earl of Moira had long continued to be involved in the Association's affairs and attended Committee meetings. At the same time he had also become increasingly involved with the Prince of Wales. In February 1811 he had supported the Regency Bill in Parliament, and applauded as executive power for ruling the country was handed to the Prince. Before long he had been appointed Governor-General of India. Just before his departure, the Committee offered to create the post of President of the African Association for him, suggesting at the same time that he might like to create an Indian branch. The noble Lord declined the offer, although in his absence he continued as a member.

It may have lost Moira, but the Committee could still call on the support of the Earl of Caledon, a former Governor of the Cape Colony; Lord Clive, a Member of Parliament and grandson of *the* Clive of India; William Hamilton, the Under-Secretary of State for Foreign Affairs, who had inherited the role of Secretary to the Association from his father; the Earls of Hardwick and Morton; the Hon. Frederick North, former Governor of Ceylon; Earl Spencer; Viscount Valentia, who had employed Henry Salt as his secretary for the voyage to India and Abyssinia; and William Wilberforce, leader of the anti-slavery movement. With such influential men to hand, it might have been expected that new missions would be planned, yet for a while nothing happened.

Burckhardt's death was reported to the Association's general meeting of 1818. William Hamilton was typically understated in his *Memoir* of Burckhardt when he observed that 'His name will be held in honourable remembrance, as long as any credit is given to those who have fallen in the cause of science . . . By the African Association his loss is severely felt, nor can they easily hope to supply the place of one whom birth, education, genius, and industry, conspired to render well adapted to whatever great enterprise his fortitude and honourable ambition might have prompted him to undertake . . .'[3] Other tributes were more expressive, with the *Quarterly Review* catching the spirit of the moment when it called Burckhardt 'this extraordinary person, whose accomplishments and perseverance were such as could not have failed, had he lived, to place him in the ranks of the most distinguished travellers of this or indeed any age'.[4] Yet Burckhardt's many achievements – the rediscovery of Petra and Abu Simbel, his mastery of Arabic and his collection of proverbs and manuscripts, his understanding of the Bedouin and his description of the Holy Land, Nubia and the Hejaz – only served to emphasise the Association's lack of progress with African geography. Between the commissioning of Burckhardt in the spring of 1808 and his death in autumn 1817, it had added less than expected to the knowledge of the interior of Africa, and had in fact failed to fill in any more of the blanks on Rennell's maps. Meanwhile, around the Association, the world had been transformed.

By 1817, Napoleon Bonaparte was taking long baths in the middle of the day at Longwood, his house of exile on St Helena, while the conquering Duke of Wellington was still being fêted around Europe. Now that the wars were over, the British government found itself with a ready supply of decommissioned officers who were only too happy to undertake an expedition that offered the prospect of fame and perhaps fortune. The alternative was far from attractive: early retirement on a meagre pension in a country with chronic unemployment and even worse war debts. Here was the most significant change of all for the African Association. When it was founded in 1788, it was the only organisation dedicated to the business of exploration: it had the field to itself. But now it faced the prospect of the British government commissioning explorers. Unsurprisingly, the man responsible for this programme of exploration was one of Banks' protégés, John Barrow.

Barrow was a bureaucrat, the son of a Lancashire farmer, who combined his talent as a linguist with an ambition to improve himself and a desire to see something of the world. In 1792 he was lucky enough to be proposed as interpreter on Lord Macartney's British embassy to China. After this journey, he left nothing to chance in making the most of his opportunities: by 1804, he was sitting behind the polished Second Secretary's desk in Admiralty House, replacing William Marsden, one of the Association's longest-standing members, who had just been promoted to First Secretary. Marsden was also a key member of the Royal Society, so it comes as no surprise when charting Barrow's progress in this age of patronage to find that he was elected a Fellow of the Society in 1806. Entry to the Royal Society also gave him access to its dining club and to the Sunday-evening meetings at Soho Square. There he came into contact with the man on whom he was to model himself: Sir Joseph Banks.

Just as Banks had been the powerhouse of British exploration in the late eighteenth century, so Barrow was to be its principal motor in the first half of the nineteenth. His travelling credentials did not quite match Banks' – unlike Cook's voyage, Macartney's Chinese embassy was a fiasco – but having already established himself as the most influential reviewer of books relating to travel and exploration, with the end of the Napoleonic wars Barrow emerged as the driving force behind the British Admiralty's commissioning of explorers.

'To what purpose,' Barrow had wondered rhetorically, 'could a portion of our naval force be, at any time, but more especially in time of profound peace, more honourably or more usefully employed than in completing those details of geographical and hydrographical science of which the grand outlines have been boldly and broadly sketched by Cook, Vancouver and Flinders, and others of our countrymen?'[5] This question is raised in Barrow's introduction to James Tuckey's *Narrative of an expedition to explore the River Zaire*. The same passage also contains the answer: exploration was both honourable and useful in post-war Europe. Tuckey, with subordinate officers and a detachment of other ranks, had been sent to sail up the Congo from its mouth in the Atlantic. Barrow was in command of commissioning the expedition while Banks was, as usual, its scientific godfather. Although Banks declared himself sceptical about Tuckey's prospects of success, he did advise on the means of transport (he was keen for a steam-powered craft to be used, though that proved impractical), the size of the mission ('it is better to adopt a Plan of sufficient extent at first than to do it after a failure', he wrote to Barrow[6]) and goals for the botanists he had decided should be sent along.

Tuckey left England in February 1816 on the appropriately named HMS *Congo*. Barrow, who penned the mission's instructions, was surely echoing Banks and Beaufoy's original plan for the African Association when he claimed, 'That a river of such magnitude should not be known with any degree of certainty beyond 200 miles from its mouth, is incompatible with the present advanced state of geographical science.'[7] To correct this failure, the captain was instructed to sail as far as he could up the Congo: Barrow was hoping this would prove his theory that it joined the Niger and also a third river which, he was sure, ran southwards through Africa towards Cape Town. In the event, the expedition provided proof of nothing beyond the deadly nature of the West African climate: by the beginning of October, twenty-one of the fifty-four-person mission, Tuckey and all his junior officers among them, had succumbed to the fevers and were dead.

Barrow was undeterred by this setback, and his attention soon returned to the question of the Niger. There were current at the time at least four different opinions as to where the river ended. Barrow was coming round to the idea that the ancient geographers would be proved right, and that the Niger would be found to flow eastwards and to meet up with the Nile. Banks, like Park before him, believed that the Niger and Congo were the same river. Rennell was sticking to his theory that it flowed into a great lake at the heart of Africa.[8] Few were still prepared to push the German geographer C.G. Reichardt's revolutionary, unfashionable but nonetheless correct view, stated as early as 1803, that the Niger would be found to flow into the Atlantic at the Bight of Benin.

Earlier in the century, Banks had urged the British government to send an expedition in from the west coast of Africa in search of a route to the Niger. This they now did, authorising a mission out of Sierra Leone led by a Major Peddie and supported by a strongly-armed squad of a hundred soldiers. Like Tuckey's before him, Peddie's expedition was a costly failure: the surgeon died before even heading inland, and most of his colleagues had shared his fate by the time the few straggling survivors made it back to the coast in 1821; no new information was acquired; and the bill, according to one estimate, ran to £40,000,[9] more than four times the total sum the Association had spent on all its geographical missionaries.

For the British government money was not the issue, and even before the survivors of Peddie's expedition had returned home, another mission was being organised. On 25 January 1817, Rear-Admiral Sir Charles Penrose wrote to John Croker, Barrow's immediate superior at the Admiralty, with news that the Pasha of Tripoli wanted to make a friendly gesture to the British government. If they would send travellers, he would be glad to see that they reached the south in safety. This offer meant considerably more than the protection offered to Simon Lucas thirty years earlier, for the Pasha had now extended his control as far as Fezzan, while the Bey of Fezzan, who recognised the Pasha's authority, had recently returned from an expedition beyond Borno. Thanks to Britain's increased political influence – a consequence of the defeat of Napoleon – it seemed as though the road south across the Sahara was finally being opened.

Banks recommended as missionary a twenty-nine-year-old doctor called Joseph Ritchie. His candidate was approved of by the Lords of the Admiralty, and by October 1818 Ritchie had landed in Tripoli accompanied by an assistant, Lieutenant George Lyon, and a carpenter recruited in the Malta dockyards. Their arrival was the most successful part of what was to come: when the travellers finally had an audience with the Pasha, he denied having made any offer of safe passage, insisted that his authority only stretched as far as Murzuq, the Fezzani trading town from where Hornemann had set off south into the desert in 1800, and warned that he could guarantee nothing. This will have come as no surprise to whichever Foreign Office mandarin had damned the Pasha by writing anonymously that 'a greater villain never infected the earth'.[10] There was worse to come, for the Bey of Fezzan, now in Tripoli, announced that he was unable to proceed further than his own town. By November the travellers were in Murzuq, but Ritchie was dead, the carpenter was deaf and dizzy and Lyon, almost out of money, had just discovered that the crates he had thought were filled with trade goods were in fact loaded with botanical and other scientific instruments, which had no resale value in the south.

Before Ritchie and Lyon had even set off for the interior, Sir Joseph Banks suffered another severe attack of gout. He had first been struck by the illness in November 1787, before the start of his African adventure. On that occasion, he had suffered for a month, provoking George III to write him the following note: 'The King is sorry to find Sir Joseph is still confined, and though it is the common mode to congratulate persons on the first fit of the Gout, He cannot join in so cruel an etiquette...'[11] After a few weeks Banks had begun to show signs of recovery, but from that moment on he was susceptible to the disease and suffered periodic relapses.

Many of Banks' family and friends were fellow sufferers from this 'most ancient and respectable of diseases',[12] among them Edward Gibbon and the geographer Rennell. Banks will not have bothered much about the propriety of the disease, an inflammation of the joints, accompanied by severe body pains and a rise in temperature, whose side-effects included depression. With his reverence for ancient writers, Banks is likely to have known that Hippocrates identified gout as a complaint mostly suffered by older men, while Pliny the Elder suspected it was passed down through the generations. In fact the swelling is caused by an excess of uric acid in the blood. Eighteenth-century doctors did not know this, but that did not stop them from endorsing a variety of cures.

In 1793, Banks submitted to Dr Edward Harrison's regime of extensive massage with old linen, a regime that was intended to restore the circulation. By the turn of the century he was using ginger, as recommended by the apothecary Pittonet, and soon after followed the milk diet of Dr David Pitcairn, physician at St Bartholomew's Hospital. His love of ancient writers seems to have led him to the cure recommended by Alexander of Tralles, a sixth-century Byzantine physician whose brother was the architect of the Aya Sophia in Istanbul: little meat, no alcohol and the use of colchicine, derived from the roots of the autumn crocus plant and its family – in 1806 he wrote that 'I now live on vegetables entirely and drink nothing but water. Since this regime has taken place I have never been confined to my bed and now I hope to be better.'

Between bouts, and even at times during them, Banks was as optimistic and energetic as ever; one friend described finding him 'in his bed, his body and head swelled apparently with dropsy, but with all his accustomed energy and true politeness of manner of a sensible Englishman'.[13] For as long as the cures had the power to fight back the gout pains, Banks was able to continue working: in 1818, at seventy-five years of age, he was still chairing the Royal Society and sitting on government committees, including one charged with finding ways of making banknotes more difficult to forge. He was also still the father of exploration, his house the unofficial home of the African Association's Committee. He closely followed the progress of exploration elsewhere in the world, of Ross and Parry in the Arctic and the survey of Australia's northern coastline, and still helped the Admiralty and Barrow to choose their explorers and equip their missions.

But death was not far away. In 1818 both his beloved sister Sarah Sophia and Queen Charlotte had died. On 26 March 1820, his long-time correspondent Sir Charles Blagden, Banks' eyes and ears in Paris, was having dinner with the chemist Berthollet – the man who had rescued Frederick Hornemann from the Cairo Citadel in 1798 – when he had a fit and dropped dead into his dish. And on 1 June that year, bowed down by age and grief and puffed up with gout, Banks finally did what 'Misogallus' had urged him to do almost two decades earlier and resigned as President of the Royal Society, only to have his resignation rejected – even the dissenters knew he would not be among them for long and were prepared to allow him to go out with dignity. This he did: at 8 a.m. on Monday, 19 June 1820, in the comfort of his house at Spring Grove, a short ride from his beloved gardens at Kew, Banks' hands finally came to rest beside his considerable trunk of a chest.

His death, at seventy-seven years of age, had been long in coming, and was not unexpected. Yet the shock of Banks' passing was felt in many spheres and many countries around the world. Even if there were other men such as himself, with the intellect, fortune and desire to straddle almost every aspect of society and of the world, they would not be able to achieve what he had managed, for the world itself had changed, and the time of amateurs was passing. Banks had seen his Australian colony flourish, many other projects come to fulfilment, the map of Africa altered considerably. And if he had not found the answers to the geographical questions he and his friends had set themselves when they created the Association for promoting the discovery of the inland parts of Africa, he had at least the satisfaction of knowing that his African project now had a life of its own.

While the great man was being buried quietly in his parish church – he had insisted there should be no pomp or ceremony, no public burial in Westminster Abbey – the people he had inspired turned their attention to another of the continent's great geographical problems.

17

The Fountains of the Sun

'Seek a land far distant, where the tawny race
Dwell near the fountains of the sun, and where
The Nigris pours his dusky waters; wind
Along his banks till thou shall reach the fall,
Where, from the mountains with papyrus crown'd,
The venerable Nile impetuous pours
His headlong torrent.'

Aeschylus, *Prometheus Bound*[1]

'ENGLAND HAS, by her different voyages of discovery, and her missions to explore distant countries, far surpassed all the nations of Europe: and a successful expedition through the interior of the African continent is alone wanting to render her triumphs complete.'[2] So Burckhardt had written in 1814 after he left Shendi market, deep in Sudan, and his words still rang true in the 1820s. What is more, in 1821 the business was given a new urgency by the creation in Paris of the Société Géographique,* an organisation with worldwide interests that was keen to pursue the exploration of West and Central Africa.

The course of the Niger might have promised greater geographical advances, but Timbuktu was still the big prize for the French, as for the British, in spite of the fact that Robert Adams, the shipwrecked American sailor who claimed to have been sold into slavery in

---

* The Société Géographique still disputes the African Association's claim to being the world's first geographical society.

Timbuktu, had had his story verified by the French Consul in Mogador. In 1824, the Société went as far as to offer the significant sum of ten thousand francs to the first person – one presumes they meant the first *French* person – to reach Timbuktu and survive. Meanwhile Barrow and his Admiralty-sponsored travellers did their best to ensure that a Briton was first into the fabled city. They also hoped to resolve the other questions that had long eluded the African Association – the course of the Niger, the greatness of Hausa and the glory of the city of Katsina. While this went on, the Committee of the African Association looked around for another geographical problem on which it could expend its energies and bring glory to the country.

How were they to proceed? Banks was no longer there to put the pieces together with his energy and money, his deft hand and extraordinary range of contacts. Only three of the dozen members of the Saturday's Club who had founded the African Association back in 1788 were still alive, and of these Earl Carysfort was incapacitated, Lord Rawdon, the Earl of Moira, was Governor-General of India, and Sir John Sinclair had retired from public life. Rennell's house in Suffolk Street became, for a while at least, a gathering place for people interested in travel, and his 'forenoon receptions', like Banks' breakfasts and evenings, attracted travellers, geographers and many others with an interest in advancing the science. And although it could not boast the sort of numbers it had enjoyed during the heady spring of 1799 after Mungo Park's safe return from the Niger, the Association still had a significant following. According to the list of 1819, the year before Banks' death, it could count on more than forty subscribers. Among them were several people we have already met, including William Hamilton, Under-Secretary of State for Foreign Affairs until 1822, the bankers Hoare and Coutts, and William Wilberforce, still the leading anti-slavery campaigner. Encouragingly, there was also new support from the likes of the Earl of Aberdeen, soon to become Foreign Secretary and a future Prime Minister, Byron's guardian the Earl of Carlisle, the wealthy Irish landowner Lord Darnley, and Lord Harrowby, a former Foreign Secretary.

The problem was less one of numbers than of intention: members needed a goal on which to focus their abilities and energies, a mission to accomplish, information to gather. Gone were the days when they could point to the map and choose their field of action without regard to others. Barrow and his Admiralty explorers had taken on projects with political or commercial potential, whether it was looking for a North-West Passage between the Atlantic and Pacific oceans or trying to find a navigable river into West Africa. And since 1807, an organisation calling itself the African Institution – 'deeply impressed with the enormous wrongs which the natives of Africa have suffered in their intercourse with Europe'[3] – had been monitoring the application of the British law suppressing the slave trade. But there was one particular problem of African geography that seemed perfectly suited to the Association's new circumstances. What's more, the Association already had a claim to it, in that Burckhardt and before him James Bruce had made headway with it. So the Committee now turned their thoughts to the whereabouts of the source and the course of the Niger's twin, the Nile.

There was no expression of indignation, no sense of shame or slur on the age, so keenly felt in 1788, as the fact that so much was known about the rest of the world and so little about the Nile. By the 1820s, the enlightened age that had seen gentleman-scholars pursue geographical knowledge for its own sake had given way to an era when science was made to serve national interests. A new age of conquest and colonisation was just beginning to dawn. But whatever was happening in Europe, America and elsewhere in the world did not change the fact that the geography of the African interior was still mostly unknown. Rennell had been trying for several decades to locate the whereabouts of the Nile's source through logic and deduction. As with the Niger, he began with his old favourite, the fifth-century BC Greek Herodotus. 'It is certain,' Herodotus had insisted, wrongly, 'that the Nile rises in the West,' though he admitted that 'beyond the above point all is uncertainty'.[4] Later geographers – the Alexandrian Ptolemy, al-Idrissi and Abul Feda – all placed the sources of the Nile to the south, claiming the river flowed from a fountain located in what were known as the

Mountains of the Moon. Everything Rennell had read seemed to agree with that: 'To us, it appears more probable that the remote sources of the Nile are rather to the *south* than the *west.*'5

So where were those lunar mountains? What was this fountain? And would it have any connection with the Niger? These were the questions that the African Association set itself to answer in the years after Banks' death.

It was helped in 1820 by a development in North African politics. As the great man lay dying in Soho Square, Muhammad Ali, several thousand miles away in Cairo, sent his son Ismail south at the head of a significant force with orders to extend Egyptian rule far into Sudan, where local unrest had interrupted the trade caravans. Ismail was a capable general in command of an Egyptian force trained by Western officers: by the following year, most of the country as far as Sennar was under Egyptian control. In case the opportunities this new situation presented were lost on people in Europe, one of the many foreigners in the Egyptian army, an American naval officer with the unlikely name of English and the equally inappropriate initials of G.B. (George Bethune), spelled them out. 'This expedition has laid open to the researches of the geographer and the anti-quarian a river and a country highly interesting and hitherto imper-fectly known to the civilised world.'6 The country may have been fascinating, but it was the river that stimulated the Committee's imagination: the Nile was just as worthy and as full of potential glory (if not gold) as the search for the Niger.

The following year, 1822, the Association published Burckhardt's *Travels in Syria and the Holy Land*. In his introduction, the new Secretary, Colonel William Leake,* a classical topographer of great repute, summed up progress along the Nile. Burckhardt had been warned off travelling south from Shendi by the threat of wild tribes. Since then, two Englishmen had made it four hundred miles further south and 'some French gentlemen' – Cailliaud and Letorzec – had travelled with the Pasha's army as far as Sennar. Leake was certain

---

* Leake became Secretary of the Association in 1822, when the former Secretary (and his good friend) William Hamilton followed in the footsteps of his namesake and took up the post of British Ambassador in Naples.

that Egyptian influence in Sennar would open the upper reaches of the Nile and remove the sort of dangers that had held Burckhardt back. 'There is reason to hope,' he wrote, 'that the opportunity will not be neglected, and that a survey of this celebrated river from its sources to the Mediterranean, may, perhaps, at length be made, if not for the first time, for the first time at least since the extinction of Egyptian science.'[7]

The dangers were as unknown as those faced by the Association's first missionaries heading for the Niger: their knowledge of the place and people was almost non-existent, their maps, like those given to Lucas and Ledyard, were founded upon speculation and hearsay, and their prospects of success were slim indeed. Given this, and knowing the long list of fatalities already attached to the Association's expeditions, one might expect that the Committee would have had difficulty in finding volunteers. Professor Blumenbach in Göttingen was so upset by the news of Jean Louis Burckhardt's death that he refused to recommend any other young men for Africa. And the Admiralty was offering better terms and could mount larger expeditions, blessed with official recognition, and so would be the first stop for a promising adventurer with contacts. But in spite of this and the fact that a traveller as remarkable as Burckhardt had thought that this was no mission for an individual – 'if the sources of the Bahr el Abyadh [the White Nile] are ever to be discovered,' he had written, 'it must be by armed force'[8] – the African Association was still approached by a steady flow of volunteers wanting to become geographical missionaries. In May 1822, soon after Leake took over as Secretary, members assembled at the Thatched House Tavern to learn that their latest traveller was already in the field.

Little is known about James Gordon, a retired naval captain from the English Midlands, before he approached the Association. But in December 1821 he left England for Egypt, commissioned 'to explore the Bahr el Abiad or Western branch of the Nile'.[9] In May 1822, Leake reported that 'no intelligence has been received from him since his departure'.[10]

Henry Salt, still British Consul in Cairo and still an honorary member of the Association, had clearly enjoyed Gordon's company, and had approved of his 'perseverance in the Arabic language and of the strength of body and enterprising spirit which concur in promising success to his undertaking'.[11] Salt had approached Muhammad Ali to obtain a firman for Gordon to travel freely through the Pasha's territories, and had also offered to advance him whatever money he might need, against the Association's account.

'He set off,' Salt later wrote to Leake, 'with sanguine expectations from Cairo dressed in a common Arab dress, having already acquired as much Arabic as would enable him to get on without an interpreter.'[12] In June 1822 Gordon stopped at Aswan and wrote to assure his employers that he was well and happy, and that his chances of success had been considerably increased by the Pasha writing letters of recommendation to his officers along the Sennar route. His plan then was to go as far as 'Shelluk on the Abiad' (White Nile), the limits of Muhammad Ali's authority, to send back his servant with his report to the Association and then to proceed alone into the unknown. The plan was adventurous and called for someone with unusual talents and abilities. Gordon may have possessed these, though no one was quite sure: after he had ascended the cataracts and entered Nubia, an official in Aswan wrote to Salt that Gordon was 'either a *rogue* or some *very* extraordinary character'.[13]

Alarmingly for Gordon, at the same time as he was making his way south through Nubia, the Egyptian Pasha's army began to lose its grip. During the previous year, Ismail, the Pasha's son, and his European-trained troops, bloodthirsty Mamluks and Turkish Janissaries at their core, had left a trail of blood along the Nile. Near Fazughli, not far from the modern-day border between Sudan and Ethiopia, Ismail came to a halt in front of the dramatic rise of the Ethiopian mountains: his scouts reported that the Blue Nile, which they had been following, flowed through a narrow gorge that not even foot-soldiers could pass. The General retreated to Sennar, from where he sent a messenger to Cairo requesting permission to return home. From Sennar, the Frenchman Frederick Cailliaud set about prospecting for gold and the General's troops rounded up slaves. Both encountered difficulties: Cailliaud failed to find any worthwhile gold deposits, while Ismail's slave drivers reported that half of thirty thousand captives sent downriver to Cairo had died on the journey.

In October 1822 Ismail received his father's permission to return to Cairo, and before the month was out had travelled north to Shendi, the limit of Burckhardt's Nile journeys, where Mek Nimr held sway. Ismail had passed this way the previous year and received Nimr's homage. Arriving with a peace offering of two fine horses, Nimr had prostrated himself before Ismail, placing the General's foot on his head as a sign of submission, only to be snubbed by the Egyptian. It was typical of Ismail's high-handed conduct during the campaign. Passing through Shendi on his way home to Cairo, Ismail now demanded that Nimr hand over thirty thousand dollars and six thousand slaves within forty-eight hours. Nimr insisted that the demands were impossible – he simply didn't have that much cash or that many slaves to hand. He would need time. Ismail rejected his complaints and hit the Mek in the face with his long wooden pipe. An outraged Nimr went to draw his sword, but was immediately overwhelmed by Ismail's Mamluk bodyguards. That night, while Ismail and his inner circle were enjoying a banquet, entertained by local dancers, Nimr set fire to the place. The General's bodyguard was cut down as it rushed out to stop the fire, while Ismail stayed inside and was burned to death.

News of the Mek's resistance caused a storm along the Nile and various tribes rose up against the occupiers. When word of Ismail's death reached his father in Cairo, Muhammad Ali demanded retribution. Mek Nimr escaped into Abyssinia, but local uprisings were put down with a rare brutality that left some fifty thousand Sudanese dead and many more mutilated – the favoured punishment for captured Sudanese was for the men to be castrated, women to have their breasts cut off and for boiling pitch to be poured onto the wounds to ensure a terrible, lingering death.

This was clearly no place for a traveller, and when rumours of these events reached Cairo, Salt wrote to London to express his concern. 'The unsettled state of the country round the territory occupied by the Pasha's armies, and the danger of being taken for a spy, will render his progress beyond that very doubtful.' Salt then expressed his concerns about Gordon's behaviour. 'I am afraid too that he exposes himself too much to the sun and night air, relying rather more than is prudent on the rude health which he seems to enjoy.' But then, Salt had done enough travelling in his time, and had seen enough people passing through Cairo to know the sort of character who was attracted to the enterprise: 'Men who make up their minds to these kind of hazardous enterprises must be left pretty much to their own opinion, for it is not by a known rule, or road, that success can be ensured, and every man prefers his own route to the *Temple of Fame* . . .'[14]

At the Association's meeting at the Thatched House on 7 June 1823, Leake gave another progress report. He had, he explained, been in touch with a Mr Bowditch, an Englishman who had spent years on the Gold Coast, had recently been in France to learn the basics of astronomy and natural history, and was on his way back to West Africa, where he intended to do some exploring. Meanwhile, Barrow at the Admiralty had assembled an official expedition to follow up on the Association's work in the north, sending out Dr Walter Oudney, British Army Major Dixon Denham and Royal Navy Lieutenant Hugh Clapperton to establish a consulate at Murzuq and then to proceed to Borno. Leake also made mention of 'Mr. Belzoni . . . now in the Kingdom of Morocco and although your Committee is entirely ignorant of the Nature of the undertaking in which he is engaged they feel confident that he will not lose any favourable opportunity of illustrating the Geography of Northern Africa'.[15]

Belzoni, it transpired, had been inspired by the Association, in particular by the death in Cairo of his friend Burckhardt, for whom he had moved the bust of Ramses II at Luxor. Having finished his excavations in Egypt and mounted an extremely popular exhibition in London, the eccentric Italian had decided to complete Burckhardt's task by reaching Timbuktu. Bowditch in the west, Belzoni in Morocco, Barrow's mission in Murzuq and Gordon heading out beyond the Pasha's authority in Sennar: 'It is,' Leake summed up, 'by simultaneous efforts on different sides of Northern Africa that we have the best prospect of obtaining a knowledge of the interior of that country.'[16]

In this the members seemed to concur; but they were wrong. Bowditch reached Bathurst at the mouth of the Gambia River in 1824, promptly caught the fevers and died soon after. Belzoni reached West Africa and also died of fever, without sending back any report of his journey. As for the Association's missionary, in December 1824 the following notice appeared in the *Gentleman's Magazine*: '1822, September 27th. At Wiled Medinet, a day's journey from Sennar, from whence he was proceeding in an attempt to penetrate up the sources of the Bahr Coltitaid [sic], Captain R.J. Gordon R.N. who had often distinguished himself during the late war ... His death adds another victim to the melancholy list of those who have perished in the cause of African discovery.'[17] So that just left Barrow's men still in the field.

On 30 April 1822, Clapperton, Denham and Oudney set out from Tripoli to Murzuq in Fezzan, accompanied by a significant caravan. Their mission was to follow Frederick Hornemann's route across the Sahara to Lake Chad, and from there to settle the question of Hausa and to explore a swathe of sub-Saharan Africa. The Moor Shabeni, who had introduced the name Hausa into Europe in the spring of 1790 during one of his discussions with Henry Beaufoy, believed that it referred both to an empire and its capital

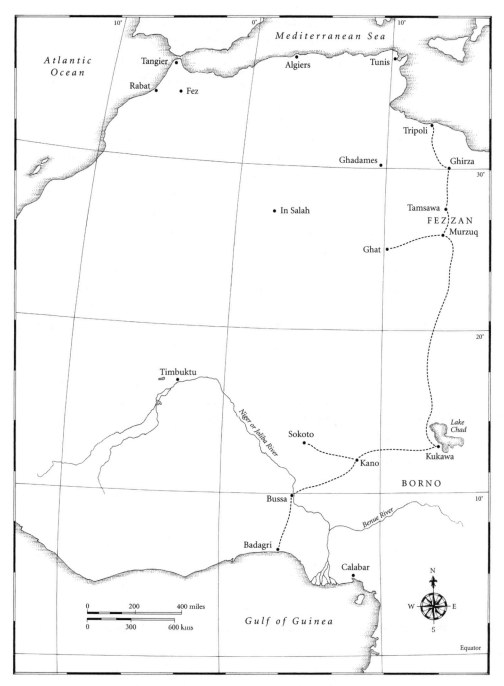

Missions to the Niger: Clapperton, Denham and
Oudney's route, 1822–25

city.* Shabeni described the city as being almost as large as London, ruled by a despot who could call on 180,000 soldiers, possessed an enormous amount of gold, gladly encouraged trade and ruled over a stable country. Since then, information had come in from Consul Matra in Morocco, Mungo Park, Hornemann and others confirming the report and adding that Cashna – more properly Katsina – was the name of the capital.

Armed with the Pasha of Tripoli's protection, with luck and not a little courage, the four men crossed the Sahara and travelled around Lake Chad, where they found a lush tropical land that corresponded with their idea of a terrestrial paradise: animals were plentiful, and so tame that they neither ran nor flew away. Here they finally reached the empire of Borno. At first sight it appeared to be everything Banks and Beaufoy had dreamed of. Muhammad al Kanami, the Shaykh of Borno – Denham called him the Skeikh of Spears – had sent a troop of cavalry to meet the foreigners. The riders made an imposing sight, several thousand of them sporting medieval armour, 'in coats of mail composed of iron chain ... some of them had helmets, or rather skull-caps, of the same metal, with chin-pieces, all sufficiently strong to ward off the shock of the spear'.[18] More surprising for the travellers was the advanced state of the people of Borno. Describing an outbreak of smallpox in a village, Denham reported, 'They are not ignorant of inoculation, and it is performed nearly in the same manner as amongst ourselves, by inserting the sharp point of the dagger, charged with the disease.'[19] Banks, had he been alive, would have been thrilled by this news.

The Pasha of Tripoli's recommendation had secured the party's safety on their journey to the *shaykh*, but it was their answer to the question of why they had come that earned his welcome. Echoing Bruce's reply to the Pasha in Cairo, they explained that they had come 'to see the country merely, and to give an account of its

---

* This suggestion that Hausa referred to both city and country merely reflected the common Arab custom: Egypt and Cairo are both known as Misr, while Morocco referred both to the country and to Marrakesh, then its capital city. Hence Tunis/Tunisia, Algiers/Algeria.

inhabitants, produce, and appearance; as our sultan was desirous of knowing every part of the globe'.[20]

While Denham attempted to circumnavigate Lake Chad to settle the question of whether the Nile flowed out of it or the Niger into it (they don't), Clapperton and Oudney headed west. The doctor, who had been ill for some time, died along the way, another martyr to science. But the naval lieutenant went on to unravel the mystery of Hausa. Contrary to Shabeni's description, it turned out to be a federation or empire of several city-states, created during a successful *jihad* by Fulani Muslims and united under a single caliph or leader: when Clapperton arrived, this was Muhammad Bello.

Clapperton first visited Kano, 'the great emporium of the kingdom of Haussa [sic]',[21] a city of some forty thousand people. He had been advised to make an impression on entering Kano, and had saved his naval dress uniform for the purpose. But 'I might have spared all the pains I had taken with my toilet,' he complained, 'for not an individual turned his head round to gaze at me.'[22] Kano was so well connected, its people so used to seeing extravagantly attired foreigners passing through, that the arrival of a six-foot-tall, red-headed Scot was not worthy of attention.

Sokoto, further west and nearer the Niger, looked every bit the capital of an empire. Lodged with the vizier, invited to the palace, Clapperton was ushered into an audience with Sultan Muhammad Bello, 'a noble-looking man, forty-four years of age, five feet ten inches high, portly in person, with a short curling black beard, a small mouth, a fine forehead, a Grecian nose, and large black eyes'.[23] Seated on a carpet, his head, nose and mouth covered by his turban, Tuareg-style, the Sultan dazzled the traveller. His father had led the *jihad* that had created the empire, but Muhammad Bello was an enlightened man who preferred words to war; he liked to write poetry and was the author of more than a hundred scholarly works on subjects as diverse as medicine, Sufism and the administration of his empire. His empire stretched from Lake Chad to the Niger River, a journey of four months from east to west, too large to be centrally controlled, so separate states were ruled by their kings or *shaykh*s, among them Muhammad al Kanami. Clapperton, writing of this visit to Muhammad Bello, is unequivocal in his admiration of the place and his affection for the man. Nor could he disguise his surprise at the Sultan's knowledge. He discussed trade possibilities with Britain, the end of the slave trade and British advances in India, explained that he would be happy to welcome a British consul and then asked to see one of the newspapers Clapperton had brought with him, which the Sultan referred to as '*Huber el dinneah*', 'News of the world'.[24]

Clapperton and Denham were back in London on 1 June 1825 with news of their extraordinarily successful journey. The *Edinburgh Review* captured the spirit of the moment when it declared, with hardly any exaggeration, that 'Regions have been surveyed, the very existence of which was before unknown and others, of which only a faint rumour had reached across the immense deserts by which they were enclosed.'[25] A great moment for Britain, then, but the Admiralty's success could hardly have cheered members of the Association, whose travellers had done so much to put Borno on the map, but who had been denied the glory of being the first to reach Sokoto and Kano.

The Association's affairs were at such low ebb during 1824 and 1825 that without a traveller in the field or any other pressing expenses, the Committee decided not to collect the annual subscription. But at the meeting in May 1826, members were asked to pay their subscriptions to help support 'a person at present employed in the interior of Africa'.[26] That person, they learned, was a Frenchman by the name of Louis-Maurice-Adolphe Linant de Bellefonds. Banks, who had so wished for an Englishman to claim the geographical prizes, might have been disappointed, although perhaps the universal scientist in him would have applauded.

Linant was only in his mid-twenties, but had considerable experience of travel in North Africa. More important, he had already made a significant Nile journey. He had served as a draughtsman in a French mission in the eastern Mediterranean in 1817, when he was just eighteen years old, and had been so struck by Cairo that he decided to stay, and secured a post with Muhammad Ali, through whom he met some of the many foreigners travelling through the city. Among them was Byron's friend and Burckhardt's admirer W.J. Bankes, who persuaded the Pasha to let Linant accompany him as draughtsman on his journey into Nubia. In March 1820, back in Cairo, Linant joined the first official Egyptian expedition to Siwa Oasis, and at the end of the year travelled with an Italian doctor, Alessandro Ricci, into Sinai. On his return to Cairo, Linant was again employed by Bankes, this time to take advantage of the Pasha's push into Sudan by following independently and at a little distance, recording all that he saw. During the winter of 1821–22 he visited Shendi, Sennar and Dongola. In the autumn of 1824 he arrived in England, still under the patronage of Bankes. Bankes did not become a member of the Association until 1826, but he was in close contact with several Committee members from the moment of his return to England, and it seems likely that he recommended Linant as a future geographical missionary. Appropriately, Linant mentions the Association for the first time in a letter written while staying at Bankes' Northop estate.* On 24 May 1825 he received his instructions from the Committee, written in English and French so that there could be no misunderstanding.

Four Committee members were supposed to sign the instructions, although in the event only Leake, Hamilton and Lord Clive put their names to it. In its ten clauses, the Committee laid out their expectations for the journey and also their understanding of the geography of the African interior. Barrow's travellers had brought back news of Lake Chad – which Rennell had previously known as Wangara and which he suspected would prove to be the endpoint of the Niger and, at one point, perhaps also the source of the Nile. The Committee were now certain that the Nile did not flow out of the lake, but that it rose to the south of Sudan in

---

* Mme Pascale Linant de Bellefonds has referred me to a letter Linant wrote on 29 December 1824, when he was staying with Bankes, now kept in the Dorchester Record Office (HJI/249).

mountains that formed a continuation of the Ethiopian highlands.*
'To throw light on this great question by personal examination of
the places and by following the course of the White Nile from its
junction with the Blue Nile up to its sources will be the first and
main object of your Mission.'[27] The main, but not the only objective
of Linant's mission.

The success of Denham's expedition around Lake Chad had
encouraged the Committee to direct their traveller westwards. So,
after locating the source of the White Nile, Linant was requested
to travel into Borno – he was to be given letters of recommendation
to the authorities of that kingdom. If he saw any opportunity to
buy antiquities, he should do so and send them down the Nile to
Salt in Cairo, who would forward them to London. But above all,
he should be diligent in charting his progress and in informing
London of all he saw and of whatever occurred. He had £150 to
equip himself and get to Cairo, and was to be paid £1 a day from
the time he left Cairo, although this would drop to half that sum
if he stayed more than a month in any one place without showing
good reason for doing so. Presumably this injunction was intended
to avoid Linant's mission developing the same way as Burckhardt's
had done. Whatever happened, the Committee only tied themselves
to this agreement for three years. To help him with the scientific
side of his mission, Linant was sent several cases of equipment,
which included:

> A chronometer in a leather case
> A silver hunting watch with second hand
> A sextant of 8 inch radius, by Watkins & Hill
> A brass-mounted case of instruments
> A miner's azimuth dial with sights
> A large gilt compass
> Two tape measures
> A reflecting circle of 10 inches diameter
> Two ivory thermometers

* 'Le Bahr el Abiad ou Nil Blanc a ses sources exclusivement dans les hauteurs qui forment
vers le couchant une continuation des montagnes de l'Abyssinie' (Louvre, mss 267/7).

A 3 foot achromatic telescope
Two herbaries
A leather-covered paste board for drawing
A complete medicine chest

To this was added several books, including the single-volume edition of W.G. Browne's *Travels in Africa, Egypt and Syria*, the two volumes of the Association's *Proceedings*, weather almanacs for 1826 and 1827, and Aaron Arrowsmith's four-sheet Map of Africa, with its author's dedication, 'To the Committee and Members of the British Association for Discovering the Interior parts of Africa.'[28]

Two years passed before the Committee had news of Linant, but the Thatched House meeting of June 1827 was told that several letters had been received, the last, dated 27 October 1826, reporting that the Frenchman had ascended all the Nile's Nubian cataracts on a boat belonging to the Association (which, presumably, he bought for them), that he was about to visit Meroe to make drawings of its antiquities and would then attempt to take his boat up the White Nile. But members were warned that 'the state of the Country however rendered it very doubtful whether M. Linant would be able for the present to prosecute his Navigation up that River at least to any great distance'.[29] If that was the case, it was hoped he would return to Cairo and consult with Salt, who had heard that the Pasha, Muhammad Ali, was planning a military expedition up the White Nile.

By the time of the meeting, however, Linant's expedition was over. Travelling in several boats with an entourage that included a Turkish soldier and a translator, he reached the junction of the Blue and White Niles early in April, and then managed to sail some 150 miles south up the White Nile. Thanks to the firman Salt had obtained from Muhammad Ali and to the willingness of officers along the river, he made good time. Then he reached the edge of territory belonging to the Shilluk. Burckhardt had been warned about this tribe, and had been referring to them when he wrote that force of arms, not personal skill, would open the way to the source of the Nile.

To compound Linant's problems, the weather started to break and storms cut up the river. Tacking, occasionally forced to hide from the wind behind islands in the stream, he and his assistants came into a stretch of the Nile populated with hippopotami that were, he thought, 'enraged' by the presence of his boats. At night he listened to lions roaring in the west, hyenas howling to the east. But all this was nothing compared to the reputation of the Shilluk, one of the few tribes Muhammad Ali had been unable to subdue. People along the river warned Linant that the Shilluk would never let him pass: they would assume he was going to make trouble and would kill him.

Linant had anticipated the problem and had devised a plan to surprise the Shilluk which, he hoped, would provide him with an opportunity to explain his mission before they were able to jump to conclusions. He moved cautiously up the river, taking with him the *shaykh* of a neighbouring tribe, a reluctant traveller who was well known to the Shilluk. The scale of his problems was soon apparent: the *shaykh* pointed out people watching them in trees along the riverbank, but when Linant looked through his telescope he could see nothing. When they landed, they found signs of recent fires and beehives that the Shilluk had collected, but saw no people. And then, on the night of 15 April, Linant saw a light in the distance: he pointed it out to 'Sheikh Nimmer, who assured me that it was certainly a party of Shiloukhs, I proposed to him to start before day, in order to catch them. The Sheikh, on the contrary, said that it would be much better to return at once, as probably it was a strong party come down to oppose us . . .'[30] As a mutiny threatened to break out, Linant drew his pistol and 'threatened to shoot the first man I should hear disputing my orders, instead of obeying them'.[31]

In the morning, Linant put his plan into action, but the Shilluk saw him coming and prepared to run for cover. 'I did all I could,' he explained to the Committee, 'to engage them to remain, and open an intercourse with us, but they only halted a moment on the beach, as if to look at us, and, the instant we approached, retired into the woods uttering loud cries.'[32] It was an extraordinary moment of first contact, the naked Shilluk and the young European looking at each other with mutual misunderstanding. One thing Linant had understood was that he could not make it through Shilluk territory on this occasion, so, with the weather turning and the rainy season started, he decided to drop back down the river to Cairo.

In May 1828 at the Thatched House in London, Colonel Leake read members an abridged version of Linant's story. As they listened, the more experienced of them might have softened their disappointment at his failure on the Nile by recognising that although he had not reached the source, he had travelled further up the White Nile than any European before him – or at least, any whose journey had been recorded.* What was more, he had returned safely and had brought valuable information on the people, flora, fauna and monuments of the country he had passed through. Among his notes on the Bahr-Abiad or White Nile is the following report: 'Sheikh Hassan of Fassoulo told me that south of the Shiloukhs the Bahr-Abiad is lost in some extensive lakes, which stretch away westward, and communicate with each other during the inundations . . .' There was more. 'Another remarkable fact seems to me to prove indubitably that it [the White Nile] comes from a system of lakes; namely, the prodigious quantity of fish which arrive with the freshes [sic] at their first appearance, for these fish can only come from lakes where they remain imprisoned when the waters are low, and escape when the inundation takes place.'[33] Here was the first mention, and from a source high up the river, of the Nile flowing out of Victoria and the other lakes of the East African highlands.

Linant arrived back in Cairo on 27 September 1827, and wrote to London the following February to assure Leake that he intended to travel south again. In the event, however, he went east and visited Petra with a Frenchman he had recently met in Cairo, Léon de

---

* Linant reached 13 degrees 6 minutes North.

Laborde, promising that he would send the Committee the drawings he had made on the way and a new map of the route from Cairo to Petra. More than a year went by, but no material arrived; in June 1829, Leake complained that 'neither these drawings nor those made by M. Linant in the Countries of the Upper Nile have yet been received by the Secretary although M. Linant has repeatedly announced that he is on the point of transmitting them and on one Occasion reported that he had actually transmitted a part of them to England'.[34] In fact, apart from his sporadic letters, the only materials from Linant's journeys that had reached London were some minerals, dried plants and shells collected on the way to Petra and some weapons and 'horse furniture' of the Bedouin of the Egyptian desert. Inevitably the Association ran out of patience and voted to inform Linant 'that he was no longer to consider himself in the service of the Association or entitled to draw for any Salary upon the Treasurer'.[35]

Linant later claimed that 'if it [the Association] quarrelled with me, it was on account of the conduct of M. Leon de Laborde [his companion on the journey to Petra] [and] also on account of Mr. Barker who did not act very uprightly towards me'.[36] Whatever the circumstances of the falling out, Linant never made another journey for the Association, nor did he send his drawings to London. The following year, he accepted an appointment from Muhammad Ali to work as his Chief Engineer for Upper Egypt.* But by then the field of African geography had been transformed, and the African Association along with it.

---

* Linant remained in Egypt and later became involved in the planning of the Suez Canal, was appointed Minister of Public Works in 1869, created a Pasha in 1873 and died in Cairo ten years later, at the age of eighty-four.

18

The Spirit of Discovery

'If I were asked, what I conceive to have been the one main-
spring, to which modern times owe their immense advantages
in Science . . . to what one faculty, or rather tendency, of the
human mind, are we most indebted for our superiority over
the ancients? I should say, it was the spirit of geographical and
nautical discovery . . .'

William Hamilton, *Address to the Royal Geographical Society* (1839)[1]

IT BEGAN WITH Sir Joseph Banks attending a dinner at the
St Alban's Tavern in June 1788, and its end was sealed by his protégé
John Barrow at a dinner thirty-nine years later. On 7 February 1827,
while Linant de Bellefonds was carrying the Association's ambitions
up the Nile into Sudan, *Romeo and Juliet* was staged at the Covent
Garden Theatre, the Cabinet went into session at the Foreign Office,
an emergency meeting was held at the Grand Masonic Lodge following the death of the Duke of York, and a group of gentlemen
gathered for dinner at the Thatched House, the African Association's favourite watering hole. It was the sort of gathering Banks
would have loved. The Orientalist and former Admiralty Secretary
William Marsden, Banks' old friend and long-time Association
member, chaired the dinner, although the idea for the gathering
belonged to Captain Sir Arthur de Capell Broke. Capell Broke was
a young man who had travelled widely in Scandinavia, was preparing to publish *A Winter in Lapland*, an account of his travels, and

liked the idea of getting together and swapping stories with other travellers. A decade earlier he would, no doubt, have been a regular guest at Banks' evenings or breakfasts in Soho Square. But since the great man's death, London had lacked a focal point where travellers could meet informally. Sir Arthur decided to rectify this and to create his own travellers' centre, the intention being 'the attainment, at a moderate expense of an agreeable, friendly and rational society formed by persons who have visited every part of the globe'.[2]

Thirty-nine travellers turned up for this first dinner, among them William Leake, William Hamilton, William Marsden and W.J. Bankes, all key African Association members. Over dinner, they discussed the creation of a club that would be named after Sir Walter Raleigh and devoted to travel. In what will, by now, be a familiar proceeding, a committee was elected and members agreed to attend dinner once a fortnight, from November to May – unless, of course, they were off searching for the source of the Nile, looking for a northern passage through to the Pacific Ocean or engaged in some other worthy geographical quest. Thomas Legh MP and Captain James Mangles of the Royal Navy, both of whom had travelled on the Nile, were among the first intake, as was Barrow of the Admiralty; the Arctic explorers John Franklin and William Parry also soon signed up.

The Raleigh Club never expected to rival the African Association, and had neither the funds nor the desire to sponsor geographical missions. Instead, it was intended as a talking shop. Above all, Capell Broke wanted its meetings to be entertaining, and suggested that members might like to bring food back from their travels. To set the right example, at the first dinner he served a haunch of reindeer venison from Spitzbergen, a jar of Swedish brandy, rye-cake from near the North Cape, a Norwegian cheese called *Gammel Ost* and preserved cloudberries that he had picked up in Lapland. Other members contributed equally exotic ingredients for subsequent dinners, and the Raleigh earned the sort of reputation for eccentricity that was the calling card of any respectable dining club. Meanwhile, behind the amusements, something serious was going on.

In May 1828, the popular London-based *Literary Gazette* published an anonymous letter in which regret was expressed at the
fact that Paris and Berlin could boast of geographical societies, but
that London could not: although the African Association was the
world's first geographical society, its area of activity was deemed
too limited in the new global environment. As the *Gazette*'s editor
suggested, 'A Geographical Society would be an excellent institution
in England ... Our numerous travellers returning home would
continually bring novelty and information; and the meetings could
not fail to be of the most agreeable and instructive kind.'[3] During
the next two years, while the African Association terminated Linant
de Bellefonds' contract and commissioned Henry Welford, a
twenty-one-year-old lieutenant in the East India Company's army,
to undertake a journey to the Mountains of the Moon, the idea of
a geographical society was discussed at the Raleigh Club's dinners
and at various other functions around town. Out of these conver-
sations, Barrow, Banks' heir as 'the Father of research, the advocate
for enquiry, and the friend of the adventurous Traveller', emerged
as the man most likely to lead such a venture. But at that time the
Admiralty Secretary's attention was focused far from London, on
West Africa.

Captain Gordon Laing had served in Sierra Leone, but returned
with a tarnished record; his commanding officer had described his
military exploits as being 'worse than his poetry'.[4] Laing and Barrow
had been at odds for some time over the course of the Niger.
Barrow, who had previously supported the idea that the Niger
would be found to flow into the Nile, now seemed persuaded of
Banks' old theory that it flowed into the Congo. Laing, on the other
hand, insisted that it flowed into the Gulf of Benin. With both men
only too happy to air their opinions, conflict was inevitable. But
however irritating Laing might have been, Barrow was still prepared
to consider him for an African mission. For one thing, he had

experience of travel in Africa, had some valuable contacts and, perhaps most important given the financial drain of some of Barrow's recent geographical disasters, he was cheap, for he had offered to waive his salary and to set up his expedition for £640.10s. Banks would have jumped at the opportunity to engage him, and Barrow now saw the sense of it, especially with the French Société Géographique taking such an interest in West Africa. So before Denham and Clapperton had reported back to London, Barrow sent Laing off to Africa with orders to become the first European into Timbuktu.

Laing certainly had the spirit for the job. 'The termination of the Niger . . . is destined for me,' he wrote, somewhat arrogantly, given that the matter had eluded the world's best travellers for the past forty years. 'Timbuctoo shall be visited, and the Niger explored within a very few months.'[5] Newly promoted to the rank of major, he arrived in Tripoli in May 1825 and proceeded to fall in love with the daughter of the British Consul, Hanmer Warrington. The Consul was not amused. Colonel Warrington was a proud man who had married one of George IV's illegitimate daughters. According to his French counterpart in Tripoli, he was also a man of violence: Laing was the last person he would wish his daughter to marry. But Warrington was also a skilled diplomat, and in the eleven years he had spent as Consul in Tripoli he had seen many explorers and adventurers go, and he knew that very few of them returned. So, instead of opposing his daughter and her lover, he agreed to the union on the condition that it would be binding only if Laing reached Timbuktu and returned. Then there would at least be some consolation in having a celebrity for a son-in-law.

On 14 July 1825, just before Laing left Tripoli, Colonel Warrington married the young Scot to his second daughter, Emma. The Consul was certainly caught up in the drama of the moment, writing to London that 'a more Wild, Enthusiastic and Romantic Attachment never before existed'.[6] But he was also clearly concerned about the arrangement, and held the young lovers to their promise not to consummate the marriage, writing to Lord Bathurst in London that 'they are not to cohabit till the Marriage is duly performed by a Clergyman of the established Church of England'.[7] He was also trying to hedge his bets and avoid making a widow of his daughter, were Laing not to return.

The traveller had no such concerns about his future. Indeed, he was so convinced of his abilities that he described himself as 'a man of enterprize [sic] and genius'.[8] He intended to take control of his destiny, too, refusing to wait, like Burckhardt, for the arrival of a caravan. If one was not ready to leave, he would assemble his own, which he did, running up alarming bills that Warrington was left to pay – the Consul clearly had a sneaking admiration for the eccentric, love-struck madman, and supported his expenses against the British government's protests. By now it was clear that the road to Timbuktu could be travelled only if, like Burckhardt and Hornemann, the explorer could pass for a Muslim. He would also need a reserve of luck and be able to call on the right sort of protection. Warrington helped considerably by arranging for the young officer to travel with Shaykh Babany, a long-time resident of Timbuktu, and a Tuareg chief by the name of Hateeta. 'The arrangements of this Mission are excellent, the success so certain,' Warrington wrote to London.[9]

In the blazing heat of a North African July, Laing left Tripoli for the south. His steady stream of letters to his prospective father-in-law, sent back along the 'road' in the care of northbound travellers, reveal a man teetering on the brink of insanity. 'For Heavens sake,' Warrington warned him, 'do not let your powerful feelings operate on you so.'[10] But powerful feelings were all that motivated this particular traveller and, throwing dire predictions at Clapperton and Denham, who had recently returned to Tripoli from the south, announcing the inevitability of his own great achievements and asking for a warship to be sent to the Gulf of Benin to wait for him to emerge from the mouth of the Niger, Laing headed for Ghadames.

It was as well that he was buoyed by his own certainties, for the journey offered few of them. Food was short; during the last few days before reaching Ghadames he had little to drink and nothing to eat. Temperatures in the desert throughout July and August were blistering and the native Tuareg were at times hostile, in spite of

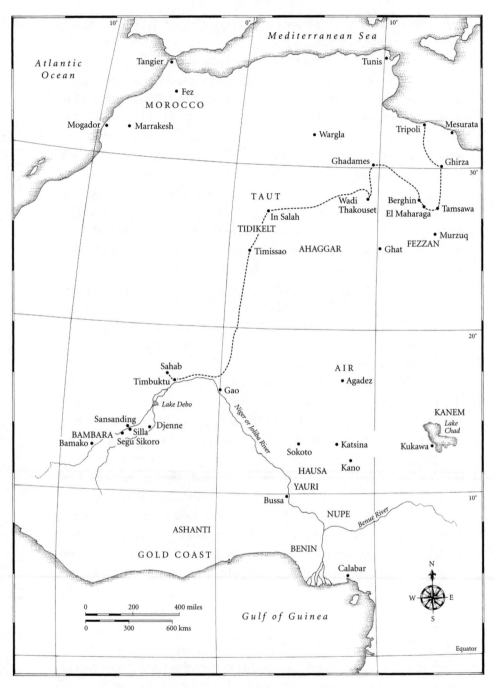

Laing's route to Timbuktu, 1825–26

his travelling with such protection; perhaps so small a caravan was just too much of a temptation.

Ghadames was reached by the middle of September, and clearly did not please the Major. Dreary, barren, dilapidated, crumbling – there was little about the place that pleased him. But whatever he had suffered so far on his journey was soon to pale beside what lay ahead.

Laing set out for Timbuktu on 3 November 1825. 'Every person tells me that this road is very different from that of Bournou – the latter is a regular trading road under the power of the Bashaw along which a child might travel, but on this there are many conflicting interests.'[11] The Bashaw's protective hand may not have extended as far as Timbuktu, but his ear certainly did, and in March the following year Warrington reported to London that Laing and his travelling companions were attacked as they entered the territory of Timbuktu.

The rumour proved to be true. Early one icy morning in January 1826 a party of Tuareg had attacked Laing's group, killing many and making off with whatever they could carry. Laing was left for dead. He was still alive, though terribly wounded. The damage? 'To begin from the top,' he wrote almost with relish to Warrington, 'I have five sabre cuts on the crown of the head and three on the left temple, all fractures from which much bone has come away; one on my left cheek which fractured the jaw bone and has divided the ear, forming a very unsightly wound; one over the right temple and a terrible gash on the back of the neck, which slightly grazed the windpipe; a musket ball in the hip, which made its way through my back, slightly grazing the backbone; five sabre cuts on my right arm and hand, three of the fingers broken, the hand cut three-fourths across, and the wrist bones cut through; three cuts on the left arm, the bone of which has been broken but is again uniting; one slight wound on the right leg and two with one dreadful gash on the left, to say nothing of a cut across the fingers of my left hand, now healed up.'[12]

Laing was saved by his camel-driver, Muhammad, who managed to round up a couple of camels, on one of which he strapped the wounded Englishman. At the next stop, Sidi al Muktar, things got worse: Laing caught the plague, 'a dreadful malady somewhat similar to yellow fever in its symptoms'.[13] Sick, wounded, robbed of his gun and most other possessions, his death should have been inevitable and speedy. But Laing clung to his belief that he was destined to reach Timbuktu, survived the plague and watched his wounds heal. On 13 August 1826, more than a year after leaving his new bride in Tripoli, having crossed more than two and a half thousand miles of wind-whipped, sand-buffed, sun-blistered, Tuareg-tormented desert, he finally entered the fabled city.

The seventeenth-century sea captain Richard Jobson had described Timbuktu's houses as lined with gold. Leo Africanus had said that the rich king of Timbuktu had many gold plates and sceptres, some weighing more than 1300 ounces. Sir Joseph Banks and his friends believed the glory of the ancient world might be rediscovered in Timbuktu's thriving markets, well-endowed libraries, magnificent court and luxurious palaces. Laing found none of these. Timbuktu had been in decline since the Moroccan emperor, Mansour al-Dahabi, 'the golden one' – that word again! – conquered the Niger kingdoms in the sixteenth century. There was still some caravan trade and some European goods were being sold in the markets, but the golden city was no more. Instead, Laing entered a town – it could not be called any more than that – surrounded by Saharan sands, its mud-brick houses baked under a relentless sun and worn by a swingeing wind. Whatever culture had once thrived there was dying, the Sultan no longer being sufficiently wealthy to keep poets and philosophers in his court.

The traveller was housed near the main mosque – you can still visit the wreck of the building, identified by a plaque erected by the African Society at the beginning of the twentieth century. He was an object of curiosity and not a little hostility, as he had been everywhere he had stopped: in Timbuktu he suffered more for being associated with 'the Christian who made war upon the people inhabiting the banks of the Niger',[14] Mungo Park.

Whatever delights or terrors Laing encountered in Timbuktu, with its salty food, its brackish water, the distant smell of the Niger, living in the shadow of the Sahara, all he wrote to Warrington, in the only letter he sent from the dream city, scribbled down on 21 September, the penultimate of the forty-odd days he spent there, was that Timbuktu had 'completely met my expectations . . . I have been busily employed during my stay here, searching the records in the town, which are abundant.'[15] But while Laing went about his researches and convinced himself 'that my hypothesis concerning the termination of the Niger is correct', the Sultan of Timbuktu trembled for his safety and strongly urged his immediate departure. It later emerged that the Sultan had been ordered to keep Europeans out of the city – perhaps, ironically, this was something Clapperton had suggested to Sultan Bello when he was in Sokoto. Whatever the origin of the ban, on 22 September 1826 Laing left town in some haste, joining a caravan heading back north. He was ready to claim his bride in Tripoli and to be fêted in Europe, but he also had a presentiment of the dangers ahead: 'I fear I shall be involved in much trouble after leaving Timbuktu.'[16] In this, at least, he was right. Two days out of the city, the Tuareg *shaykh* to whom he had been entrusted by the Sultan of Timbuktu turned against him. This time there was no mistake: the infidel was strangled with a turban, his head was cut off and his remains were devoured by vultures. The desert will have polished his bones.

News of Laing's death, carried by an African survivor of the attack, took two years to reach Tripoli. By then he had become another celebrity-traveller, missed and then mourned like Mungo Park. By then, also, a Frenchman, René Caillié, was on his way inland from Sierra Leone, across the Futa Jallon on his way to Timbuktu. Caillié had long been inspired by the legends of Africa, by the work of the African Association and by the exploits of Park and his contemporaries. Unlike most other admirers, he was determined to emulate them. Although he had no backing from his government or the Société Géographique, he was no doubt encouraged by the Société's offer of a reward for the first Frenchman to reach Timbuktu. Travelling alone and with few possessions, disguised as a Muslim returning to Mecca after being held captive by Europeans, Caillié suffered what will, by now, seem the usual hardships and privations, the sunburn and windchill, fevers and maladies, including a touch of scurvy. In spite of these setbacks, he succeeded in reaching the Niger and sailing down to Timbuktu.

'On 20 April [1828], at sunset, I entered Timbuktu the mysterious and I could hardly control my joy. My idea of the city's grandeur and wealth did not correspond with the mass of mud houses, surrounded by arid plains of jaundiced white sand, which I found before my eyes.'* The golden city, it was now known for sure, was nothing but a mirage; Timbuktu was a dusty little town with neither gold nor grandeur, nor even the mud wall, twelve-foot deep trench and camel-skin gates the Moor Shabeni had described to Banks back in 1790.

In spite of the fact that the saga of Timbuktu ended not in the discovery of a great empire on the Niger (although one had been discovered slightly to the east and some way from the river) but in mud and dust, Caillié returned to France in the autumn of 1828 to be hailed a hero. This however was not the end of the story: later that year, the pages of the *Bulletin de la Société Géographique* were filled with claim and counter-claim as Barrow fought to defend Laing's memory by disputing the Frenchman's right to call himself the first to reach Timbuktu.[17] The Admiralty Secretary had his last word a couple of years later when he reviewed Caillié's *Journal* in the *Quarterly Review*: 'The French have contributed so little, of late years, to the improvement of geography, that when the mountain has brought forth the mouse, the tiny animal is so fondled and dandled, and crammed, that it swells out to the unwieldy size of an elephant.'[18] No one, Barrow insisted, cared in the least for Caillié's achievements. An Englishman had been first in Timbuktu, and that was what counted. But there was more. Barrow went on to dispute or refute almost every claim and piece of intelligence Caillié had given in his account. 'We shall offer no opinion whether M. Caillié did or did not reach Timbuctoo – that question we are willing to

---

* 'C'est le 20 avril, au coucher du soleil que j'entrai à Tombouctou la mystérieuse, et j'avais peine à contenir ma joie. Je m'étais pourtant fait de la grandeur et de la richesse de la ville une idée à laquelle ne correspondait guère l'amas de maisons de terre, entouré d'arides plaines de sable d'un blanc jaunâtre, que j'avais sous les yeux' (Caillié, pp.167–8).

leave the critics in Paris to decide; but we do not hesitate to say, that, for any information he has brought back, as to the geography of Central Africa, or the course of the Joliba [Niger], he might just as well have staid [sic] at home.'[19]

On 7 April 1830, almost two years to the day after Caillié entered Timbuktu (for we are now convinced that he did), *The Times* announced the death of a man who had done more than most to further the cause of African geography. James Rennell, the eighty-seven-year-old geographer who had spent much of these last few years crippled by gout, had fallen badly while walking in his home and had broken his femur. Laid up, watched over by his daughter, his mind still sharp, he had continued to tease away at the puzzles of geography until the end. Unlike Banks, who had requested a private funeral, Rennell was buried with both pomp and ceremony, his remains pulled to Westminster Abbey by six horses, the hearse draped with silk-velvet hangings and ostrich feathers and followed by thirty carriages carrying relations, friends and admirers.

It was at this time, in the spring of 1830, while Rennell's death was still fresh and keenly felt, with the city nervously watching while France faced yet another political crisis, as news arrived of Vesuvius erupting, on the day that the King offered the feeble excuse to Parliament that his hand was too weak to hold a pen to sign Parliament's Bills, that the Raleigh Travellers' Club met at the Thatched House. The extraordinary meeting was so heavily attended by members and guests that John Barrow had to speak up to assert some order in the unusually crowded room. Taking the chair, he announced that 'a Society was needed whose sole object should be the promotion and diffusion of that most important and entertaining branch of knowledge – geography'. By the end of the meeting, London finally had its Geographical Society.

The new Society had an immediate effect on the old Association. Although the Association had set itself a new mission in the discovery of the sources of the White Nile, by 1830 it had just fourteen active members, and was therefore barely able to mount properly supported expeditions. The Geographical Society had no such problem, for where the Association had always cherished its exclusivity – right to the end, admission was controlled by the African Club – the new Society addressed itself to 'the public at large'.[20] No longer would the majority of people be restricted to applauding celebrity-travellers when they returned or mourning their loss when they did not: it was now possible for anyone with a serious interest in geographical progress to play a part in the process by joining the Geographical Society.

The public at large soon responded, and within a few weeks 460 people had signed up, among them many leading politicians. This in itself might not have brought about the end of the Association. But at a meeting held on 16 July – not at the Thatched House, but at the Horticultural Society's rooms in Regent Street* – Barrow broke the news that the King, William IV, had agreed to extend his patronage, something his predecessors had not done for the African Association, and that the new organisation would now be known as the Royal Geographical Society.

A year passed before the final act was played out. The Association's annual general meeting, held at the Thatched House on 9 July 1831, was attended by just six members, among them Burckhardt's old friend the Reverend Renouard (now Foreign and Honorary Secretary of the Royal Geographical Society) and his editor William Leake (its Vice-President). The first item on the agenda was a despatch that had been received from the British Commander-in-Chief in the Mediterranean reporting the death of their traveller Henry Welford at Sennar. Members failed to hide their disappointment: it was noted in the minutes that their last geographical missionary had died 'without having effected anything in the object of African discovery'.[21]

With a little over £700 in the bank, scant chance of increasing membership and none at all of raising the subscription, with Barrow

---

* The Horticultural Society had grown from another seed Banks had planted.

doing so well in West Africa and the country being so dangerous in the East, the Association in its current state had little chance of making any further contributions to African geography. What's more, the new Society shared the same ambitions as the Association, but intended to nurture what William Hamilton called 'the spirit of geographical discovery' on a global scale. Faced with the inevitable, the half-dozen members discussed 'the expediency of effecting a junction of the Association with the Royal Geographical Society'.[22] Banks, I suspect, would have enjoyed the prospect of the change, especially given the Society's royal seal of approval. The Association's remaining members did as well, and agreed unanimously to vote themselves into the Society, and the Association out of existence.

Epilogue

'I do not much wish well to discoveries, for I am always afraid
they will end in conquest and robbery.'

Samuel Johnson, letter to W.S. Johnson, 14 March 1773

IT STARTED WITH a desire to acquire knowledge about Africa's
people, politics and potential, to fill in some blanks on the map
and to remove a slur from the Age of Enlightenment. It ended with
the creation of the world's foremost geographical society. Overland
exploration had come of age and the African Association had played
a key role in its maturity. Alexander von Humboldt was making
his way across South America while the Royal Geographical Society
considered its next moves in Africa. Timbuktu had been found –
and dismissed – and the Niger question was resolved in 1831, the
year the Association merged with the Royal Geographical Society,
when Clapperton's servant Richard Lander, and his brother John
returned to London, having traced the river to its end in the Atlantic. The sources of the Nile and the whereabouts of the Congo
remained mysteries.

It is tempting to consider what might have happened had the
African Association enjoyed greater success early on: had Houghton
not been murdered, or had Park found a way of opening a regular
connection between the Gambia and the Niger, British business
could have traded directly with the African interior. Beaufoy's hope

that they would discover the descendants of the ancient Egyptians and Phoenicians, their culture intact, living happily in the heart of Africa, was always fanciful.* The Association was on firmer ground with its desire to find an alternative to the trade in slaves.† Through the Gambia–Niger connection, they could have built up viable, though junior, trading partners. Once events in Europe stoked Anglo–French rivalry in West Africa – and elsewhere in the continent with the Germans and Portuguese – the desire for trading partners quickly gave way to thoughts of colonisation. Just eleven short years separated the Association's early, utopian musings – remember his comment that 'something we may have to learn' from Africans – from Banks' speech, made after Mungo Park's return and with Europe unsettled by Napoleon, that two hundred British redcoats 'would be able to overcome the whole Forces which Africa could bring against it'.

The British government allowed the Association for Promoting the Discovery of the Interior Parts of Africa a free hand in the interior of the continent for the first twenty-seven years of its existence. Until the end of the Napoleonic wars in 1815, the Association influenced and, at certain moments, dictated official British policy towards Africa. Thanks to Banks' unique position as President of the Royal Society, a friend of King George III and as adviser to successive governments, the Association's missions took on an increasingly official nature: Daniel Houghton had an interview with Prime Minister Pitt before heading for the Gambia in 1790, while Mungo Park's first journey was originally going to be made in the company of 'a consul for Senegambia' and under the protection of a detachment of British troops, another of the Association's ideas to promote British trade into the interior along the Gambia River. Park's last journey was an official expedition, proposed and paid

---

* Which isn't to say the hope was unfounded: traces of those ancient cultures are being found only now, from the Dogon in Mali to the ancient goldmines in Zimbabwe.
† Remember that in 1788, when the Association was founded, the loss of the American colonies was still painfully recent. Banks supported colonies for prisoners (Botany Bay) and freed slaves (Sierra Leone), but there is nothing to suggest that the African Association's travellers were outriders of Empire.

for by the British government, but organised by Banks and the Association.

The promise of political and commercial gains in this part of Africa was never fulfilled. Beaufoy's confident prediction that a mighty empire would be found and that trade worth £1 million would soon be conducted was always more wishful thinking than serious proposal. The information on which those predictions were based was already several hundred years out of date by the time the Association was founded. The days were long past when the ruler of Timbuktu owned, as Leo Africanus tells it, 'many golden Plates and Scepters, some whereof are 1300 Ounces in Weight', or when the King of Mali carried so much gold when he travelled that he could depress Cairo's gold market for a generation. All that was no more than a reverie, a tale to be told at palavers and around campfires. The Timbuktu trade did exist and could have been dominated, but it was clear, even before the end of the Association, that there were bigger profits to be made elsewhere in Africa.

The African Association's more significant achievements, its lasting legacy, are to be found in the field of exploration and geographical investigation. Its members' passion for knowledge was remarkable. They didn't just want to know where to find Timbuktu: they wanted to know everything about it and its inhabitants. Before the Association, most exploration had a broad focus and was conducted by governments – Captain Cook's voyages were proof of how successful those could be. The African Association showed what could be achieved over time by a group of determined individuals with common interests and sufficient funds. Banks, Beaufoy and their colleagues recognised that several missions might have to be sent out before they made any breakthroughs. Rather than expect to make significant advances with each mission, the Association was prepared to collect information systematically, over years, that would allow it to achieve its goals. In this way it has more in common with modern geographical enquiry than did anything that had gone before.

Thanks to Banks' interests, his position at the Royal Society and his conviction as a universal scientist, the scientific aspect of the journeys became increasingly important. The Association's travellers were among the first overlanders to carry cutting-edge equipment. The reason for their lack of progress is easily found, for they were usually relieved of their equipment long before they were able to make full use of it. Only Park was lucky enough to hold onto his compass beyond the first few weeks of his journey – and only then because Ali of Ludamar was scared of its magical properties. In spite of this, the Association's travellers became the archetype, the model of the modern, scientifically aware explorer. Culturally aware too, as Burckhardt's achievements show.

When the Committee sent Ledyard and Lucas to Africa, they considered the climate and Africa's intimidating geography to be the most difficult obstacles they would have to overcome. Over the course of several missions, several deaths, it became clear that the Moors, Muslim intermediaries between Europe and black Africa, were in fact the biggest obstacle. By studying language and customs, and perfecting disguise, Hornemann and Burckhardt showed a way forward. This was something that Richard Burton understood as he passed through Cairo's Bab an-Nasr cemetery at the end of Ramadan in 1853. Five years later Burton and his colleague John Speke reached Lake Tanganyika, and within twenty years most of Africa's geographical puzzles – the Nile, Zambezi and Congo among them – had been solved. By then exploration marched hand in hand with imperial destiny, and the scramble by European nations to occupy Africa was under way. Seen from this historical perspective, the age of the African Association is almost blessed with innocence. Slavery was about to be abolished, of that the members were certain, but the idea of a white-dominated Africa was too far-fetched to be considered.

History has not been generous to the African Association. Apart from the transcription of its records in the 1960s and a few very brief mentions in various histories of African exploration, little has been written about it. Yet the Association made great advances in geography, launched some of the first truly scientific geographical expeditions, established a model for the Romantic explorer, paved the way for new commercial ties and helped create what remains one of the world's foremost societies for geography and exploration. One of the Association's 'geographical missionaries' was the first European to record the whereabouts of the Niger River. Elsewhere in Africa, the Association was first to begin the exploration of the Sahara and a systematic search for the sources of the White Nile. Burton and Speke's discovery of the great lakes Victoria and Tanganyika was only made possible by the achievements of earlier explorers. The Association's geographical travellers opened the way, showed what could be achieved and how it could be done. The great age of African exploration may have peaked in the second half of the nineteenth century, but it began in June 1788, when Sir Joseph Banks and the other members of the Saturday's Club sat down to dinner at the St Alban's Tavern.

NOTES

ABBREVIATIONS

AAC   Minute Book of the Committee of the African Association

NHM BL DTC   The Banks Archive at the Natural History Museum, Dawson Turner Copies. By permission of The Trustees of The Natural History Museum

NLS   National Library of Scotland

PAA   *Proceedings of the African Association* (unless otherwise stated, this is the 1810 edition)

PRO   Public Record Office

RAA   *Records of the African Association*, Hallett, 1964

SP   Sutro Papers in the Royal Geographical Society

PREFACE: *Talking Timbuktu*

1 *Burton, p.168.*
2 *Ibid., p.123.*

1: *Exploration's Godfather*

1 Lincolnshire Archives Office, Hill Colln, 2.28.
2 Johnson (no page numbers).
3 Hallett, *Penetration*, p.81.
4 Horace Walpole to Sir Horace Mann, 10 July 1774.
5 Wilford, p.42.
6 Carter, 1988, p.124.

2: *The Charge of Ignorance*

1 Innes, p.11.
2 *The Prelude*, Book 7.
3 *The Times*, 116, p.2.
4 H. Beaufoy, pp.36–7.
5 RAA, 14n.
6 RAA, 46.
7 RAA, 45.
8 RAA, 46.

9 The British Library General Catalogue of Printed Books to 1975, Saur, 1983, pp.135–7.
10 Sinclair, I, p.204.
11 Hallett, *Penetration*, p.139.
12 Davidson, p.76.
13 Moore, appendix, pp.69–70.
14 PAA, Vol. I, p.205.
15 Moore, appendix, p.23.
16 Ibid.

3: *A Friend to Mankind*

1 Sinclair, Vol. I, p.204.
2 Lyte, p.210.
3 Ibid.
4 'Sir Joseph Banks and the Emperor of Morocco'.
5 Lincolnshire Archives Office, 2Haw2/B/64, copy of the will of Miss Banks, 21 September 1818.
6 D'Arblay, Vol. iv, p.128.
7 AAC, 17 July 1788.
8 AAC, 26 July 1788.
9 PRO State Papers, 97/54.

10 Ledyard, *Cook*, p.157.
11 Ledyard, *Russia*, p.92.
12 Ibid., p.187.
13 PAA, Vol. I, pp.19–22.
14 RAA.
15 Lyte, pp.188–9.
16 Ledyard, *Russia*, p.249.
17 Ibid.
18 RGS.
19 RAA, 52.
20 Sparks, pp.395–6.
21 RAA, 62.
22 PAA, Vol. I, p.258.
23 Ledyard, *Russia*, p.253.
24 Sparks, pp.399–400.
25 Kinglake, *Eothen*.
26 RAA, 57.
27 Ibid.
28 RAA, 59.
29 RAA, 60.
30 Sparks, p.405.
31 PAA, Vol. I, p.41.
32 Ibid.
33 Ibid.

4: *The Oriental Interpreter*

1 SP, 70/RAA, 48.
2 Hallett, *Penetration*, p.176.
3 BM Add MS 33978, 208–9.
4 PAA, Vol. I, pp.20–1.
5 PAA, 1790, Vol. I, p.48.
6 Tully, pp.2–3.
7 Ibid., p.55.
8 Hallett, *Penetration*, p.207.
9 PAA, Vol. I, p.79.
10 Ibid.

5: *The Moors' Tales*

1 E. Gibbon, Vol. 5, p.192.
2 *Gentleman's Magazine*, Vol. 59, p.565.
3 PAA, Vol. I, pp.9–11.
4 RAA, 70–1.
5 RAA, 72.
6 NHM BL DTC, 6, pp.184–5.
7 Ibid.
8 SP, 83.
9 SP, 83/RAA, 76.
10 Ibid.

11 Matra to Banks, 13 February 1789, BM Add MS 33978, 228.
12 Ibid.
13 RAA, 81.
14 RAA, 81–2.
15 PAA, 1790, Vol. I, p.118.
16 PAA, Vol. I, pp.114–15.
17 PAA, 1790, Vol. I, p.124.
18 Ibid., p.178.
19 Ibid., p.72.
20 RAA, 105.
21 Ibid.
22 RAA, 113.
23 PAA 1790, Vol. I, p.211.
24 Ibid.
25 PAA, 1790, Vol. I, p.223.
26 Ibid., p.226.
27 Ibid., p.200.
28 Ibid., p.202.
29 Ibid., p.203.
30 Ibid., p.9.
31 Ibid., p.205.
32 PAA, Vol. I, p.202.
33 Ibid., pp.205–6.

6: *The Gambia Route*

1 Sinclair, I, p.204.
2 NHM BL DTC, 6, p.133.
3 NHM BL DTC, 8, pp.8–10.
4 BM Add MS 33979, 29–30.
5 NHM BL DTC, 11, pp.293–6.
6 Lancashire Record Office, Ddho/A23, 7 February 1779.
7 Ibid., 4 June 1778.
8 PAA, 1792, Vol. I, p.15.
9 Ibid., p.122.
10 RAA, 127.
11 PAA, 1792, Vol. I, p.5.
12 PAA, Vol. I, pp.242–4.
13 Ibid., pp.318–22.
14 PAA, 1792, Vol. I, p.7.
15 PAA, Vol. I, pp.318–22.
16 Ibid., pp.300–4.
17 Ibid., pp.318–22.
18 Ibid.
19 PAA, 1792, Vol. I, p.8.
20 Ibid.
21 Hallett, *Penetration*, p.32.
22 Ibid.
23 Ibid.

24 PAA, 1792, Vol. I, p.12.
25 Ibid., p.9.
26 Ibid., p.10.
27 Ibid.
28 Ibid., p.13.
29 PAA, Vol. I, p.252.
30 PAA, 1792, Vol. I, p.14.

7: *The Political Player*

1 Astley, Vol. II, pp.66–74.
2 Ibid.
3 Ibid, p.147.
4 Ibid, pp.145–6.
5 Ibid.
6 Ibid, pp.148–58.
7 Stone.
8 Ibid.
9 NHM BL DTC, 7, pp.213–15.
10 Ibid.
11 PAA, Vol. I, pp.318–22.
12 Ibid., p.254.
13 Ibid., pp.254–5.
14 Ibid., p.256.
15 Ibid., p.266.
16 Ibid., p.281.
17 Ibid., p.283.
18 Ibid., p.284.
19 Ibid., p.256.
20 Ibid., pp.286–7.
21 Ibid., p.292.
22 SP, 193–4.
23 SP, 197.
24 RGS, AAGM, 22.
25 PAA, Vol. I, pp.300–4/RAA, 138.
26 Park, p.84.
27 RGS, AAGM, 25 May 1792/RAA, 142.
28 Rees, p.138.
29 NHM BL DTC, 7, pp.213–15.
30 RGS, AAGM, 26 May 1792/RAA, 142.
31 SP, 231–4.
32 AAC, 6 March 1796.
33 Ibid.
34 Ibid.
35 AAC, 6 March 1796, paper 16.
36 PAA, Vol. I, p.258.
37 Ibid., pp.258–9.

8: *No Mean Talents*

1 NLS, Ms No.10782, f.180, quoted in Lupton, p.36.
2 Park, p.1.
3 NLS, Ms No.10782, f.180.
4 Ibid.
5 PAA, Vol. I, p.304.
6 Park, pp.1–2.

9: *Pity the White Man*

1 Park, p.5.
2 Ibid., p.6.
3 Ibid.
4 Park (1799), p.9.
5 Park, p.14.
6 Ibid., p.7.
7 Lupton, p.41.
8 RAA, 161.
9 Park, p.21.
10 Ibid.
11 Ibid., p.24.
12 Ibid., p.26.
13 Ibid., p.27.
14 Ibid., p.35.
15 Ibid., p.40.
16 Ibid., p.51.
17 Ibid., p.61.
18 Park (1799), p.95.
19 Ibid., p.102.
20 Ibid., p.103.
21 Ibid.
22 Park, p.85.
23 Ibid., p.86.
24 Lupton, p.63.
25 Park, p.91.
26 Park (1799), p.119.
27 Ibid., p.122.
28 Park, p.110.
29 Park (1799), p.163.
30 Ibid., p.172.
31 Ibid., p.173.
32 Ibid., pp.173–4.
33 Park, p.148.
34 Ibid., p.149.
35 Park (1799), p.195.
36 Park, p.153.

10: *The Golden Harvest*

1 NHM BL DTC, 10(1), pp.77–9.
2 Park, p.194.
3 Ibid.
4 Ibid., p.275.
5 Carter, 1988, p.354.
6 BM Egerton MSS 2641, 159–61.
7 Park, postscript.
8 Ilchester, Vol. I, p.172.
9 *Gentleman's Magazine*, Vol. 70, 1800, p.702.
10 NHM BL DTC, 10(1), pp.53–4.
11 Ibid.
12 Ibid.
13 DNB, 1889, Vol. 17, p.112.
14 NHM BL DTC, 10(2), pp.229–30.
15 BM Egerton MSS 2641, 159–61.
16 NHM BL DTC, 10(1), pp.201–2.
17 PAA, Vol. I, p.403.
18 AA Comm/RGS/21 April 1795.
19 PAA, Vol. I, pp.404–5.
20 Leo, Vol. VI, p.7.
21 PAA, Vol. I, p.416.
22 Ibid., p.524.
23 Ibid., p.537.
24 RAA, 163.
25 Ibid.
26 RAA, 164.
27 Lupton, p.104.
28 NHM BL DTC, 11, p.80.
29 Ibid., p.79.
30 Ibid., p.80.
31 Ibid., p.88.
32 Ibid., p.78.
33 Lupton, p.105.
34 NHM BL DTC, 11, p.84.
35 Ibid.
36 Ibid., p.113.
37 Ibid., pp.114–15.
38 Ibid., pp.181–2.
39 Park, p.xv.
40 *Gentleman's Magazine*, Vol. 85, May 1815, p.438.
41 *Gentleman's Magazine*, Vol. 69, August 1799, pp.680–1.
42 Park, p.1.
43 *Quarterly Review*, Vol. 13, April 1815, p.122.
44 NHM BL DTC, 11, pp.217–18.
45 PAA, Vol. II, p.2.
46 RAA, 168.
47 RAA, 146.
48 Ibid.
49 RAA, 168.
50 RAA, 169.
51 Curtin, p.6.
52 Gascoigne, *Science in . . .*, p.188.
53 BM Add MS 38233. 94.
54 SP, A2:76.
55 RAA, 169.
56 Dutot, 1840, pp.324–38.
57 Hallett, *Penetration*, p.303.

11: *The Göttingen Connection*

1 NHM BL DTC, 6, pp.89–90.
2 Banks to Sir John Stepney, 20 July 1794, SP, 300.
3 Hallett, *Penetration*, p.189.
4 SP, 435.
5 AAC, 3 June 1796.
6 SP, 377.
7 AAC, 3 June 1796.
8 BM Add MS 8098, 313.
9 NHM BL DTC, 10(1), pp.91–2.
10 NHM BL DTC, 10(2), p.25.
11 BM Add MS 8098, 317.
12 SP, 444.
13 AAC, 20 March 1797/RAA, 178–9.
14 Hallett, *Penetration*, p.57.
15 PAA, Vol. I, p.159.
16 Ibid., p.163.
17 Hallett, *Penetration*, p.252.
18 SP, 419.
19 SP, 499–500/RAA, 179.
20 AAC, 20 March 1797/RAA, 178.
21 RAA, 181.
22 RAA, 180.
23 NHM BL DTC, 10(1), p.154.
24 Hallett, *Penetration*, p.252.
25 SP, 438.
26 NHM BL DTC, 10(2), p.24.

12: *Juset ben Abdallah*

1 NHM BL DTC, 10(2), pp.111–12.
2 Ibid., pp.179–81.
3 Sattin, p.23.
4 Ibid.
5 NHM BL DTC, 10(1), p.183.
6 Ibid., pp.196–200.

7 NHM BL DTC, 10(2), p.165.
8 NHM BL DTC, 10(1), pp.196–200.
9 NHM BL DTC, 10(2), p.165.
10 RAA, 266.
11 Jabarti/Cuoq, p.30 (my translation).
12 Ibid., p.31.
13 PAA, Vol. II, p.8.
14 Moorehead, *Blue Nile*, p.76.
15 Ibid.
16 Ibid., p.91.
17 Rodenbeck, p.153.
18 Charles-Roux, pp.38–9.
19 *The Times*, 15 October 1798.
20 PAA, Vol. II, p.9.
21 Sinclair, *Correspondence*, 1831.
22 Moorehead, *Blue Nile*, p.102.
23 PAA, Vol. II, p.9.
24 NHM BL DTC, 11, pp.66–7.
25 Ibid., pp.64–5.
26 Ibid., p.67.
27 Ibid., pp.64–5.
28 PAA, Vol. II, p.12.
29 NHM BL DTC, 12, p.66.
30 NHM BL DTC, 11, pp.64–5.
31 PAA, Vol. II, p.40.
32 Ibid.
33 Ibid., p.41.
34 Ibid.
35 Ibid., p.42.
36 Ibid., p.44.
37 Ibid., p.43.
38 Ibid., pp.42–3.
39 AAC, 3 June 1796/RAA, 177.
40 Browne, pp.531–2.
41 PAA, Vol. II, p.67.
42 Ibid., p.69.
43 Ibid., p.70.
44 Ibid., p.75.
45 Ibid., p.85.
46 Ibid., p.86.
47 Ibid., p.89.
48 Ibid., p.90.
49 Ibid., pp.90–1.
50 Ibid., p.94.
51 Ibid., p.126.
52 Ibid., p.130.
53 Hallett, *Penetration*, p.260.
54 NHM BL DTC, 11, p.268.
55 PAA, Vol. II, p.127.
56 Ibid.
57 Lane, p.348.
58 PAA, Vol. II, p.148.
59 Ibid., p.144.
60 Ibid., p.133.
61 NHM BL DTC, 11, pp.266–74.
62 Ibid., p.268.
63 Ibid., p.294.
64 NHM BL DTC, 12, p.65.
65 NHM BL DTC, 11, pp.281–5.
66 Ibid., p.326.
67 Ibid., p.324.
68 RGS archive, 408 (6).

13: *Many Deaths*

1 Golbéry, vol. I, p.56.
2 PAA, Vol. II, p.327.
3 Carter, p.410.
4 NHM BL DTC, 12, pp.240–2.
5 Lyte, p.213.
6 Ibid.
7 NHM BL DTC, 12, pp.240–2.
8 CO 2/1. Banks to Sullivan, 1 August 1802.
9 CO 2/1. Rennell to Sullivan, 17 October 1802.
10 Park, p.283.
11 NHM BL DTC, 14, p.161.
12 Ibid., pp.140–1.
13 Park, p.6.
14 NHM BL DTC, 15, pp.242–5.
15 Ibid.
16 *Quarterly Review*, Vol. 13, April 1815, p.128.
17 Lupton, p.150.
18 *Quarterly Review*, Vol. 13, April 1815, p.128.
19 Park, p.308.
20 Ibid., p.352.
21 Ibid.
22 Ibid., p.358.
23 Ibid., p.357.
24 Ibid., p.362.
25 Ibid.
26 *Quarterly Review*, Vol. 13, April 1815, p.129.
27 Ibid.
28 Ibid.
29 BL Add MS 37232, f.163.
30 Ibid.
31 *Quarterly Review*, Vol. 13, April 1815, p.130.

32 PAA, Vol. II, p.320.
33 Ibid., p.363.
34 RGS, AAGM, 29 May 1803/RAA, 191.
35 AAC, 9 June 1804/RAA, 192.
36 PAA, Vol. II, pp.386–7.
37 Ibid., p.387.
38 Ibid.
39 Ibid., p.388.
40 Ibid., p.410.
41 *The Times*, 10 July 1806, p.2.
42 *The Times*, 1 September 1806, p.2.
43 *The Times*, 6 July 1858, p.9.
44 RAA, 210.
45 PAA, Vol. II, p.384.
46 Ibid., pp.417–18.
47 Ibid., p.420.
48 *Quarterly Review*, Vol. 18, 1818, p.372.
49 Lyon, p.132.
50 *Quarterly Review*, Vol. 18, 1818, p.372.
51 PRO/FO76/15; and *Quarterly Review*, Vol. 18, 1818, p.372.
52 Lyon, p.132.
53 NHM BL DTC, 11, pp.64–5.

14: *The Swiss Gentleman*

1 Carter, p.483.
2 Ibid., pp.529–30.
3 *Edinburgh Review*, Vol. 1, October 1802, pp.134–5.
4 Ibid., pp.136–7.
5 NHM BL DTC, 13, p.306.
6 *Edinburgh Review*, Vol. 1, October 1802, p.138.
7 NHM BL DTC, 12, p.28.
8 RGS, AAGM, 28 May 1804/RAA, 267.
9 NHM BL DTC, 9, p.81.
10 Burckhardt-Sarasin, p.96.
11 AAC, 21 March 1808/RAA, 219.
12 Burckhardt, *Nubia*, p.v.
13 Burckhardt-Sarasin, pp.94–112.
14 Burckhardt, *Syria*, p.i.
15 Burckhardt, *Nubia*, p.v.
16 Ibid.
17 Introduction to *Lyrical Ballads*, 1800.
18 Burckhardt-Sarasin, pp.94–112.
19 Sim, p.54.
20 AAC, 244–50/RAA, 221.
21 Burckhardt, *Nubia*, p.x.
22 Ibid., p.xii.
23 Ibid.

24 Ibid., p.xxii.
25 Ibid., p.xxiii.
26 Sim, p.73.
27 Ibid.
28 Burckhardt, *Nubia*, p.xxvi.
29 Otter, p.592.
30 Burckhardt, *Nubia*, p.xxxi.
31 Ibid.
32 Otter, p.590.
33 Ibid., p.592.
34 Ibid., p.591.
35 Ibid., p.592.
36 Burckhardt, *Nubia*, p.xxxii.
37 Burckhardt, *Arabia*, pp.51–2.
38 Ibid., p.52.
39 Burckhardt, *Nubia*, p.xlii.
40 Burckhardt, *Arabia*, p.147.
41 Burckhardt, *Nubia*, p.xlvi.
42 Hallett, *Penetration*, p.370.
43 Burckhardt, *Arabia*, p.419.
44 Ibid., p.420.
45 Ibid., p.424.
46 Ibid., p.425.
47 Ibid., p.428.
48 Ibid.
49 Ibid., p.421.
50 Burckhardt, *Nubia*, p.1.
51 Burckhardt, *Arabia*, p.430.
52 Ibid., p.456.
53 Legh, p.11.

15: *Shaykh Ibrahim ibn Abdallah*

1 Burckhardt, *Nubia*, p.lxvi.
2 Ibid., p.lii.
3 NHM BL DTC, 18, p.288.
4 Ibid.
5 Burckhardt, *Nubia*, p.3.
6 Legh, p.83.
7 Ibid.
8 Burckhardt, *Nubia*, p.68.
9 Ibid., p.83.
10 Burckhardt-Sarasin, pp.145–8.
11 Burckhardt, *Nubia*, p.li.
12 Ibid., p.167.
13 Ibid., p.241.
14 Ibid., p.240.
15 Ibid., p.258.
16 Ibid., p.254.
17 Ibid., p.265.
18 Ibid., p.308.

19 Ibid., p.257.
20 Ibid.
21 Ibid., p.322.
22 Ibid., p.327.
23 Ibid., p.328.
24 Ibid., p.338.
25 Ibid., p.454.
26 Ibid., p.lviii.
27 Ibid., p.lvii.
28 Ibid., p.3.
29 Sim, p.279.
30 Burckhardt, *Arabia*, p.130.
31 Ibid., p.134.
32 Ibid., p.184.
33 Ibid., p.183.
34 Ibid., p.184.
35 Otter, p.613.
36 Burckhardt, *Nubia*, p.lx.
37 Sim, p.343.
38 Hallett, *Penetration*, p.391.
39 RAA, 226.
40 PRO/FO24/6, f.53.
41 Manley, p.70.
42 Letter to Valentia, quoted in ibid., p.73.
43 Hamilton, *Aegyptica*, p.177.
44 Usick, p.51.
45 Manley, p.87.
46 *Quarterly Review*, Vol. 24, October 1821, p.142.
47 Clarke, 1825, Vol. 2, p.306.
48 Burckhardt, *Nubia*, p.lxxiv.
49 Ibid., p.lxxvii.
50 Sim, p.405.
51 Burckhardt, *Nubia*, pp.lxxxi–lxxxii.
52 Ibid., p.lxxvii.
53 Ibid., pp.lxxix–lxxx.
54 Adams, p.xi.
55 Ibid., p.xii.
56 Ibid., p.xix.
57 Burckhardt-Sarasin, p.166.
58 Ibid., p.171.
59 Burckhardt, *Nubia*, p.xciv.
60 Ibid., p.xcv.
61 Halls, 1834, Vol. II, p.50.

16: A New World Order

1 Carter, 1988, p.494.
2 Ibid., p.528.
3 Burckhardt, *Nubia*, pp.xcvi–xcvii.
4 *Quarterly Review*, Vol. 18, p.364.
5 Tuckey, p.ii.
6 Quoted in Carter, 1988, p.499.
7 Tuckey, p.xxxi.
8 RAA.
9 Fleming, p.93.
10 Ibid., p.95.
11 Carter, 1988, p.525.
12 *Oxford Companion to Medicine*, 1986, p.480.
13 Carter, p.534.

17: *The Fountains of the Sun*

1 PAA, Vol. I, p.257.
2 Burckhardt, *Nubia*, p.257.
3 African Institution, p.1.
4 Rennell, p.31.
5 Ibid., p.35.
6 English, p.xii.
7 Burckhardt, *Syria*, p.xviii.
8 Burckhardt, *Nubia*.
9 RGS AAGM, 25 May 1822/RAA, 232.
10 Ibid.
11 RAA, 233.
12 Halls, 1834, Vol. II, p.211.
13 Ibid.
14 Ibid.
15 RGS AAGM, 7 June 1823/RAA, 234.
16 RAA, 234.
17 *Gentleman's Magazine*, Vol. 94, 1824, p.574.
18 Denham, Vol. I, p.210.
19 Ibid., p.425.
20 Ibid., p.212.
21 Ibid., Vol. II, p.266.
22 Ibid.
23 Ibid., pp.332–3.
24 Ibid., p.352.
25 *Edinburgh Review*, Vol. 44, No. 86.
26 RGS AAGM, 27 May 1826/RAA, 236.
27 Louvre, mss 267/7.
28 Tooley, p.9.
29 RGS AAGM, 16 June 1827/RAA, 237.
30 RGS, JRGS 1832, Vol. 2, p.179.
31 Ibid.
32 Ibid., p.180.
33 Ibid., p.187.
34 RGS AAGM, 13 June 1829/RAA, 239.
35 RGS AAGM, 13 June 1829/RAA, 240.
36 RGS archive (LBR.MSS), letter from M.

Linant to Lord Prudhoe, dated Cairo,
17 August 1839.

18: *The Spirit of Discovery*

1 Hamilton, 1839, pp.41–2.
2 Mill, p.8.
3 *Literary Gazette*, 24 May 1828.
4 PRO/CO2/15, Turner to Bathurst, 9
April 1825.
5 PRO/CO2/20, Laing to Warrington, 15
October 1825.
6 PRO/FO/76/19, 1725.
7 Ibid.
8 Bovill, *Missions*, p.178.
9 PRO/FO/76/19, 1727.

10 RS, 374 (La).
11 Ibid., 95.
12 PRO/CO2/20, Laing to Warrington, 10
May 1826.
13 Ibid., 1 July 1826.
14 RS, 374 (La), 113.
15 PRO/CO2/20, Laing to Warrington, 21
September 1826.
16 RS, 374 (La), 113.
17 *Bulletin de la Société de Géographie*, Vol.
10, Paris, 1828, p.230ff.
18 *Quarterly Review*, Vol. 42, 1830, p.450.
19 Ibid., p.464.
20 Markham, *Fifty Years . . .*, p.19.
21 RAA, 243.
22 RGS AAGM, 9 July 1831/RAA, 244.

BIBLIOGRAPHY

AFRICAN ASSOCIATION PUBLICATIONS

PRIVATE PUBLICATIONS FOR MEMBERS ONLY:

The Association for Promoting the Discovery of the Interior Parts of
  Africa (London, 1788)
Proceedings of the Association for Promoting the Discovery of the Interior
  Parts of Africa, 2 vols (Macrae, London, 1790)
Proceedings of the Association for Promoting the Discovery of the Interior
  Parts of Africa (T. Cadell, London, 1791)
Elucidations of the African Geography; from the communications of
  Major Houghton and Mr Magra, 1791 (Bulmer, London, 1793)
Proceedings of the Association for Promoting the Discovery of the Interior
  Parts of Africa (Bulmer, London, 1798)
Voyages et Découvertes dans l'Intérieur de l'Afrique (Tavernier, Paris,
  AnVII, 1798/99)
African Researches, or the Proceedings of the Association for Promoting
  the Discovery of the Interior Parts of Africa (Bulmer, London, 1802)
Extract from the Proceedings of the African Association, May 26, 1804
  (Bulmer, London, 1804)
African Association, Report, June 1, 1805 (Bulmer, London, 1805)
Proceedings of the Association for Promoting the Discovery of the Interior
  Parts of Africa, 2 vols (Nichols, London, 1810)

PUBLICATIONS OFFERED FOR SALE:

The Journals of Frederick Hornemann's Travels from Cairo to
  Mourzouk, the Capital of the Kingdom of Fezzan in Africa. In the
  years 1797–8 (Bulmer, London, 1802)
Proceedings of the Association for Promoting the Discovery of the Interior
  Parts of Africa (Bulmer, London, 1810)
Travels in Nubia; by the late John Lewis Burckhardt (John Murray,
  London, 1819)

Travels in Syria and the Holy Land by the late John Lewis Burckhardt (John Murray, London, 1822)

Travels in Arabia by the late John Lewis Burckhardt (Colburn, London, 1829)

Arabic Proverbs, or The Manners and Customs of the Modern Egyptians by the late John Lewis Burckhardt (Murray, London, 1830)

Notes on the Bedouins and Wahabys, collected during his travels in the east, by the late John Lewis Burckhardt (Colburn & Bentley, London, 1831)

Adams, Robert, *The Narrative of Robert Adams, a Sailor, who was shipwrecked on the western coast of Africa* (John Murray, London, 1816)

Ajayi, J.F.A., and Crowder, Michael (eds), *History of West Africa*, Vol. I (Longman, London, 1971)

Annesley, George, Viscount Valentia, *Voyages and Travels to India, Ceylon, the Red Sea, Abyssinia and Egypt* (Bulmer, London, 1809)

Anonymous, *A Historical and Philosophical Sketch of the Discoveries and Settlements of the Europeans in Northern & Western Africa at the close of the Eighteenth Century* (Brown, Edinburgh, 1799)

Anonymous, *The Picture of London for 1802* (Phillips, London, 1802)

d'Arblay, Frances (Fanny Burney), *Diary and Letters of Madame d'Arblay* (Colburn, London, 1842–46)

Astley, Thomas, *A new General Collection of Voyages and Travels* (Astley, London, 1745)

Badia, Domingo, *Voyages d'Ali Bey el Abbassi* (Didot, Paris, 1814)

Baldwin, George, *Narrative of Facts relating to the Plunder of the English Merchants by the Arabs, and other subsequent outrages of the Government in Cairo* (London, 1780)

Banks, Sir Joseph, *The History of Science and Technology, Series Two: The Papers of Sir Joseph Banks, 1743–1820* (Adam Matthew, Marlborough, 1995)

Beaufoy, Gwendolyn, *Leaves from a Beech Tree* (Blackwell, Oxford, 1930)

Beaufoy, Henry, *The Speech of Mr Beaufoy, Tuesday, the 18th of June,*

1788, in a Committee of the Whole House, on a Bill for Regulating the Conveyance of Negroes from Africa to the West-Indies (Phillips, London, 1789)

Beaver, Philip, *African Memoranda* (Baldwin, London, 1805)

Belzoni, Giovanni, *Narrative of the Operations and Recent Discoveries within the Pyramids, Temples, Tombs and Excavations in Egypt and Nubia; and of a Journey to the Coast of the Red Sea, in search of the ancient Berenice; and another to the Oasis of Jupiter Ammon* (John Murray, London, 1821)

Bennett, J.A., *The Divided Circle: A History of Instruments for Astronomy, Navigation and Shipping* (Phaidon/Christie's, Oxford, 1987)

Blumenbach, J.F., *The Anthropological Treatises* (Longman, Green, London, 1865)

Bovill, E.W. (ed.), *Missions to the Niger*, Vol. 1 (Hakluyt Society, Second Series, No.CXXIII, Cambridge University Press, London, 1964)

Bovill, E.W., *The Gold Trade of the Moors* (Oxford University Press, London, 1968)

Boyle, T.C., *Water Music* (Granta, London, 1993)

Browne, W.G., *Travels in Africa, Egypt and Syria* (Cadell & Davies, London, 1806)

Burckhardt-Sarasin, Carl, and Schwabe-Burckhardt, Hansrudolph, *Scheik Ibrahim, Johann Ludwig Burckhardt, Briefe an Eltern und Geschwister* (Helbing & Lichtenhehn, Basel, 1956)

Burton, Richard Francis, *Personal Narrative of a Pilgrimage to el-Medinah and Meccah* (Longman, London, 1855)

Caillié, Réné, *Travels through Central Africa to Timbuctoo* (Colburn & Bentley, London, 1830)

Carpenter, Kirsty, *Refugees of the French Revolution* (Macmillan, London, 1999)

Carter, Harold B., *Sir Joseph Banks: A Guide to Biographical and Bibliographical Sources* (St Paul's/British Museum, London, 1987)

Carter, Harold B., *Sir Joseph Banks, 1743–1820* (British Museum/ Natural History, London, 1988)

Chambers, Robert, *A Biographical Dictionary of Eminent Scotsmen* (Blackie, Glasgow, 1835)

Charles-Roux, F., *Bonaparte: Governor of Egypt* (Methuen, London, 1937)

Clifton, Gloria, *Directory of British Scientific Instrument Makers 1550–1851* (Zwemmer, London, 1995)

Cooley, William, *Negroland of the Arabs* (Arrowsmith, London, 1841)

Curtin, Philip, *The Image of Africa* (Macmillan, London, 1965)

Davidson, Basil, *The African Past* (Longmans, London, 1964)

Dawson, W.R., *The Banks Letters: A Calendar of the Manuscript Correspondence of Sir Joseph Banks* (British Museum/Natural History, London, 1958)

Denham, Major, Captain Clapperton and the late Dr. Oudney, *Narrative of Travels and Discoveries in Northern and Central Africa* (John Murray, London, 1828)

Edwards, Edward, *Lives of the Founders of the British Museum* (Trubner, London, 1870)

English, G.B., *Narrative of the Expedition to Dongola and Sennar* (John Murray, London, 1822)

Equiano, Olaudah, *The Interesting Narrative of the Life of Olaudah Equiano, or Gustavus Vassa, the African. Written by Himself.* (Wilkins, London, 1789)

Feltham's Picture of London for 1805

Fleming, Fergus, *Barrow's Boys* (Granta, London, 1998)

Flint, John E. (ed.), *The Cambridge History of Africa*, Vol. 5 (Cambridge University Press, Cambridge, 1976)

Foreman, Amanda, *Georgiana, Duchess of Devonshire* (HarperCollins, London, 1998)

Gascoigne, John, *Joseph Banks and the English Enlightenment* (Cambridge University Press, Cambridge, 1994)

Gascoigne, John, *Science in the Service of Empire* (Cambridge University Press, Cambridge, 1998)

Gibbon, Edward, *Miscellaneous Works* (John Murray, London, 1814)

Gibbon, Lewis Grassic, *Niger: The Life of Mungo Park* (Porpoise Press, Edinburgh, 1934)

Golbéry, Sylvain de, *Fragments d'un voyage en Afrique* (Treuffel et Würtz, Paris, 1802)

Grant, Douglas, *Fortunate Slave* (Oxford University Press, Oxford, 1968)

Gray, William, *Travels in Western Africa* (John Murray, London, 1825)

Hallett, Robin, *Records of the African Association* (Nelson, London, 1964)

Hallett, Robin, *The Penetration of Africa*, Vol. 1 (Routledge & Kegan Paul, London, 1965)

Halls, J.J., *The Life and Correspondence of Henry Salt Esq. FRS, His Britannic Majesty's Late Consul-General in Egypt* (Richard Bentley, London, 1834)

Hamilton, William R., *Remarks on Several Parts of Turkey: Aegyptiaca or some account of the antient and modern state of Egypt* (T. Payne, Cadell & Davies, London, 1809)

Hamilton, William R., *Address to the Royal Geographical Society of London* (Clowes, London, 1839)

Herodotus, *The Histories* (trans. Aubrey de Sélincourt) (Penguin, London, 1972)

Hoare, Prince, *The Memoirs of Granville Sharp* (Henry Colburn, London, 1820)

Ilchester, Earl of (ed.), *The Journal of Elizabeth, Lady Holland* (Longmans, London, 1908)

Innes, C.L., *A History of Black and Asian Writing in Britain, 1700–2000* (Cambridge University Press, Cambridge, 2002)

al-Jabarti, Abd al-Rahman, *Chronicle of the First Seven Months of the French Occupation of Egypt* (trans. S. Moreh) (E.J. Brill, Leiden, 1975)

Jackson, J.G., *An Account of the Empire of Morocco* (Longmans, London, 1809)

Jackson, J.G., *An Account of Timbuctoo and Housa* (Longmans, London, 1820)

Jobson, Richard, *The Golden Trade, or a Discovery of the River Gambia, and the Golden Trade of the Aethiopians* (Penguin, London, 1932)

Johnson, Samuel, *A Dictionary of the English Language*, 6th Edition (Rivington et al., London, 1785)

Journal d'un notable du Caire Durant l'expédition française, 1798–1801 (trans. Joseph Cuoq) (Albin Michel, St Juste-la-Pendue, France, 1979)

Labat, J.B., *Nouvelle rélation de l'Afrique occidentale*, 5 vols (Guillaume Cavelier, Paris, 1728)

Lane, Edward William, *Manners and Customs of the Modern Egyptians* (Charles Knight, London, 1842)

Last, Murray, *The Sokoto Caliphate* (Longmans, London, 1967)

Lawrence, A.W., *Trade Castles and Forts of West Africa* (Jonathan Cape, London, 1963)

Ledyard, John, *John Ledyard's Journal of Captain Cook's Last Voyage* (ed. James Kenneth Munford) (Oregon State University Press, Oregon, 1963)

Ledyard, John, *John Ledyard's Journey through Russia and Siberia, 1787–1788* (ed. Stephen W. Watrous) (University of Wisconsin Press, Wisconsin, 1966)

Legh, Thomas, *Narrative of a Journey in Egypt and the Country Beyond the Cataracts* (John Murray, London, 1816)

Leo Africanus, *The History and Description of Africa* (Hakluyt Society, London, 1896)

Lodge, Edmund, *Portraits of Illustrious Personages of Great Britain* (Harding & Lepard, London, 1835)

Lupton, Kenneth, *Mungo Park the African Traveller* (Oxford University Press, Oxford, 1979)

Lyon, G.F., *A Narrative of Travels in Northern Africa in the years 1818, 1819 and 1820* (John Murray, London, 1821)

Lyte, Charles, *Sir Joseph Banks* (David & Charles, Devon, 1980)

Manley, Deborah, and Rée, Peta, *Henry Salt* (Libri, London, 2001)

Markham, Clements R., *Major James Rennell* (Cassell, London, 1895)

Markham, Clements R., *The Fifty Years' Work of the Royal Geographical Society* (John Murray, London, 1881)

Martin, Eveline, *The British West African Settlements, 1750–1821* (Longmans, London, 1927)

Meagher, Alan (ed.), *Historic Sights of the Gambia* (National Council for the Arts and Culture, Banjul, 1998)

Middleton, John, *Encyclopaedia of Africa South of the Sahara* (Scribner's, New York, 1997)

Mill, Hugh Robert, *The Record of the Royal Geographical Society, 1830–1930* (RGS, London, 1930)

Moore, Francis, *Travels into the Inland Parts of Africa* (Stagg, London, 1738)

Moorehead, Alan, *The White Nile* (Hamish Hamilton, London, 1960)

Moorehead, Alan, *The Blue Nile* (Harper & Row, New York, 1962)

Murray, Hugh, *Historical Accounts of Discoveries and Travels in Africa* (Longman, Hurst, Rees, Orme & Brown, London, 1818)

Norry, Charles, *An Account of the French Expedition to Egypt* (Ridgway, London, 1800)

O'Brian, Patrick, *Joseph Banks: A Life* (Collins Harvill, London, 1987)

Ogot, B.A. (ed.), *UNESCO General History of Africa*, Vol. 5 (Heinemann/UNESCO, California, 1992)

Oliver, Roland, *The African Experience* (Weidenfeld & Nicolson, London, 1991)

Otter, Rev. William, *The Life and Remains of Rev. Edward Daniel Clarke, LL.D.* (Cowie, London, 1824)

Park, Mungo, *Travels in the Interior of Africa* (Eland, London, 1983; new edition 2003)

Park, Mungo, *Travels in the Interior Districts of Africa*, 2nd edition (Nichols, London, 1799)

Pindar, Peter, *Sir Joseph Banks and the Emperor of Morocco: A Tale* (Kearsley, London, 1788)

Pyne, Stephen J., *The Ice* (Weidenfeld & Nicolson, London, 2003)

Rees, Siân, *The Floating Brothel* (Headline, London, 2001)

Rennell, James, *The Geographical System of Herodotus* (Nichols, London, 1800)

Riley, James, *Loss of the American Brig* Commerce, *with an Account of Tombuctoo* (Murray, London, 1817)

Rodenbeck, Max, *Cairo: The City Victorious* (Picador, London, 1998)

St John, James Augustus, *The Lives of Celebrated Travelers* (J. & J. Harper, New York, 1832–33)

Sainville, Léonard, *Histoire du Sénégal depuis l'arrivée des Européens jusqu'à 1850* (CRDS, Senegal, 1972)

Salt, Henry, *A Voyage to Abyssinia and Travels into the Interior of that Country* (Rivington, London, 1814)

Sancho, Ignatius, *Letters of the late Ignatius Sancho, an African* (Nichols, London, 1783)

Sattin, Anthony, *Lifting the Veil* (Dent, London, 1988)

Schama, Simon, *A History of Britain*, Vol. 3: *The Fate of Empire, 1776–2000* (BBC, London, 2002)

Segal, Ronald, *The Black Diaspora* (Faber & Faber, London, 1995)

Segal, Ronald, *Islam's Black Slaves* (Atlantic, London, 2001)

Sim, Katharine, *Desert Traveller: The Life of Jean Louis Burckhardt* (Gollancz, London, 1969)

Sinclair, Rev. John, *The Life and Works of Sir John Sinclair* (Blackwood, Edinburgh, 1837)

Sinclair, Sir John, *The Correspondence of the Rt Hon. Sir John Sinclair, Bart.* (Colburn & Bentley, London, 1831)

Smith, William, *A Dictionary of Greek and Roman Geography* (John Murray, London, 1873; reprinted AMC, New York, 1966)

Sparks, Jared, *Memoirs of the Life and Travels of John Ledyard from his Journals and Correspondence* (Colburn, London, 1828)

Starkey, Janet and Okasha El Daly (eds), *Desert Travellers from Herodotus to T.E. Lawrence* (ASTENE, Durham, 2000)

Stone, T.G., 'Journey of Cornelius Hodges in Senegambia, 1689–90', in *English Historical Review*, Vol. XXXIX (1924)

Summers, Judith, *Soho* (Bloomsbury, London, 1989)

Suttor, George, *Memoirs Historic and Scientific of the Right Honourable Sir Joseph Banks, Bart.* (E. Mason, Parramatta, 1855)

Tardy, l'Abbé, *Manuel du voyageur à Londres* (L'Homme, London, 1800)

Tooley, R.V., *Collectors' Guide to Maps of the African Continent and Southern Africa* (Carta Press, London, 1969)

Tuckey, J.H., *Narrative of an expedition to explore the River Zaire* (John Murray, London, 1818)

Tully, Miss, *Letters Written during a Ten Years' Residence at the Court of Tripoli*, 3rd edition, 2 vols (Colburn, London, 1819)

Usick, Patricia, *Adventures in Egypt and Nubia: The Travels of William John Bankes (1786–1855)* (British Museum Press, London, 2002)

Walckenaer, Baron, *Notice historique sur la vie et les ouvrages de M. le Major Rennell* (Institut de France, Paris, 1842)
Wheatley, Henry, *London Past and Present*, 3 vols (John Murray, London, 1891)
Wheatley, Henry, *Hogarth's London* (Constable, London, 1909)
Wilford, John Noble, *The Mapmakers* (Pimlico, London, 2002)

Yule, Col. Sir Henry, 'Major James Rennell, FRS', in 'Sundry Military Biographies', *Royal Engineers' Journal* (January 1882)

African Institution Annual Report, 1807
Cobbett's Annual Register (Hansard, London, 1810)
Edinburgh Review
Gentleman's Magazine
Journal of the Royal Geographical Society
Quarterly Review
Report of the Committee of the African Institution (Hatchard, London, 1811)
The Times
Transactions of the Linnaean Society

MANUSCRIPT SOURCES

Dawson Turner Copies of Sir Joseph Banks' correspondence, in The Banks Archive Research Project at the Natural History Museum, London
Minute Books of the African Association. The originals are in Cambridge University Library (Add. MSS 7085–7087). Photocopies in the archives of the Royal Geographical Society, London
Rennell's papers at the Royal Geographical Society include 'Data for a

Memoir of Major Rennell, collected by his Grandson' (London, 184[blank])

Sutro Papers: Some original Banks correspondence and papers relating to the African Association are held in the Sutro Library, California, but photocopies are held in the Royal Geographical Society and/or Natural History Museum

INDEX